Online Banking Security Measures and Data Protection

Shadi A. Aljawarneh
Jordan University of Science and Technology, Jordan

A volume in the Advances in Information Security, Privacy, and Ethics (AISPE) Book Series

IGI GLOBAL
DISSEMINATOR OF KNOWLEDGE

www.igi-global.com

Published in the United States of America by
IGI Global
Information Science Reference (an imprint of IGI Global)
701 E. Chocolate Avenue
Hershey PA 17033
Tel: 717-533-8845
Fax: 717-533-8661
E-mail: cust@igi-global.com
Web site: http://www.igi-global.com

Library of Congress Cataloging-in-Publication Data

Names: Aljawarneh, Shadi, editor.
Title: Online banking security measures and data protection / Shadi A. Aljawarneh, editor.
Description: Hershey, PA : Information Science Reference, 2017. | Includes bibliographical references and index.
Identifiers: LCCN 2016028381| ISBN 9781522508649 (hardcover) | ISBN 9781522508656 (ebook)
Subjects: LCSH: Internet banking--Security measures. | Electronic funds transfers--Security measures. | Data protection. | Computer networks--Security measures. | Computer security.
Classification: LCC HG1708.7 .O55 2017 | DDC 332.1/7028558--dc23 LC record available at https://lccn.loc.gov/2016028381

This book is published in the IGI Global book series Advances in Information Security, Privacy, and Ethics (AISPE) (ISSN: 1948-9730; eISSN: 1948-9749)

British Cataloguing in Publication Data
A Cataloguing in Publication record for this book is available from the British Library.

Advances in Information Security, Privacy, and Ethics (AISPE) Book Series

ISSN: 1948-9730
EISSN: 1948-9749

Mission

As digital technologies become more pervasive in everyday life and the Internet is utilized in ever increasing ways by both private and public entities, concern over digital threats becomes more prevalent.

The **Advances in Information Security, Privacy, & Ethics (AISPE) Book Series** provides cutting-edge research on the protection and misuse of information and technology across various industries and settings. Comprised of scholarly research on topics such as identity management, cryptography, system security, authentication, and data protection, this book series is ideal for reference by IT professionals, academicians, and upper-level students.

Coverage

- Network Security Services
- Cookies
- Tracking Cookies
- Security Classifications
- Electronic Mail Security
- Internet Governance
- Computer ethics
- Access Control
- Global Privacy Concerns
- Information Security Standards

IGI Global is currently accepting manuscripts for publication within this series. To submit a proposal for a volume in this series, please contact our Acquisition Editors at Acquisitions@igi-global.com or visit: http://www.igi-global.com/publish/.

The Advances in Information Security, Privacy, and Ethics (AISPE) Book Series (ISSN 1948-9730) is published by IGI Global, 701 E. Chocolate Avenue, Hershey, PA 17033-1240, USA, www.igi-global.com. This series is composed of titles available for purchase individually; each title is edited to be contextually exclusive from any other title within the series. For pricing and ordering information please visit http://www.igi-global.com/book-series/advances-information-security-privacy-ethics/37157. Postmaster: Send all address changes to above address.

Titles in this Series

For a list of additional titles in this series, please visit: www.igi-global.com

Developing Next-Generation Countermeasures for Homeland Security Threat Prevention
Maurice Dawson (University of Missouri-St. Louis, USA) Dakshina Ranjan Kisku (National Institute of Technology, India) Phalguni Gupta (National Institute of Technical Teachers' Training & Research, India) Jamuna Kanta Sing (Jadavpur University, India) and Weifeng Li (Tsinghua University, China)
Information Science Reference • copyright 2017 • 428pp • H/C (ISBN: 9781522507031) • US $210.00 (our price)

Security Solutions for Hyperconnectivity and the Internet of Things
Maurice Dawson (University of Missouri-St. Louis, USA) Mohamed Eltayeb (Colorado Technical University, USA) and Marwan Omar (Saint Leo University, USA)
Information Science Reference • copyright 2017 • 347pp • H/C (ISBN: 9781522507413) • US $215.00 (our price)

Managing Security Issues and the Hidden Dangers of Wearable Technologies
Andrew Marrington (Zayed University, UAE) Don Kerr (University of the Sunshine Coast, Australia) and John Gammack (Zayed University, UAE)
Information Science Reference • copyright 2017 • 345pp • H/C (ISBN: 9781522510161) • US $200.00 (our price)

Security Management in Mobile Cloud Computing
Kashif Munir (University of Hafr Al-Batin, Saudi Arabia)
Information Science Reference • copyright 2017 • 248pp • H/C (ISBN: 9781522506027) • US $150.00 (our price)

Cryptographic Solutions for Secure Online Banking and Commerce
Kannan Balasubramanian (Mepco Schlenk Engineering College, India) K. Mala (Mepco Schlenk Engineering College, India) and M. Rajakani (Mepco Schlenk Engineering College, India)
Information Science Reference • copyright 2016 • 375pp • H/C (ISBN: 9781522502739) • US $200.00 (our price)

Handbook of Research on Modern Cryptographic Solutions for Computer and Cyber Security
Brij Gupta (National Institute of Technology Kurukshetra, India) Dharma P. Agrawal (University of Cincinnati, USA) and Shingo Yamaguchi (Yamaguchi University, Japan)
Information Science Reference • copyright 2016 • 589pp • H/C (ISBN: 9781522501053) • US $305.00 (our price)

Table of Contents

Detailed Table of Contents

In recent years, online banking has become an alternative channel for most traditional entities. The increase in the number of users and rapid expansion has resulted in a successful strategy among financial institutions. This chapter discusses the use of technology in the finance industry and the various factors associated with it, as well as introducing the reader to the basic characteristics of online financial services. We review the current literature identifying the relevant research questions for our purpose.

Banks provide service not only through branches in the countries but also offers banking services to customers over the internet. However, customers concern using internet banking because of the various troubles and adversities that may occur on the web and because of their habits. The using of internet banking is still not reached the desired level due to various reasons such as security, troubles on web and habits of customers. In this research, bankers using rate of internet banking and bankers approach on internet banking are determined. According to the survey results in Turkey, almost all of the bankers use internet banking but using of mobile applications does not appear to fully spread. Even though the using of internet banking is very

challenges in the development of online banking system. The adoption of online banking can decrease the operating expenses and offer good and rapid services to their customers. The framework factors have been classified as facilitators and barriers of adoption of online banking. Performance expectancy, effort expectancy and social influence have been classified as facilitators whereas security concerns, privacy concerns and legal concerns have been classified as barriers. The results revealed various significant suggestions for online banking service providers, designers and developers.

The insufficient preparation for the information and communication technologies revolution led to few offering online transaction platforms, information security features, and credit facilities. One of the security concerns is a lack of data validation. Data that is not validated or not properly validated is the main issue for serious security vulnerabilities affecting online banking applications. In this chapter, the influences of security issues on world banks will be discussed. A number of data validation methods will be also reviewed to date to provide a systematic summary to banking environment. Based on the advantages and disadvantages of each method, the IT developer will decide which is best suited to develop the systematic online banking application. From this analysis, a global view of the current and future tendencies of data validation will be obtained and therefore provision of possible recommendations for solving the security and privacy issues for the online banking services.

This chapter introduces about a Proposal to any bank of any country for fast but secured transfer of money anytime anywhere any-amount by anybody to anybody on the spot with confirmation from the payee on the spot. The work here is on a new method of real time payment system, which is highly secured and fast, and 100% technology-based without any paper format or paper work of the bank. This breaking scheme is entitled as "5A-RTP scheme" where '5A' stands for Anytime Anywhere Any-amount Anybody to Anybody and 'RTP' stands for Real-Time Payment. There is no paper-work at all. It is completely secured, realization of payment (debit + credit)

Online banking system has created an enormous impact on IT, Individuals, and networking worlds. Online banking systems and its exclusive architecture have numerous features and advantages over traditional banking system. However, these new uniqueness create new vulnerabilities and attacks on an online banking system. Cross-site scripting request forgery or XSS attack is among the top vulnerabilities, according to recent studies. This exposure occurs, when a user uses the input from an online banking application without properly looking into them which allows an attacker to execute malicious scripts into the application. Current approaches use to mitigate this problem, especially on effective detection of XSS vulnerabilities in the application or prevention of real-time XSS attacks. To address this problem, the survey of different vulnerability attacks on online banking system performed and also presents a concept for the prevention, detection, removal and recovery of XSS vulnerabilities to secure the banking application.

Compared to the last five to six years, the massive scale by which innocent users are being subjected to a new age threat in form of digital extortion has never been seen before. With the rise of Internet, use of personal computers and devices has mushroomed to immense scale, with cyber criminals subjecting innocent users to extortion using malware. The primary victim to be hit the most has been online banking, impacting the security and reputation of banking and financial transactions along with social interactions. Online security revolves around three critical aspects – starting with the use of digital data and files, next with the use of computer systems and finally the internet as an unsecure medium. This is where Ransomware has become one of the most malicious form of malware for digital extortion threats to home and corporate user alike.

Insider threat poses huge loss to organizations since malicious insiders have enough knowledge to attack high sensitive information. Moreover, preventing and detecting insider attacks is a hard job because malicious insiders follow legal paths to launch attacks. This threat leads all kinds of attacks in banking systems in the amount of loss it causes. Insider threat in banking systems poses huge harm to banks due to

turned key informant on how to decrease the rising incidence of cybercrime. A major finding is that credit card fraud is all too easy to enact and merchants need to conduct better staff training to catch fraudsters early. With increases in global online purchasing, international carding networks are proliferating, making it difficult for law enforcement agencies to be "policing" unauthorized transactions. Big data may well have a role to play in analyzing behaviors that expose cybercrime.

Preface

Do not worry about your difficulties in Mathematics. I can assure you mine are still greater. – Albert Einstein

The corresponding book publication summarizes the recent research papers on online banking security techniques, approaches and technologies and Case studies entitled, "Online Banking Security Measures and Data Protection." This comprehensive and timely publication aims to be an essential reference source, building on the available literature in the field of e-banking security while providing for further research opportunities in this dynamic field. It is hoped that this text will provide the resources necessary for policy makers, technology developers and managers to adopt and implement security techniques and technologies in developing banks across the globe.

This book summarizes some current trends in the online banking security such as online banking security services, data protection techniques, applications and technologies, and explores one key area of growth: Online Banking. To illustrate the role of Applications and Services in the growth of online banking industries, a number of examples focusing on the learning, government, industry and security are used. Recommendations for future areas are presented.

This book is intended for researchers and practitioners who are interested in issues that arise from using technologies of online banking security advancements. In addition, this book is also targeted to anyone who wants to learn more about the online banking security measures and data protection research advancements in design and applications. For example, policy makers, academicians, researchers, advanced-level students, technology developers, bank officers and government officials will find this text useful in furthering their research exposure to pertinent topics in e-banking security and assisting in furthering their own research efforts in this field. Online banking security has become a hot topic in recent years and people at different levels in any organization need to understand online banking in different ways and different perspectives.

BOOK DESCRIPTION, MISSION, AND OBJECTIVES

Although the e-banking field has been found Information Systems literature since the mid-1990s, there is still a lack of advanced research into banking security adoption and associated organizational issues. In addition, there is a shortage in case studies surveying the real experience of firms and organizations in deploying e-banking security. As e-banking is an IT product for development and evolution, this sort of gap in the advanced research makes some sensitive issues and challenges for banking sector, particularly these that currently develop e-banking security because the weaknesses and actual limitations in subject to this field normally mean difficulties in planning and developing e-banking security measures and controls.

The use of the Internet as a main distribution channel raises the necessity of securing e-banking since it becomes a vital issue to the environment and could make organizations more vulnerable to system attacks and threats. Although there are several techniques and methods to security as a whole whose value is evident – there is an expectation that security can be more efficiently managed if the concentration goes beyond technical-oriented solutions.

E-banking can not only offer various benefits to customers in terms of ease and cost of transactions, but it also poses new challenges for banks in supervising their financial systems and in designing and implementing necessary security measures and controls. Therefore, understanding security communication in e-banking issues is important for senior management because it would assist them enhance their approach to e-banking security. This edited book addresses this issue by reporting exploratory case studies about developing and implementing security in e-banking. Particularly, this edited book of advanced research aims to explore how e-banking security measures and controls takes place within the bank, what are the standards and procedures that play an important role to the success of e-banking security and what key lessons come out of their experience which could be generalized.

This book also looks to discuss and address the difficulties and challenges that banks have faced in implementing security techniques, technologies and applications. The editor will seek chapters that address different aspects of e-banking adoption, ranging from Phishing of Banking Information, Pharming of Banking Websites, Adaptive Authentication in Banking, "Watering Hole" Attacks, Malware-Based Attacks, Zeus Trojan, Mobile Banking Security, Identity Theft, and Related Topics.

This book focuses on advanced research in the practical applications and the theoretical foundations of online banking security, through presentation of the most up-to-date advances and new directions of research in the field from various scholarly, professional, and practitioner perspectives. An interdisciplinary look at online banking, including engineering and business aspects, such book covers and encourages high-quality research exposition on such topics as virtualization technologies for online banking, online banking security utilities, real case studies on online banking security vulnerabilities as well as data protection techniques, and business perspectives for online banking security.

The main mission of this book is to be the premier and authoritative source for the most innovative scholarly and professional research and information pertaining to aspects of online banking security measures and data protection. Such book presents advancements in the state-of-the-art, standards, and practices of online banking security, in an effort to identify emerging trends that will ultimately define the future of "the Cloud of Online Banking" and "the Gog of Online Banking". The main topics are discussed through original papers, review papers, technical reports, case studies, and conference reports for reference use by academics and practitioners alike.

This book is intended to reflect new directions of research and report latest advances. It is a platform for rapid dissemination of high quality research / application / work-in-progress articles on Online Banking Security solutions for managing challenges and problems within the highlighted scope.

The objectives of this book are multi-folds, including:

1. Establish a significant channel of communication among Online Banking Security researchers, engineers, practitioners and IT policy makers;
2. Provide a space to publish and share the latest high quality research results in the area of Online Banking Security;
3. Promote and coordinate international collaboration in the standards of Cloud and Fog Computing of Online Banking to meet the need to broaden the applicability and scope of the current and future research of Online Banking Security.

Topics to be discussed in this book include the following:

- Techniques, technologies, and services
- Applications
- Architecture
- Standards
- Management
- Cloud and Fog engineering
- Business
- Security Vulnerabilities and threats

WHAT THIS BOOK COVERS

In this book, we will present the current state of online banking security research advancements on design, and applications. So that we will summarize each advanced research, its influence in the science of online banking security measures and data protections as follows:

Chapter 1: Online Banking and Finance

In recent years, online banking has become an alternative channel for most traditional entities. The increase in the number of users and rapid expansion has resulted in a successful strategy among financial institutions. This chapter discusses the use of technology in the finance industry and the various factors associated with it, as well as introducing the reader to the basic characteristics of online financial services. We review the current literature identifying the relevant research questions for our purpose.

Chapter 2: Internet Banking Usage Level of Bankers: A Research on Sampling of Turkey

Banks provide service not only through branches in the countries but also offer banking services to customers over the internet. However, customers concern using internet banking because of the various troubles and adversities that may occur on the web and because of their habits. The using of internet banking is still not reached the desired level due to various reasons such as security, troubles on web and habits of customers. In this research, bankers using rate of internet banking and bankers approach on internet banking are determined. According to the survey results in Turkey, almost all of the bankers use internet banking but using of mobile applications does not appear to fully spread. Even though the using of internet banking is very common among the bankers, some of the participants said that they encountered some problems while using internet banking. Solutions of systemic deficiencies, password security problems and other security problems will increase the using of internet banking.

Chapter 3: Internet Banking and Financial Customer Preferences in Turkey

The first online banking service was introduced in Turkey by İş Bank in 1998. However, the number of internet users has been increasing rapidly in Turkey, the number of online banking users did not increase with a similar pace. Although banks are taking measures for the security of online banking transactions, many financial consumers are still concerned about the security of these transactions therefore preferring not to use online banking. This study reveals the development of internet banking in Turkey and consumer percentages. Previous research on the factors affecting the usage of e-banking are also addressed in this study. It was found that the majority of these studies focus on the correlation between the security concerns which result in avoiding using internet banking.

Chapter 4: Expectation and Perception of Internet Banking Service Quality of Select Indian Private and Public Sector Banks: Comparative Case Study

This research paper mainly deals with expectation and perception of service quality of select Indian Banks i.e. SBI and HDFC on the customer satisfaction. The research survey was based on IS-QUAL dimensions a diagnostic model developed in 2014, which measures service quality and internet service quality in terms of customer expectations and perceptions of banking services. This present research tends to evaluate the overall idea of expected and perceived services of the two banks. This study is a cross-sectional survey that employed the use of pre-structured questionnaire to collect primary data from a sample of 120 respondents through personal contact, field survey and email. Collected data have been analyzed through SPSS 21 software by different statistical tools like Reliability test for judgment of internal consistency of collected data and paired t-test.

Chapter 5: Towards Fully De-Materialized Check Management

Banks worldwide are putting a big effort into de-materializing their processes, in order to streamline the processes and thus reducing overall costs. In this chapter, the authors describe how the de-materialization can be a big opportunity for banks, describing the European context. Furthermore, the de-materialization of check handling is taken as example, proposing a review of existing technologies and describing the advantages that a real framework can give to the users and to the bank systems.

Chapter 6: Emerging Challenges, Security Issues, and Technologies in Online Banking Systems

Online banking security is a critical issue over request-response model. But the traditional protection mechanisms are not sufficient to secure the online banking systems that hold information about clients, and banks. The infrastructure of networks, routers, domain name servers, and switches that glue these online banking systems together could be fail, and as a result, online banking systems will no longer be able to communicate accurately or reliably. A number of critical questions arise, such as what exactly the infrastructure is, what threats it must be secured against, and how protection can be provided on a cost-effective basis. But underlying all these questions is how to define secure online banking systems. In this chapter, emerging challenges, security issues and technologies in Online Banking Systems will be analyzed and discussed systematically.

Chapter 7: The Influences of Privacy, Security, and Legal Concerns on Online Banking Adoption: A Conceptual Framework

Business globalization and the rising new technology enforced traditional banking to head towards online banking services, which facilitates customers to obtain access to their accounts from their business sites and personal computers to online banking services. The objective of this chapter is to construct a framework of adoption of online banking and represent the major influences of privacy, security, and legal concerns on online banking adoption. Furthermore, the chapter reveals the main challenges in the development of online banking system. The adoption of online banking can decrease the operating expenses and offer good and rapid services to their customers. The framework factors have been classified as facilitators and barriers of adoption of online banking. Performance expectancy, effort expectancy and social influence have been classified as facilitators whereas security concerns, privacy concerns and legal concerns have been classified as barriers. The results revealed various significant suggestions for online banking service providers, designers and developers.

Chapter 8: Analysis of Data Validation Techniques for Online Banking Services

The insufficient preparation for the information and communication technologies revolution led to few offering online transaction platforms, information security features, and credit facilities. One of the security concerns is a lack of data validation. Data that is not validated or not properly validated is the main issue for serious security vulnerabilities affecting online banking applications. In this chapter, the influences of security issues on world banks will be discussed. A number of data validation methods will be also reviewed to date to provide a systematic summary to banking environment. Based on the advantages and disadvantages of each method, the IT developer will decide which is best suited to develop the systematic online banking application. From this analysis, a global view of the current and future tendencies of data validation will be obtained and therefore provision of possible recommendations for solving the security and privacy issues for the online banking services.

Chapter 9: Anytime Anywhere Any-Amount Anybody to Anybody Real-Time Payment (5A-RTP) with High Level Banking Security

This chapter introduces about a Proposal to any bank of any country for fast but secured transfer of money anytime anywhere any-amount by anybody to anybody on the spot with confirmation from the payee on the spot. This breaking scheme is entitled as "5A-RTP scheme" where '5A' stands for Anytime Anywhere Any-amount Anybody to Anybody and 'RTP' stands for Real-Time Payment. There is no paper-work at all. It is highly secured, fast and 100% technology-based. It is completely secured, realization of payment happens immediately very fast, without any man-hour or manpower of the bank. It is claimed that 5A-RTP scheme, if incorporated in all the banks in any country, will give the country a huge momentum of customers' satisfaction, huge momentum in country's growth and economic progress. The revolutionary breakthrough in 5A-RTP scheme is that it dominates all of the existing banking instruments. The 5A-RTP scheme may even slowly cause a natural death of the existing instruments.

Chapter 10: An Algorithm for Securing Hybrid Cloud Outsourced Data in the Banking Sector

The Cloud has become a significant topic in the banking computing; however, the trend has established a new range of security issues that need to be addressed. In Cloud, the banking data and associated software are not under their control. In addition, with the growing demands for Cloud networks communication, it becomes increasingly important to secure the data flow path. The existing research related to security mechanisms only focuses on securing the flow of information in the communication banking networks. There is a lack of work on improving the performance of networks to meet quality of service (QoS) constrains for various services. The security mechanisms work by encryption and decryption of the information, but do not consider the optimized use of the network resources. In this chapter the authors propose a Secure Data Transmission Mechanism (SDTM) with Preemption Algorithm that combines between security and quality of service for the banking sector. Their developed SDTM enhanced with Malicious Packets Detection System (MPDS) which is a set of technologies and solutions.

Chapter 11: Prevention, Detection, and Recovery of CSRF Attack in Online Banking System

Online banking system has created an enormous impact on IT, Individuals, and networking worlds. Online banking systems and its exclusive architecture have numerous features and advantages over traditional banking system. However, these new uniqueness create new vulnerabilities and attacks on an online banking system. Cross-site scripting request forgery or XSS attack is among the top vulnerabilities, according to recent studies. This exposure occurs, when a user uses the input from an online banking application without properly looking into them which allows an attacker to execute malicious scripts into the application. Current approaches use to mitigate this problem, especially on effective detection of XSS vulnerabilities in the application or prevention of real-time XSS attacks. To address this problem, the survey of different vulnerability attacks on online banking system performed and also presents a concept for the prevention, detection, removal and recovery of XSS vulnerabilities to secure the banking application.

Chapter 12: Ransomware: A Rising Threat of New Age Digital Extortion

Compared to the last five to six years, the massive scale by which innocent users are being subjected to a new age threat in form of digital extortion has never been seen before. With the rise of Internet, use of personal computers and devices has mushroomed to immense scale, with cyber criminals subjecting innocent users to extortion using malware. The primary victim to be hit the most has been online banking, impacting the security and reputation of banking and financial transactions along with social interactions. Online security revolves around three critical aspects – starting with the use of digital data and files, next with the use of computer systems and finally the internet as an unsecure medium. This is where Ransomware has become one of the most malicious forms of malware for digital extortion threats to home and corporate user alike.

Chapter 13: Insider Threat in Banking Systems Complete Recognition Capability

Insider threat poses huge loss to organizations since malicious insiders have enough knowledge to attack high sensitive information. Moreover, preventing and detecting insider attacks is a hard job because malicious insiders follow legal paths to launch attacks. This threat leads all kinds of attacks in banking systems in the amount of loss it causes. Insider threat in banking systems poses huge harm to banks due to the importance and attractiveness of assets that banks have. This chapter discusses insider threat problem in banking sector, and introduces important surveys and case studies that show the severeness of this threat in this sector. Moreover, the chapter demonstrates some policies, technologies and tools that may prevent and detect insider threat in banking systems.

Chapter 14: Achieving Security to Overcome Attacks and Vulnerabilities in Mobile Banking Security

Mobile Banking is a means of connectivity between bank and its customers. It would be impractical to expect customers to regularly visit banks or connect to a web site for regular upgrade of their mobile banking application. Mobile Banking is a provision and availability of both banking and financial services with the help of mobile telecommunication devices as an Application. It would be expected that the mobile application itself check the upgrades and updates and download necessary patches. Mobile banking has brought the advantage to have an alternate to debit and credit card usage. Mobile banking has the below three inter-related concepts: Mobile accounting, Mobile brokerage, Mobile financial information services. Mobile banking services are Account information provision, Monetary Transaction, Investment facilitation, Support and Content services. The threats involved in Mobile Banking are categorized as, Threats against end user and end user device, Threats against communication network, Threats against remote banking service.

Chapter 15: Credit Card Fraud: Behind the Scenes

In 2004, Dan DeFilippi was arrested for numerous counts of credit card fraud. This chapter will include a full length interview transcript between Katina Michael and Dan DeFilippi. The transcript will cover areas to do with: (1) how Dan became involved with credit card fraud, (2) the techniques used by fraudsters to evade detection; (3) the socio-ethical impacts of the fraud; (4) how he was detained by the FBI; and (5) how he reformed by becoming a key informant and evading jail. The interview is 12,000 words in length, and has numerous sections. It contains numerous illustrations and primary documentation of the offences of credit card fraud, and victim statements.

Acknowledgment

The editor would like to acknowledge the help of all the people involved in this project and, more specifically, to the authors and reviewers that took part in the review process. Without their support, this book would not have become a reality.

First, the editor would like to thank each one of the authors for their contributions. Our sincere gratitude goes to the chapter's authors who contributed their time and expertise to this book.

Second, the editor wishes to acknowledge the valuable contributions of the reviewers regarding the improvement of quality, coherence, and content presentation of chapters. Most of the authors also served as referees; we highly appreciate their double task.

Shadi A. Aljawarneh
Jordan University of Science and Technology, Jordan

Chapter 1
Online Banking and Finance

Marta Vidal
Complutense University of Madrid, Spain

Javier Vidal-García
University of Valladolid, Spain

ABSTRACT

In recent years, online banking has become an alternative channel for most traditional entities. The increase in the number of users and rapid expansion has resulted in a successful strategy among financial institutions. This chapter discusses the use of technology in the finance industry and the various factors associated with it, as well as introducing the reader to the basic characteristics of online financial services. We review the current literature identifying the relevant research questions for our purpose.

DOI: 10.4018/978-1-5225-0864-9.ch001

INTRODUCTION

The integration of internet in business strategy is promoting the use and development of new means of purchase, such as mobile, that are enabling the rapid growth of home shopping to the consumer and providing a range of additional benefits over traditional channels (Xu, Wikes, & Shah., 2006, p. 19). Among the variety and breadth of products made available to the user, financial services are, by their very nature, particularly attractive to be marketed via internet, because they offer a number of advantages, including the possibility that the user check their bank accounts from anywhere and at any time, the facility to compare between different investment alternatives or financing options, which saves time and money (Ainin, Lee, & Wee, 2000; Gerrard & Cunningham, 2003).

Previous research suggests that internet division is the most profitable section within a bank (Pikarrainen, Pikarrainen, Karjaluoto, & Pahnila, 2004). The success of online banking can be revealed by analyzing the number of current and potential users of these services. Although there is still a high degree of ignorance from financial institutions on which aspects are most valued by their customers, together with barriers to its adoption, banks do not perform an efficient allocation of resources that enable them to gain competitive advantage.

In this chapter we introduce the reader to e-banking services and financial services through the internet. For our purpose, we reviewed the current literature identifying the relevant topics for the chapter.

BACKGROUND

The development of web technologies has led to the proliferation of new business models and complementary distribution channels alternative to the traditional banking, the financial sector remains one of the fastest in incorporating technological innovations. The development of e-banking is due to progress in the accessibility of communication technologies and information (Bradley & Steward, 2002), so that is the most modern provision of financial services. Since the revolution which represented the debit and credit cards, the ability to pay with them in stores, and the introduction of ATMs, it was thought that there was no more revolutionary service in the banking sector. The use of the term e-banking and no remote banking is due to the latter term is defined by the Law Society Services of Information and Electronic Commerce (LSSI, 2002) as the "supply of banking services without personal contact between employees of the bank and its customers." However, this concept can also include remote banking systems ATMs, POS terminals and banking through mobile devices. On the other hand, e-banking includes various types of technologies such as: phone banking (through both fixed line and mobile telephone), electronic funds transfer, and online banking or online (Weitzman, 2000). However, the commitment of the various banks for online banking has not adapted to the needs of each user, but have standardized services already offered, allowing only operations which allow to see the account balance and historical transactions, pay bills, transfer funds between accounts, apply for credit cards and order checks (Chou & Chou, 2000). Banks hope to achieve greater market share and show a more innovative image, although not always achieve these objectives for two reasons. The first is that banks still consider the business of e-banking as a secondary channel; while the second is the suspicion that a large number of potential customers have in the system (Rexha, John, & Shang, 2003). In this study we aim to show the importance for the development and dissemination of online banking that users have on their operation, use and usefulness. We analyze the need to introduce and develop e-banking to distribute financial products and services, focusing on the factors that have influenced the development of this technology by financial institutions (such as the availability of internet in homes or the possibility of reducing economic costs) along with the advantages and disadvantages of this new channel. A review of the personal attitudes of users to innovation, experience, learning and knowledge it is also necessary regarding this service offered by banks. We will raise the different forms of learning that can take the users of these services, reaching a number of conclusions as to whether financial institutions are somehow promoting the use of online banking.

MAIN FOCUS OF THE CHAPTER

The Importance of E-Banking

The global banking system has been characterized in the last decade by an increase in competition between the main companies due to the increase in the number of competitors. To address these threats financial organizations have developed competitive strategies, understanding these as the set of actions, offensive or defensive, aimed at maintaining the competitive position of these entities in the sector in which they operate, improve or search a new position in order to achieve greater performance. Therefore, each type of entity will develop its competitive strategy (focus on quality, diversification of products and services, image enhancement, etc.) depending on its mission and objectives. However, the continued fall in interest margins has forced banks to implement cost control policies, increase staff productivity and offices, and investment in technology (Hobson, 2012, p. 15). Thus, most financial institutions have seen the development of online banking as a growth strategy, because despite the large initial investment required, it yields improved levels of productivity and profitability, and reduce staff costs and facilities (Bradley & Steward, 2003). Furthermore, the strong concentration process that this sector has experienced in recent years, has resulted in a new scenario: first, the development of online banking by smaller financial institutions; and second, the investments needed for mergers limit the budget available to develop e-banking technological development (Hart, 2005, p. 36). Following this line, the acceptance and spread of online banking also has its origin in the changes that have occurred in the behavior and needs of customers. These are becoming more demanding and value very positively "the savings in time and the possibility of analyzing more information about the quality and price of various products and services" that are offered by banks. Thus, customers can conduct their banking transactions such as paying bills or selling their shares and securities, at the most convenient time and place, depending on their lifestyles (Kallstrom, 2000, p. 20). In many cases, the lack of services provided through the internet is perceived by customers as a decline in the quality of the company. However, all this would not be possible without the availability of internet technology in most homes, thanks to the measures taken by the different governments for adoption (Laopodis, 2013, p. 26). An example of an initiative in this sense is that some banks have signed an agreement with the local government to finance the purchase of computers with internet access, at no cost to customers who must be individuals residing in the area and who can prove they have children enrolled in public education centers. As a result, the internet has become an important resource for information among consumers due to its ease of use, accessibility and cost reduction in recent years (Bonn, Furr, & Susskind, 1999). With all this, we can define what is meant by user of online banking, distinguishing between those who have access to companies that operate only on the internet and users accessing banks that use the internet as a complementary channel. In any case, generally, a user of online banking is a internet user during a reference period that makes use of any of the services offered by banks via the Internet, both for information and to perform any transaction. Thus, the most visited websites correspond to those companies which also provide information about business transactions. Finally, online banking is limited to the activities carried out over the internet. In this sense, these activities aim to achieve two objectives: first, to improve the quality of these services provided via internet, perfecting and increasing them quantitatively and qualitatively; and second, to achieve a process of technological modernization and redesign the business model needed to grow its productivity (see Friedman (2000)).

Benefits and Challenges of E-Banking

The introduction of information and communication technologies in the banking sector has given rise to a number of competitive advantages (see Liao, Yuan, & Chen, 1999):

1. Increased competition in banking markets,
2. Appearance of new possibilities for expansion into other markets,
3. Cost savings to production structure,
4. Improved data management
5. New product design and risk control, and
6. Introducing a new product distribution system (Krantz, 2013, p. 19).

But a consequence of these effects is:

1. The significant decrease of the strategic value of the network of bank branches and, consequently, the problem of excess capacity in the banks; together with
2. Not being able to expand the customer base, but to move from traditional banks to the new entities over the internet, with lower margins (Chavan, 2013).

Therefore, there are a series of risks, classified as strategic and business, operational, reputation and legal (Sarlak, & Astiani, 2011, p. 29). Strategic and business risks that this sector faces relate, as its name suggests, to the decisions that would affect the future profitability of the banks (Lassar, Lambert, Woodford, & Moschovitis, 2005, p. 15). Operational risks are described as exposure of the entities failures in the operation of the technology, its misuse by third parties or employees, and a possible fault in the external systems necessary to use the means available to users. Regarding reputational risks, they are closely linked to the two previous. In banking, brand reputation is crucial when customers decide between the product of a financial institution or its competitor, so any strategy or operational failure can question the reliability or the security of the transactions. They can occur due to:

1. A transfer of customers to other competing institutions, which will be difficult to recover in a competitive environment like banking;
2. loss of potential customers by bad experiences that can be described as dissatisfied customers.

Finally, the legal risks relate to:

1. The likelihood of facing lawsuits from customers who suffered any type of fraud or misuse of information, and
2. Breach of the legislation in certain countries as a consequence of not knowing the rules properly.

For all these risks, even though online banking increases the efficiency and competitiveness of banks, it should also increase efforts to achieve lower costs and increase productivity and efficiency to meet rising competition among financial institutions. Technological changes in communication have made possible the development of internet use in financial transactions. Consequently, consumers of banking services are increasingly using the internet, even if they have not yet used to this service for their daily financial transactions, due mainly to the lack of trust, the impersonal care and insecurity that characterizes this system of commercial transaction, an often as a result of ignorance of the system.

The Need for Knowledge of Users and Managers of Online Banking

Although e-banking is an innovative tool in which all financial institutions are investing heavily, two major problems were observed, on the one hand the creation of prior knowledge of the customer for the service is not well promoted by the institutions, so that its implementation does not become fully effective; and secondly, financial institutions do not have all the necessary information about users in order to offer more products and services tailored to their needs. To this, there is still an additional challenge to overcome by institutions. Customers often lack the financial knowledge necessary to understand the dimensions of the products offered, which are each day more sophisticated. Thus, it becomes a pressing need to provide clear and understandable information on financial services offered and establish periods of reflection that allow them to analyze the conditions and compare offers from other banks.

To improve the adoption of online banking and try to solve the first problem, financial institutions should promote a process of learning to capture a greater number of users of their services through online banking and have a real cost reduction. The problem arises in how to generate knowledge about electronic banking users. From our point of view, banks can perform two different learning processes:

- Prior learning by training or training. It refers to all the information clients can receive as potential user before using the electronic banking service. In this way, clients can eliminate the uncertainty which may involve using these services for the first time.

The tools that can be used to achieve this goal would provide learning by users:

- Manuals on the operation of the website of the organization, how to perform different tasks.
- Courses in the bank with computers connected online.
- Explanations before opening an account.
- Articles in magazines and journals.
- Recommendations from other users in forums created by the banks.
- Helping with the process of opening and account and the creation of passwords.
- Training online or learning by doing.

With these initiatives it is intended that the information required by the client to use online banking is available right on the time these clients have any questions or concerns regarding the operation of the service. Thus, that these customers do not become failed users or discontent. Financial institutions should aim to show the ease of use and speed with which clients can carry out simple transactions thus saving time (opportunity cost) (Liao & Cheung, 2002), this would be the purpose of such training. In this case, the potential initiatives to follow might be:

- Telephone contact for clients.
- Forum aid on the same website.
- Guide online on how to use the service step by step.
- Demos online.

With these techniques we can even begin to solve the second problem that affects the utilization of online banking. Keep in mind that banks are interested in knowing who is using online banking, the features of these users and why some use it more easily than others (Lassar, Manolis, & Lassar, 2005). In the case of learning by training, the bank will meet the profile of these users, and the potential level of use of online systems according to their characteristics, as will be offering them a prior information controlled by the bank; but if what is used is learning by doing, it would require that institutions make a small initial questionnaire to provide them with the most interesting data on the profile of the customer to know the possible utilization of the system, such as training, age, and even some aspect that helps to measure their level of financial risk. All this information will help them deliver products and services more tailored to their needs.

However, it is not only the lack of knowledge that justifies the utilization of online banking is so low yet. In this regard, a number of studies identifying other reasons are:

1. Ease of use (Liao & Cheung, 2002, Wang, Wang, Lin, & Tang, 2003),
2. The speed of the transaction (Liao & Cheung, 2002),
3. Security (Liao & Cheung, 2002) and credibility of electronic banking (Wang et al., 2003), and
4. The precision (Liao & Cheung, 2002).

It is also important to consider the personal characteristics of the user, as his innate ability to innovation and its potential to adopt new products.

In conclusion, each portal or website for e-banking vary between different financial institutions, it varies based on the profile of each organization and the needs of each user, thus the knowledge required to use online banking changes in each case.

Means of Electronic Payment

In this section we will try to analyze the means most used in electronic banking payment, as they not only have great significance in the world of commerce be it traditional or electronic, but since the beginning of the traditional banking sector the different means of payment have contributed greatly to the financial results of the companies. Financial institutions operating within payment systems have a great opportunity to learn through customer transactions, and thus to make databases and segment their customers by priorities based on the bank's strategy, this information is undoubtedly a great asset available to financial institutions to analyze and know their customers (Lee, Kwon, & Schumann, 2005).

From the point of view of the means of payment present today, regardless of the degree of use of these, we can distinguish between the traditional system, payment cards, payment via mobile phone, payments via internet, and finally the means of payment within the traditional payment systems, which is still the most widely used within the financial sector. With the new type of means of payment the bank loses the close relationship with its user. Payment information always passes through the network of the institution itself, which keeps the user safe and alien to its competitor's business relationship.

The cards are another means of payment used massively by clients, there are several types of cards: credit, debit and cash cards. Cards have two characteristic elements such as, linking the user to a bank account of a financial institution and a degree of difficulty in the acceptance process between all parts of the transmission. Card use requires prior authorization from the bank that issues the card, in addition to the authorization of this system requires the presence of a system operator (MasterCard, Visa, etc), and management of information between banks. One of the major drawbacks of this type of means of payment over the internet is offering insecurity as to perform data transfers, which is necessary to write the card details on the website where the operation is being performed.

The mobile phone is the ultimate means of payment which currently is expanding thanks to new phone models that potential users own, these are called smartphone or latest phones that offer the user a high portability banking, security, penetration, connectivity, etc., plus a minimum cost per transaction to the user. This type of payment system has many advantages in other business sectors such as taxi services, food delivery, etc., where the mobility of the means of payment is very important.

Mobipay, born in 2001, could be defined as a technology which aims to create a technological standard for activating means of payment, to thereby obtain the user to make payments electronically independently of the kind of technological support that uses (mobile, POS, etc.), this technology or system is unique as an independent entity from the bank interacts between the two sides of the transaction, this system could be considered a new payment channel.

And finally mention the means of payment over the internet, where they often use mechanisms or systems such as e-payments, PayPal, etc. The average PayPal secure payment transaction is performed through a web page so that the user does not have to show his personal card details to the other side of the transaction, this method has been exceptionally extended thanks that is free of charge, provides safety and comfort for the user and basically allows anonymity when trading via the internet where it is common to ignore the other side of a commercial transaction (Fontanills & Cawood, 2009, p.43).

BIG DATA AND ONLINE FINANCIAL SERVICES

Bid data could be defined as the process of extracting value from a large database, which allows the creation of further knowledge and speed decision making, thanks to digitalization and the development of new analysis technologies with greater capacity storage, search and segmentation information.

Banks has spent years managing large amounts of information (data mining), however, the big difference is no longer current data volume, but the speed of information and analysis not only structured but also unstructured (internet and networks social, mobile, geo-locations, etc.), making it necessary to adopt new techniques and tools of analysis and information management.

If banks are able to acquire this ability to handle big data, they can aspire to be a game changer in the emerging digital business models, because banks have more data about their customers than any other company in any other sector (Packin & Lev, 2016).

The enhancement of the data is part of the strategy of the bank against new players, with the ultimate goal of maintaining their historical position and increasing it to new sectors of the digital market.

Banks can be defined as authentic capturing machines and store valuable data about their customers and other agents of the value chain, because:

- Any trade or operation by clients, is recorded by the bank (card payments, direct debits, transfers, charges) which records the locations where clients perform operations, weather, date and time, etc.).
- The banking structure favors large-scale registration of the customer data. What it could be seen as a factor of high cost, becomes a powerful weapon for relational and commercial development with customers.

However, banks need to achieve the ability to process all this data, as it implies a cultural change in most financial institutions. In this sense, many banks are now opening new departments and recruiting new staff which focuses exclusively on big data with the intention of obtaining profitability from its client's data. In this sense, banks are facing a race against time, but they can react taking some actions in the field of big data:

- Partner with logical or technological partners to shorten the adoption of big data processes and get quicker returns. Banks can use providers of these technologies, who will be able to use structure data more efficiently, and in this way focus the traditional business on the big data. For example, creating a new system of credit scoring with the new data available.
- Trying to collect data about its clients purchasing behavior. The bank can leverage the data already stored but not used, or can purchase data from external providers to enrich the information, or even rewarding clients for providing with this kind of data.

- The management of clients through Real Time Analytics to generate competitive advantages. The future of banks will not rely on an extensive network of offices and automatic teller machines, but it will depend increasingly on the ability giving access to bank services in the right time, which requires mastery of Real Time Analytics

The great improvement in the banking automation will not consist solely of the incorporation of advanced technologies or interfaces, but in the ability to anticipate customer needs. The big data is certainly the oil of the century.

The Big Data is the Key to Transforming the Marketing of Products

If banks do not reach the excellence in the distribution of its products, they will be relegated to becoming utilities where his role will be residual within the overall process of financial transactions. For example, the bank account is simply a commodity that receives the funds from our payroll and transmits it to our digital wallet managed by a third party. With this method of payment and with advice on the product purchased, that could well provide Google or Amazon, the purchase paid in cash not necessarily from the bank. The customer is increasingly feeling that is unique and does not belong to any segment and therefore needs to perceive the bank as it is unique. For this, the big data allows banks to develop marketing strategies that:

- The client is a moving target and banks need to offer value services available within few clicks. The client might have a virtual life (facebook, etc), but the bank can always find him through his mobile phone.
- Segmentation by the behavior of banking customers. The big data allow to segment customers in new ways. The segmentation of clients for its purchasing power is not so useful and segmentation for client behavior (the relationship with the bank) becomes more attractive for financial institutions.
- Tailoring of products and offers to the clients. Not even the segmentation of clients due to its behavior is good enough, as segmenting clients is a technique to simplify the client's message when not all the data is available. Nowadays, banks have a lot of data to personalize offer to products to clients.

Risks of Internet Banking

The incorporation of new technologies has brought great changes to the financial and banking activity, which highly benefits customers, but involves changes for banks. Internet banking does not create new risks, but rather emphasizes existing risks in a bank. Note that there are different types of additional security to the information that must be taken into account by the banks risks, but in most cases are not considered.

The risks to which they are exposed institutions are classified in three profiles depending on the type of services offered through internet banking:

1. **Low Risk:** Corresponds to the financial institutions that offer information about products and services of the bank.
2. **Moderate Risk:** Refers to financial institutions that offer information with savings accounts, and require data from clients, such as an address, or phone, among others. As in this case the user is entering the main systems of the bank, the risk is material.
3. **Increased Risk:** Corresponds to the financial institutions allowing customers to conduct financial transactions which involve increased risk.

The main risks to which financial institutions are exposed to offer internet banking services include:

1. **Strategic Risk:** Originated by adverse business decisions or inadequate implementation of business decisions when banks do not fully understand the strategic and technical aspects of the internet banking and pressures of competition can introduce these services without a prior cost-benefit analysis; in addition, the structure of the company may not be ready to provide this type of services.
2. **Transaction Risk:** Arises from fraud, error, negligence and inability to maintain expected service levels. There may be a high level of transactional risk banking products online because financial institutions need to have sophisticated internal controls and its use is constant, since the platforms of internet banking mostly are based on new platforms that use complex interfaces to link with previous systems, which increases the risk of errors in transactions. Furthermore, they must ensure data integrity and non-repudiation of transactions (Schwartz, 2010, p. 156).
3. **Compliance Risk:** It is due to violations of laws, regulations and ethical standards; and could lead to affect the reputation, actual monetary losses and reduced business opportunities. Banks need to carefully understand and interpret existing laws in their countries that apply to internet banking and ensure consistency with traditional banking through offices. In this regard, customers are very concerned about the privacy of your data and banks need to be seen as reliable guardians of such data.
4. **Reputation Risk:** Arises from negative public opinion. The reputation of a bank can be damaged by internet banking services that are not up to the expec-

tations of the customers, which generated distrust in the bank. For example, limited availability or software problems. It should be noted that customers have higher expectations regarding the performance of the internet channel.

5. **Risk Information Security:** Caused by weak security processes information, that expose the institution to internal malicious attacks or hackers, viruses, data theft, among others. The rate of change of technology and the fact that the channel is universally accessible internet makes this quite critical risk.
6. **Credit Risk:** As internet banking allows customers to apply from anywhere in the world, it is difficult to verify the customer's identity when offering instant loans through the network.
7. **Interest Rate Risk:** It arises from movements in interest rates. Furthermore, as rates are published on the internet, it is much easier to compare one bank to another, adding pressure on interest rates, stressing the need to react quickly to changes in the same market.
8. **Liquidity Risk:** It arises from the inability of a bank to meet its obligations. Internet banking may increase the volatility of deposits and assets, in the case of customers who keep their accounts just because they are getting a better rate, and which can be removed if they get better, because it is easier to compare between banks through the network.
9. **Price Risk:** It arises from the change in value of financial instruments traded (Benklifa & Olmstead, 2013, p. 33).
10. **Risk of Foreign Currency:** When a currency assets are founded on liabilities in another currency. Internet banking could encourage speculation, because of the ease and low cost of transactions.

In this context, top management of banks should be concerned with managing these risks and establish an effective monitoring of the risks associated with e-banking activities, and therefore do not leave it to be managed by the Management of Information Technology. They should be aware of the role of internet banking to achieve the strategic goals of the organization, and before implementing these services should perform a cost-benefit analysis, have knowledge of the importance of monitoring the technical and administration risk.

Security in E-Banking and Finance

Security controls in internet banking are very important because it is in the open network.The main steps for security checks are:

1. **Authentication:** Ensuring that customers can verify their identities before making internet transactions. At this stage, authentication methods are com-

monly used passwords (passwords), biometric methods, and challenge-response systems. Most financial institutions, apart from having a password of 6 numeric digits to enter our savings accounts, have a calculator where the key is checked, in which the position of the numbers varies each time that enters the system; and when required to make transfers must confirm the password, and the third error entry is blocked (Lee, 2012, p.14).

2. **No Rejection:** It means that the bank must cover if the customer rejects the transaction, claiming that has not been completed by accepting digital certificates (PKI technique); however their applicability in many countries is still doubtful. For example, many banks when required withdrawals or subscriptions of mutual funds are prompt clients to accept a digital service contract about mutual funds, before the transaction is completed.
3. **Segregation of DUTIES:** It is vital to prevent fraud.

Similarly, banks should keep records of audit e-banking transactions, and preserve the confidentiality of customer data via methods available such as firewalls and controls of physical and logical access (Williamson, 2006).

It is noteworthy that the security controls in electronic banking principles contained in the Risk Management Basel Committee report, which referred to previously treated.

The risks arising from internet banking are not restricted to the areas of information security, so that risk management should be directed by senior management, and control procedures need to be aligned with the rapid changes in technology.

Web applications and their protection are for many years one of the biggest challenges for financial institutions programmers. The big problem lies in the application of online banks is that they use the protocol "http" for communication between the banking user and server virtual bank and the base protocol is not safe and they do not have a monitoring mechanism in the communication session, so online banking uses the validation mechanism discussed above (signature) to prevent a possible attack or kidnapping of a user session electronic banking.

In the online operations there are two levels of validation most commonly used by companies being either virtual banks, online banks or the internet channel of a traditional bank.

In the first level of validation applications use online banking passwords mentioned above (username and password) for the user to access their private area and be able to access personal data such as account status, client balance etc., data which typically cannot be modified by the user without using other user validation. Thus the user's browser gets a series of session IDs and other data, which will serve the online bank server to track the customer or user. The problem with this system is that validation is not completely secure as this session tracking is vulnerable and likely to be captured directly or indirectly by other users or intruders outside and thus it is possible phishing banking user.

In the second level of validation, the aim is to avoid possible session hijacking on the first level validation, using within the "session" or "private area" another user authentication to carry out all those operations that may reflect economic risk, such as transfer operations, purchase of securities, etc. This identification unlike the first level of validation cited above, is not used to log on to the application but used whenever the user wants to perform a risk within a session previously validated. This second level of validation is always considered safe since in this case an attacker could hijack a user session but in no case could perform operations that would entail some risk to the banking user.

Having described the protection and safety systems most used by online banking worth briefly describe the types of network attacks against the security of electronic banking. The most common fraud are called "phishing", this type of fraud is the most important to the online banking community and involves spoofing the banking client online, in which it seeks steal data when the user access the service. What happens in this type of fraud is that an individual sends an email to the bank customer requesting update their personal access data by pretending to be an employee or manager of the bank, so it gets a client using a false link, which it is apparently identical to the bank, where the bank user requested access codes and these pass hands of the fraudster.

Of course this type of threat is not the only one in the online banking sector, other types of threats such as "trojan horses" or "pharming" are also very present today. The trojan is a software application that lies within a harmless program that often appear to be photos, music or games, and this is activated when the lid application, thus runs are achieved to obtain passwords and access the user's computer files from internet.

Authentication Measures

Authentication is the process by which it is confirmed that who connects and requests access to a service is really who they say they are, that is, the legitimate user. The following items are responsible for authenticating the process from the beginning (after the connection to the target server).

The choice of one or the other will always depend on the infrastructure provided by trade or online bank and the possibilities of the connection or device by which the process is carried out.

1. **Passwords:** So far, the element used to check the legitimacy of the user requesting the transaction has been the use of passwords. There are many mechanisms that have been improved and taken over the years, the most significant examples are:
    a. **PIN (Personal Identification Number), PIN or Password:** The PIN is the simplest and classical measure of identification: the bank or online store provides a numerical code or alphanumeric code to identify clients; it should be introduced in the appropriate form at the time of authentication.
    b. **TAN (Transaction Authentication Number) or Transaction Authentication Number:** It is an evolution of the PIN. It consists of a list or code table, depending on the circumstances; they may have been previously generated and distributed physically (paper or card) or distributed moments before the transaction through digital media or electronic devices. A different key is requested in each transaction.
2. **Tokens:** They are independent or USB connection to a PC. They can generate random private keys in a pattern or by synchronizing with an external server. At one point the bank requests that the password generated by the token customer is introduced. Clients only need to activate a button to its calculation.
3. **Smartcards:** They are also known as intelligent cards. These are identification devices, the same size as credit cards, which have a chip on which store information. Many of the new credit cards are actually smartcards, gradually abandoning the obsolete magnetic stripe for identification. This type of card reader attached to the computer allows identification when software or web is being used. Its potential is the ability to hold private information within the chip and, depending on the type of chip used, it can then be reprogrammed to add or update the internal data. Its main function is to keep personal user certificates. A clear example of smartcard is the current electronic ID of some countries.
4. **Biometric Devices:** Biometric devices are based on quality and incorporate a factor authentication, they look for a precise and unambiguous way to identify the client using for this part of his body. The most commonly used are:
    a. Fingerprint readers.
    b. Readers palm.
    c. Retina readers
    d. Voice tags.

Although they may seem devices for large companies and organizations, they are actually being adopted at all levels gradually and there are existing banking initiatives to implement them as the primary measure of user identification.

5. **Virtual Keyboards:** These are an identification system in itself but a means of introducing (more or less safely) user credentials, such as your PIN. This method is receiving wide acceptance in many banking sites for password entry forms or when applying the coordinates. Virtual keyboards also exist within the operating system or antivirus software as a means of entering data virtually without using the physical keyboard. Its aim is to avoid keyloggers on the keyboard.
6. **Digital Signatures:** These firms are intended to check the integrity of data transferred during a call. They show whether the statement on the transaction has been altered at some point in their passage through networks that separate origin and destination. They work with digital certificates and the different systems of encryption available.
7. **Digital Certificates:** Along with digital signatures, they are an essential element to initiate a secure connection. Digital certificates are files that identify users, businesses, agencies and, most commonly, the page that is accessed. In short, it is a series of personal data linked to a public key, and all signed by an entity that gives them validity. Normally certificates are issued by the Certification Authorities. The certificates can be used:
    a. Through browsers that use digital certificates (personal or corporate) installed on your computer when needed.
    b. Through smartcards or smart cards where they live and adding a physical layer security. A typical certificate comprises:
        i. Full name of the person or body to be identified.
        ii. Name of Certification Authorities.
        iii. Serial number.
        iv. Digital signature of the Certification Authorities.

It is most often used by technology standard certificates is ITU-T X.509, which regulates its content before being assigned by a Certification Authority.

8. **PKI Infrastructure:** It is an abstract concept. It is a combination of different mechanisms and protocols, both hardware and software, which enable electronic transactions with security, based on public key cryptography. Globally it refers to the set of certificate authorities and other elements involved in communication:
    a. The certificate and the different certificate authorities.
    b. The key, public or not.
    c. Servers certification.
    d. The encryption used.
    e. Digital signatures.

f. Secure channels transport information.
g. The guarantees of acceptance of the transaction (not revoked).

Security Measures During the Transaction

Currently encryption is the most suitable element known to ensure the process from start to finish, ensuring the integrity and confidentiality of the transaction. Encryption is the disruption of communications so that their understanding is difficult for unauthorized people if they are intercepted. Any online transaction must be cryptographically encrypted, since it is the only mathematical method which, if performed in the absence of malware or other distorting elements ensures safe operation.

SSL AND HTTPS

Through SSL "Secure Socket Layer" protocol, encryption and authentication protocol between Web servers and clients (browsers), it has been developed HTTPS, a security protocol based application SSL (or TLS) and derived from HTTP. It is commonly identified by the operator using the https: // at the beginning of the URL instead of the usual http: //.

During an HTTPS connection, there is a first phase agreement or "handshake" where the details of the client-server communication are established. Mainly, it is defined the authentication and encryption known by the two sides (server and browser) and which of them can be used. Whenever one of them cannot support one version, it will be attempted with a previous version, and usually not so secure. It is therefore particularly important to use updated software that supports the latest secure versions of all protocols.

It is necessary that the site possesses a valid certificate of public key and properly signed by a Certification Authority. It is the browser that is in charge of checking. Once secure communication is established, data is sent encrypted to the server until the connection closes.

Security Vulnerabilities that Threaten the Online Banking System

Banks need the means to get protected information flowing through the network in terms of authenticity, integrity and confidentiality. Authenticity is the property that the two users of a communication can see that on the other side the person or organization who claims to be is that person. Thus, a user accessing the web from a bank can be sure that the server that is sending the bank information actually belongs to that institution. It is also possible for the bank to perform a check that the user is who he claims to be, but is rarely used except in professional environments. After the user verifies that is in communication with the bank through the statement in a closed padlock or text or background in green, which appears in the address bar of the browser, the client can proceed to enter the user data to access the secure financial information form.

Integrity is the property that allows clients to check on the receiving end that the information received is correct, sent by the sender and has not been in transit through networks or been altered or modified by third parties. This property is the ensuring that the information reaching the user corresponds to the sent by the server and vice versa and therefore is correct.

Finally, confidentiality is the property that allows clients to encrypt the information to a third party who has the means to intercept the data exchanged between the ends and may not be able to extract hidden information traveling by encryption on data transmitted.

Both SSL and TLS authenticity property is achieved by using digital certificates based on digital signature cryptographic algorithms. An electronic certificate can contain information that identifies a user, a server or a physical machine connected to the internet. In order to verify that the information is true, it has some certification authorities that audits this information and, once validated, is signed by a mathematical algorithm that allows the user to verify that the information is correct to validate this signature. Thus, the user trusts the certificate authority in verifying the identification information contained in the certificate

There are vulnerabilities in the technological solutions that support the transmission of encrypted information over the internet. These tools are essential for the safe use of online services and applications, as they provide confidentiality that allows the transfer of sensitive information securely. The high number of vulnerabilities detected is an indicator of interest existing in various fields for access to the encrypted information flowing through the network.

There are two techniques by which the detected vulnerabilities allow access to information that is encrypted over the internet.

The first is to be done with encryption keys. Once clients have this information, is a pretty straightforward operation as the encryption algorithms are generally public information and anyone (especially a hacker) may implement or use software to decode the information once he has the keys with which encryption has been performed.

The other technique is known as "man in the middle" through whom the attacker gets interposed between the user's computer and the server that clients want to access.

To do this, the attacker must get to convince that the user is contacting the desired server, when it is actually accessing an intermediate machine that intercepts traffic. The attack orchestra works in two steps. In the first, the attacker manages to redirect user traffic to the intermediate machine. In the second, the attacker gets to pose as the real server, which is where the detected vulnerabilities are applicable.

The first step is generally accomplished by alteration of the operation of the DNS service designed to convert web addresses into numeric IP addresses. Another alternative is far more complex, the managers of the internet infrastructure in a controlled manner divert traffic destined for a server to another machine under its control inadvertently user and the service provider.

The result in both cases is that the traffic between the user's computer and the server clients want to access, instead of going directly to the latter, reaches an intermediate machine. This intermediate machine, where the data is decrypted, is responsible for retransmitting the genuine server and send the server response decrypted once the user.

In checking the authenticity is where the detected vulnerabilities are useful for the attacker. Since the machine brought the attacker sends a certificate manipulated to interpret the computer user who has connected to the server and genuinely exploits the vulnerabilities, thus the computer is not able to detect the handling certificate. From this point the connection and all information exchanged supposedly safely with the server falls into the hands of the attacker when is established.

All computer system is likely to have vulnerabilities and encryption tools of information are not exempt. Regardless of its commercial or free nature and whether it is open source or not, these vulnerabilities are not only detecting but are being exploited to gain access to confidential information.

Vulnerabilities of encryption tools are particularly sensitive because they affect the most precious in the systems: information. In addition, its operation can provide significant economic benefits for stealing financial, confidential information, commercial or intellectual property, which is of great interest to criminals.

The appearance of multiple vulnerabilities has alerted developers have about the information security. However, there is an evident lack of dedicated to the comprehensive review of systems and applications preventively resources.

There is growing interest in vulnerabilities having systems to diffuse rapidly throughout the network so that those involved can implement solutions as early as possible.

Finally, it is important to remember that the exploitation of such vulnerabilities in many countries, even only for analysis or investigation, can be a criminal offense. Those interested in analyzing the problem must maintain the necessary steps to do so in a controlled environment or property and to obtain precautions authorization of the rightful owners of the systems under analysis.

CONCLUSION

The introduction of online banking in society is a key aspect in the era of telecommunications, in which we are immersed. Investment in new technologies is very important for financial institutions to expand their business, reduce costs and provide better service to their customers. The problems arise in two ways, first ignorance of the channel by users, and then waste the opportunity to customize offerings to customers by financial institutions.

Technological development in recent years has meant a radical change in financial environment and the geographical barriers of time and communication have been clearly surpassed. The behavior of individual investors has also undergone a profound change, especially in relation to financial institutions (Appei, 2009, p.7). Interactive services are a new form of relationship between a customer and a financial institution. These services, which may take various forms depending on the area to which they are linked, among others: telephone banking, electronic cash, electronic wallet, payment, credit cards and debit cards and Internet.

The incorporation of new technologies will enable the bank to provide the following benefits to consumers:

1. Cost savings due to increased competition between companies
2. Transparency of information, that is, fast, accurate, easy-to-compare and responds perfectly to orders that gives the customer
3. The ability of customers to choose as to how to manage finances anytime, channel of communication with the bank, through appropriate payment, selection of financial assets, etc.
4. Offer personalized products and services. The website of the bank, which has pages of confidentiality with its own password for clients, this is a clear example of customization
5. Financial innovation, favored by the presence of the technologies and their application, for creating and developing new products and services

The influence of perceived risk in buying online services depends on the type of potential risks and that clients are considering, with the perceived risks of financial, social and psychological having a more significant influence. The influence of the financial risk is documented in previous studies that point, as the main obstacle facing the consolidation of electronic transactions, lack confidence in the security of the internet payment system on the web (Laforet & Lee, 2005; Sathye, 1999). In addition, the inability to control third party access to personal data provided during the navigation process can explain the negative influence of perceived psychological risk in adopting online banking.

Although consumers increasingly develop more positive attitudes towards online banking, a large part of bank customers perceive an added value on personal interaction with employees and directors of physical branches in time for a financial transaction. Social interaction increases satisfaction with the completion of transactions in traditional channels and induces consumers to continue to visit the physical branches.

Signing systems used for online banking or online banking today are still quite far from being a robust solution to prevent hacking, as all of these systems suffer from the same weakness, which could be summarized as all use of a base protocol "http" which was designed to be functional but in no case to be sure. Something to keep in mind by financial institutions is that it is far the superior damage to confidence and credibility that this type of fraud can lead to electronic banking in general than the specific economic damage that can affect a financial institution.

REFERENCES

Ainin, S., Lim, C. H., & Wee, A. (2005). Prospects and challenges of E-Banking in Malaysia. *The Electronic Journal of Information Systems in Developing Countries*, *22*, 1–11.

Appei, M. (2009). *Investing with exchange trade funds made easy: A start to finish plan to reduce costs and achieve higher returns* (2nd ed.). Upper Saddle River, NJ: Pearson Education Inc.

Benklifa, M., & Olmstead, W. (2013). *Learn how to trade options (Collection)*. Upper Saddle River, NJ: Pearson Education.

Bonn, M. A., Furr, H. L., & Susskind, A. M. (1999). Predicting a behavioural profile for pleasure travellers on the basis of interne use segmentation. *Journal of Travel Research*, *37*(4), 330–340. doi:10.1177/004728759903700403

Bradley, L., & Stewart, K. (2002). A delphi study of the drivers and inhibitors of internet banking. *International Journal of Bank Marketing*, *20*(6), 250–260. doi:10.1108/02652320210446715

Bradley, L., & Stewart, K. (2003). The diffusion of online banking. *Journal of Marketing Management, 19*(9-10), 1087–1109. doi:10.1080/0267257X.2003.9728252

Chavan, J. (2013). Internet banking - Benefits and challenges in an emerging economy. *International Journal of Research in Business Management, 1*, 19–26.

Chou, D., & Chou, A. Y. (2000). A guide to the internet revolution in banking. *Information Systems Management, 25*, 352–360.

Fontanills, G., & Cawood, R. (2009). *Trade options online*. Hoboken, NJ: Wiley.

Friedman, B. M. (2000). Decoupling at the margin: The threat to monetary policy from the electronic revolution in banking. *International Finance, 3*(2), 261–272. doi:10.1111/1468-2362.00051

Gerrard, P., & Cunningham, J. B. (2003). The diffusion of internet banking among Singapore consumers. *International Journal of Bank Marketing, 21*(1), 16–28. doi:10.1108/02652320310457776

Hart, C. M. (2005). *I want to make money in the stock market: Learn to begin investing without losing your life savings*. Denver, CO: Outskirts Press.

Hobson, R. (2012). *The dividend investor: A practical guide to building a share portfolio designed to maximise income*. Hampshire, United Kingdom: Harriman House Ltd.

Krantz, M. (2013). *Investing online for dummies*. Hoboken, NJ: Wiley.

Laforet, S., & Li, X. (2005). Consumers' attitudes towards online and mobile banking in China. *International Journal of Bank Marketing, 23*(5), 362–380. doi:10.1108/02652320510629250

Laopodis, N. (2013). *Understanding investments: Theories and strategies*. New York, NY: Routledge.

Lassar, P., Lambert, L., Woodford, C., & Moschovitis, C. J. P. (2005). *The internet: A historical encyclopedia*. Santa Barbara, CA: ABC-CLIO.

Lassar, W. M., Manolis, C., & Lassar, S. S. (2005). The relationship between consumer innovativeness, personal characteristics, and online banking adoption. *International Journal of Bank Marketing, 23*(2), 176–199. doi:10.1108/02652320510584403

Lee, E., Kwon, K., & Schumann, D. (2005). Segmenting the non-adopter category in the diffusion of internet banking. *International Journal of Bank Marketing, 23*(5), 414–437. doi:10.1108/02652320510612483

Liao, S., Shao, Y. P., Wang, H., & Chen, A. (1999). The adoption of virtual banking: An empirical study. *PERGAMON International Journal of Information Management, 19*(1), 63–74. doi:10.1016/S0268-4012(98)00047-4

Liao, Z., & Cheung, M. T. (2002). Internet-based e-banking and consumer attitudes: An empirical study. *Information & Management, 39*(4), 283–295. doi:10.1016/S0378-7206(01)00097-0

Packin, N. G., & Lev, A. Y. (2016). Big data and social netbanks: Are you ready to replace your bank? *Houston Law Review*.

Pikkarainen, T., Pikkarainen, K., Karjaluoto, H., & Pahnila, S. (2004). Consumer acceptance of online banking: An extension of the technology acceptance model. *Internet Research: Electronic Networking Applications and Policy, 14*(3), 224–235. doi:10.1108/10662240410542652

Rexha, N., Kingshott, R. P. J., & Shang Shang Aw, A. (2003). The impact of the relational plan of adoption of electric backing. *Journal of Services Marketing, 17*(1), 53–67. doi:10.1108/08876040310461273

Sarlak, M. A., & Astiani, A. A. (2011). *E-banking and emerging multidisciplinary processes: Social, economical, and organizational models*. Hershey, PA: IGI Global. doi:10.4018/978-1-61520-635-3

Sathye, M. (1999). Adoption of internet banking by Australian consumer's an empirical investigation. *International Journal of Bank Marketing, 17*(7), 324–334. doi:10.1108/02652329910305689

Schwartz, R. A. (2010). *Micro markets: A market structure approach to microeconomic analysis*. Hoboken, NJ: Wiley. doi:10.1002/9781118268131

Wang, Y., Wang, Y., Lin, H., & Tang, T. (2003). Determinants of user acceptance of internet banking: An empirical study. *International Journal of Service Industry Management, 14*(5), 205–219. doi:10.1108/09564230310500192

Williamson, D. G. (2006). Enhanced authentication in online banking. *Journal of Economic Crime Management, 4*, 1–42.

Xu, M. X., Wikes, S., & Shah, M. H. (2006). *E-Banking application and issues in Abbey National PLC. E-Technologies. Encyclopedia of E-Commerce, E-Government, and Mobile Commerce*.Hershey, PA, USA: IGI Global.

ADDITIONAL READING

Kallstrom, O. (2000). *Business solution for mobile e-commerce*. Ericsson Review 2000-03-27.

Lee, S. (2012). *E-banking security*. Information Security (InfoSec) Government of Hong Kong Working Paper, Hong Kong.

Weitzman, J. (2000). Cendant unit helps banks offer internet access. *American Banker*, *165*, 11.

KEY TERMS AND DEFINITIONS

Angel Investor: An investor who provides funding for small startups or entrepreneurs.

Crowdfunding Platform: Internet platforms that enable companies to advertise over the internet and obtain investments from registered users in return.

E-Banking: The performance of banking business through the internet. It is also known as "Internet banking" or "Online banking".

Electronic Commerce: A business model that enables to conduct business over the internet.

Financial Institutions: An institution that provides financial services to potential clients.

Online Trading: Individual investors buy and sell stocks over an electronic network through a brokerage company.

Online Security: Computer security involving related to the internet browsing and network security. It is designed to use to establish measures against attacks through internet.

Information Technology: It is the use of any computers, storage, networking and other processes to create, store and exchange electronic data.

Chapter 2
Internet Banking Usage Level of Bankers:
A Research on Sampling of Turkey

Ahu Coşkun Özer
Marmara University, Turkey

Hayrünisa Gürel
Marmara University, Turkey

ABSTRACT

Banks provide service not only through branches in the countries but also offers banking services to customers over the internet. However, customers concern using internet banking because of the various troubles and adversities that may occur on the web and because of their habits. The using of internet banking is still not reached the desired level due to various reasons such as security, troubles on web and habits of customers. In this research, bankers using rate of internet banking and bankers approach on internet banking are determined. According to the survey results in Turkey, almost all of the bankers use internet banking but using of mobile applications does not appear to fully spread. Even though the using of internet banking is very common among the bankers, some of the participants said that they encountered some problems while using internet banking. Solutions of systemic deficiencies, password security problems and other security problems will increase the using of internet banking.

DOI: 10.4018/978-1-5225-0864-9.ch002

INTRODUCTION

Internet banking has emerged as an extension with the development of electronic banking. It is an alternative distribution channel for banks and customers can do all banking operations from outside of the bank office.

The historical process of developing internet banking dates back to 1980's. The researches of internet banking started in US and Europe in the historical process. When the development of internet banking in 35 years is considered, it is the fact that there are major advances. Despite all these developments, both technical problems and security issues are being experienced. This is the subject that cause less numbered users especially in developing countries.

Over 400 million people in the world use the internet banking. There are researches on increasing the number of using internet banking and identifying the problems in internet banking. This research is aimed to determine the problems experienced in internet banking. Bankers are surveyed about internet banking to determine using levels and problems experienced internet banking.

BACKGROUND

Development of Internet Banking in the World

The application of internet technologies to businesses for improvements in their performances is not something new. As stated by Saffu et al. (2008), there is an increase in applications of e-commerce in businesses in the past ten years. The benefits of e-commerce include reduction in cost, increasing business opportunities, reducing lead time and providing a more personalized service to the consumers (Turban et al., 2008). One e-commerce tool that is being adopted by the banking industry is online banking or e-banking. IT tools such as online banking have provided an improvement in services among the banking industry (Dawes & Rowley, 1998). There are currently more than thousands of e-banking websites all over the world (Gurau, 2002). Although online banking has been implemented in many developed countries such as the United States and those in Europe (Pikkarainen et al., 2004), according to the Gurau (2002) there is a growing trend in the adoption of online banking by banks in developing countries too (as cited in Yee-Loong Chong, Ooi, Lin, & Tan, 2010).

Internet banking has emerged as an extension with the development of electronic banking. It is an alternative distribution channel all retail and commercial banking operations can be done outside of the bank office.

According to the Cartwright (2000), The idea of internet banking emerged with telephone banking in 1980 for the first time, increased with the using of the internet in the homes. Sarel and Marmorstein (2003) state that banking and financial institutions in Europe and the US have begun to research and programs about the concept of "home banking" in the 1980s. Because the computer and internet were not very much improved, fax machines and telephones are used by banks to help the customers. Gefen, and Straub (2000) states in the United States "NetBank" is the first internet banking application, in 1996, it was founded under the name of "Atlanta Internet Bank". Rooted banks such as Citibank and Wells Fargo have begun to offer this service to customers in 2001. According to the Batchelor (2010), Gartner Group's Report in 2009 indicate that 47% of adults in the US, 30% of adults in the UK are using internet banking. Gerrard, Barton Cunningham, and Devlin (2006) state that financial services provided via the internet in Singapore were started in 1997 by the DBS Bank. Then UOB and OCBC followed DBS Bank. As stated Polatoğlu and Ekin (2001), at the beginning of 1990 parallel with technological progress, the Turkish banks have expanded continuously automation standards around the worldwide. Turkey's first private bank Türkiye İş Bank have introduced their customers with electronic banking in 1987(as cited in Pala & Kartal, 2010).

In 1997, China Merchants Bank was first to launch the internet payment system in China and thereafter, the internet banking and telephone banking system spread rapidly within mainland China. Although the proficiency of using the internet is relatively low and electronic banking is still in its infancy (Nielsen Consult, 2002), with the advantages of being convenient, safe, efficient and economical, Chinese domestic banks are confident that electronic banking benefits would outweigh traditional banking services in the future and therefore, are eager to implement the new technology and services in order to grasp, penetrate the market and gain competitive advantage. Most retail banks in China now provide online banking as add-on services to the existing branch activities while mobile banking is in the initial stage of implementation (Laforet & Li, 2005).

When the world statistics are analyzed, it shows the global online banking penetration as of April 2012, by world region. Globally, 423.5 million people accessed online banking sites during April 2012, reaching 28.7 percent of the internet audience. In North America, 45 percent of internet audiences accessed banking sites (Statista, 2012).

Considering that population is approximately 310 million people in the US, according to the Pew Online Banking Research Company data, 87 percent of adults use the internet in the US and 61 percent of internet users provide access to online banking sites. 35 percent of mobile phone users use mobile banking.

When we checked the prevalence of online banking in European countries, it is seen that 91 percent of the population in Iceland access to the online banking site in 2014, and Iceland are the most common use of internet banking in Europe. This is followed by Norway with 89 percent. It is seen that 86 percent of the Finnish population, 84 percent of the Danish population, 83 percent of the Dutch population access to internet banking. The lowest rate of the population using internet banking in 15 EU member countries is Germany is with 49 percent. Assessed the 27 EU member countries statistic, the country has the lowest rate using internet banking is Romania with 4 percent of the population, this is followed by Bulgaria with 5 percent and Greece by 13 percent (The Statistics Portal, Statista, Online Banking Penetration in Selected European Markets in 2014).

Development of Internet Banking in Turkey

Internet banking has been implemented for the first time by Türkiye İş Bank in Turkey, in 1997, and in the same year it was followed by Garanti Bank. Then respectively, the Ottoman Bank, Pamuk Bank, Esbank, Akbank and Yapi Kredi Bank offered internet banking services to their customers. Akbank's began first internet banking for retail customers in 1999. Today İş Bank, Garanti Bank, Akbank, Vakıfbank, Denizbank, Koçbank, HSBC and other banks offer a wide range of internet banking services in the Turkey financial markets. Internet banking is perceived as an alternative distribution channel by Turkey Commercial Banks with increasing computer using, regulations in the financial sector, reduction of transaction costs, and customers wish to use electronic banking services. However, because of several reasons such as customers are not accustomed to internet banking and security concerns, the expansion of internet banking in Turkey is limited (Pala & Kartal, 2010).

Security entrance mechanism with two stage is applied in internet banking in Turkey. After the customers enter ID and password from the website of the bank they get a single-use password from the mobile phone and then customers are allowed to entrance of their bank account. Under these conditions, third persons entering a customer's account is difficult. Also, banks take special measures and security software for protection of customer information and assets.

According to the current internet banking statistics on The Banks Association of Turkey (TBB), the number of registered internet banking services to retail customers was 15 million 368 thousand 206 for the end of June 2006. According to the report published on TBB, the total number of active users of internet banking in December 2010 (log in at least once in the last three months) was 6 million 694 thousand. The total number of active users of internet banking reached 13 million 683 thousand in September 2014. It means that the number of users of internet banking has increased more than doubled in last 5 years in Turkey.

Concerns About Internet Banking

Concerns with internet banking are same around the world. Security and privacy, access to paper money and credit transactions are still concerned about internet banking.

Security of internet transactions is of paramount concern to most customers particularly where financial information is involved (Hedberg & Taylor, 2001). Banks must convince their customers that their websites are secure and sufficient safeguards have been taken to assure security at the transaction level. Also, safeguarding the privacy of customer's financial information and profile are imperative if the public is to embrace internet banking (Nath, Schrick & Parzinger, 2001). According to Fysh (1999), even with the best the internet has to offer in banking services, consumers still need to visit an ATM or a bank branch to withdraw cash. Customers also have to deposit checks by mail, through an ATM or by visiting a bank branch (as cited in Nath, Schrick & Parzinger, 2001, p. 26).

Online trust issues affect customers' relationship commitment to banks and willingness to engage in online transactions. Perceived privacy and security concerns could hinder customers from engaging in commercial transactions on the Web. Perceptions of opportunistic behavior of online banks and lack of proper communication also affect the overall level of trust towards the online banks and their systems. The issue of trust is therefore increasingly recognized as a critical success factor in the emerging retail bank space (Mukherjee & Nath, 2003).

Generally, consumers' knowledge to access channel, convenience, and consumers' experience, waiting time on the website of banks, privacy, and service qualities are important factors for using internet banking around the world.

MAIN FOCUS OF THE CHAPTER

Issues, Controversies, Problems

The using of internet banking is still not reached the desired level due to various reasons such as security, troubles on web and habits of customers. In this research, bankers using rate of internet banking and bankers approach on internet banking are determined. For this reason, 387 bankers are surveyed.

Research Methods and Methodology

Sample Size

In this research, bankers' utilization rate of internet banking and their approach to internet banking has been investigated. A survey was applied to the bankers who work in İstanbul branch of banks, in January 2015, by the random sampling method. According to the statistic of Banks Association of Turkey, the number of employees across the country in September 2014 was 199.000. The necessary sample size was calculated as 383 in 95 percent of confidence level and the range of + -5 confidence interval. 387 bankers participated for the survey research.

Research Results

Sample Characteristics

Considering the age range of participants, 47 percent of participants are between the 20-30 years old, 38 percent are in the age range 31-40, 14 percent are between 41-50 years old. When we evaluated age groups, it is seen that the age range is 20-30 years old mostly using the internet banking and lowest using rate in ages between 51-60 (1 percent of the respondents). When we asked education levels of participants, 8 percent of the participants said that they have associate degrees, 84 percent of participants have bachelor's degree, 5 percent of the participants have a graduate degree.

Survey Results

All participants (387) in the survey reported that they are using the internet banking. The rate of using mobile applications of internet banking is 80 percent. 310 participants stated that they use the mobile internet banking application, 77 participants (20 percent) said that they are not using mobile applications of internet banking. The utilization rate of internet banking is 100s percent among bankers, the utilization rate of mobile applications of internet banking is 80 percent so it is determined that using mobile applications has not yet been fully widespread among the bankers.

Survey question 'How did you meet with Internet banking? (How did you to start using internet banking?)' is responded, 68 percent of the respondents (263 people) said that they met internet banking through the work of institutions, 11 percent of respondents said they met internet banking through banks, 8 percent of respondents through advertising, 8 percent of them through friend's recommendation, 4 percent of them through the internet. It is seen that mostly the banks that bankers work is effective on bankers starting to use internet banking.

Survey question 'What kind of facilities have occurred in your life with internet banking?' is responded, 35 percent of participants (the vast majority) stated that they have time savings through internet banking. The 30 percent of bankers stated that it helps to pay costs, 22 percent of bankers said that they can make transactions faster, 6 percent stated that they can make operation 24 hours and 7 days in a week, 4 percent of them said that it makes easy to follow up payments, 3 percent stated that it is increasing convenience to the expense in banking costs.

Within this research, it is aimed to determine that whether there have been problems in the use of internet banking and what types of problems occur. According to the survey results, 33 percent of respondents face with problems while they are using of internet banking. The rate is 67 percent stated that they have no problems using internet banking. Considering the problems occurred while using of internet banking, the first problem is about the password procedures and systemic failures. 10 percent of bankers faced with password operation problems while they are using internet banking, and other 10 percent of bankers stated that they faced systemic disruptions during the using internet banking, 4 percent of bankers face to problems because of the complex the interface, 5 percent reported that they experience problems due to the lack of some functions.

Security problems experienced in internet banking cause the raising of concerns among bankers. For the question of 'Do you think that internet banking is safe? ', 3 percent of the respondents answered No, 6 percent of respondents answered 'partially safe'. 9 percent of bankers think that internet banking is not safe and 91 percent of the bankers think internet banking is safe.

According to the survey results, bankers want to much security about internet banking in the future.12 percent of them stated that they wanted to increase the security in applications related to internet banking. The correction of the systemic problem is the second expectation of bankers for the future. 5 percent of participants wants to be the corrected of systemic problems, 5 percent of participants want to apply for a loan through internet banking without going to a branch of the bank, 4 percent of bankers stated that they want a richer menu on the internet.

SOLUTIONS AND RECOMMENDATIONS

It is important that using of the internet banking should be brought safety level and concerns of the customers about internet banking should be eliminated.

The problems on system failures experienced by customers using Internet banking should be eliminated and that will increase customer loyalty to banks.

It is important that banks should reach out to customers to inform them about online banking and new developments on online banking. Banks will increase their customers by this way.

Banks should increase the services offered by online banking, allow to customers without going to the bank office for many applications like deposits, loan or credit drawing from online banking.

The services facilitate daily life, provided through bank branches can be performed on the internet and these applications will greatly increase the number of the users internet banking.

FUTURE RESEARCH DIRECTIONS

Further research is carried out on the customers to determine the problems experienced in internet banking. In addition to this, the research can be improved on services which banks will provide in the future from the web. That will improve the competitiveness of banks in the future.

CONCLUSION

When the world statistics are analyzed, it shows 423.5 million people accessed online banking sites during April 2012, it represents 28 percent of the internet audience. Considering that population is approximately 310 million people in the US, according to the Pew Research Company data, 87 percent of adults use the internet in the US. 61 percent of internet users provide access to online banking sites. When we checked the prevalence of online banking in European countries, it is seen that 91 percent of the population in Iceland access to the online banking site in 2014, and Iceland are the most common use of internet banking in Europe. This is followed by Norway with 89 percent. Among the 27 EU member countries statistic, the country has the lowest rate using internet banking is Romania with 4 percent of the population, this is followed by Bulgaria with 5 percent and Greece by 13 percent.

Internet banking has been implemented for the first time in 1997 in Turkey. Internet banking is perceived as an alternative distribution channel by Turkey commercial banks with increasing computer using, regulations in the financial sector, reduction of transaction costs, and customers wish to use electronic banking services. However, because of several reasons such as customers are not accustomed to internet banking and security concerns, the expansion of internet banking in Turkey is limited. The total number of active users of internet banking in December 2010 (log in at least once in the last three months) was 6 million 694 thousand. The total number of active users of internet banking reached 13 million 683 thousand in September 2014. It means that the number of users of internet banking has increased more than doubled in last 5 years in Turkey

When the overall the survey results are evaluated, 33 percent of bankers face with problems while they are using internet banking in Turkey. The rate is 67 percent stated that they have no problems. Considering the problems in the use of internet banking, the first problem is about the password procedures and systemic failures. Also complex interface and lack of some function on websites of banks are important problems in Turkey. Security problems experienced in internet banking cause raising of concerns among bankers. 9 percent of bankers think that internet banking is not safe and 91 percent of the bankers think internet banking is safe.

REFERENCES

Batchelor, B. (2010). The History of Internet Banking. *Ehow.com*. Retrieved 0 from http://www.ehow.com/about_5109945_history-ebanking.html

Cartwright, I.R. (2000). Mastering Customer Relations. London: McMillan.

D., Gefen,, & Straub, D. (2000). The Relative Importance of Perceived Ease-ofUse in IS Adoption: A Study of E-Commerce Adoption. *Journal of the Association for Information Systems*, *1*(8), 1–30.

Dawes, J., & Rowley, J. (1998). Enhancing the customer experience: Contributions from information technology. *Management Decision*, *36*(6), 350–357. doi:10.1108/00251749810220568

Fysh, G. (1999, June 3). Customers Cash in on Increased Availability of Internet Banking. Knight-Ridder/Tribune Business News.

Gerrard, P., Barton Cunningham, J., & Devlin, J. F. (2006). Why Consumers Are Not Using Internet Banking: A Qualitative Study. *Journal of Services Marketing*, *20*(3), 160–168. doi:10.1108/08876040610665616

Gurau, C. (2002). Online banking in transition economies: The implementation and development of online banking systems in Romania. *International Journal of Bank Marketing*, *20*(6), 285–296. doi:10.1108/02652320210446742

Hedberg, A., & Taylor, N. (Eds.). (2001). *Net Banking Must Do Better*. Marketing Week. Retrieved from https://www.marketingweek.com/2001/02/08/net-banking-must-do-better/

Laforet, S., & Li, X. (2005). Consumers' Attitudes Towards Online and Mobile Banking in China. *International Journal of Bank Marketing*, *23*(5), 362–380. doi:10.1108/02652320510629250

Sarel, D., & Marmorstein, H. (2003). Marketing Online Banking Services: The Voice of The Customer. *Journal of Financial Services Marketing*, *8*(2), 106–118. doi:10.1057/palgrave.fsm.4770111

Mukherjee, A., & Nath, P. (2003). A model of trust in online relationship banking. *International Journal of Bank Marketing*, *21*(1), 5–15. doi:10.1108/02652320310457767

Nath, R., Schrick, P., & Parzinger, M. (2001, Fall). Bankers Perspectives on Internet Banking. *e-Service Journal*, *1*(1), 21–36. Retrieved from http://muse.jhu.edu/journals/eservice_journal/v001/1.1nath.pdf doi:10.2979/ESJ.2001.1.1.21

Nielsen Consult. (2002). China Online Banking Study. Retrieved from http://estore.chinaonline.com/chinonlbanstu.html

Pala, E., & Kartal, B. (2010). Banka Müşterilerinin İnternet Bankacılığıyla ile İlgili Tutumlarına Yönelik Bir Araştırma. *Journal of Management and Economy, 17*(2). Retrieved from http://www2.bayar.edu.tr/yonetimekonomi/dergi/pdf/C17S22010/43_61.pdf

Pikkarainen, T., Pikkarainen, K., Karjaluoto, H., & Pahnila, S. (2004). Consumer Acceptance of Online Banking: An Extension of the Technology Acceptance Model. *Internet Research, 14*(3), 224–235. doi:10.1108/10662240410542652

Polatoğlu, V. N., & Ekin, S. (2001). An Empirical Investigation of Turkish Consumers' Acceptance of Internet Banking Services. *International Journal of Bank Marketing, 19*(4), 156–165. doi:10.1108/02652320110392527

Saffu, K., Walker, J. H., & Hinson, R. (2008). Strategic Value and Electronic Commerce Adoption Among Small and Medium-Sized Enterprises in A Transitional Economy. *Journal of Business and Industrial Marketing, 23*(6), 396–404.

Statista. (2012). Global Online Banking Penetration in April 2012, By region. Retrieved http://www.statista.com/statistics/233284/development-of-global-online-banking-penetration/

Statista, The Statistics Portal. (n. d.). Online Banking Penetration in Selected European Markets in 2014. Retrieved from http://www.statista.com/statistics/222286/online-banking-penetration-in-leading-european-countries/

The Banks Association of Turkey. (n. d.) Retrieved from http://www.tbb.org.tr/tr/banka-ve-sektor-bilgileri/istatistiki-raporlar/59

The Financial Brand. (n. d.). PEW Research Online Banking Users Demographic Trends. Retrieved from http://thefinancialbrand.com/32428/pew-research-online-banking-users-demographic-trends/

Turban, E., King, D., Lee, J., Warkentin, M., & Chung, M. H. (2008). *E-Commerce: A Managerial Perspective*. Upper Saddle River, NJ: Prentice-Hall.

Yee-Loong Chong, A., Ooi, K. B., Lin, B., & Tan, B. I. (2010). Online banking adoption: An empirical analysis. *International Journal of Bank Marketing, 28*(4), 267–287. doi:10.1108/02652321011054963

ADDITIONAL READING

Godfried, B.W. (2005). *Online Business Security System*. Springer. Retrieved from https://books.google.com.tr/books?id=HW9UeQdKX0cC&pg=PA12&dq=online+banking+security&hl=tr&sa=X&ved=0CCMQ6AEwAGoVChMIiYnQ25qayQIVC90sCh1pKApH#v=onepage&q=online%20banking%20security&f=false

Great Britain, Parliament: House of Lords, Science, and Technology Committee. (2006). Personal Internet Security. Retrieved from https://books.google.com.tr/books?id=W--x_sFoMK8C&pg=PA55&dq=online+banking+security&hl=tr&sa=X&ved=0CCsQ6AEwAWoVChMIiYnQ25qayQIVC90sCh1pKApH#v=onepage&q=online%20banking%20security&f=false

Jahankhan, H., Watson, D., Me, G., & Leonhardt, F. (2010). *Handbook of Electronic Security and Digital Forensics*. Retrieved from https://books.google.com.tr/books?id=ZgpV6Rvw2FoC&pg=PA163&dq=online+banking+security&hl=tr&sa=X&ved=0CDMQ6AEwAmoVChMIiYnQ25qayQIVC90sCh1pKApH#v=onepage&q=online%20banking%20security&f=false

KEY TERMS AND DEFINITIONS

Customer Loyalty: Customer loyalty is both an attitudinal and behavioral tendency to favor one brand over all others, whether due to satisfaction with the product or service, its convenience or performance, or simply familiarity and comfort with the brand.

Customers: An individual or business that purchases the goods or services produced by a business. The customer is the end goal of businesses since it is the customer who pays for supply and creates demand.

Internet Banking: The performance of banking activities via the internet.

Mobile Banking: Mobile banking refers to the use of a smartphone or another cellular device to perform tasks while away from your home computer, such as monitoring, transferring, bill payment.

Online Banking: The performance of banking activities via the internet. Online banking is also known as "Internet banking" or "Web banking." A good online bank will offer customers just about every service traditionally available through a local branch, including accepting deposits, paying interest on savings and providing an online bill payment system.

Password Problems: Password is secret series of characters that enables a user to access to online banking. Password problems experienced problems such as hacked password or forgotten password.

Security Problems: Banks have set up security systems to ensure that transactions conducted online are protected from internet security threats. Most banks use an industry-standard Secure Transaction software and protocol to manage the security on their systems.

The Web: The World Wide Web (www) is an open source information space where documents and other web sites and web resources are identified by URLs, interlinked by hypertext links. People can access the web via the Internet. It has become known simply as the Web.

Chapter 3
Internet Banking and Financial Customer Preferences in Turkey

İsmail Yıldırım
Hitit University, Turkey

ABSTRACT

The first online banking service was introduced in Turkey by İş Bank in 1998. However, the number of internet users has been increasing rapidly in Turkey, the number of online banking users did not increase with a similar pace. Although banks are taking measures for the security of online banking transactions, many financial consumers are still concerned about the security of these transactions therefore preferring not to use online banking. This study reveals the development of internet banking in Turkey and consumer percentages. Previous research on the factors affecting the usage of e-banking are also addressed in this study. It was found that the majority of these studies focus on the correlation between the security concerns which result in avoiding to use internet banking.

DOI: 10.4018/978-1-5225-0864-9.ch003

INTRODUCTION

Banking industry plays an important role in the global economy. The industry is open to internal and external changes in many countries. Among the most significant external changes concerning the industry are economic, social and technological changes. As banks are not able to directly interfere with external factors, their success depends on their ability to adapt to these changes (Jayawardhena & Foley, 2000). Generally speaking, the use of new technologies in banking services allows for changes in corporate structure, standardization of the communication system, and improved efficiency. Nevertheless, new technologies make it possible for prevention of repeated transactions while reducing the time spent for a transaction; reduction of the need for mid-level managers; and distribution of the responsibility of executives in order to assign different tasks, authority, and responsibilities to each group.

With the use of technology becoming crucial for the banks, they are now using new methods they have developed in order to offer better services for their customers. Among some of these services are automated teller machines (ATM), credit cards, phone banking and online banking. Internet banking is a web-based banking method which has been developing with new solutions for security issues replacing the interactive software which allows for home and office banking.

Information technologies are an important competitive tool for banking corporations. As the use of internet changes the business mentality and the methods used, banks are also developing their marketing and sales strategies in accordance with this process. Banks have started offering services to their consumers through internet as the use of internet became widespread. Following the new technologies meticulously, banks are now aiming for the maximum efficiency through internet banking in an era where speed, time and costs are of utmost importance.

Internet banking is the brand new distribution network which facilitates the sales of banking services. Internet banking involves several services such as account balance checking, money transfers, payment, and gathering information on several subjects which bank customers can perform from their homes and offices through a telecommunication network (Aparikyan, 2000). Widespread use of internet banking and the resulting distribution of banking transactions offer both banks and their customers significant advantages when compared to conventional branch banking (Gan, Clemes, Limsombunchai et al., 2006).

However, many banks in Turkey offer online banking services, the use of internet banking remains at a relatively low level. This study addresses the current status of internet banking in Turkey. In addition, previous research on the factors affecting the usage of e-banking are also addressed in this study.

Internet Banking

Internet banking can be defined as a channel used for distribution of banking services remotely (Çabuk & İnan, 2005). Banking industry faces major changes due to factors such as competitive prices, limited time consumers are willing to spend on banking transactions, increasing number of alternatives, consumers' need for more sophisticated products and hard-to-satisfy consumers in a competitive market. In the light of these market conditions, internet banking has become a channel which all banks need to use.

The ease of investment through internet banking directly contributes to a nation's economy. An example of this is the derivative transactions which are only available to investors in developed economies and which contribute to the stability of an economy. Technological infrastructure is a must in order for these transactions to be available for the investors. Active use of technology in the banking industry of a nation contributes significantly to the development of the economy and the market (Mermod, 2011).

When assessed from the financial consumer perspective, internet banking allows for cost savings and makes it possible to perform several banking transactions without being limited with time and location.

Some other advantages of the internet banking particularly for the banking corporations are as follows (Gurau, 2002; Singh, 2004):

- Development of new product and services
- Acquiring new customers therefore increasing sales
- Retaining the current customer base
- Reinforcing the brand image
- Ability to access more customers
- Opportunities for product marketing and customer relations
- Increasing operating effectiveness
- Offering more efficient customer services
- Ability to take banking services beyond the limits of conventional banking
- Ability to rapidly respond to the changes in the market
- Reducing the load on the branches
- Reduction of the number of branches and employees
- Increasing customer loyalty

The advantages it offers aside, the issue of privacy and security proves challenging for the adoption of online banking by the consumers. Factors such as the perception that it is relatively advantageous, its convenience for the lifestyle and working methods, the perception of security and risk, previous experiences with the

Internet, the need for a convenient and suitable channel such as Internet, the ability to use Internet efficiently play an important role in the adoption of internet banking.

Internet Banking in Turkey

Turkish banking industry has been growing not only in numbers but also with the range of services it offers to its local and international customers thanks to the technological advancements. Banking activities in Turkey had been conducted mainly in bank branches until 1987. The first private bank established in Turkey, Türkiye İş Bankası, has introduced ATMs in 1987 laying the foundations of electronic banking in Turkey. Telephone banking which offers any banking transaction except money withdrawal had gained widespread recognition as of the last quarter of 1997. Internet banking, on the other hand, was introduced by Türkiye İş Bankası in 1997 in Turkey and Garanti Bankası also offered e-banking to its customers the same year. Osmanlı Bankası, Pamukbank, Esbank, Akbank, Yapı Kredi Bankası and other banks followed and offered online banking services to their customers (Polatoğlu & Ekin, 2001).

It was only possible to perform a limited amount of banking transaction using internet banking when it was first introduced in 1997. The number of services offered through internet banking is increasing every other day with the bank competing to improve the service range they offer online. It is now possible to perform almost all of the transactions one can perform in a branch using internet banking (Aksoy, 2000).

The Banks Association of Turkey (TBB), a legal entity which represents all the banks operating in Turkey, reports on the statistics it compiles about the internet and mobile banking users regularly. Including the data from 28 banks, this report is significant for it shows that the increasing number of transactions and transaction volume especially in the mobile banking.

The Use of Internet Banking in Turkey

The total number of individual customers who are registered in the internet banking system and who signed in at least once is 42,917,000 as of 2015. The number of individual customers who logged in at least once in the past year is approximately 23,900,000. The number of active internet banking users has increased by 3.1 million in the last year.

16 million individual customers have logged in to the internet banking system at least once between October and December, 2015. This number adds up to 38% of the total number of registered individual customers. The number of active individual customers has increased by 2,989,000 between October and December, 2015

when compared to the same period of time the previous year while increasing by 1,171,000 when compared to the previous quarter (Turkiye Bankalar Birligi, 2016)

The total number of corporate customers who are registered in the internet banking system and who signed in at least once is 2,766,000 as of December, 2015. 1,251,000 of these corporate customers (45%) have logged in at least once between October and December, 2015. The number of corporate customers who logged in at least once in the past year is approximately 1.5 million.

38% of the total number of customers (individual and corporate) are registered and logged in at least once in the system between October and December, 2015. The number of total active customers has increased by 3.1 million between October and December, 2015 when compared to the same period of time the previous year while increasing by 1,210,000 when compared to the previous quarter.

Table 1. The number of Internet banking users in Turkey

	2011	2012	2013	2014	2015
Number of Individual Customers (Thousand)					
Active (A) (Logged in at least once in the last 3 months)	7.803	9.630	11.422	13.181	16.170
Registered (B) (Logged in at least once)	18.106	22.611	28.190	34.048	42.917
Registered (C) (Logged in at least once in the past 1 year)	10.389	13.884	16.824	19.615	23.900
Active (A) / registered (B) customer ratio (%)	43	43	41	39	38
Number of Corporate Customers (Thousand)					
Active (A) (Logged in at least once in the last 3 months)	803	922	1.014	1.134	1.251
Registered (B) (Logged in at least once)	1.892	2.193	2.235	2.324	2.766
Registered (C) (Logged in at least once in the past 1 year)	968	1.131	1.217	1.399	1.548
Active (A) / registered (B) customer ratio (%)	42	42	45	49	45
Total Number of Customers (Thousand)					
Active (A) (Logged in at least once in the last 3 months)	8.606	10.552	12.436	14.315	17.420
Registered (B) (Logged in at least once)	19.998	24.804	30.425	36.371	45.683
Registered (C) (Logged in at least once in the past 1 year)	11.358	15.015	18.041	21.014	25.448
Active (A) / registered (B) customer ratio (%)	43	43	41	39	38

Source: Turkiye Bankalar Birligi (2016)https://www.tbb.org.tr/tr.

Internet Banking Transactions

Financial Transactions

As of the period between October and December, 2015, the total number of internet banking transactions was approximately 141 million which adds up to a volume of 770 billion Turkish Liras. Money transfer transactions such as EFT, bank wire and foreign exchange transactions accounted for 71% of the financial transaction volume.

The number of financial transactions has increased by 3,869,000 when compared to the same period of time the previous year while increasing by 9,609,000 when compared to the previous quarter. The total transaction volume, on the other hand, has increased by 156 billion TL when compared to the same period of time the previous year while increasing by approximately 76 billion TL when compared to the previous quarter.

Investment Transactions

As of the period between October and December, 2015, the total number of internet banking transactions was approximately 11 million which adds up to a volume of 145 billion Turkish Liras. The transaction volume was increased by 10 billion TL when compared to the period between July and September, 2015.

Foreign exchange transactions account for the highest trade volume with approximately 43 billion TL (3,271 transactions) in the 3rd quarter. Deposit accounts, investment funds and stock transactions follow foreign exchange transactions in terms of their trade volume.

Table 2. Financial transactions in Internet banking

	2014		2015	
	# of Transactions (Thousand)	**Transaction Volume (Million TL)**	**# of Transactions (Thousand)**	**Transaction Volume (Million TL)**
Money transfer	63.281	488.705	68.534	600.081
Payments	48.748	30.390	45.612	37.421
Investment transactions	10.759	127.800	10.812	155.279
Credit card transactions	11.711	16.393	12.176	17.634
Other financial transactions	2.890	27.374	4.124	35.961
Total	137.389	690.662	141.258	846.376

Source: Turkiye Bankalar Birligi (2016)https://www.tbb.org.tr/tr.

Table 3. Investment transactions in Internet banking

	September 2015		December 2015		Net Difference		December 2015
	# of Transactions (Thousand)	Transaction Volume (Million TL)	# of Transactions (Thousand)	Transaction Volume (Million TL)	# of Transactions (Thousand)	Transaction Volume (Million TL)	Average Transaction Volume (Thousand TL)
Investment Funds	1.848	26.547	1.941	29.051	93	2.504	15,0
Foreign Exchange Transactions	3.285	45.680	3.271	43.760	-13	-1.920	13,4
Deposit accounts	945	41.061	934	42.377	-11	1.316	45,4
Stock transactions	3.312	17.976	4.146	26.323	834	8.348	6,3
Repo transactions	102	5.080	100	4.964	-2	-115	49,8
Bill and bond transactions	59	808	58	775	-1	-33	13,4
Gold	282	1.778	230	1.257	-52	-521	5,5
VIOP	132	6.160	132	6.770	0	610	51,3
Total	9.964	145.089	10.812	155.279	848	10.190	14,4

Source: Turkiye Bankalar Birligi (2016)https://www.tbb.org.tr/tr.

The highest average transaction volume accounts for VIOP transactions with TL51,000. Repo transactions follow VIOP with approximately TL50,000. The average transaction volume is TL45,000 for deposit accounts.

30% of the active individual internet banking users and 35% of the active corporate internet banking users resides in Istanbul. Ankara and Izmir are respectively follows Istanbul for both customer groups.

THE ATTITUDE OF FINANCIAL CONSUMERS TOWARDS INTERNET BANKING

There is research in the literature which studies the factors affecting the use of internet banking. The fact that internet is an easy-to-access technology raises the question of security of the website. Security problems lead to customer complaints. Nevertheless, it is widely accepted that the transactions must be conducted in privacy and they should not be traceable by others. The trust in internet banking plays an important role in the preference of customers to perform banking transactions online. Trust is defined as the willingness of a bank to act on its customers' expectations with respect to the internet banking.

Customers want to trust the bank itself and the website of the bank. The convenience of the Internet technology, ease-of-use, accessibility and the quality of the internet connection are also important factors regarding the use of internet banking. Being aware of the services offers by the Internet technology contributes to the use of Internet banking. Among the other factors affecting the use of Internet banking are the existence of people who use Internet banking in the social sphere of a person and that the person is computer literate.

The research on the consumer attitude and the adoption of Internet banking shows that there are several factors affecting the consumer attitude towards Internet banking. Demographic characteristic of the consumer and their experience in the use of computer and new technologies are among these factors. Nevertheless, the attitude of the consumer towards the Internet banking is also in relation with their motivation for and attitude towards the banking technologies.

Security Factor

There is research on the security concerns as a factor affecting the usage of e-banking by financial consumer. Among these are Zhu (2009), Reid (2008), Ekberg, Li and Morina (2007), Polasik and Wisniewski (2008), Flavian, et al. (2006), Shergill and Li (2006), Rotchanakitumnuai and Speece (2003), Sohail and Shanmugham (2003), Matilla, Karjaluoto and Pento (2003), Suh and Han (2002), Karjaluoto et all. (2002), Sathye (1999). Among the studies which use the technology acceptance model are Yoon and Steege (2013); Alsajjan and Dennis (2010); Gu, et al. (2009), Cheng et al. (2006); Luarn and Lin (2005); Pikkarainen et al. (2004); Eriksson et al. (2004). Several researchers reported that the reliability factor plays an important role in the access to information and financial transactions through Internet banking (Wang et al., 2003; Casalo et al., 2007; Al-Somali, Gholami, & Clegg, 2008).

Yoon and Steege (2013) in their study, listed openness, availability of the website, and security concerns of the customers as the factors affecting the use of Internet banking.

Alsajjan and Dennis (2010) used the technology acceptance model in their study. They collected the data through a survey distributed to 618 university students in Saudi Arabia. It was found that trust and advantages were among the factors affecting the use of Internet banking.

Zhu (2009) reported three factors regarding the security of Internet banking. The first factor is the necessity to make sure that the messages received by the bank and the customer to be legal (authenticity). The second is the necessity that the financial data sent through Internet cannot be accessible to any third parties other than the bank and the customer (privacy and honesty). The last factor is the necessity to prove that a transaction was made by a person after the transaction is completed. Zhu, in his study, states that Internet banking is not offering a secure media and that modern mobile phones need larger screens and improved computer features in order to secure the transactions.

Vrechopoulous and Atherinos, (2009) reported that the design of the online banking website has an effect on the Internet usage behavior.

Gu, et al. (2009) investigated the attitude of Korean consumers towards mobile banking adding several external variables along with trust variable to the technology acceptance model. The study showed that perceived ease-of-use and perceived convenience had an impact on the intention while perceived convenience had a correlation with perceived ease-of-use.

Reid (2008) stated that the trust in the system and the ability of the individuals to conduct banking transactions online are among the most important factors affecting the use of Internet banking.

Polasik and Wisniewski (2008) suggested that factors such as perceived security level, having an experience with Internet at an average level, and demographic variables play a significant role in the adoption of Internet banking.

Ekberg, Li and Morina (2007) in their study involving 4 leading banks operating in Sweden, investigated the principles banks take into consideration when deciding on using Internet banking. They reported that security concerns have an impact on the use of Internet banking.

Nor and Pearson (2007) in their study conducted in Malaysia, reported that factors such as confidence, relative superiority, trialability have an impact on the use of Internet banking.

Sanmugam (2007) suggested that the most important factor in the adoption of Internet banking is the social norms.

Casalo et al. (2007) showed that security and privacy played an important and immadiate role in earning the trust of customers in Internet banking. Security concerns also affect the growth and development of the e-commerce. Therefore, it is of utmost importance to offer Internet banking transactions without the risk of security breaches which also affect the use of Internet banking. Privacy is defined as the protection of the data collected during the interaction of the customer and the Internet banking system in several ways (w/o the user being informed about it).

Flavian, et al. (2006) concluded that the trust in a bank; and the income level, age and gender of the customer affects the preference of the customer to use the Internet banking services provided by the bank the customer is working with.

Shergill and Li (2006) conducted a research with the aim to identify the factors affecting the confidence and loyalty New Zealanders place in Internet banking. In their study they found that shared values were the most important factor influencing the trust bank customers place in Internet banking. On the other hand, they have found that factors such as customer satisfaction from Internet banking, confidence, brand image and expenses played an important role in the customer's loyalty to the bank.

Cheng, et al. (2006) investigated the factors influencing the intention of bank customers in Hong Kong to use Internet banking including a perceived web security variable to the technology acceptance model. This study showed that variables such as perceived convenience and perceived web security had an effect on the intention to use while perceived ease-of-use had an indirect impact.

Luarn and Lin (2005) investigated the factors affecting the intention to use Internet banking in Taiwan including variables such as credibility, perceived self-efficacy, perceived financial cost along with perceived convenience and perceived ease-of-use. This study showed that perceived credibility had a more significant effect when compared to the traditional variables of the technology acceptance model.

Pikkarainen, et al (2004) added four new variables to the technology acceptance model (perceived playfulness, knowledge about Internet banking, security and privacy, quality of the Internet connection) and investigated the factors affecting the adoption of Internet banking in Finland. According to this study, knowledge about Internet banking has an effect on the adoption of online banking; while the effect of factors such as perceived playfulness, security and privacy, quality of the Internet connection were statistically insignificant. In another study, Eriksson, et al. (2004) investigated the viewpoint of bank customers in Estonia towards Internet banking using the technology acceptance model. This study emphasized that users of Internet banking services agree on the advantages of Internet banking. Therefore, the study states the key role perceived convenience plays in the use of Internet banking.

Rotchanakitumnuai and Speece (2003) investigated the obstacles to the adoption of Internet banking for corporate bank customers in Thailand. The study revealed that concerns about Internet security is the most important obstacle for the widespread use of Internet banking.

Sohail and Shanmugham (2003) in their study conducted in Malaysia, reported that factors such as accessibility, knowledge about Internet banking, resistance to change, capital costs of computers and access to Internet, trust in the bank, security concerns, advantages and ease-of-use influence the adoption of Internet banking.

Matilla, Karjaluoto and Pento (2003) conducted a study on the Internet banking customers aged 65+ who are living in Finland. Aspects such as inconvenience, security and being deprived of personalized services are among the obstacles of using Internet banking.

Suh and Han (2002) investigated the viewpoint of consumers in Korea using a survey embedded to the websites of 5 banks. They reported that advantages and ease-of-use have an impact on the use of Internet banking by financial consumers. They also stated that the element of trust was one of the most important measures influencing the use of Internet banking.

Karjaluoto et al. (2002) conducted a study on the Internet banking customers living in Finland. They reported that security concerns did not have a significant impact on the use of Internet banking.

Sathye (1999) in the study conducted in Australia, reported that factors such as security concerns and not being sufficiently informed about Internet banking were among the obstacles of adopting Internet banking.

FACTORS AFFECTING THE USE OF INTERNET BANKING BY FINANCIAL CUSTOMERS IN TURKEY

Majority of the studies conducted in Turkey reports that the security concerns affect the use of Internet banking. Among the studies which show that security concerns affect the use of Internet banking are Yıldırım (2015), Akın and Karaboğa (2011), Ustasüleyman and Eyüboğlu (2010), Pala and Kartal (2010), İlter, Saatçıoğlu and Kuruoğlu (2009), Usta (2005)

Yıldırım (2015), in his research, developed surveys in order to collect data and they were delivered to academics working in Turkish universities. According to the findings of the analysis, the most important factor affecting the intention to use internet banking for financial consumers in Turkey is the perception of trust. Ease-of-use, convenience and security considerations were among the other factors affecting the intention to use internet banking.

Akın and Karaboğa (2011), in their study focusing on the decision to use the branchless banking services, concluded that the most important factors for the preference to use branchless banking services are security and computer literacy.

Pala and Kartal (2010) studied the attitude of the customers of bank towards the Internet banking along with the factors affecting the process to register an Internet banking account and the selection of the bank which is offering the services in a study which involved 196 active Internet users. The results of the study showed that aspects such as convenience and security affect the use of Internet banking.

Ustasüleyman and Eyüboğlu (2010) aimed to identify the factors which affect the use of Internet banking using the Technology Acceptance Model based on the structural equation modeling. Results of the analysis showed that convenience significantly and positively affects perceived usefulness while perceived usefulness significantly and positively affects the trust. Nevertheless, it was found that variables such as trust, perceived usefulness, perceived ease-of-use and perceived web security affect the intention to use Internet banking.

İlter, Saatçıoğlu and Kuruoğlu (2009), in their study which was aimed at the factors affecting the use of Internet banking, analyzed factors such as efficiency, security and trust, convenience and accuracy, internalization and relating, and privacy. The study reports that security and trust is the most important factor in this respect.

Usta (2005), aimed to define the reasons why individuals do not use Internet banking in his study. The study concluded that the security concerns have the most important effect on the use of Internet banking. This study also showed that security concerns differ depending on the gender of the consumer.

When both national and international literature is analyzed, it was found that factors such as customer satisfaction, service quality, 24/7 accessibility from any location, saving from time, convenience, and ease of access prove to be important factors affecting the use of Internet banking. The most important factor affecting the widespread use of Internet banking, on the other hand, is obviously the perception of risk regarding the transactions made using the Internet, i.e. reliability. According to the common conclusions of the studies conducted on this subject, factors such as being unaware of the service, lack of ability to use Internet, being afraid of making mistakes, finding the bank's website rather confusing, and lack of controls and trust are found to be affecting the use of Internet banking unfavorably.

CONCLUSION

Competitive prices, limited time consumers are willing to spend on banking transactions, and competitive market have led to major changes in the banking industry rendering the Internet banking a must. The first online banking service was introduced in Turkey in 1998 and the number of users is ever increasing.

The reasons behind the financial consumers prefer Internet banking are that banking transactions costs less, one can go into more detail in the service provided and that it is possible to perform transactions rapidly without the need for visiting a branch. Despite the security measures banks employ for Internet banking, there still may be breaches in the banks' information systems. The customer himself/herself seems to be the weakest link in this process regarding their negligence to protect their passwords.

However, Internet banking offers several favorable features, it would be hard to claim that it is adopted by the consumers at an expected level. Therefore, in order for the banks to be able to utilize all the opportunities Internet banking has to offer, it is a must to first identify the factors affecting the adoption of Internet banking and to manage their marketing efforts accordingly.

Security concerns need to be eliminated in order for the financial consumers to use Internet banking. Many previous studies showed that security concerns limit the use of Internet banking. It is possible to increase the intention to use Internet banking taking necessary measures on this subject.

In order to eliminate the security concern of the bank customers to deposit their money to virtual world, banks not just need to secure the system but also need to inform the consumers about the security. In this context, public relations efforts through newscasts rather than conventional advertisements may prove efficient.

REFERENCES

Akın, F., & Karaboğa, K. (2011). Bireysel Müşterilerin Şubesiz Bankacılık Hizmetlerini Kullanma Kararına Etki Eden Faktörlerin Belirlenmesi Üzerine Bir Araştırma: Bilecik Örneği, Marmara Üniversitesi İ.İ.B.F Dergisi, Cilt XXX. *Sayı*, *I*, 301–320.

Aksoy, T. (2000). *Elektronik Ticaret*. Ankara: Sistem Yayınları.

Al-Somali, S. A., Gholami, R., & Clegg, B. (2009). An investigation into the acceptance of online banking in Saudi Arabia. *Technovation*, *29*(2), 130–141. doi:10.1016/j.technovation.2008.07.004

Alsajjan, B., & Dennis, C. (2010). Internet Banking Acceptance Model: Cross-Market Examination. *Journal of Business Research*, *63*(9-10), 957–963. doi:10.1016/j.jbusres.2008.12.014

Aparikyan, B. (2000). Bankacılıkta Teknoloji Kullanımı. *Banka ve Para Teknolojileri Dergisi*, 6(2).

Çabuk, S., & İnan, H. (2005). İnternet Aracılığıyla Bankacılık Hizmetlerinin Pazarlaması. *Marmara Üniversitesi Sosyal Bilimler Enstitüsü Dergisi*, *6*(23), 23–34.

Casalo, L. V., Flavian, C., & Guinaliu, M. (2007). The role of security, privacy, usability and reputation in the development of online banking. *Online Information Review*, *31*(5), 583–603. doi:10.1108/14684520710832315

Cheng, T.C.E., Lam, D.Y.C., & Yeung, A.C.L. (2006). Adoption of Internet Banking: An Empirical Study in Hong Kong. *Decision Support Systems*, *42*(3), 1558–1572. doi:10.1016/j.dss.2006.01.002

Eriksson, K., Kerem, K., & Nilson, D. (2004). Customer Acceptance of Internet Banking in Estonia. *International Journal of Bank Marketing*, *23*(2), 200–216. doi:10.1108/02652320510584412

Flavian, C., Guinaliu, M., & Torres, E. (2006). How Bricks and Mortar Attributes Affect Online Banking Adoption. *International Journal of Bank Marketing*, *24*(6), 406–423. doi:10.1108/02652320610701735

Gan, C., Clemes, M., Limsombunchai, V., & Weng, A. (2006). A Logit Analysis of Electronic Banking in New Zealand. *International Journal of Bank Marketing*, *24*(6), 360–383. doi:10.1108/02652320610701717

Gu, J., Lee, S., & Suh, Y. (2009). Determinants of Behavioral Intention to Mobile Banking. *Expert Systems with Applications*, *36*(9), 11605–11616. doi:10.1016/j.eswa.2009.03.024

Gurau, C. (2002). Online Banking in Transition Economies: The Implementation and development of Online Banking Systems in Romania. *International Journal of Bank Marketing*, *20*(6), 285–296. doi:10.1108/02652320210446742

İlter, B., Saatçıoğlu, Ö. Y., & Kuruoğlu, E. (2009). Who Uses Internet Banking in Turkey and Why? *Proceedings of theEuropean and Mediterranean Conference on Information Systems* (pp. 1-18).

Jayawardhena, C., & Foley, P. (2000). Changes in the Banking Sector: The Case of Internet Banking in the UK. *Internet Research: Electronic Networking Applications and Policy*, *10*(1), 19–30. doi:10.1108/10662240010312048

Karjaluoto, H., Matilla, M., & Ve Pento, T. (2002). Electronic banking in Finland: Consumer beliefs and reactions to a new delivery channel. *Journal of Financial Services Marketing.*, *6*(4), 346–361. doi:10.1057/palgrave.fsm.4770064

Li, S., Ekberg, P., & Morina, P. (2007). Online banking access system: Principles behind choices and further development, seen from a managerial perspective.

Luarn, P., & Lin, H.-H. (2005). Toward an Understanding of the Behavioral Intention to Use Mobile Banking. *Computers in Human Behavior*, *21*(6), 873–891. doi:10.1016/j.chb.2004.03.003

Matilla, M., Karjaluoto, H., & Pento, T. (2003). Internet Banking Adoption among Mature Customer: Early Majority Or Laggards? *Journal of Services Marketing*, *17*(5), 514–528. doi:10.1108/08876040310486294

Mermod, A. Y. (2011). *Elektronik Bankacılık ve Riskler*. İstanbul: Beta Basım Yayım Dağıtım A.Ş.

Nor, K.Md. & ve Pearson, J.M. (2007). The Influence of Trust on Internet Banking Acceptance. *Journal of Internet Banking and Commerce*, *12*(2), 1–10.

Pala, E., & Kartal, B. (2010). Banka Müşterilerinin İnternet Bankacılığı ile İlgili Tutumlarına Yönelik Bir Pilot Araştırma. *Yönetim ve Ekonomi.*, *2*(17), 43–61.

Pikkarainen, T., Pikkarainen, K., Karjaluoto, H., & Pahnila, S. (2004). Consumer Acceptance of Online Banking: An Extension of the Technology Acceptance Model. *Internet Research*, *14*(3), 224–235. doi:10.1108/10662240410542652

Polasik, M., & Wisniewski, T.P. (2008). Empirical Analysis of Internet Banking Adoption in Poland. *International Journal of Bank Marketing*, *27*(1), 32–52. doi:10.1108/02652320910928227

Polatoğlu, V. N., & Ekin, S. (2001). An empirical investigation of the Turkish consumers acceptance of İnternet banking services. *International Journal of Bank Marketing*, *19*(4), 156–165. doi:10.1108/02652320110392527

Reid, M. (2008). Integrating Trust and Computer Self-Efficacy with TAM: An Empirical Assessment of Customers' Acceptance of Banking Information Systems (BIS) in Jamaica. *Journal of Internet Banking and Commerce*, *12*(3).

Rotchanakitumnuai, S., & Speece, M. (2003). Barriers to Internet Banking Adoption: A Qualitative Study Among Corporate Customers in Thailand. *International Journal of Bank Marketing*, *21*(6), 312–323. doi:10.1108/02652320310498465

Sanmugam, A. (2007). Factors Determining Consumer Adoption of Internet Banking. Retrieved from http://papers.ssrn.com/sol3/papers.cfm?abstract_id=1021484#

Sathye, M. (1999). Adoption of Internet Banking by Australian Consumers: An Empirical Investigation. *International Journal of Bank Marketing*, *17*(7), 324–334. doi:10.1108/02652329910305689

Shergill, G. S., & Li, B. (2006). Internet Banking-An Empirical Investigation of a Trust and Loyalty Model for New Zealand Banks. *Journal of Internet Commerce*, *4*(4), 101–118. doi:10.1300/J179v04n04_07

Singh, A. M. (2004). Trends in South African internet Banking. *Aslib Proceedings: New Information Perspectives*, *56*(3), 187–196. doi:10.1108/00012530410539368

Sohail, M. S., & Shanmugham, B. (2003). E-Banking and Customer Preferences in Malaysia: An Empirical Investigation. *Information Science*, *150*(3-4), 207–217. doi:10.1016/S0020-0255(02)00378-X

Suh, B., & Han, I. (2002). Effect of trust on customer acceptance of Internet banking. *Electronic Commerce Research and Applications*, *1*(3-4), 247–263. doi:10.1016/S1567-4223(02)00017-0

Turkiye Bankalar Birligi. (2016). Retrieved from https://www.tbb.org.tr/tr

Usta, R. (2005). Tüketicilerin İnternet Bankacılığını Kullanmama Nedenleri Üzerine Bir Araştırma. *Doğuş Üniversitesi Dergisi*, *6*(2), 279–290.

Ustasüleyman, T., & Eyüboğlu, K. (2010). Bireylerin İnternet Bankacılığını Benimsemesini Etkileyen Faktörlerin Yapısal Eşitlik Modeli ile Belirlenmesi. *BDDK Bankacılık ve Finansal Piyasalar*, *2*(4), 11–38.

Vrechopoulous, A., & Atherinos, E. (2009). Web Banking Layout Effects on Consumer Behavioural Intentions. *International Journal of Bank Marketing*, *27*(7), 524–546. doi:10.1108/02652320911002340

Wang, Y. S., Wang, Y. M., Lin, H. H., & Tang, T. I. (2003). Determinants of user acceptance of internet banking: An empirical study. *International Journal of Service Industry Management*, *14*(5), 501–519. doi:10.1108/09564230310500192

Yıldırım, İ. (2015). Factors Affecting the Way Financial Consumers in Turkey Regard Internet Banking. *Journal of Business Research Turk*, *7*(3), 21–35. doi:10.20491/isader.2015315711

Yoon, H. S., & Steege, L. M. B. (2013). Development of a quantitative model of the impact of customers' personality and perceptions on Internet banking use. *Computers in Human Behavior*, *29*(3), 1133–1141. doi:10.1016/j.chb.2012.10.005

Zhu, F. (2009). Smart Card Based Solutions for Secure Internet Banking with a primitive reader or mobile phone, Retrieved from http://www.cs.ru.nl/bachelorscripties/2009/Feng_Zhu

KEY TERMS AND DEFINITIONS

Financial Consumer: The customer who enjoys the products or services provided by banks.

Internet Banking: It is the use of Internet by the bank customers in order to buy banking services. It has been widely used due to increasing availability of the Internet and shopping opportunities. Internet banking involves several banking transactions and is conducted through a computer with Internet connection without to need to visit a branch of the bank.

Mobile Bank: An application developed for smartphones and tablets in order to make it possible to conduct banking transactions using these devices.

Bank: An establishment which can loan and borrow money with interest, can conduct discount and exchange transactions, can offer safe deposits for money, valuable documents and goods, and can perform any commercial, financial and economic activity.

Deposit: Any money deposited to a bank or a credit company in order to be withdrawn after a specific period of time or notice period.

Chapter 4
Expectation and Perception of Internet Banking Service Quality of Select Indian Private and Public Sector Banks:
A Comparative Case Study

Nilanjan Ray
Netaji Mahavidyalaya, India

ABSTRACT

This research paper mainly deals with expectation and perception of service quality of select Indian Banks i.e. SBI and HDFC on the customer satisfaction. The research survey was based on IS-QUAL dimensions (Ray & Ghosh,2014) a diagnostic model developed in 2014, which measures service quality and internet service quality in terms of customer expectations and perceptions of banking services. This present research tends to evaluate the overall idea of expected and perceived services of the two banks. This study is a cross-sectional survey that employed the use of pre-structured questionnaire to collect primary data from a sample of 120 respondents through personal contact, field survey and email. Collected data have been analyzed through SPSS 21 software by different statistical tools like Reliability test for judgment of internal consistency of collected data and paired t- test.

DOI: 10.4018/978-1-5225-0864-9.ch004

INTRODUCTION

Customer satisfaction is a serious issue for the success of any organization. Service quality is the main indicator to measure the client satisfaction. The relation between expectations and perceptions are very important in business especially in service industry to identify the service quality. In modern business environment, providing high service quality is the major key for a sustainable competitive advantage. Being a service industry catering to the millions of customers, banks are constantly offering new products to satisfy their diverse client bases with varied tastes and preferences. In recent years, internet banking is one of the facilities are offering to their clients to ensure client satisfaction along with improved business. The internet banking or online banking is a win-win solution for both the banks and their clients. The clients are advantaged because of the convenience, flexibility and literally 24-hour banking solutions in their hands and the banks get benefitted because of lower operating costs, wider geographical reach and reduced client pressure on their branches. Present status of Indian commercial banks demonstrates that maximum amount of branches is computerized and with CBS (Core Banking Solution). Commercial banks working in rural areas also providing most of internet banking services like mobile banking, NEFT, RTGS, ATM, credit cards, POS etc. Basically e-banking includes all non-traditional and electronic means of banking such as ATM, internet banking (IB), mobile banking, banking through credit cards and debit cards etc.

SURVEY OF EXISTING LITERATURE

The major reason for customers to choose banks for investment funds is because of the dependability and reputation of banks. Banks always promise customers a high level of security during transactions. Banking service can increase customers' confidence and trust if employees are able to provide appropriate service to each customer. For instance, understanding the needs of each individual customer, such as knowing the customers' expected retirement age, annual income, and hobbies are required to help provide a good match of insurance and fund products for customers. Assurance is the knowledge and courtesy of employees and their ability to inspire trust and confidence. Bank commitments are important, as customers may save a large sum of money in banks. For complicated products such as insurance, funds, and margins, employees must provide a clear explanation of each product to customers, so that customers can feel confident about the services provided by banks. The final dimension is empathy, which represents the individualized attention that firms provide to its customers. Employees who show understanding of customer needs and are knowledgeable to solve customer problems are success factors for the service industry. Friendly customer service pleases customers when they walk into a bank. The purpose of this dimension is to retain customers to keep using the bank service (Van Iwaarden et al., 2003). Customer satisfaction provides an essential link between cumulative purchase and post-purchase phenomena in terms of attitude change, repeat purchase and brand loyalty (Churchill & Surprenant, 1982). Service quality has a positive influence on customer satisfaction (Yee et al., 2010). Customer satisfaction is defined as the attitude resulting from what customers believe should happen (expectations) compared to what they believe did happen (performance perception) (Neal, 1998). Satisfaction reinforces quality perception and drives repeat purchases. Zaim, Bayyurt, and Zaim (2010) found that tangibility, reliability and empathy are important for customer satisfaction, but Mengi (2009) found that responsiveness and assurance are more important. Siddiqi (2010) examined the applicability of service quality of retail banking industry in Bangladesh and found that service quality is positively correlated with customer satisfaction; empathy had the highest positive correlation with customer satisfaction, followed by assurance and tangibility. On the other hand, Lo, Osman, Ramayah and Rahim (2010) found that empathy and assurance had the highest influence on customer satisfaction in the Malaysian retail banking industry. Arasli, Smadi and Katircioglu (2005) found that reliability had the highest impact on customer satisfaction. A number of studies have identified the dimensions of service quality as the antecedents of customer satisfaction. Kotler and Armstrong (2012) preach that satisfaction is the pos-purchase evaluation of products or services taking into consideration the expectations. Researchers are divided over the antecedents of service quality and satisfaction. Whilst some believe service quality leads to satisfaction, others think otherwise (Ting, 2004). The studies of Lee et al. (2000); Gilbert and Veloutsou (2006); Sulieman (2011) and Buttle (1996) suggest service quality leads to customer satisfaction. To achieve a high level of customer satisfaction, most researchers suggest that a high level of service quality should be delivered by the service provider as service quality is normally considered an antecedent of customer satisfaction. As service quality improves, the probability of customer satisfaction increases. Quality was only one of many dimensions on which satisfaction was based; satisfaction was also one potential influence on future quality 2 perceptions (Clemes, 2008). Service quality is an important tool to measure customer satisfaction (Hazlina et al., 2011). Badri M, (2003) made an assessment and application of the SERVQUAL model in measuring service quality in information technology centre. For their research gap they used a larger sample which also differs from other studies that addressed the dimensionality problem of the IT centre-adapted SERVQUAL instruments. Curry et al., (2002, p.197) in an attempt to assess the quality of physiotherapy services used the SERVQUAL model and three physiotherapy services in Dundee, Scotland. They considered the ten original criteria for evaluation and combined them into five; tangibles, reliability, responsiveness, assurance (including competence, courtesy, credibility, and security) and empathy (including access, communication, and understanding). Avkiran (1999) used service quality instrument developed in Australia to measure service quality in retail banking as perceived by customers (BANKSERV). It was adapted from SERVQUAL to specifically suit the Australian banking industry. Wang et al. (2002) found in Chinese banks that reliability was the key drivers of the product quality &followed by tangibility. The authors argued in favor of improving service quality &product quality to build and enhance company reputation.

Research Objectives

This study can be ascertained by the following research objectives:

1. To discuss the impact of banking service quality dimensions on client satisfaction.
2. To analyze IS-QUAL dimensions on customer satisfaction.

Research Methodology

Data for the study undertaken has been collected from the primary source, which is again collected through pre-structured questionnaire. The questionnaires include information on their name, sex, age, country and occupation. Based on the objectives, 20 questions were set up and to make the analysis more transparent the sample size was restricted to 120 respondents. This study is representative in nature so far as the banks are concerned and focuses on client satisfaction of internet banking services and not on a particular bank's internet banking services.

Measures and Analysis

Primary data were collected using a predetermined personally administered questionnaire. The questionnaire was designed to capture sample characteristics and the objectives. It has a mix of quantitative and qualitative feedbacks. For the quantitative feedbacks, a five point Likert scale from 1 to 5 was used, where 1 was for the lowest satisfaction level and 5 was for the highest satisfaction level. Collected data has been analyzed by SPSS 21 using paired t- test to identify the impact of internet banking service quality on client satisfaction. The structured questionnaire contained IS-QUAL dimensions (Ray & Ghosh 2014) were grouped and designed to measure the respondents' expectations and perceptions regarding quality of services offered by the bank. Descriptive statistics analysis was used to measure clients' expectations and perceptions scores. Paired *t*-test was carried out to test the significant difference between the two means of expectations and perceptions of the services offered by the bank.

IS-QUAL Dimensions

ANALYSIS AND DISCUSSION

For internal reliability of the questionnaire was tested by Cronbach's Alfa. If Alfa value greater than 0.70, it depicts that higher internal consistency in the measured dimension. Here the above table Cronbach's Alfa is .744. It is clear that the questionnaire used in this study had strongly internal reliability and it could be used with confidence for the application of next statistical analysis and interpretation.

Table 3 depicts that, the means difference scores, *t*- values and the significance obtained through the evaluation of each service dimensions. The gap scores (PM-EM) for each dimension was calculated by subtracting the expected and perception

Table: 1 IS-QUAL dimensions

IS-QUAL Dimensions	Descriptions
Trustworthiness	Privacy, Safe transactions, Secured login, Clear information, Degree of client's belief that the bank's site is safe, Billing accuracy
Awareness	Promotional offers i.e. internet banking, mobile banking, NEFT, RTGS, debit cards, credit cards
Accessibility	24X7X365 basis service, Online assistance, Account Access when aboard, ATM Access, Mobile Banking
Rigidity	Flexibility of timings, Easy fund transfer
Navigation	Continuous up-gradation of online system, user-friendly interface
Communication	Updated status, Availability, emails, SMS
Web Customization / Personalization	Accurate online transaction, easy login, functions that clients needed, pattern of online shopping

Source: Ray N, Ghosh D (2014): Internet Service Quality (I-SQ) Dimensions and their Impact on Consumer Satisfaction: Case from Banking Industry, Asian Journal of Research In Banking and Finance, Vol.4, Issue. 8, 212-221.

Table 2. Reliability test

Cronbach's Alpha	Cronbach's Alpha Based on Standardized Items	N of Items
.744	.743	7

means. Above table also depicts that all dimensions are positive so it indicates that customers are satisfied i.e. expectations are matched with perceptions. *T*- values are also positive of all dimensions and *P*- values are significant i.e. P< 0.05. It indicates that customers are significantly satisfied with internet banking in HDFC. Again Table 4 depicts that, the means difference scores, *t*- values and the significance obtained through the evaluation of each service dimensions. The gap scores (PM-EM) for each dimension was calculated by subtracting the expected and perception means. Above table also depicts that all dimensions are negative so it indicates that customers are not satisfied with internet banking. *T*- values are negative of all dimensions and *P*- values are significant i.e. P< 0.05. It indicates that customers are significantly not satisfied with internet banking in SBI.

According to our research respondents, it is very important that their transactions and personal information must be fully secured. Trustworthy and secured online system would make the decision easy for a client moving to internet banking from

Table 3. T-Test for customers' perception and expectation in HDFC bank

IS-QUAL Dimensions	Expectations Mean	Perceptions Mean	Gap (PM-EM)	T -Value	Sig.
Trustworthiness	3.8941	4.3273	0.4332	7.043	.002
Awareness	3.9243	4.2765	0.3522	6.244	.001
Accessibility	3.8433	4.3324	0.4891	7.543	.001
Rigidity	4.0361	4.5303	0.4932	5.341	.000
Navigation	3.7098	4.1324	0.4226	8.354	.000
Communication	2.8943	4.0873	1.193	7.542	.002
Web Customization	3.5686	4.2144	0.6458	7.553	.003

Table 4. T-test for customers' perception and expectation in state bank of India

IS-QUAL Dimensions	Expectations Mean	Perceptions Mean	Gap (PM-EM)	T -Value	Sig.
Trustworthiness	4.8941	3.6372	-1.2569	-6.033	.000
Awareness	4.9353	3.1746	-1.7607	-7.324	.000
Accessibility	4.7423	3.2313	-1.511	-5.332	.000
Rigidity	4.0361	2.4201	-1.616	-7.432	.000
Navigation	4.5248	3.2321	-1.2927	-8.253	.000
Communication	4.2952	3.1832	-1.112	-7.341	.000
Web Customization	4.4382	3.1123	-1.3259	-7.421	.000

traditional modes of banking. According to respondents' internet banking in HDFC is more flexible than SBI as most of the SBI branches are not implemented net banking. Again, clients of some banks, offering internet and mobile banking services through ATMs in countries like India and Bhutan, found that it was inconvenient to access ATM when they are abroad. A simple navigable website would be encouraging for clients and they would desire to use online services. The banks should also ensure that there is no communication gap between a bank and its client and during any need or query, a client can easily access the management or the bank's staff. According to respondents SBI banking staffs sometimes are not willing to mitigate the problems of customers. If banks work on these dimensions, then it would surely ensure the increase of client-flow towards internet banking. According to the respondents, the service efficiency dimension of internet banking is reasonably good in HDFC net banking system. They were found to be highly satisfied with the service efficiency in areas like providing information, updating records, quick confirmation of payments, prompt reply of emails, 24X7X365 basis online support, etc. Clients' trust in Internet dealing with record trades have a kind estimation, that is, the nonspecific method for the online environment, the wide use of advancement, and the inborn insecurity of using an open establishment for trades. This gives a fascinating test to banks to find ways to deal with begin and foster electronic relationship with clients. Problem solving attitude should also prevail in banks, as this factor has an impact on assured service dimension. Most of the respondents like E-managing account administrations like Promotional offers i.e. web saving money, portable managing an account, NEFT, RTGS, platinum cards, credit cards. Thus, the nonappearance of client trust, both in the properties of the bank and in the general online environment has been, and remains, a deterrent in the no matter how you look at it gathering of Internet sparing cash. Client retention is potentially one of the most influential factors that financial institutions can utilize to gain a strategic advantage and survive in today's ever-increasing competitive business environment. Moreover, banks need to develop strategies that enhance loyalty of their clients. Therefore, banking organizations should always attempt to ensure that their clients remain extremely satisfied. In all above respect according to the respondents that they are most satisfied with HDFC bank rather than SBI bank.

CONCLUSION

The nature of administration can be accessed through steady criticism instrument for diverse administration measurements and this can help the banks to perform all the more adequately and productively. Clients are the spirit of any business organization and banks being in the administration division are likewise customer driven and are continually overhauling their operations to guarantee better client fulfillment. Be that as it may, expanding standards, regulations, advancements, rivalry and vicinity of tech-adroit customers make a bank more helpless against diverse parts of administration quality. This requires an inside and outside examination of present managing account operations to oblige new administration quality measurements in both conventional and virtual banking operations. Easy navigated website would be soothing for customers and they would like better to use online services. Trustworthy and secured online system, if provided, would make the decision easy for the customer moving to internet banking. It is very significant that their transactions and personal information must be fully secured. In case of any query there must not be communication gap and customer have access to the management and banking staff when needed. If banks works on these determinants that it would surely increase its customers using online banking.

REFERENCES

Arasli, H., Smadi, S. M., & Katircioglu, S. T. (2005). Customer service quality in the Greek Cypriot banking industry. *Managing Service Quality*, *15*(1), 41–56. doi:10.1108/09604520510575254

Churchill, G., & Surprenant, C. (1982). An investigation into the determinants of customer satisfaction. *JMR, Journal of Marketing Research*, *19*(4), 491–504. doi:10.2307/3151722

Clemes, M. D. (2008). An empirical analysis of customer satisfaction in international air travel. *Innovative Marketing*, *4*, 49–62.

Gilbert, G. R., & Veloutsou, C. (2006). A Cross-Industry Comparison of Customer Satisfaction. *Journal of Services Marketing*, *20*(5), 298–308. doi:10.1108/08876040610679918

Hazlina. (2011). Impacts of service quality on customer satisfaction: Study of Online banking and ATM services in Malaysia. *International Journal of Trade Economics Finance*, 2(1).

Kotler, P., & Armstrong, G. (1999). *Principles of Marketing*. Upper Saddle River, NJ: Prentice Hall.

Lee, M. C., Lee, Y., & Yoo, D. (2000). The determinants of perceived service quality and its relationship with satisfaction. *Journal of Services Marketing*, *14*(3), 217–231. doi:10.1108/08876040010327220

Lo, L. K., Osman, M., Ramayah, T., & Rahim, M. (2010). The impact of service quality on customer loyalty: A study of banks in Penang, Malaysia. *International Journal of Marketing Studies*, *2*(2), 57–66.

Mengi, P. (2009). Customer satisfaction with service quality: An empirical study of public and private sector banks. *Journal of Management Research*, *8*(9), 7–17.

Neal, W. D. (1998). Satisfaction be damned, value drives loyalty. *Paper presented at the ARF Week of Workshops*, New York.

Ray, N., & Ghosh, D. (2014). Internet Service Quality (I-SQ) Dimensions and their Impact on Consumer Satisfaction: Case From Banking Industry. *Asian Journal of Research In Banking and Finance*, *4*(8), 212–221.

Siddiqi, K. O. (2010). Interrelationships between service quality attributes, customer satisfaction and customer loyalty in the retail banking sector in Bangladesh. *Paper presented at theInternational Trade and Academic Research Conference*, London.

Sulieman. (2011). Banking Service Quality Provided by Commercial Banks and Customer Satisfaction. *American Journal of Scientific Research*, 27(2), 68-83.

Ting, D. H. (2004). Service Quality and Satisfaction Perceptions: Curvilinear and Interaction Effect. *International Journal of Bank Marketing*, *22*(6), 407–420. doi:10.1108/02652320410559330

Van Iwaarden, J., van der Wiele, T., Ball, L., & Millen, R. (2003). Applying SERVQUAL to Web sites: An exploratory study. *International Journal of Quality & Reliability Management*, *20*(8), 919–935. doi:10.1108/02656710310493634

Yee, R. W. Y., Yeung, A. C. L., & Cheng, T. C. E. (2010). An empirical study of employee loyalty, service quality and firm performance in the service industry. *International Journal of Production Economics*, *124*(1), 109–120. doi:10.1016/j.ijpe.2009.10.015

Zaim, H., Bayyurt, N., & Zaim, S. (2010). Service quality and determinants of customer satisfaction in hospitals: Turkish experience. *The International Business & Economics Research Journal*, *9*(5), 51–58.

ADDITIONAL READING

Kaiser, H. F., & Cerny, B. A. (1979). Factor analysis of the image correlation matrix. *Educational and Psychological Measurement*, *39*(4), 711–714. doi:10.1177/001316447903900402

Nunnally, J., & Bernstein, I. (1994). *Psychometric Theory*. New York: McGraw-Hill.

Nuseir, M. T., Akroush, M. N. (2010). The Effect of E-service Quality on Customers' Satisfaction in Banks Operating in Jordan: An Empirical Investigation of Customers' Perspectives. *International Journal of Services, Economics and Management.*

Philipos, L. B. (2013). Customer satisfaction and electronic banking service on some selected banks of Ethiopia. Retrieved from www.ijrcm.org

Rotchanakitumnuai, S., & Speece, M. (2003). Barriers to Internet banking adoption: A qualitative study among corporate customers in Thailand. *International Journal of Bank Marketing*, *21*(6/7), 312–323. doi:10.1108/02652320310498465

Salman, S., & Kashif, S. (2010). *Electronic banking and e-readiness adoption by commercial banks in Pakistan*. Linnaeus University, School of Computer Science, Physics and Mathematics.

Sampson, E. (2005). *Technological developments and global banking innovation*. Zenith Economic Quarterly.

KEY TERMS AND DEFINITIONS

Client Satisfaction: It is a measure of how products and services supplied by a company meet or surpass customer expectation.

Internet Banking: Internet Banking is an automated payment system that enables customers of a financial institution to conduct financial transactions on a website operated by the institution, such as a retail bank, virtual bank, credit union or building society.

ISQUAL Dimensions: ISQUAL is Internet Service Quality Dimensions are Trustworthiness, Awareness, Accessibility, Rigidity, Navigation, Communication and Web Customization/Personalization.

Chapter 5
Towards Fully De-Materialized Check Management

Fulvio Frati
Università degli Studi di Milano, Italy

Ernesto Damiani
Information Security Research Center, Khalifa University, UAE

Claudio Santacesaria
Research & Development Department, Rototype S.p.A., Italy

ABSTRACT

Banks worldwide are putting a big effort into de-materializing their processes, in order to streamline the processes and thus reducing overall costs. In this chapter, the authors describe how the de-materialization can be a big opportunity for banks, describing the European context. Furthermore, the de-materialization of check handling is taken as example, proposing a review of existing technologies and describing the advantages that a real framework can give to the users and to the bank systems.

DOI: 10.4018/978-1-5225-0864-9.ch005

INTRODUCTION

In the last few years, banks have done a big effort to improve services they supply to customers, reducing costs at the same time. As a part of this effort, a trend is emerging towards progressive de-materialization of banking processes and artifacts. For instance, the term certificates dematerialization refers to investors converting into digital form the physical certificates of shares they have given in custody to a financial institution acting as a depository. In Europe, investors can dematerialize any certificate provided that (i) is registered in their name and (ii) belongs to the list of securities admitted for dematerialization by regulatory authorities like the European Central Bank. De-materialization of banking processes has started to affect loan and investment procedures that traditionally involved face-to-face meetings with customers at bank branches, and can now be carried out online via sophisticated Web portals. In turn, dematerialization has led to downsizing, allowing banks to reduce personnel and other operational costs.

More recently, banks started de-materializing physical artifacts, like receipts, that can now be sent as email and not directly delivered to users, and checks. Processes involving checks are potentially very profitable for banks, as check clearing is carried out within the banking system, without the need of sharing profits with intermediaries. However, two big issues of checks management have hindered their diffusion in the last years:

- From the bank side, checks involve high management costs with respect to other payment methods (UK Payments Administration, 2008);
- From the customer side, checks are considered vulnerable to frauds.

Nevertheless, Vines et al. (2012) have shown how checks are perceived by many customers as an attractive payment method. Continued customer interest in checks as a handy payment instrument motivates the development of de-materialization technologies targeted to reducing check management costs and prevent known frauds.

In this chapter, the authors propose a novel framework based on secure traditional encryption algorithms, digital signatures, and online verification systems, to be applied to checks in substitution of obsolete solutions like magnetic ink, ultra-violet verifiers, and watermarks.

BACKGROUND

Traditional Checks

The notion of check as a payment method dates back to the 18th century, when the Bank of England produced the first batch of pre-printed and numbered checks. Printed serial numbers were introduced later as a way to prevent frauds. In the Sixties, the use of Magnetic Ink Character Recognition techniques (MICR) for printing and reading serial numbers allowed banks to start using mechanical verifiers, reducing check management costs. Then, in the Nineties, use of checks plummeted due to the increase of credit cards payments and the diffusion of frauds. Recent changes in tax regulations, which authorize cash payments only up to a fixed threshold, boosted again the interest in checks of bank and users alike.

Several stakeholders have started investigating new technologies for de-materializing checks into digital images, allowing an easier transmission of them trough digital channels. De-materialization changes the traditional check lifecycle, removing physical barriers to the collection process.

In the traditional check handling process (see Figure 1), a check is issued by the Drawee Bank and it is characterized by a unique identification number: the check serial number and the Drawee Bank code. All these data are saved in the check magnetic code line. The Drawee Bank produces and issues the check, which is assigned to a specific customer (Drawer). The Drawer fills the check to pay the Payee, writing the amount, the Payee, the payment date. The Payee in turn asks the

Figure 1. Check life cycle

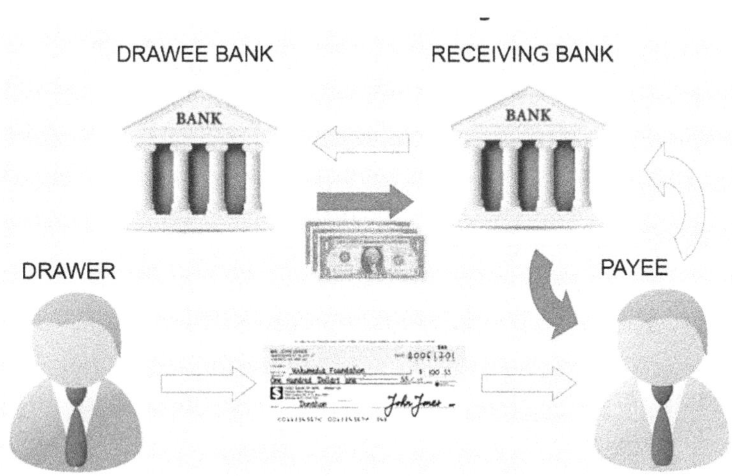

collection of the amount to his/her bank (Receiving Bank). Finally, the latter agrees with the Drawee Bank the transfer of money from the Drawer to the Payee account.

All steps involving the Drawee and Receiving Bank have been fully digitized, paving the way to digital secure checks described in this chapter. In many European countries laws, like Repubblica Italiana (2011), give to digital checks the same value as the traditional ones, giving to Payees the possibility to electronically submit digital checks to collection. A secure check framework should exploit advanced cryptographic techniques to avoid the tampering of checks assigning a unique distinctive code to be associated to them, and an online framework that can be used to Payee and Drawer to verify check integrity.

Known Issues of Traditional Checks

With respect to cash, checks have lower handling costs and are more easily traceable. With respect to credit card transactions, handling checks requires virtually no profit sharing as it does not involve intermediaries. Also, checks have the advantage of not having strict limits on maximum amount for single operation or for time periods. On the other hand, checks have the limit of high production cost, needed to prevent frauds and misuses. Traditional checks are subject to a number of attacks:

- **Check Forgery:** The attacker tries to forge a check that is similar to a legitimate one. The forger tries to replicate a check issued by a bank generating a fake codeline and number, or copies data from a real check to obtain a check clone. In addition, there have been cases of checks issued by non-existing banks.
- **Check Modification:** The attacker modifies the amount or the Payee name. This attack is executed by physically intercepting a check that was sent, for example, by traditional mail.
- **Blank or Missing Checks**: This attack exploits blank checks that are lost or stolen. Those checks can be blocked by banks upon receiving a request from law enforcement authorities, but this generates an additional cost for drawees.
- **Dud Checks:** this attack happens when a Drawer signs and issues a check without having enough money on her bank account to cover it. This will trigger a costly procedure for the Drawer bank that has to block the payment, contact the Drawer, and open an action against her.

Early Approaches to Partial Dematerialization

In the Nineties, check handling started to include sending a digital image of the check to both sides. Digital images where stored by the Receiving Bank and sent to Drawee Bank instead of moving the check hardcopy. This evolution supported automated handling, and paved the way to the definition of more complex and secure techniques. Next, the authors provide an overview of the early approaches that lead to a partial dematerialization of check handling.

NetCheque

NetCheque is a seminal system originally developed by the University of Southern California (Neuman, 1993). It was originally designed for the distributed management of access to computation resources in a University computation center and was based on the Kerberos authentication framework, and was extended for the management of virtual checks.Under NetCheque, each check is identified by the following fields:

- The amount indicated on the check,
- The currency used,
- The check date,
- The Drawer's account number,
- The beneficiary's name,
- The digital signature of the account holder, validated by the Drawee Bank,
- The endorsement of the beneficiary and of the banks used.

Kerberos session tickets are exchanged between the customer and the Receiving Bank, and between the two banks in order to exchange and encrypt/decrypt the check data.

BANK INTERNET PAYMENT SYSTEM (BIPS)

In the BIPS framework, the virtual checkbook is represented by a smart card and an encrypted file in the customer's workstation. BIPS defines a remote payment system that exploits the Internet (Web or email), as communication channel and covers a large number of bank services (FSTC, 1998).BIPS supports the following types of transactions:

- Direct debits, related to payments initiated by a creditor and already agreed by a debtor;
- Fund transfer, related to business-to-business payments that rely on fund transfers only;
- Payments authorized remotely through a computer connection, for example for the payment of bills.

The architecture of a BIPS system relies on (i) a mail or a web server to manage customer requests, (ii) a front-end module for the management of BIPS messages, that acts also as a proxy for the Electronic Payment Handler (EPH), (iii) an EPH server dedicated to the validation of digital signatures and certificates of the BIPS messages, (iv) a payment system interface that translates the incoming payment messages into the format of the selected payment mechanism, (v) an event log module for the monitoring of actions and events, and (vi) a repository for the storage of all transactions.

eCheck

eCheck is a virtual check framework sponsored and recognized by the US Treasury Department at the end of the Nineties (Jaffe&Landry, 1997). The system allows a debtor to transfer fund to a creditor using standard email messages.

eCheck implements the traditional process and exchange of the management of checks in a fully dematerialized way. Figure 2 depicts the eCheck process. The payer sends a signed eCheck to the Payee (steps 1 and 2), which is then deposited by the Payee in her bank (step 3). Clearance and settlement go through the traditional financial network (step 4). Because banking clearance takes the usual electronic path, payment to the creditor does not occur before the debtor's bank completes all the necessary verifications. Finally, the creditor's bank sends an electronic ac-

Figure 2. Dematerialized check negotiation with e-Check
Hashem Sherif, 2003.

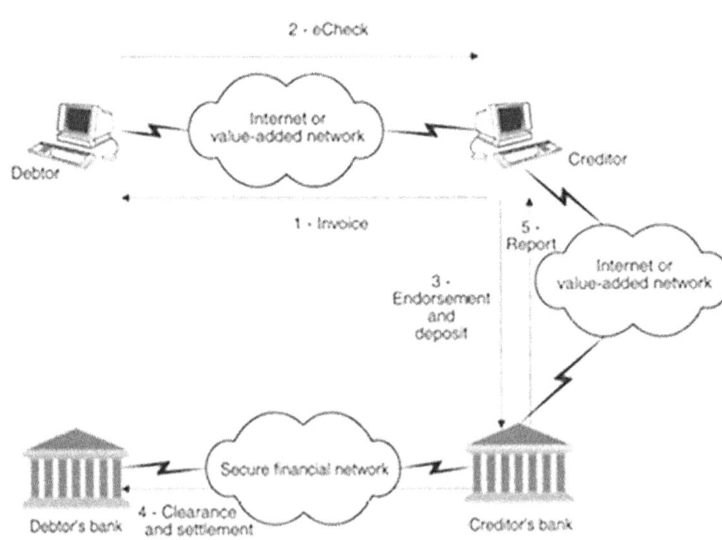

knowledgement message to the creditor to notify the result (positive or negative of the operation (step 5).

eCheck provides a mean for attaching some free-format files or messages to the payment message to give needed information regarding billing statements or purchase orders to the creditor and to the banks. eCheck messages adopts the Financial Services Markup Language (FSML) (FSTC, 2015), defined within the framework of SDML (Signed Document Markup Language), which specifies how to sign digital documents (W3C, 1998). In turn, SDML is based on SGML of ISO 8879 (1986), and it is not compatible with standard XML.

The European Context

After 2000, dematerialized checks have become accepted in most Western countries. Dematerialization of check handling has been introduced in all countries belonging to the Group of Ten (G-10) including ten key International Monetary Fund (IMF) members: Belgium, Canada, France, Germany Italy, Japan, the Netherlands, Sweden, the United Kingdom, and the United States. In particular, a further innovation has been introduced by the Italian the Decree Law n. 70, 23 May 2011 (see Repubblica Italiana, 2011), which has given to digital checks the same legal value as traditional ones at all stages of the handling process.

This law has opened an entirely new perspective with respect to previous implementations of check handling. As described in (Hashem Sherif, 2003), it allows using dematerialized checks from collection included, improving the efficiency and reducing costs of collection. The law defines a set of requirements that the digital copies of checks need to satisfy:

- Black and white scan of the check with a resolution of at least 200 dpi;
- XML metadata describing the check images including codeline, amount, Payee, and issuing date;
- Special finishing or watermarking to allow the automatic identification of front and back sides of the checks;
- Inclusion of special graphical codes (e.g., QR codes) for supporting security features.

In the future, the introduction of de-materialized checks worldwide will allow banks to keep and exchange digital versions of checks only. The acquisition of images will happen in the bank branches, or directly at the Payee's side using smartphones or personal computers. This procedure will trigger a drastic reduction in check handling costs for banks and, consequently, for customers, making dematerialized checks a viable alternative to credit card payments. Standard techniques like magnetic or infrared inks are not feasible in case of de-materialized checks, new solutions have been proposed to provide them with all security features that are common in case of classic digital communication. Available solutions range from special laser puncturing of the check, where the pattern of the puncture is related to the codeline of the check, with high implementation costs, to QR codes, printed on the front side of the check, that contains digest and security certificate that are stored and used by the banks to validate the checks.

Full Check Dematerialization

The main target of full check dematerialization is to reduce the overall effort and costs of manual operations thus making the check handling as automatic as possible, given (i) the wider diffusion of self-service deposit kiosks, where checks are presented to an Automated Teller Machine (ATM) and any kind of manual handling is required, and (ii) the possibility that might be given to the Payee to present the check to her bank without physically bringing it to the branch but just sending a picture of the check and the main data; also in this case, the possibility to avoid human handling is required is highly appreciated by the bank.

A secondary target is also to achieve complete security on both the paper and the dematerialized version of the check thus solving the traditional problem of fraud handling and the consequential loss of customers' trust, and extending the security to virtual checks where the image cannot bring the traditional security features that are normally carried by the paper version (e.g., watermarks and special inks).

The analysis of existing literature and the most common frameworks for checks dematerialization led us to comparative assessment of check handling and payment services provided by online banking systems through Secure Electronic Transactions (SETs) based on SSL/TLS.

First of all, SETs are designed to manage interactive transactions on the Web, while virtual checks can be used either on the Web or by e-mail, moving the security requirement from the connection to the exchanged messages.

Also, SETs require real-time authentication and online verification of the provided certificates. On the other side, in the case of virtual checks authentication is not necessarily needed in real time, thus reducing the constraints imposed on the system.

Finally, encryption of transaction data hides the information on the user's account from the merchant's server but not from the payment gateway. In fact, in SET, the payment gateway plays the role of a trusted third party, without knowing the details of the transaction. Thus, it verifies the agreement between the buyer and the merchant using the appropriate digests. In the case of virtual checks, no trusted third parties are required, and the process is managed at the level of the interested banks.

In our vision, a fully dematerialized check will allow automatic processing and will be instantly payable as a Banker's check. To achieve this goal, on top of technology it is essential the role of the Drawer, which needs to write in the check details, such as amount, Payee and date, into an online database: a small distributed effort that has somehow to be rewarded.

The bank may incentivize this process by paying the checks that have been treated with this technology with a faster payment cycle thus allowing the use of the check to pay goods and services in real time like you can do with a credit card but without same limits. Self-creating a Banker's check is quite an advantage also for the customers to justify the data entry effort in her mobile phone.

AN IMPLEMENTATION FOR FULLY DEMATERIALIZED SECURE CHECKS

In this section it is describe a framework, Secure Checks (Figure 3), that brings modern encryption techniques to traditional checks, guaranteeing a secure and reliable de-materialization process. The framework is considered as a solution to the issues identified in the previous section, as summarized in Table 1.

A check compliant to the Secure Checks framework (see an example in Figure 3) will be printed by the Drawee Bank and will be equipped with a QR code carrying the following information:

Figure 3. A check secured by Secure Checks security features

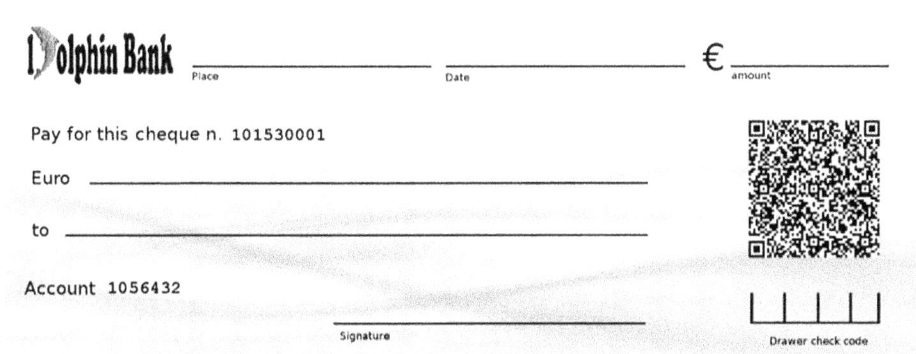

Table 1. Main challenges of virtual checks full dematerialization

Main Challenges	SETs	Virtual Checks Full Dematerialization
1	Manage interactive transactions on the Web	Manage interactions via web and email
2	Require real-time authentication and online verification	Do not require verification in real time
3	Require a trusted third party (payment gateway)	No trusted third parties are required, the process is managed at the level of the banks

- The check codeline;
- identification of the Drawee Bank;
- A digital signature, calculated using as input the private key of the Drawee Bank and the specific features of the printed check, to ensure that the check is authentic and actually issued by the Drawee Bank.

This information can be used to prevent check forgery. In fact, the signature contained in the QR Code is generated using the private key of the Drawee Bank. Specific applications can test the authenticity using the public key of the bank to verify the signature.

Traditional check vs Secure Check

A traditional check (see Figure 4) includes a codeline as unique check identifier, printed with magnetic ink suitable to be readable by a magnetic head. It often includes a bank ID and the progressive number of the check. There are also some

Figure 4. Example of traditional check

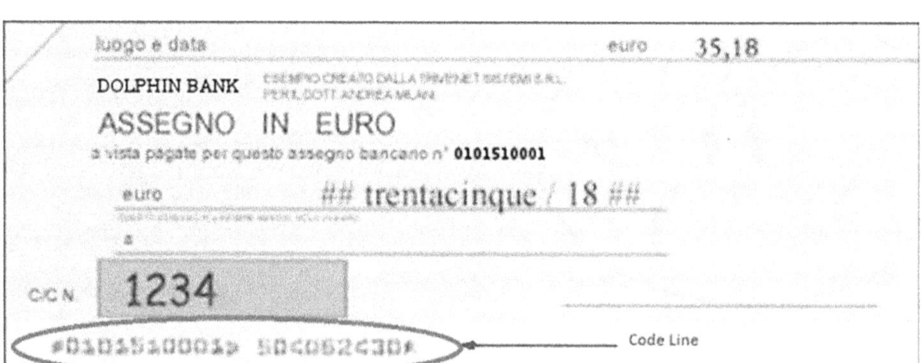

blank fields (amount, date, Payee, Drawer signature) meant to be filled in by the Drawer.On the other side, our secure check (see Figure 3) includes two additional fields only:

- QR code;
- Drawer Check Code meant to be filled in by the Drawer.

QR Code and Bank Digital Signature

When a Secure Check is printed by the Drawee Bank, a unique QR code is computed and printed on the front side. It contains:

- The check codeline;
- The Drawee Bank ID;
- A cryptographic signature on specific fields based on the private key of the issuing bank, thus guaranteeing that the check is authentic and issued by Drawee Bank.

By using an asymmetric cryptography algorithm, end users will be able to verify check authenticity by using mobile devices (Figure 5). Scanning the QR code with an appropriate application and using the bank public key will return the confirmation of the authenticity of the check.

Figure 5. Digital signature verification

This solution prevents frauds based on check forgery; an attacker who does not hold the private key to generate the signature, will never be able to generate a check that passes the check verification process.

Drawer Check Code

In order to address other types of frauds, it is needed the check code to be generated when the Drawer writes the check. Also, it is needed to guarantee that the Drawer itself has written the check without altering the critical fields. To this end, an application for mobile device will be supplied by the bank to the Drawer. The bank will generate and store a secret key for each Drawer, to ensure that each Check Code will be different and strongly associated to the corresponding Drawer.

The Drawer scans the QR code with the software and inserts amount, Payee name and date in the mobile device. The software will communicate with the Bank web service that will generate and provide the Drawer with the Check Code to be copied on the check. At the same time amount, Payee and date will be stored on the bank server (see Figure 6).

Later, the Payee, with the same application, can verify the Check Code by scanning QR code, inserting Drawer Check Code (to prove she is actually holding the check) and getting the check details from the server.

Storing the amount, Payee and date on the server and adding the Drawer Check Code as a digital signature of the Drawer will protect our Secure Checks against well-known types of frauds like Check Modification and Missing Check. It is important to remark that, when issuing the Drawer Check Code, the bank can also verify that the Drawer has enough funds.

This approach carries a huge benefit in terms of dematerialization, since the check details are known to the Drawee Bank immediately when its customer issues

Figure 6. Drawer check code generation

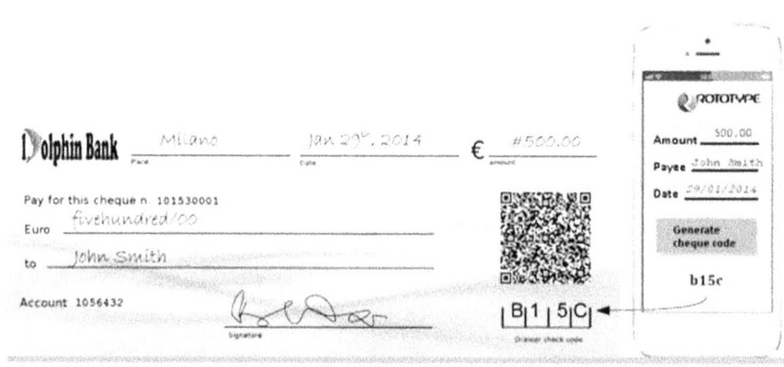

the check. Also, storing the key information on a central server achieves all purposes of dematerialization, removing the tradition lock-in on the physical paper check.

System Architecture and Benefits

Our system architecture is centered on a secure server, where the bank stores the private key and generates the digital signatures to be printed in QR codes. The bank also publishes a public web server connected to a database. The database contains the list of issued checks and for each check stores the reference to the Drawer and the status of the check including Payee, Amount and Date that are filled in when the Drawer writes the check.

A client software, available for workstations and mobile devices, will allow process actors (namely the Payee and the Receiving Bank) to verify the authenticity of the check, filled by the Drawer, ensuring that it has not been modified and it will not bounce due to lack of funds. Furthermore, the bank will be able to retrieve data about the amount, Payee, and date without retrieving them directly from the check handwriting.

The benefits for the users include faster and secure payment of the check, while the benefits for the banks are twofold:

1. Alleviation of frauds, and
2. The reduction of check handling effort, since data will be stored in the server by the Drawer itself and therefore all check truncation and check payment steps will involve verification and validation without any data entry.

Bank Signature Details

Several alternatives are possible for encoding signature information. XML (eXtensible Markup Language) is ideal format to represent information in machine-to-machine exchanges (see Figure 7). For the signature, ECDSA protocol with Base64 encod-

Table 2.

XML Code	QR Code
<cs> <check BID="DOLPHINBANK" CL="a0101510001d504062430e"></ check> <sign ALG="ECDSA"> MD0CHCcbRmjyYulLLzD6THRBOOQpKCQfwK4AO4Dk/ LQCHQD1CLADTH5TUxN3y/pgvoOj7ztbnn0S92mZAm4T</sign> </cs>	<Figure_QR.tif>

Figure 7. QR code digital signature

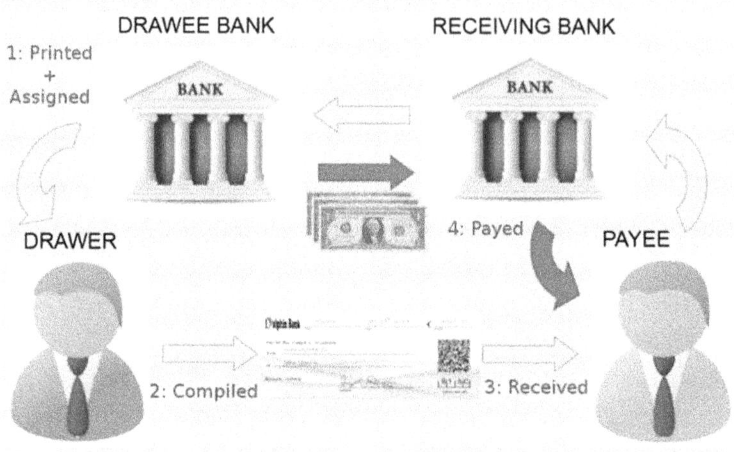

ing has been selected, because it is compact and secure. It is interesting to note that high security can be achieved with a smaller key and more limited computational power than RSA and other protocols: for example, with a 256 bit key, the ECDSA signature is about 64 bytes long and it is comparable, in terms of security, to a signature generated with RSA algorithm with a key of 3072 bit. Table 3 shows the security equivalence in terms of key length with different protocols.

The QR code is a bi-dimensional barcode used to store information easy to fast decode with smartphones and mobile devices. It handles error correction and it is more compact than other similar codes. The combination of QR code and ECDSA signature generates a compact bi-dimensional code that can easily fit in the limited space available on the checks.

Table 3. Comparison with different cryptographic protocols

	Block Cipher	RSA	Elliptic Curve	DSA
Export Grade	56	512	112	512/112
Traditional recommendations	80	1024	160	1024/160
	112	2048	224	2048/224
Lenstra/Verheul 2000	70	952	132	952/125
Lenstra/Verheul 2010	78	1369	146/160	1369/138

Drawer Check Code Details

The Drawer Check Code depends on the values written on the check and in particular "Amount" "Payee" name, and "Date" and "Codeline."

These data are concatenated in a single string. In the following example the encoding of a check of 500 USD issued to John Smith on January 29th 2014 is shown. The check codeline is also included so that two checks with the same Payee, amount, and date will generate different Drawer check codes.

The bank uses a different secret key for each user in order to have Drawer Check Code different for different Drawer, even for checks where other details are the same. The following operations are performed:

- Amount is espressed in cents
- Date is formatted as: yyyy/mm/dd
- Amount, Payee, Date and Codeline are made uppercase and concatenated
- No space or punctuation mark is applied
- The resulting string is ASCII encoder and written in a 128 byte array which is 0 padded to the right

Below, the example with the corresponding encoding:

- **Amount:** 500.00;
- **Payee:** John Smith;
- **Date:** 29-01-2014;
- **Codeline:** 01a0101530001d504062430e.

50000JOHNSMITH2014012901a0101530001d504062430e

Then, the concatenated string above is encrypted with the private personal key of the user and hashed to 4 digits, for example, applying a CRC16. It is important to note that the user private key is generated and maintained by the bank in a secure database connected to the web service.

The same algorithms could be used for bank signatures; in this case, the choice fell on the RSA algorithm. Even if the length of the key and signature are not relevant since everything is cut to 16 bits, the generation of a unique pattern remains fundamental. ECDSA cannot be used because it generates a different signature with the same input date each time that the algorithm is run; this would imply a different Drawer Check Code each time that the algorithm is executed, which is not the objective of the framework.

Check code is generated by the function $f = CRC16(RSA(M,k))$, where M s is the above built string (amount, Payee, date, codeline) and k is the private RSA key of the Drawer. RSA signature is based on SHA-1 and 2048 bit key. Although this is very robust, CRC16 reduces the robustness to a 16 bit equivalent (a brute force attack will require trying all the 2^{16} combinations of CRC16).

The short Drawer Check Code of 4 digits was selected because it is easy for the Drawer to copy it manually on the check. The verification is done by running the function again and checking the result against the supplied Drawer Check Code. Since RSA is computationally heavy, theoretically a better choice would be to use a symmetric algorithm in this context, such as AES. Practically, the Drawer will contact the web service with its mobile banking authentication to generate the Drawer Check Code: this process is executed "online" and allows to store the check details on the bank server for later usage and complete dematerialization.

As an alternative procedure, the user can download the private key on her mobile device and therefore being able to perform an "offline" generation of the Drawer Check Code: the security is similar but the dematerialization in this case is not performed, since nobody can send to the bank server the check details.

There is actually another security advantage in the online generation of Drawer Check Code: the server will only allow to do such generation once. If a second generation with different data is attempted, an alert can be raised that there might be two copies of the same check in the field. This way, not even a fraudster Drawer will be able to generate two copies of the same check and issue them to different parties.

When verifying a check Payee will only be allowed to enter the Drawer Check Code a limited number of times: this prevents a brute force attack since the Drawer Check Code is short and guessing might be possible. Anyway for "online" model, even in case of successful guessing the attacker can read the data from the server but cannot modify it.

Dematerialised Check Lifetime Management

With this model the bank is also able to manage the check lifecycle by knowing exactly where the check is at any time. A check can be in five different states (See Figure 8):

- **Printed:** Check has been generated by the printing facility and its codeline is stored in the database, thus initiating the lifecycle by entering the check in the database.
- **Assigned:** Check has been assigned to a customer, and her account is associated to the codeline.

Figure 8. Check lifecycle

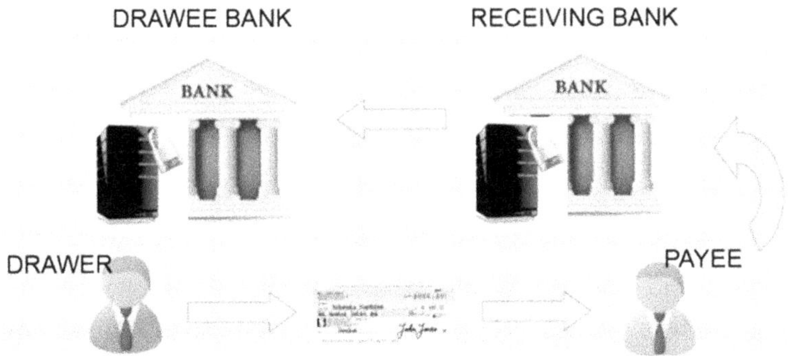

- **Written:** This state is specific of the secure check framework and it happens when the Drawer uses her mobile device to generate the Drawer Check Code, and check details are stored in the server
- **Received:** When the Payee checks the details, the server can assume that the check has been delivered to the Payee.
- **Paid:** When the Receiving Bank contacts the server with bank credentials, the server knows that the check has been paid and the bank will be able to close to lifecycle by depositing the requested amount from Drawer account to Receiving Bank

Web Service

In order to achieve security and dematerialization of checks, the bank has only to implement the web service. Most banks already provide and maintain a mobile application and therefore adding the check writing and verification to the same is not an issue. The web service must support the following users:

- **Drawee Bank:** Manages the server and have all privileges included adding new checks.
- **Receiving Bank:** Can access a function to obtain check details by simply sending check codeline (automatically read from QR code).
- **Drawer:** Upon checking that a specific check is assigned to the user requesting to write the check, the Drawer check code generation function is active. The Drawer sends writing details that are stored in the database and the Drawer Check Code is generated.
- **Normal Customers:** Can read QR code, send QR code derived codeline and manually entered Drawer Check Code and read the check details to compare

to those written on the check. The web service generates the Drawer check code based on the writing details stored in the database and in case of positive match with the digits provided by the user, return the check writing details to the user.

The Multi Bank Scenario

Using the web service described above, each bank can manage the entire check handling process. Let us now discuss what happens when a check is issued by a Drawer from her account at a Drawee Bank and then presented by the Payee to her Receiving Bank (different from the Drawee Bank). In this scenario (Figure 9), each bank needs to establish trust relationship with the servers at the other banks and the same web services may be used in a multibank scenario by simply forwarding the requests to the right bank.

In this scenario, the Payee does not need to know anything about the Drawee Bank although the check she needs to verify belongs to that bank and is stored in its database; the Payee does not have an account nor username and password to access Drawee Bank services. The Payee uses the mobile application (and related authentication) from her bank (the Receiving Bank) and addresses the check verification request to her bank.

The receiving bank web service detects that the check belongs to the Drawee Bank and forwards the request (might be the QR code signature verification or the Drawer Check Code verification) to the Drawee Bank using a mutual trust username and password that Drawee bank has assigned to Receiving Bank. The Drawee Bank web service performs the checks in the same way whether the verification requests comes from a user or from another bank. Finally, the Receiving Bank waits for the reply and forwards it back to the Payee.

Figure 9. The multi bank scenario

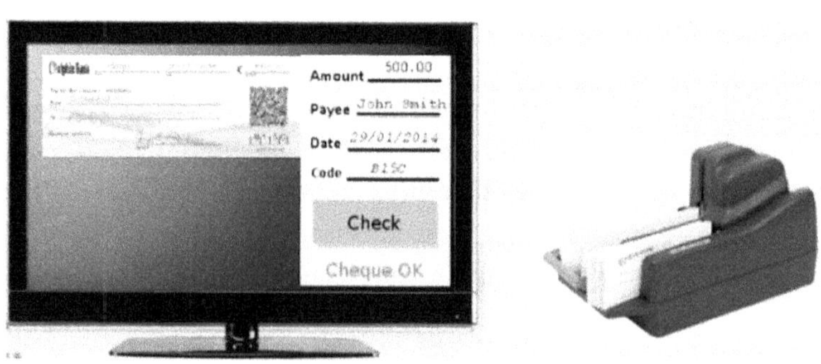

Figure 10. Receiving Bank desk scanning application

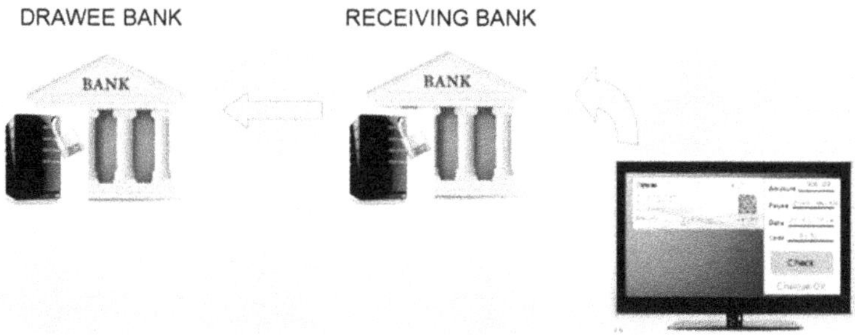

The web service interface is the same for the Drawee Bank customers and for the Receiving Bank, and the multibank scenario only affects the business logic and user credentials without impacting on the service interface (Figure 10). Furthermore, when the check is presented to the receiving bank, it is usually scanned with a desk scanner and the receiving bank will directly extract information about the check (Drawee Bank and codeline) from QR code sending a request to the Drawee bank web service to query the check writing details.

Our web service will recognize the receiving bank credentials and will provide amount, Payee and date as stored on their server. The Receiving Bank teller will compare the data from the server and the data written on the physical check. The

Figure 11. Receiving Bank desk scanning application

check truncation process proceeds then as usual by sending the check image and the data back to the Drawee Bank for payment.

The web service interface is the same for the Drawee Bank tellers and for the Receiving Bank tellers and the multibank scenario only affects user credentials without impacting on the service interface (see Figure 11).

CONCLUSION

Before 2000, many financial institutions manually exchanged checks for clearing purposes. Each day, banks sent checks issued by customers of banks other than that of the beneficiary (often called interbank checks) to one of the so-called national clearing houses made available to them by national Central Banks. At the time of the switch to the European common currency in 2000, banking establishments decided to modernize this obsolete system and dematerialize their exchanges in order to reduce the time and cost of check handling.

So, image-based check handling systems (such as the French "Echange d'Images Chèques" or "Exchange of Checks' Images") have been introduced to reduce physical circulation of checks, decreasing administrative costs as well as check processing time for some critical check handling procedures like interbank check clearing. In this chapter, the authors outlined a solution based on XML encoding of checks handled by Web services that aims to completely dematerialize all check handling procedures.

REFERENCES

Financial Services Technology Consortium – FTSC. (1998). BIPS Specification V.1.0. Retrieved from http://www.echeck.org

Financial Services Technology Consortium – FTSC. (2015). FSML Version 2.0. Retrieved from http://echeck.org/echeck-specs-and-references-fsml-2-0-logging-proposal/

Hashem Sherif, M. (2003). *Protocols for Secure Electronic Commerce* (2nd ed.). London, UK: CRC Press. doi:10.1201/9781420040012

Jaffe, F., & Landry, S. Electronic checks: the best of both worlds (1997). *Electron. Commerce World*. Retrieved from http://www.echeck.org/kitprint/article.htm

Neuman, B. C. (1993). Proxy-based authorization and accounting for distributed systems. *Proc. 13th Int. Conf. on Distributed Comput. Syst. 1993* (pp. 283–291). doi:10.1109/ICDCS.1993.287698

Repubblica Italiana. (2011). *Decreto Legge 13 maggio 2011 n.70 "Prime disposizioni urgenti per l'economia"*. Retrieved from http://www.gazzettaufficiale.it/

Standard Generalized Markup Language (SGML). (1986). ISO 8879 Information Processing Text and Office Systems. Retrieved from http://www.iso.org/cate/d16387.html

UK Payments Administration. (2008). *Fact sheet for people who still write cheques backed by a guarantee card*. London, UK: UK Payments Administration.

Vines, J., Dunphy, P., Blythe, M., Lindsay, S., Monk, A., & Olivier, P. (2012). The Joy of Cheques: Trust, Paper and Eighty Somethings.*Proceedings of the ACM 2012 conference on Computer Supported Cooperative Work*, Seattle, Washington, USA (pp. 147-156). doi:10.1145/2145204.2145229

W3C. (1998). SDML-Signed Document Markup Language, Version 2.0. Retrieved from http://www.w3.org/TR/NOTE-SDML/

Chapter 6
Emerging Challenges, Security Issues, and Technologies in Online Banking Systems

Shadi A Aljawarneh
Jordan University of Science and Technology, Jordan

ABSTRACT

Online banking security is a critical issue over request-response model. But the traditional protection mechanisms are not sufficient to secure the online banking systems that hold information about clients, and banks. The infrastructure of networks, routers, domain name servers, and switches that glue these online banking systems together could be fail, and as a result, online banking systems will no longer be able to communicate accurately or reliably. A number of critical questions arise, such as what exactly the infrastructure is, what threats it must be secured against, and how protection can be provided on a cost-effective basis. But underlying all these questions is how to define secure online banking systems. In this chapter, emerging challenges, security issues and technologies in Online Banking Systems will be analyzed and discussed systematically.

DOI: 10.4018/978-1-5225-0864-9.ch006

INTRODUCTION

Online banking security is a critical issue over HTTP request-response model. But the traditional protection mechanisms are not sufficient to secure the online banking systems that hold information about clients, and banks (Aljawarneh et. al, 2016; Aljawarneh et. al, 2014). The infrastructure of networks, routers, domain name servers, and switches that glue these online banking systems together could be fail, and as a result, online banking systems will no longer be able to communicate accurately or reliably. A number of critical questions arise, such as what exactly the infrastructure is, what threats it must be secured against, and how protection can be provided on a cost-effective basis. But underlying all these questions is how to define secure online banking systems (Aljawarneh et. al, 2014; Aljawarneh, 2011a; Aljawarneh, Alkhateeb, & Al Maghayreh, 2010).

Cryptography and watermarking seem to be the alternative solutions for reinforcing the security of multimedia documents against tampering attacks (Aljawarneh et. al, 2007; Chen, Lin, Sirakriengkrai et al., 2015). When the hidden or encrypted information is revealed or even suspected, the purpose of cryptography and watermarking are defeated (Hodgson, 2015). It difficult to employ end-to-end encryption or end-end watermarking on all banking data to achieve end-to-end security because proxies, web servers, and web browsers involve decrypting some or all data to read and even modify some of them to provide client-server services such as executing client and server scripts, transforming and filtering web pages. However, if sensitive data is exposed (decrypted) to untrustworthy proxies, web servers, and web browsers for processing, it can result in information leakage and tampering (Aljawarneh et. al, 2007; Aljawarneh et. al, 2008).

This chapter presents the description of online banking content, and the HTTP request-response model. It also discusses the online banking security issues, objectives, and technologies. Placing an online banking security in perspective is important, because it is a central issue and necessary to banks, clients and even home users now and in the future. Indeed, what is online banking security? Having it is clearly good; everyone says so. But few people realize it exactly. Core to online banking security are the issues of confidentiality, integrity and availability, which refer to keeping data secret, ensuring data remains intact and ensuring systems, are responsive.

WEB HISTORY

In the late 1960s, the Advanced Research Projects Agency (ARPA) of U.S. Defense Ministry sponsored a project for implementing the ARPANET, the legacy of Internet. The main purpose of the ARPANET project was to allow multiple users to make request and response messages simultaneously over the same communication channel via phone lines. The information was divided into a number of packets and then routed to their destinations. Each packet consisted of sender address, destination address, additional information for checking the integrity of communication, and part of the data. The communication protocol, which was used in ARPANET project, is called Transmission Control Protocol (TCP). The aim of this protocol is to ensure that the messages are correctly routed from sender to receiver over the communication channel of the ARPANET system (Aljawarneh et. al, 2007; Aljawarneh et. al, 2008).

However, some challenges arose such as how to communicate across a network of networks. ARPANET improved the TCP protocol to be Internet Protocol/Transmission Control Protocol (IP/TCP) protocols. Currently, they are the basic architecture of the Internet (Kumar Bhajantri, Sujatha, Yaligar et al., 2016).

After that, Berners Lee developed World Wide Web (WWW) at the European organization for Nuclear Research in 1990, as well as the concept of hypertext. The WWW is a distributed environment that allows users to communicate and view multimedia-based documents over the Internet. In 1993, web-based services were explored by the Mosaic browser, which had a graphic Interface. Currently, most major web browsers (such as Microsoft Internet Explorer and Netscape Navigator) are used to explore the web-based services (Spinellis, 2016).

The WWW Consortium (W3C) was founded in 1994 to make the web universally accessible and available regardless of ability, language, or culture. W3C also participates to check the validation of web technologies including Hyper Text Markup Language (HTML), Extensible Hyper Text Markup Language (XHTML), Cascading Style Sheet (CSS) and Extensible Markup Language (XML) (Spinellis, 2016).

Web technology has introduced a new distributed computing paradigm. This is suitable for various web-oriented applications, web administrative applications and general web applications including e-Commerce, e-Banking, e-Shopping, e-Ticketing, e-Finance, and e-Management. Web technology has incorporated database connectivity to be able to access much information in online state. This information is stored on a server using Database Management Systems (DBMS) database application for processing (Aljawarneh et. al, 2007; Aljawarneh et. al, 2008).

Online Banking Content

Online Banking content is a textual or multimedia content that is encountered as part of the user experience on online banking systems. It includes text, images, sounds, videos, objects and animations (Aljawarneh et. al, 2014). Rosenfeld and Morville defined content broadly as "the stuff in your Web site." This may include documents, data, applications, e-services, images, audio and video files, personal Web pages, archived e-mail messages, and more. And we include future stuff as well as present stuff.

The use of hypertext concept, hyperlinks concept and a page-based model of sharing information help to define web content, and to form the architecture of web sites. Currently, the categorization of web sites is based on a type of web site where web content is dominated by the page concept. When the web address is requested, a range of web pages are viewed, but in each page could have embedded tools to view "video clips" (Spinellis, 2016).

For example, e-Commerce sites could contain textual material and embedded with graphics displaying a picture of the item(s) for sale. However, there are few sites that are composed page-by-page using some variant of HTML. Generally, web pages are composed as they are being served from a database to a customer using a web browser. However, a user sees the mainly text document arriving as a web page to be rendered in a web browser.

In this Chapter, we are intended to explore two kinds of online banking content, dynamic and static. A dynamic online banking content is the content (text, images, form fields, etc.) that can modify on a web page in response to different conditions such as user interaction. There are two ways to create this kind of interactivity (Aljawarneh et. al, 2007; Aljawarneh et. al, 2008):

- Using client-side scripting to change interface behaviors within a web page, in response to mouse or keyboard actions or at specified events. In this case the dynamic behavior occurs within the presentation of a web page.
- Using server-side scripting to change the supplied page source between pages, adjusting the sequence or reload of web pages or web content supplied to a web browser. Web server responses may be determined by such conditions as data in a posted HTML form, parameters in the Uniform Resource Locator (URL), the type of web browser being used, the passage of time, or a database or server state.

The result of either technique is described as a dynamic online banking page, and both may be used in parallel. In first kind of interactivity, web pages must use presentation technology called rich interfaced web pages. Client-side scripting languages such as JavaScript used for Dynamic HTML (DHTML) and flash technologies are normally used to activate media types (sound, animations, changing text, etc.) of the presentation. The scripting also allows use of remote scripting, a technique by which the DHTML page requests additional information from a server, using a hidden frame, XMLHttp Requests object, or a web service (Aljawarneh et. al, 2007; Spinellis, 2016).

Web pages that adhere to the second kind are almost generated with the help of server-side languages such as Active Server Page (ASP or ASP.NET), Java Server Page (JSP), and other server scripting languages. These server-side languages typically use the Common Gateway Interface (CGI) to generate dynamic web pages. These kinds could also use on a client-side (Aljawarneh et. al, 2007; Spinellis, 2016).

The Client-side dynamic content is generated on a client's machine. A web server retrieves the page and sends it as is. A web browser then processes the code embedded in the page and displays the page to a user. However, some users have scripting languages disabled in their web browsers due to possible security threats. In addition, some web browsers do not support the client-scripting language or they do not support all commands of the language (Aljawarneh et. al, 2007).

On the other hand, server-side dynamic content is a little bit more complicated. The following steps illustrate how the server-side dynamic content is produced:

1. A web browser sends an HTTP request.
2. A web server retrieves the requested script or program.
3. A web server application executes the script or program, which typically outputs an HTML web page. The program usually obtains input from the query string or standard input, which may have been obtained from a submitted web form.
4. A server sends the HTML output to a web browser.

Server-side has many possibilities for dynamic content, but the use of it can be a strain on low-end, high-traffic machines. If not properly secured, server-side scripts could be exploited to gain access to a machine (Aljawarneh et. al, 2007; Aljawarneh et. al, 2008).

Another type of content is referred to as "static". A static web page is a web page that always comprises the same information in response to all downloaded requests from all users. The most obvious requests are the transmission of images and blocks of text. This is the data that is found on virtually every first page in a site and which forms the basis of virtually every page. This type of page is usually called "static HTML" (Aljawarneh et. al, 2007; Aljawarneh et. al, 2008).

HTML LANGUAGE

HTML is a legacy language of a web technology. Each electronic document (or web document) contains a predefined set of HTML tags that might be embedded Active Contents modules. It is accessible by URL. HTML technology supports multimedia documents including video, sound, text and dynamic links as well as the textual interface (Spinellis, 2016; Lee et. al, 2015). HTML and HTTP are the core technologies of the WWW so the global hypertext system is the center of the e-Business revolution.

A web document is platform-independent, based on HTML language and its successor XML. Various web browsers on various operating systems can view it. HTML is a content mark-up language, not a desktop publishing environment that is used to describe the layout of a web document.

HTML analyzer and Script analyzer process web documents. The HTML analyzer is to process the HTML tags, while the Script analyzer is to process the embedded scripts either in the client-side or in the server-side (Yang, Huang, Wang et al., 2002).

HTML documents consist of two sections, head and body. Each section includes HTML elements and HTML sub-elements to describe a web layout. HTML supports form element <form> that permits for user interaction. This element contains sub elements such as <input>, <select>, <textarea> and others. HTML form has two fundamental functions:

1. Providing area on a web page to enter a particular data that is sent to a web server for processing.
2. Allowing validation of input data by invoking script element, which resides on a web document.

HTML also supports script element that was provided by Netscape 2.1 for input data validation. This element supports powerful scripting languages (such as JavaScript and Visual Basic script) to perform interactive tasks. One of the main tasks of scripting language is to check the user input errors on the client-side rather than on the server-side, because if a server finds any input error, a server returns an error message to a web browser, therefore, the client-side validation modules saves round-trips over a network.

Furthermore, <applet> and <object> HTML elements provide a link to embed Java Applets, multimedia objects, and ActiveX object. For example, a web browser downloads ActiveX object after rendering using <object>) element to run inside a web page. However, ActiveX is vulnerable to a security risk, because the ActiveX object is not restricted and directly can access operating system resources on a client machine. However, Microsoft Internet Explorer verifies this control using Authenticode technology. The digital signatures and the Public Key Infrastructure (PKI) support this technology. It can sign the ActiveX control, which is run in a machine code or in a Java Bytecode. Therefore, Authenticode can download the control or do not (Oppliger & Gajek, 2005).

However, HTML is not a specific high level domain language to validate the user interaction, because it does not support specific HTML validation tags. In addition, HTML does not offer the extensibility of own user tags and attributes. HTML is not also suitable for complex data entry that consists of many forms. Therefore, W3C has developed XML language. It is a purely declarative and high-level domain language. This means that, XML supports extended tags and attributes for validation modules without the need to programming skills.

HTTP Request-Response Models

HTTP request-response model is constructed from three parts, a web browser, a web server and a communication channel between a client and a server (Oppliger & Gajek, 2005). Figure 1 illustrates the components of HTTP request-response model architecture.

Figure 1. HTTP request-response model

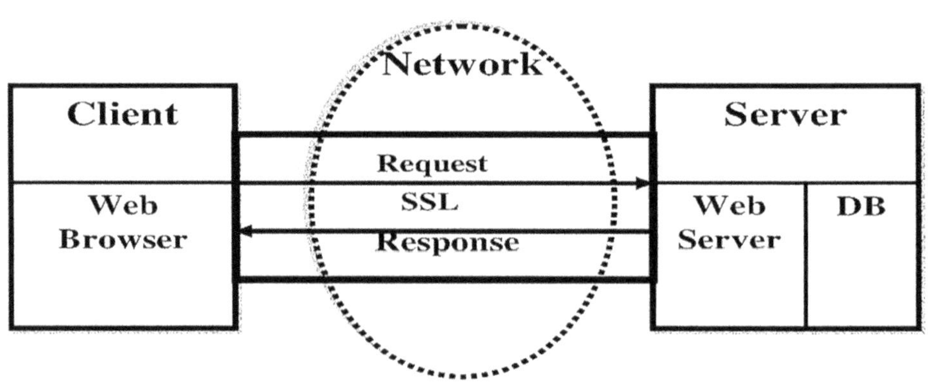

A web browser is a software application that is used to access WWW and has three basic functions (Oppliger & Gajek, 2005):

- Obtaining information on the Internet using URL and speaking with HTTP.
- Rendering HTML source code that is receiving in the form of HTTP response from a web server.
- Current web browsers provide Graphic User Interface (GUI) tool for performing different tasks such as saving web documents, searching, and others.

A web server is an independent platform that is structured from software and hardware. For example, Apache web server is used in many Internet/Intranet settings. However, a web server has several basic functions (Oppliger & Gajek, 2005):

1. Logging activities.
2. Authenticating users.
3. Protecting files from criminals.
4. Responding web documents to authorized users.

All HTTP operations are based on the HTTP request-response Model. In a web environment, a request is defined as "an operation to be performed on URL". Meanwhile, a response is defined as web server answers or replies for request operation to a web browser (Oppliger & Gajek, 2005).

The data integrity relies on the integrity of the HTTP request-response Model. Therefore, if this model fails, the data integrity might be violated (Hassinen & Mussalo, 2005). A user can access a client through a web browser to make a request by clicking on hyperlink text or hyperlink image, clicking on a submit button or command button, redirecting using the action attribute of form element, or by setting the requested URL at the address bar of a web browser (Hassinen & Mussalo, 2005).

Data is sent to a web server via the communication channel. It is assumed that the communication channel is secure and controlled by some communication protocols including TCP/IP, and SSL (Oppliger & Gajek, 2005). The aim of a web server is to manage and control all user requests, communicate with the correct user, save the request information on a server database, and then control the access of user to web page resources. For sensitive web content, a web server authenticates a request that contains a username and a password and then:

1. Accept the request, and then allow making the connection if they are correct, otherwise,
2. Refuse the request and then close the connection.

This request is processed on a web server by an application written in server-side programming language. As a result, data query may save data into a backend database. Finally, a web server sends the appropriate web page to a web browser, which renders it (Oppliger & Gajek, 2005).

Note that the Multipurpose Internet Mail Extensions (MIME) types are used to define the types of a particular fragment of information being sent from a web server to a web browser. Each web browser has a different configuration for mapping the types of data to particular function. Major web browsers can process various types of HTML documents, and CSS but other types are sent to various programs via the plug-in mechanisms such as sound player, video player (Oppliger & Gajek, 2005).

Uniform Resource Locater (URL)

Uniform Resource locator (URL) is a method of addressing web documents in the WWW. URL consists of:

1. Protocol (such as HTTP, and Gopher).
2. Host name.
3. Internet port number of service. If not specified, the default port number (80 for HTTP) is used.
4. Location of resource on a server (path/query).

The URL components can be specified in HTML/XHTML form element through action attribute. The URL can be specified in a Link element through HREF attribute of A tag.

The HTTP Request

There are three parts of HTTP request operation, a request line, request header and request body (this part is optional depending on form author) (Oppliger & Gajek, 2005). The request line starts with request method, followed by a resource identifier and the protocol version, For Example:

1. Get/default.html HTTP/1.
2. Post/index.html HTTP/1.

The form element has a number of methods to send the user input from a web browser to a web server as follows (Oppliger & Gajek, 2005):

- GET, is the default request type, which notifies a web server to fetch a document and send it back to a web browser. It is normally used to retrieve data such as search engine or data query. This type appends the form information directly to the end of the URL. The input field name and input field value are represented as a pair of parameter name and its value at end of URL after the question marker.
- POST, is used to process any kind of data in various form services such as sorting, updating, ordering a product, sending e-mail, or responding to a query. Another advantage, POST method is used, if the total size of a request is huge, because the URL contains limited parameters.
- HEAD, is used to retrieve header information of a web document such as a version of a document, and availability of hyperlinks.
- DELETE, is used to delete a recourse identified by a URL during the need of a web server.

For utilization of request operation, a user can send additional information about a web browser and user itself. This additional information is called request header fields such as Accept, Encoding, Authorization, Authentication, Host, and User Agent (Oppliger & Gajek, 2005).

Behind the Scenes of a Web Page

This example shows a simple web page that contains a list of hyperlinks of universities in United Kingdom. A web server responses and sends back the HTML file and the header file to a web browser. A web browser parses this URL (http://www.findaschool.org/index.php?Country=United+Kingdom). Table 1 shows meaning of each part of URL:

A web browser connects to findaschool.org using the HTTP protocol. The default port for HTTP is 80 if it is not specified. Table 2 shows the structure of request message:

In the Other hand, a web server returns header file "header information" and HTML file to a web browser as shown in Table 3.

Table 1. The meaning of the URL

Content	Meaning
http	Hyper Text Transfer Protocol
WWW	World Wide Web
findaschool.org	Host name
index.php	A document path in a server
?Country=United+Kingdom	A query path, which contains the parameter names and their values. The values of parameters are URL-encoded, space becomes +, non-alphanumeric chars become \%hexcode for encryption.

Table 2. The structure of the request message

GET/ HTTP/1.0 (Request Get, HTTP protocol, Protocol version 1.0)
Connection, keep-Alive (TCP Connection is open until to disconnect)
User-Agent, Microsoft Internet Explorer 6.0 (Win XP)
Host, findaschool.org- (hostname on server)
Accept, image/gif, */* (>Media Type to be accepted)
If-Modified-Since, Friday, 10-Feb-16 11,12,30 GMT (last modified)

Table 3. The structure of the response message

HTTP/1. 200 ok (Protocol version, status code)
Date, Sat, 10 Feb 2006 13,00,10 GMT (Current Time on the Server)
Server, Apache/1.1.1 (type of software running on server)
Content-Type, text/html (type of document that being sent to web browser)
Content-Length, 327(size of document-byte unit)
Last-modified, Sat, 10 Feb 2016 13,30,10 GMT ->the recent modification time
<!DOCTYPE html PUBLIC "-//W3C//DTD XHTML 1.0 STRICT//EN"
"http,//www.w3.org/TR/xhtml1/DTD/xhtml1-strict.dtd">
<html><head>
<title>GEO I Colleges and Universities I United Kingdom</title>
...
</head><body>
...
</body></html>

Response Classes

The response classes rely on the status code in a header file. In respect to the first digit of status code, the type of response classes is determined as follows:

1. 1xx, (Informational) request received, still in process
2. 2xx, (Success) the operation is successfully received, parsed and accepted
3. 3xx, (Redirection) further process required for competing the request
4. 4xx, (Client Error) the header file of request contains syntax error and cannot be performed well. Or,
5. 4xx, (Server error) the server failed to perform a valid request.

ONLINE BANKING SECURITY

Any discussion of online banking security necessarily starts from a statement of requirements (i.e. what it really means to call an online banking system secure). Generally, secure online banking systems will control, through use of specific security policies, access to information such that only properly authorized individuals, or processes operating on their behalf, will have access to read, write, create, or delete information (Aljawarneh et. al, 2007).

Banks are being increasingly worried for their reputations, and losing money if a system is subverted. This is because the current security tools may not prevent the online banking system vulnerabilities (Aljawarneh et. al, 2007). For example, by the end of 2006, more than half (55.78%) of the phishing attacks have fake web sites hosted in the U.S. and with 7,247 vulnerabilities disclosed in 2006, total vulnerability count increased nearly 40% over the previous year. This trend of increase is expected to continue throughout the next years (Aljawarneh et. al, 2007).

A number of online banking security definitions from the user's perspective. For some, online banking security is the ability to view banking content in peace and safety. For others, it is the ability to conduct safe business and financial transactions. For web authors, it is the confidence that individuals will not damage their sites.

In generic, a Gehling and Stankard (Gehling & Stankard, 2005) defined a web security as "technique for ensuring that the data stored in a computer transmitted between computers cannot be read or compromised by unauthorized users". There are no guaranteed solutions for making the online banking environment safe. The current technologies such data validation schemes, firewalls, intrusion detections and cryptographic techniques alone are not sufficient to secure the integrity of online banking content on the server (Aljawarneh et. al, 2007; Aljawarneh et. al, 2008).

Online Banking Security Risks

Clients and banks are suffering from a growing number of attacks that abuse data on the Internet. These attacks become a source of threat for online banking systems. A bank that has established a strong reputation may suffer from persistent destruction to its reputation after attacking event. According to CERT many web sites (such as the U.S. Central Intelligence Agency, the U.S. Air Force, and NASA) have been subject to malicious attacks.

Online banking security vulnerabilities result from poorly configured operating systems, limitations of web servers and web browsers, weakness of web technologies, and weakness of software engineers. There are three types of security risk (Oppliger & Gajek, 2005):

- Source code problems in a web server that enable an adversary to:
  - Read and copy confidential documents on a web server and this causes loss of data confidentiality.
  - Run malicious code on a server. This permits tampering with web documents and subsequent loss of data integrity.
  - Obtain header response information from a web server that will permit breaking into online banking system recourses. As a result, there is a loss of data availability.
  - Activate denial-of-service attacks that might break into the online banking system.
- Browser-side risks including:
  - Enable active content vulnerabilities on a web browser such as malicious Java Applet attack, and script attacks.
  - Loss of data integrity at the form level.
- Network-side risks that cause the eavesdropping problem (i.e. listening to someone else's conversation from any point including:
  - A web browser connection.
  - A web server connection.
  - Communication channel of online banking systems.

Online Banking Security Issues

Studies and surveys indicate that web security (such as online banking security) objectives are easily violated on a web environment, and as a result, the e-commerce environment is suffering financial losses. There are three basic security issues (Gehling & Stankard, 2005):

1. **Data Confidentiality**: Any data that viewed, modified, or copied by unauthorized user that cause to loss of confidentiality such as credit card details. The data confidentiality objective refers to limiting information access and disclosure to authorized users. Confidentiality involves limiting the disclosure of data by ensuring that authorized users only know it. A common method to ensure confidentiality is to encrypt data known as the plaintext with a secret key known only to the authorized users to produce encrypted text known as the cipher text. A good encryption scheme will make it difficult or impossible to recover the original data from the encrypted data without knowledge of the key.
2. **Data Integrity**: Any data that are tampered with either on a client or on a server that cause to loss of integrity. The data integrity objective ensures that an authorized client can only legally alter the data.
3. **Data Availability**: Any data, which available on insecure online banking system might be compromised. It refers to information system that is not available when you need it.

Cryptography is not always sufficient to ensure the confidentiality of data. It is possible to imagine online banking system in which simply the presence of an encrypted message implicitly conveys information about the value of confidential data. In this situation an adversary may never need to discover the key or break the encryption algorithm in order to attack the system.

In data integrity, malicious data corruption is more difficult to counter. A simple hash function such as MD5 is insufficient because hash functions are assumed to be public knowledge and easy to compute. An adversary would still be able to corrupt the data provided they also recomputed the corresponding hash. An alternative is to encrypt the hash value with a secret key to form a Message Authentication Code (MAC). Only authorized parties own the key and can generate and verify matching MACs. It is possible to use a hash function to build a MAC using an algorithm such as HMAC. In this Chapter, we have attempted to address only the data integrity issue.

The privacy and security issues (confidentiality, integrity, and availability) are exploited for the lack of a web browser and limitation of web technologies. For example, Java is the safest security model because it supports sandbox class model to protect the Java Applet from some potential security vulnerabilities. Furthermore, Java Applet does not support direct or indirect connection to operating system environment. On the other hand, JavaScript and ActiveX is the least security model. Indeed, JavaScript supports methods to capture the user details (confidentiality issue) by reading the user files. Integrity problems might result from JavaScript methods that altering, destroying the user details. While data availability problems result from JavaScript methods that destroying the user session by reading the cookie details or running an infinite loop to open infinite number of windows and then crash the operating system.

Malicious Attack

A malicious attack is any code launched to disrupt or harm an intended request-response conversation on online banking system, including attack scripts, Java Applet attack, input validation attacks and ActiveX control attack. A malicious attack causes disruption to the HTTP request-response operations, or causes eavesdropping problem (McGraw & Morrisett, 2000).

Due to the insecurities of the communication protocol, the open architecture of the Internet and the lack of online banking security mechanisms, the web environment is vulnerable to security risks. However, criminals successfully find security holes in the web environment infrastructure because they have a strong arsenal of attack tools that use very systematic plans of actions including (McGraw & Morrisett, 2000):

- Analyze the server architecture, server type, operation system types and limitations of web browsers.
- Study the web environment architecture such as studying the HTTP Request type (GET, POST, and DELETE) and user input interaction. A criminal searches for security holes in a feedback form, an inquiry form or a login form.
- Study input validation modules. These modules determine whether a certain form data is safe or unsafe data is rejected during the validation processing. Therefore, a criminal could apply reverse engineering algorithms on validation modules.

Java Security

Java was designed to work in a network-computing environment such as downloading Applets over networks. Currently, Java is a safe programming language that protects users from some security vulnerabilities. In addition, Java supports the code signing using JDK 1.1 for securing the integrity of Java Applets (Oppliger & Gajek, 2005).

Java cannot own solutions to protect online banking system from intentionally malicious code (McGraw & Morrisett, 2000). So that, it is necessary to apply a security policy on web pages which are downloaded on a client machine. The existing Java security policy contains a number of classes to limit what a downloaded web page can do, including the Sandbox class, SecurityManager class, Bytecode Verifier, and Loader class (Oppliger & Gajek, 2005). When Java programs are launched, a Bytecode Verifier is run to validate for any unauthorized operations. Bytecode is a name given to machine code for compiling a Java program in the Java Virtual Machine (JVM) and then interpreted on the running machine. Figure 2 illustrates how to compile Java program and then download on an online banking system.

Java includes JVM platform to provide a trusted environment for running the Applets, which are embedded in a web page. However, JVM cannot secure a web page against a malicious Applet. The malicious applet is "Any applet that performs an action against the will of the user who invoked it should be considered malicious". It is important to understand the architecture of java security model to know how to detect the Java Applet vulnerabilities. Therefore, the Java policy in JVM prevents most security critical operations, but it does not prevent untrusted Applets from disrupting the users.

Another Java security issue is that Java allows a web designer to give unnecessary details and choices such as extras details to specify the form field attributes or Applet attributes. Therefore, Java is not a small high-level domain specific language for securing the data integrity.

Java does not also support pointers and multiple inheritances to keep the Java program simple, readable and less error prone features. Therefore, if a web application is properly constructed and implemented using Java, it might be safer or more secure than other programming languages. However, a web developer should

Figure 2. Java program architecture

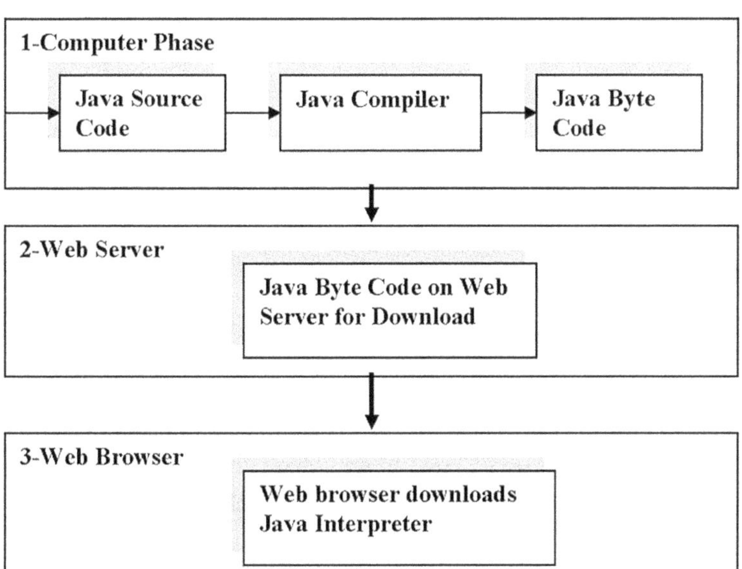

check the bounds of dynamic array and then throw any unpredicted element through Exceptions class. Otherwise, this can cause a buffer overflow attack and as a result, this attack leads to loss of data availability and then loss of data integrity (McGraw & Morrisett, 2000).

Java supports a Servlet application to work over an online banking system. Servlet is used to generate dynamic web pages on demand (each time, the page is requested) (Oppliger & Gajek, 2005). The contents of a dynamic web page can be different each time at each request, because the construction of dynamic page relies on a user interaction. The Servlet includes HTTPservlet class that manages the multiple requests. This feature solves the sessionless HTTP drawback. Therefore, Servlet is developed instead of CGI for better scalability and security. A Servlet structure contains HTML tags that are embedded in the Java source code. Furthermore, it has full access to HTTP Layer and then it has the ability to trace each request-response conversation. However, the change of web page needs to change in Java code rather than HTML code. As a result, a designer needs to be familiar with Servlet structure or Java Programming language.

JavaScript Security

JavaScript is a Netscape object-oriented language that is developed to make animation, well-designed form, form field validation and other interactive features (Oppliger & Gajek, 2005). JavaScript programs reside in HTML files, usually surrounded by both <script></script> in a web document. A web browser can render JavaScript commands in HTML file. JavaScript supplies additional objects:

- **Client-Side JavaScript**: JavaScript supplies objects to control a web browser and a Document Object Model (DOM). For example, an object can be extended to have some user-defined methods. This object is invoked by event-handler on a form element including on click, on mouse over.
- **Server-Side JavaScript**: extends by supplying objects to run on a server. For example, the request information could be stored on a backend database after communicating the application to a web server. Another example, the JavaScript might incorporate with Server Active Page (ASP) to apply validation modules on a server-side.

JavaScript has introduced several security problems including Denial-of-Service attacks, input validation attacks, script attacks, and privacy violations. For example, JavaScript methods can launch Denial-of-Service attacks on a client machine through a web page or an electronic mail. A simple JavaScript Denial-of-Service is to invoke alert() method inside a loop statement. Each time, the loop is executed; a message window appears on the screen of a web browser. This attack can cause loss of data availability and then the data integrity is compromised (Oppliger & Gajek, 2005).

In addition, JavaScript has indirect access to operating system resources and user data through a set of JavaScript methods and objects such as "history", "navigator", and "cookie". For example, "history" object allows a user to discover the URL of all of the other web pages that have been visited during a session. This feature could be combined with a previous feature to perform a form of automated eavesdropping problem (Oppliger & Gajek, 2005).

For JavaScript popularity, simplicity, and high efficiency, web applications are still used JavaScript language for user input validation on the client-side. However, the form content might be faked by cancelling the validation modules on the client-side. The server fooled and then accepts the faked form. This is possible, because any user can display HTML and JavaScript code using tools of a web browser (Oppliger & Gajek, 2005).

Furthermore, a safe-type programming language (such as Java) can explicitly declare type of user inputs during program writing and then this gives less error and fewer security risks. On other hand, JavaScript considers all user inputs have the same type and it is possible to apply any operation (such as mathematical addition, and string concatenation) on any type of user input. Consequently, this leads to escape harmful meta-characters via user inputs. Therefore, JavaScript form inputs are vulnerable to validation attacks (Oppliger & Gajek, 2005).

Common Gateway Interface Security

CGI is a communication protocol between a web page and a program that is executed on a web server. It permits the input data of HTML forms to be sent to a server, which runs a CGI script and passes this data to it through the standard input or standard query. The CGI program can then process the data, and return it in HTML form format through the standard output to a web browser. CGI can be written in any language (such as JavaScript, C, C++ and Perl) and can be run on various types of operating systems such as Mac, NT, UNIX or any operation system that runs on a web server (Oppliger & Gajek, 2005; Yang, Huang, Wang et al., 2002).

One advantage of CGI is that it is used to generate dynamic web pages in relation to user interaction. For example, the creation of a web search engine, which reads a search string from a user, searches a database of web pages, and returns HTML data listing the matching sites (Oppliger & Gajek, 2005; Yang, Huang, Wang et al., 2002).

CGI returns the output data as part of the URL, and then output data is encoded to binary format. The blanks are represented by +, and the other special characters are represented as XX where XX is the ASCII value of a character in hexadecimal format. A CONTENT_LENGTH environment variable determines the number of bytes to be read on standard input or standard output. However, data tampering could be taken place when data have been altered either on the client-side or the server-side for poor design and implementation of data validation modules. For example, an adversary might bypass the data validation modules in a client, alter data input, and then the CGI scripts are tampered with. A tampered CGI script can disrupt a server, and might be exploited to gain access to a back-end database. Another related problem is that the huge amount of input data is sent to a server. This causes overflow in the CGI buffer and then the CGI script is destroyed (Oppliger & Gajek, 2005; Yang, Huang, Wang et al., 2002).

Due to the CGI scripts only run a server, more opportunities to abuse data on a server that may be the target of interest to adversaries rather than data on a client. Therefore, many web sites adopt double-checking of data validation modules to ensure the integrity of an online banking system. However, the generated dynamic web content is an issue because the double-checking validation scheme is not able to ensure the data integrity against tampering. This scheme is beneficial for basic input data.

Another security risk is that the HTTP is sessionless (Oppliger & Gajek, 2005; Yang, Huang, Wang et al., 2002; Aljawarneh et. al, 2007). HTTP only provides once the type of request/response communication. Therefore, each time, there is a new connection between a web browser and a web server. CGI supports the maintenance of state through the use of hidden variables or cookies that keep track of the current information for each request. However, this possible solution could be broken through saving the HTML form to a disk, tampering the hidden values, and then reloading this altered form into a web browser for rendering.

Online Banking Security Technologies

In this Chapter, we have focused on two technologies of an online banking security, hashing and Message Authentication Code (MAC). Hashing is a web security technology to ensure the integrity of data. The hash function generates computationally unique hash values similar to fingerprint signature. The hash value is called a message-digest or a checksum that is expressed in hexadecimal or binary format.

In this Chapter, the form of hash function is \$h = H (wc)\$ where \$h\$ is the checksum, and \$wc\$ is the variable length a web content. The checksum is compared to the previous calculated hash value of a web content for checking the web content integrity. The hash function is an effective cryptographic hash method for the following features (Oppliger & Gajek, 2005; Yang, Huang, Wang et al., 2002):

1. **One-Way Hash Function**: The adversary cannot decrypt the checksum because it is not irreversible.
2. **Random Values**: It gives different checksums even though the binary string inputs are similar.
3. **No Collision**: It computationally finds the values of two binary strings x and y in different locations, even though the $h(x)$ and $h(y)$ are similar.

Table 4 shows a comparison between a set of hash functions:

Message Authentication Code (MAC)

MAC is a very small code to ensure the integrity of data beside the cryptography techniques. It is a one-way hash function that involves a private key. Only the parties that know the private key can compute the MAC value. Therefore, a private key can be produced by one of the parties, and then sent in an encrypted format to other using the public key encryption method. A sender computationally generates a number (fixed-length data item) that is formulated from a combination of the key and the message. On the other hand, a receiver uses the same key with a computational procedure to re-compute this number, and this is called authentication code. If the matching is true, then the message is not altered (Oppliger & Gajek, 2005; Yang, Huang, Wang et al., 2002).

Table 4. A list of hash functions

Hash Function	Hash Sum Size (bits)
MD4	128
MD5	128
RIPEMD-128	128
RIPEMD-160	160
SHA-1	160
SHA-256	256
SHA-384	384
SHA-512	512
Tiger / Tiger2	192

CONCLUSION

This chapter has discussed the data flow over the HTTP request-response model. This is because the data integrity relies on the integrity of the HTTP request-response model. Therefore, if this model fails, the data integrity might be violated.

We have explained that the popularity of the web technologies (HTML/XHTML, Java, JavaScript, and CGI) refers to a number of reasons, fully openness of web technology, the easy to use features of the web browsers including the simple navigation and access of information, and fully integration of text, sound, and graphics. However, online banking security issues such as data tampering in the web technologies are currently evolving rapidly for some factors, the need for data protection over the HTTP request-response model, and for ensuring data integrity against tampering attacks.

We have also tried to place online banking security in perspective, because it is central issue and necessary to banks, clients and even home users now and in the future. We have offered a review of online banking security issues, focusing on particular areas of concern, such as server security and data integrity issue. There are three basic security issues, confidentiality, availability, and integrity of data. In this Chapter, we have focused on one of these issues is a data integrity because it has received little attention in the information security research. A loss of data integrity is possible for statelessness of HTTP, openness of web technologies (such as the transparency of a code on a web browser), and limitations of web browser and web server.

Furthermore, we have explored the two standard technologies of online banking security, hashing and MAC. In this Chapter, we suggest to use a SHA1 hash function with a changeable private key (MAC technology) as a solution to any secure system.

REFERENCES

Alhaj, A., Aljawarneh, S., Masadeh, S., & Abu-Taieh, E. (2013). A Secure Data Transmission Mechanism for Cloud Outsourced Data. *International Journal of Cloud Applications and Computing*, *3*(1), 34–43. doi:10.4018/ijcac.2013010104

Aljawarneh, S. (2011a). Cloud security engineering: Avoiding security threats the right way. *International Journal of Cloud Applications and Computing*, *1*(2), 64–70. doi:10.4018/ijcac.2011040105

Aljawarneh, S. (2011b). A web engineering security methodology for e-learning systems. *Network Security*, *2011*(3), 12–15. doi:10.1016/S1353-4858(11)70026-5

Aljawarneh, S., Al-Rousan, T., Maatuk, A. M., & Akour, M. (2014). Usage of data validation techniques in online banking: A perspective and case study. *Security Journal*, *27*(1), 27–35. doi:10.1057/sj.2012.10

Aljawarneh, S., Alkhateeb, F., & Al Maghayreh, E. (2010a). A semantic data validation service for web applications. *Journal of Theoretical and Applied Electronic Commerce Research*, *5*(1), 39–55. doi:10.4067/S0718-18762010000100005

Aljawarneh, S., Dababneh, M., Hosseny, H., & Alwadi, E. (2010b). A web client authentication system using smart card for e-systems: initial testing and evaluation. *Proceedings of the Fourth International Conference on Digital Society ICDS '10* (pp. 192–197). IEEE. doi:10.1109/ICDS.2010.40

Aljawarneh, S., Laing, C., & Vickers, P. (2008). Design and experimental evaluation of Web Content Verification and Recovery (WCVR) system: A survivable security system.*Proceedings of ACSF* (pp. 1–7).

Aljawarneh, S., Laing, C., & Vickers, P. (2007). Security policy framework and algorithms for web server content protection.*Proceedings of ACSF'07*.

Aljawarneh, S. A. (2012). Survivability of Web Content: Theoretical and Practical Approaches Protection of static and dynamic data against tampering.

Aljawarneh, S. A., Moftah, R. A., & Maatuk, A. M. (2016). Investigations of automatic methods for detecting the polymorphic worms signatures. *Future Generation Computer Systems*, *60*, 67–77.

Brabrand, C., Moller, A., Ricky, M., & Scwartzbach, M. I. (2000). Powerforms: Declarative client-side form field validation. *World Wide Web (Bussum)*, *3*(4), 205–214. doi:10.1023/A:1018772405468

Chen, Y.-H., Lin, C.-Y., Sirakriengkrai, W., & Weng, I.-C. (2015). Repairable Image Authentication Scheme. *International Journal of Network Security*, *17*(4), 439–444.

Gehling, B., & Stankard, D. (2005, September). eCommerce security.*Proceedings of the 2nd annual conference on Information security curriculum development* (pp. 32-37). ACM. doi:10.1145/1107622.1107631

Hassinen, M., & Mussalo, P. (2005, November). Client controlled security for web applications. *Proceedings of the 30th Anniversary IEEE Conference on Local Computer Networks* (p. 7). IEEE. doi:10.1109/LCN.2005.38

Hodgson, G. (2015). Breaking Encryption and Gathering Data: International Law Applications. *Journal of Technology Law & Policy*.

Kumar Bhajantri, V., Sujatha, C., Yaligar, S., & Pawar, M. K. (2016). An Experiential Learning in Web Technology Course. *Journal of Engineering Education Transformations*.

Lee, W., Park, S. S., Lim, C., Kim, J., & Kang, S. (2015). Proxy Server Authentication for Blocking HTTP-Cache-Poisoning Attacks. *Applications of Mathematics*, *9*(2L), 483–492.

McGraw, G., & Morrisett, G. (2000). Attacking malicious code: A report to the Infosec Research Council. *IEEE Software*, *17*(5), 33–41. doi:10.1109/52.877857

Oppliger, R., & Gajek, S. (2005, September). Effective protection against phishing and web spoofing. In *Communications and Multimedia Security* (pp. 32–41). Springer Berlin Heidelberg. doi:10.1007/11552055_4

Spinellis, D. (2016, January). Addressing Threats and Security Issues in World Wide Web Technology. In Communications and Multimedia Security (Vol. 3, p. 33). Springer.

Yang, J. T., Huang, J. L., Wang, F. J., & Chu, W. C. (2002). Constructing an object-oriented architecture for Web application testing. *Journal of Information Science and Engineering*, *18*(1), 59–84.

Chapter 7
The Influences of Privacy, Security, and Legal Concerns on Online Banking Adoption:
A Conceptual Framework

Khalid Alkhatib
Jordan University of Science and Technology, Jordan

Ahmad Alaiad
Jordan University of Science and Technology, Jordan

ABSTRACT

Business globalization and the rising new technology enforced traditional banking to head towards online banking services, which facilitates customers to obtain access to their accounts from their business sites and personal computers to online banking services. The objective of this chapter is to construct a framework of adoption of online banking and represent the major influences of privacy, security, and legal concerns on online banking adoption. Furthermore, the chapter reveals the main challenges in the development of online banking system. The adoption of online banking can decrease the operating expenses and offer good and rapid services to their customers. The framework factors have been classified as facilitators and barriers of adoption of online banking. Performance expectancy, effort expectancy and social influence have been classified as facilitators whereas security concerns, privacy concerns and legal concerns have been classified as barriers. The results revealed various significant suggestions for online banking service providers, designers and developers.

DOI: 10.4018/978-1-5225-0864-9.ch007

INTRODUCTION

Global internet access of more than 1000 million people by the end of 2014 (Internet World Stats, 2015), offering new markets for online based services such as online banking. Online banking is defined as the use of banking services through the computer network (the Internet) offering a variety of prospective benefits to financial institutions (Aladwani, 2001; Yiu, Grant, & Edgar, 2007). With online banking, consumers can execute, electronically, a range of transactions, such as standing orders, paying bills, transferring funds, statements requests, and account balances queries through the bank's website banking system. Online banking expected to be attractive to customers with several benefits including cost savings, better service delivery control, waiting time reduction, higher levels of customization understanding, and convenient access to bank services. In addition, by offering online banking services traditional financial institutions look for a reduction in operational costs, improve consumer-banking services, maintain consumers and expand market share of consumers, and increase consumers' loyalty and satisfaction.

Despite the anticipated value of online banking in many countries to both consumers and banks, its adoption rate is still small. According to comScore, more than 420 million people globally accessed online banking sites during the month of April 2012, reaching 28.75% of the Internet users. This comprised of 45% of the Internet users in North America, 37.8% in Europe, 25.1% in Latin America, 22% percent in Asia Pacific, 8.8 percent in Africa. In comparing the adoption rate of online banking between developed and developing countries' consumers, developing countries are clearly far lower. Such a low adoption rate is a worrying factor to banking institutions and it is due to several reasons. For example, consumer demand for online banking services in North America hindered in 2005, this perhaps due to a rise in security concerns related to a rise in identity fraud, phishing and online frauds (ZDNet, 2005). Therefore, the success of the implementation of online banking hinders on whether we can understand the adoption issues prior to the actual implementation of the system. The deficiency of understanding such issues is one of the main reasons for the failure of many information technology systems (Aart & Gorman, 2007, Berg et al., 2013).

Since online banking is still in its premature phase of dispersion in developing countries, it is important that we explore what influence its consumer adoption' decision-making process. Online banking systems that are undesirably considered by consumers are inappropriate similar to any product or service, and consumers of online banking ought to be contented; otherwise, they will go somewhere else to accomplish tasks they are aiming to complete. Therefore, to increase the adoption rate in developing countries, banks in these countries need to better manage factors that influence consumers' adoption of the online banking, which is the goal of this chapter. Despite some general technology adoption theories (Wu et al., 2008; Zhou, 2012; Kijsanayotin et al., 2009, Lin et al., 2011), the literature survey reveals that there is a gap of theory that explains the adoption of online banking in developing countries by specifically addressing the unique characteristics of the technology. Further, previous research had explored the adoption behavior of online banking in developed countries with limited concerned on developing countries considering the bag differences between both. Additionally, limited research explored the impact of security, privacy and legal concerns on the consumer adoption in developing countries. Thus, the aim of this chapter is to fill this knowledge gap by developing a framework to explain the adoption behavior of the online banking in developing countries by its consumers.

This chapter offers several contributions to the online banking literature. First, it enhances the effectiveness of technical implementation of online banking in developing countries by identifying both facilitators and obstacles to the adoption of online banking. Second, it enriches the theoretical foundation of online banking research by proposing a conceptual framework to explain online banking adoption, enabling theory-driven design and development of the systems. Third, it introduces various new factors such as security, privacy and legal concerns, which can help improve consumers' acceptance and reduce their resistance to the online banking technology in the developing countries; fourth, it enables online banking system designers and developers had better understand consumers' security and privacy needs.

THEORETICAL FOUNDATION

Technology acceptance is defined as "an individual's psychological state with regard to his or her voluntary or intended use of a particular technology." Traditionally, acceptance models have been used to assist explain and forecast adoption of new technologies. In information systems research, various theories have been proposed to explore the acceptance of the user for a new IT and its usage. With its foundation in the field of social learning, Social Cognitive Theory (SCT) is based on the acquisition of knowledge through observation. (Fishbein & Ajzen, 1975) develop the Theory of Reasoned Action (TRA) which is drawn from social psychology. Theory of Planned Behavior (TPB) extends TRA by adding the construct of perceived behavioral control (Fishbein & Ajzen, 1975).

(Thompson, Higgins, & Howell, 1991) revealed a substitute to TRA and TPB, the Model of PC Utilization (MPCU). The model is mostly suited to forecast individual acceptance and use of a variety of information technologies. The Technology Acceptance (TAM) model is more customized to information technology research contexts and is mainly designed to forecast information technology acceptance

(Davis, 1989). (Taylor & Todd, 1995) developed a theory known as a Combined TAM-TPB, or C – TAM – TPB. It combined the predictive elements of TPB with the concept of perceived usefulness from TAM.

With the intention to formulate, a comprehensive model that considers the variables included in all the previous models, Venkatesh, Morris, Davis and Davis (2003) developed research to test each of the constructs described above. They presented a summary of previous model comparison studies and an empirical synthesis of the different models. Finally, with the variables that presented the largest impact, they defined a new model termed Unified Theory of Acceptance and Use of Technology (UTAUT)

In the context of online banking, authors of a number of prior studies have applied such IS theories to explore the adoption of online banking. However, none of the studies had explained online banking security and privacy adoption and no one has considered the legal and ethical matters for explaining the adoption behavior.

PERFORMANCE EXPECTANCY

Performance expectancy is the extent to which a user believes that using online banking will help him/her improve job performance. Performance expectancy has four sub-constructs based on the literature: usefulness, extrinsic motivation, relative advantage, and outcome expectations. Table 1 provides a brief description about each of the sub-constructs.

Several previous studies demonstrate the influence of performance expectancy on usage intent (Alshehri et al., 2012, Alawadhi & Morris, 2008, Rezaie & Abadi, 2012, Jahangir & Begum, 2008) and found that performance expectancy being the strongest predictor of intention to use IT (Venkatesh et al., 2003). In the context of

Table 1. Sub-constructs and descriptions of performance expectancy

Sub-Constructs	Definition
Usefulness	The degree to which a person believes that using the technology would improve his or her job/ personal performance.
Relative advantage	The degree to which using an innovation is considered as being better than using its antecedent.
Motivation	The perception that person will want to perform an activity because it is perceived to be instrumental in achieving valued results that are different from the activity itself, such as improved job performance, pay, or promotions
Outcome expectations	Relate to the implications of the conduct.

online banking, performance expectancy shows that using online banking is expected to help users gain benefits, increase the whole output, execute tasks rapidly and flexibly, and effectively access services.

Effort Expectancy

Effort expectancy refers to the degree of ease a user feels with respect to the use of online banking. Effort expectancy has three sub-constructs based on the literature: complexity, ease of use and learning. Table 2 provides a brief description about each of the sub-constructs.

According to Venkatesh et al. (2003), the three previous constructs that underlie effort expectancy are perceived ease of use (TAM/TAM2), complexity (MPCU), and ease of use (IDT) (Venkatesh et al, 2003). Several previous studies have proven that effort expectancy has impact on intention to use technology in other domains (Kijsanayotin et al., 2009, Alshehri et al., 2012). In the context of online banking, their adoption depends on their ease of use and freeing from errors. If the use of online banking systems is complex, the interaction with them would not be understandable, which would influence negatively on the users' adoption.

SOCIAL INFLUENCE

Social influence is defined as the extent to which a user perceives that significant others believe he or she should use online banking. Social influence has two sub-constructs based on the literature: subjective norm and subjective culture. Table 3 provides a brief description about each of the sub-constructs.

Social and emotion support is instrumental for the people who receives banking services. Thus, the users' decision to use online banking is influenced by their peers and friends in their community. Various previous studies propose that social influence is significant in shaping an individual's intention to use a new technology (Kijsanayotin et al., 2009, Thompson, Higgins, & Howell, 1991).

Table 2. Sub-constructs and descriptions of effort expectancy

Sub-Constructs	Definition
Complexity	The degree to which the technology is perceived as relatively difficult to understand and use.
Ease of use	The degree to which a person believes that using the technology would be free of effort.
Learning	The degree to which using an innovation is perceived as being difficult to learn.

Table 3. Sub-constructs and descriptions of social influence

Sub-Constructs	Definition
Subjective norm	The person is noticing that most people who are significant to him believe he should or should not adopt the technology.
Subjective culture	The individual's internalization of the reference group's subjective culture, and specified personal deals that the individual has made with others, in specific social condition.

Privacy Concerns

Privacy refers to the right to be left alone (Hossain & Prybutok, 2008). (Hossain & Prybutok, 2008) revealed four types of privacy were information privacy, bodily privacy, privacy of communications, and territorial privacy. The most pertinent of which to online banking adoption is information privacy, which refers to as the users' scarcity of control over the gathering and use of their personal information after they have adopted the system. In addition, privacy concerns subsume four sub-constructs emerged from the literature: confidentiality, unauthorized use by third party, lack of meeting of standards, and improper use of data. Table 4 provides a brief description about each of the sub-constructs.

Online banking systems forms several warnings to personal information privacy. Two privacy issues that influence the adoption of such technology has been identified (Hossain & Prybutok, 2008), user's personal information leaks and tracing of the user's physical location. In addition, there is a chance to collect, store, unauthorized access and secondary use of personal data when using online banking systems. The information collected could be potentially accessible by third parties (Al Eroud & Karabatis, 2012). Online banking systems service providers could share or misuse their user data which raise a concern on the user side. If personal identifiable data are dynamically traced by the system, a third party can possibly abuse the data

Table 4. Sub-constructs and descriptions of privacy concerns

Sub-Constructs	Definition
Confidentiality	The degree to which a person believes that his/ her personal data isn't kept credible and privatc
Unauthorized use by a third party	The degree to which a person believes that somebody else uses the data illegally
Standardization	The degree to which a person believes that the technology lacks of meeting of privacy standards
Improper use of data	The degree to which a person believes that the personal data be disclosed and/or misused improperly.

in order to build behavioral profiles of the users, which can successively be used to deduce the user's daily behaviors, their lifestyle, and so on. Several previous studies had approved that privacy is predictor of the intention (Alzahrani & Goodwin, 2012, Xu & Gupta, 2009)

Security Concerns

Security is defined as the protection against security threats, and referred to as a "circumstance, condition, or event with the potential to cause economic hardship to data or network resources in the form of destruction, disclosure, modification of data, denial of service, and/or fraud, waste, and abuse" (Hossain & Prybutok, 2008). Based on this definition, we define security concerns as the degree to which users believe that the online banking system is vulnerable to online threats/attacks. Based on the literature, security concerns are composed of four sub-constructs: safety, security threats/attacks, encrypted information, and security measures. Table 5 provides a brief description about each of the sub-constructs.

Security threats can occur through online banking and data transactions spasms and through unauthorized access (Al Eroud & Karabatis, 2012). Security is a leading matter relating to the adoption of online banking. Several previous studies provided empirical evidence for the impact of security on the intention of adoption of technology in other domains (Sanayei & Bahmani, 2012, Jahangir & Begum, 2008). The use of online banking presents potential security threats because personal information can be stolen or modified knowingly or unknowingly, especially in an environment that lacks of security measures to prevent any kind of harm. Users assess the risk-benefit of the technology from their point of view. They accept security risks if they believe that the benefits accrued are worth the risk (Hossain & Prybutok, 2008). In effect, prospect users estimate the benefits and risk exposure before they willingly adopt a system. Therefore, user adoption of online banking is

Table 5. Sub-constructs and descriptions of security concerns

Sub-Constructs	Definition
Safety	The degree to which a person believes that the data collected by the system is subject to unintended use.
Security attacks	The degree to which a person believes that his/her use of the system is subject to risky threats such as stealing data, or modifying data.
Encryption	The degree to which a person believes that his/her personal information isn't kept in encrypted way.
Security measures	The degree to which a person believes that there is a lack of protection against any kind of harm caused by using the system.

influenced by their perceived importance of security and their willingness to get the gains resulting from the usage of the technology against the potential risk of failure or harm. If users are concerned more about security threats of the system, they are less likely to adopt it (Lo & Yang, 2005).

Legal Concerns

Legal concerns generally described as conduct basics or action stipulated or officially renowned as obligatory or imposed by a controlling body (Booth et al., 2009). Legal concerns have four sub-constructs based on the literature: laws for privacy, reliability, liability and contract. Table 6 provides a brief description about each of the sub-constructs.

Legal concerns consider the legal coverage for reliability, quality, privacy, and tort-liability (Dickens & Cook, 2006). Users are concerned about whether federal, state, and/or local laws cover these components. There are several legal apprehensions ought to be considered by the rules and regulations to improve the online banking adoption. For instance, the level of guarantee of quality of services, the law protection for the quality of service through privacy contract or official protection, and the compensation in case of faults. In collecting the enormous volumes of banking and lifestyle information by online banking, an attention should be drawn to who controls the information, who inputs them, and where that information is stored. If online banking goes wrong and damages occurs, who to address this issue ethically and legally.

Table 6. Sub-constructs and descriptions of legal concerns

Sub-Constructs	Definition
Laws for privacy	The degree to which a person believes that laws don't provide coverage to protect his/her private information collected by the technology.
Reliability	The degree to which a person believes that laws don't provide coverage for the mistakes, quality of services and errors made by the technology.
Liability	The degree to which a person believes that laws don't provide coverage for harmful errors and mistakes made by the system.
Contract	The degree to which a person believes that there exists an official protection plan or a contract protected by law for the use of the system.

FRAMEWORK DEVELOPMENT AND PROPOSITIONS

Based on the identified constructs and sub-constructs discussed earlier, we develop a conceptual framework of online banking adoption as depicted in Figure 1. In particular, to explain the online banking adoption, we modified the authentic UTAUT model by allowing changes on its constructs and sub-constructs. Furthermore, we determined three new factors or constructs, comprising privacy, security and legal concerns. For data collection, primary data sources from literature review and interviews with domain experts. We then grouped the factors into two major categories, facilitators and barriers for the adoption. For instance, performance expectancy, effort expectancy and social influence are classified as facilitators for the adoption of online banking whereas security, privacy and legal concerns are classified as barriers.

As depicted in the framework, online banking adoption is the dependent variable, which connects to the way the users aim to use online banking. Online banking adoption is significant predictor to the actual user and is influenced by several independent factors as shown in the model including privacy, security, and legal concerns. The influential relationship between the independent and dependent fac-

Figure 1. A conceptual framework of online banking adoption

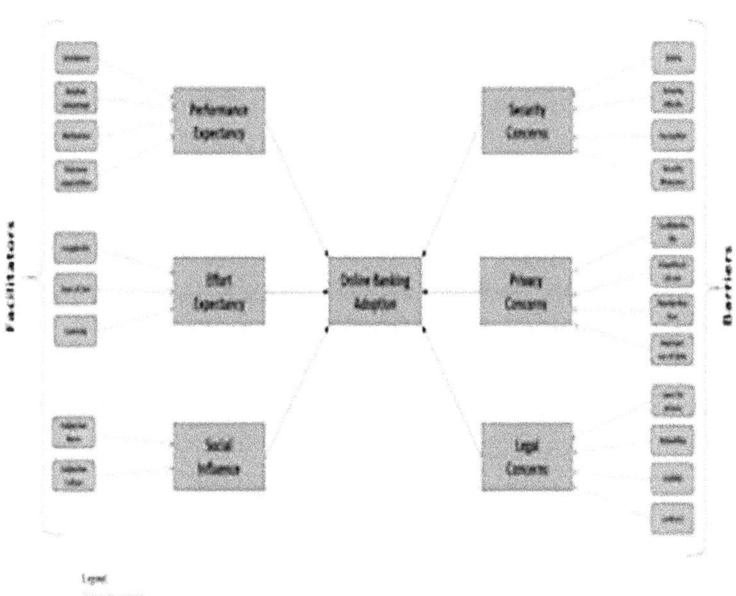

Table 7. Research propositions

Proposition No.	Proposition
Proposition 1	There would be a positive relationship between performance expectancy and online banking adoption.
Proposition 2	There would be a positive relationship between effort expectancy and online banking adoption.
Proposition 3	There would be a positive relationship between social influence and online banking adoption.
Proposition 4	There would be a negative relationship between security concerns and online banking adoption.
Proposition 5	There would be a negative relationship between privacy concerns and online banking adoption.
Proposition 6	There would be a negative relationship between legal concerns and online banking adoption.

tors can be positive or negative depending on whether the influencing factor is being classified as facilitators or barriers. Therefore, we propose a set of propositions that explain the nature of influential relationship between the independent and dependent factors. Table 7 provides a summary of the research propositions.

The identified propositions can be used in a further quantitative study to validate the significance of the relationships.

CONCLUSION

This chapter attempted to construct a framework of adoption of online banking. The chapter framework extends UTAUT with new factors and domain. The framework factors have been classified as facilitators and barriers of adoption of online banking. Performance expectancy, effort expectancy and social influence have been classified as facilitators whereas security concerns, privacy concerns and legal concerns have been classified as barriers. Furthermore, this chapter has some valuable theoretical and practical implications.

In terms of theory, the chapter produces a framework for explaining users' online banking adoption, besides improving the theoretical basis of online banking research, also to develop the application of technology adoption theories to this new field. Further, we identified new facilitators and barriers to users' adoption of online banking, including privacy, security and legal concerns, which can be used to guide future research in this area.

In practice, the chapter provides various practical implications for online banking users, service providers, and designers and developers of online banking systems. Users are the target beneficiaries of online banking. Therefore, it's very important to involve them, from the beginning, in the technology design and development and understand their security and privacy perceptions about the technology in creating a more secure effective design and to promote its diffusion. Specifically, the knowledge gained by this chapter can potentially lead to an online banking system that is acceptable by users by matching to their security and privacy needs and preferences. In addition, the chapter provides a framework that decision and policy makers in banking institutions can use as part of a feasibility study before formally adopting and using online banking systems. Finally, the chapter suggest various design practices for online banking designers and developers towards a more acceptable and secure technology design and development to accelerate the adoption of the online banking systems. In particular, the chapter proposes the low level dimensions of security, privacy and legal concerns that show how users perceive these concerns in the online banking systems.

REFERENCES

Aarts, J., & Gorman, P. (2007). IT in health care: Sociotechnical approaches to err is system. *International Journal of Medical Informatics*, *76*(1), s1–s3. doi:10.1016/S1386-5056(07)00078-0 PMID:17466251

Ajzen, I. (1991). The theory of planned behavior. *Organizational Behavior and Human Decision Processes*, *50*(2), 179–211. doi:10.1016/0749-5978(91)90020-T

Al Eroud, A., & Karabatis, G. (2012). Discovering Unknown Cyber Attacks using Contextual Misuse and Anomaly Detection. The ASE science Journal.

Aladwani, A. M. (2001). Online banking: A field study of drivers, development challenges, and expectations. *International Journal of Information Management*, *21*(3), 213–225. doi:10.1016/S0268-4012(01)00011-1

Alawadhi, S., & Morris, A. (2008). The use of the utaut model in the adoption of e-government services in Kuwait.*Proceedings of the 41st Hawaii International Conference on System Sciences* (p. 219). doi:10.1109/HICSS.2008.452

AlEroud, A., & Karabatis, G. (2012). Contextual Anomaly Detection Approach to Discover Zero-Day Attacks. Proceedings of the ASE/IEEE international conference on cyber security, Washington DC. doi:10.1109/CyberSecurity.2012.12

Alshehri, M., Drew, S., Alhussain, T., & Alghamdi, R. (2012, December 3-5). The effects of website quality on adoption of E-government service: An empirical study applying UTAUT model using SEM. *Proceedings of the23rd Australasian Conference on Information Systems.*

Alzahrani M, & Goodwin R. (2012) Towards a UTAUT-based Model for the study of E-government citizen acceptance in Saudi Arabia. *International Journal of Economics and Management Sciences*. 64, 109-115.

Berg, M., Aarts, J., & Van Der Lei, J. (2013). ICT in health care: Sociotechnical approaches. *Methods of Information in Medicine*, *4*(42), 297–301. PMID:14534625

Booth, K., Whicker, L., Wyman, T., Pugh, D., & Thompson, S. (2009). *Medical assisting: administrative and clinical procedures* (3rd ed.). McGraw-Hill.

Compeau, D. R., & Higgins, C. A. (1995). Computer self-efficacy: Development of a measure and initial test. *Management Information Systems Quarterly*, *19*(2), 189–211. doi:10.2307/249688

Davis, F. D. (1989). Perceived usefulness, perceived ease of use, and user acceptance of information technology. *Management Information Systems Quarterly*, *13*(3), 319–339. doi:10.2307/249008

Davis, F. D., Bagozzi, R. P., & Warshaw, P. R. (1992). Extrinsic and intrinsic motivation to use computers in the workplace. *Journal of Applied Social Psychology*, *22*(14), 1111–1132. doi:10.1111/j.1559-1816.1992.tb00945.x

Dickens, B., & Cook, R. (2006). Legal and ethical issues in telemedicine and robotics. *International Journal of Gynaecology and Obstetrics: the Official Organ of the International Federation of Gynaecology and Obstetrics*, *94*(1), 73–78. doi:10.1016/j.ijgo.2006.04.023 PMID:16777109

Fishbein, M., & Ajzen, L. (1975). *Belief, attitude, intention and behavior: An introduction to theory and research.* Reading, MA: Addison-Wesley.

Hossain, M., & Prybutok, V. (2008). Consumer acceptance of RFID technology: An exploratory Study. *IEEE Transactions on Engineering Management*, *55*(2), 316–328. doi:10.1109/TEM.2008.919728

Internet World Stats. (2006). Internet Usage Statistics, 2006. Retrieved from http://www.Internetworldstats.com/stats.htm

Jahangir, N., & Begum, N. (2008). The role of perceived usefulness, perceived ease of use, security and privacy, and customer attitude to engender customer adaptation in the context of electronic banking. *African Journal of Business Management*, *2*(1), 32–40.

Kijsanayotin, B., Pannarunothai, S., & Speedie, S. (2009). Factors influencing health information technology adoption in Thailand's community health centers: Applying the UTAUT model. *International Journal of Medical Informatics*, *78*(6), 404–416. doi:10.1016/j.ijmedinf.2008.12.005 PMID:19196548

Lin, F., Lu, L., & Hsieh, P. (2011). Understanding the adoption of wireless sensor network service in households.*Proceedings of 2011 International Joint Conference on Service Sciences* (pp. 218–222). doi:10.1109/IJCSS.2011.50

Lo, B., & Yang, G. (2005) key technical challenges and current implementations of body sensor network. *Proceedings of theInternational Workshop on Wearable and Implantable Body Sensor Networks.*

Moore, G. C., & Benbasat, I. (1991). Development of an instrument to measure the perceptions of adopting an information technology innovation. *Information Systems Research*, *2*(3), 192–222. doi:10.1287/isre.2.3.192

Rezaie, H., & Abadi, D. (2012). Investigate the customers' behavioral intention to use mobile banking based on TPB, TAM and Perceived Risk (A case study in Meli bank). *International Journal of Academic Research in Business and Social Sciences*, *2*(10), 312–322.

Sanayei, A., & Bahmani, E. (2012). Integrating TAM and TPB with perceived risk to measure customers acceptance of internet banking. *International Journal of Information Science and Management*, *2012*, 25–37.

Taylor, S., & Todd, P. A. (1995). Assessing IT usage: The role of prior experience. *Management Information Systems Quarterly*, *19*(2), 561–570. doi:10.2307/249633

Thompson, R. L., Higgins, C. A., & Howell, J. M. (1991). Personal computing: Toward a conceptual model of utilization. *Management Information Systems Quarterly*, *15*(1), 124–143. doi:10.2307/249443

Venkatesh, V., Morris, M. G., Davis, G. B., & Davis, F. D. (2003). User acceptance of information technology: Toward a unified view. *Management Information Systems Quarterly*, *27*(3), 425–478.

Wu, J., Shen, W., Lin, L., Greenes, R., & Bates, D. (2008). Testing the technology acceptance model for evaluating healthcare professionals' intention to use an adverse event reporting system. *International Journal for Quality in Health Care*, *20*(2), 123–129. doi:10.1093/intqhc/mzm074 PMID:18222963

Xu, H., & Gupta, S. (2009). The effects of privacy concerns and personal innovativeness on potential and experienced customers' adoption of location-based services. *Electronic Markets*, *19*(2), 137–149. doi:10.1007/s12525-009-0012-4

Yiu, C. S., Grant, K., & Edgar, D. (2007). Factors affecting the adoption of Internet banking in Hong Kong – Implications for the banking sector. *International Journal of Information Management*, *27*(5), 336–351. doi:10.1016/j.ijinfomgt.2007.03.002

ZDNet. (2005). Security worries holding back online banking. Retrieved from http://news.zdnet.co.uk/Internet/security/0,39020375,39216740,00.htm

Zhou, T. (2012). Examining location based services usage from the perspectives of unified theory of acceptance and use of technology and privacy risk. *Journal of Electronic Commerce Research*, *13*(2), 135–144.

Chapter 8
Analysis of Data Validation Techniques for Online Banking Services

Shadi A Aljawarneh
Jordan University of Science and Technology, Jordan

ABSTRACT

The insufficient preparation for the information and communication technologies revolution led to few offering online transaction platforms, information security features, and credit facilities. One of the security concerns is a lack of data validation. Data that is not validated or not properly validated is the main issue for serious security vulnerabilities affecting online banking applications. In this chapter, the influences of security issues on world banks will be discussed. A number of data validation methods will be also reviewed to date to provide a systematic summary to banking environment. Based on the advantages and disadvantages of each method, the IT developer will decide which is best suited to develop the systematic online banking application. From this analysis, a global view of the current and future tendencies of data validation will be obtained and therefore provision of possible recommendations for solving the security and privacy issues for the online banking services.

DOI: 10.4018/978-1-5225-0864-9.ch008

BACKGROUND

The rate of successful act of bypassing protection mechanisms and gaining access to computer system is sharply increased. Good examples can be found in Saudi Arabia, the United Arab Emirates, Lebanon, and Jordan. Above 20% of banks operating in the North Africa and Western Aisa, offer online services, from simple banking facilities to payment schemes (Ben-Jadeed & Molina, 2004). For instance, Lebanese banks now offer online services by moving some documentary credit procedures online to facilitate and guarantee e-commerce procedures (Aljawarneh et al, 2014).

The recent online banking facilities have not yet found their way to Libyan banking. Amongst the Arab nations, Libya has the finest reputation in the bankers but the worst banking services (Libyan investment, 2007). Essential electronic banking services, such as ATMs and mobile banking are limited unless in some commercial banks. Most Libyan banks are still using manual banking techniques to carry out their services. It seems that there is no good networking among Libyan banks and their branches due to poor IT infrastructure. Consequently, security measures are not up to the standard required in the Libyan banking industry. There is a great concern about security issues that regulate e-banking activities in Libya, such as potential fraudulent activities, errors in conducting customer transactions, in addition to the lack of security measures such as e-laws and legislation (Abukhzam & Lee, 2010).

The United Arab Emirates Central Bank has adopted Secure Sockets Layer (SSL), Public Key Infrastructure (PKI), and smart card technology to activate online banking, and payment gateways that are being implemented by some of the large national players (Dutta & Coury, 2003).

However, because of information security concerns, most Small and Medium Enterprises (SMEs) in the Arab world ((refers to Arabic-speaking states and populations in North Africa and Western Asia) depend on conventional interactions and have not moved their operations online. Almost all of Arab banks websites are still informational without any online interaction among their customers. With little training and poor levels of awareness, SMEs do not take benefits from online accessing to new markets and inter-Arab trade potential (Dutta & Coury, 2003), for example as in Egypt and the western region of North Africa including five countries: Morocco, Algeria, Tunisia, Libya, and Mauritania. As a result, the insufficient preparation for the Information and communication technologies (ICT) revolution led to few offer transaction platforms, security features, and credit facilities for SMEs to motivate access technology.

For example, generally speaking, the major drawback of e-commerce in Libya is the lack of security, which scared people to use the Internet. Web applications need to be secured and people should be educated regarding security issues (Hamed, 2010). The several banks (such as Citibank, HSBC, Lloyds TSB, National Bank of Abu Dhabi and Emirates NBD) across the United Arab Emirates are currently fighting to restore lost confidence in its online banking system after criminals used counterfeit credit cards to withdraw large quantities of funds from cash machines. Losses are expected to be several million dollars. This estimation of increase is expected to continue (Internet Security.ca, 2011).

In this chapter, we will focus on the main security issue which is the lack of data validation. Data that is not validated or not properly validated is the main issue for serious security vulnerabilities affecting online banking applications.

Therefore, the banks that have a web presence are increasingly worried for their reputations if the web system is subverted. This is because current security tools may not prevent the web system vulnerabilities. For example, with 4,396 new vulnerabilities disclosed in first half of 2010, total vulnerability count increased nearly 36% over the first half of previous year. This trend of increase is expected to continue (IBM, 2010).

Because inadequate data validation is a challenge, the Open Web Application Security Project (OWASP) mentioned the top ten security vulnerabilities effecting web. Several security issues in applications are caused by inadequate input validation including:

- Parameter manipulation, and therefore subversion of logic or security controls.
- Code injection, such as Cross Site Scripting, Structured Query Language (SQL) (MySQL, n. d.) Injection and Operating System command injection attacks (OWASP – 4 and 6).
- Legacy C/C++ vulnerability classes, such as buffer overflows, integer wrap and format string vulnerabilities.

It should be noted that the ad-hoc security products such as firewall and Anti-virus are not sufficient to solve this problem because fundamentally they are designed to provide protection at the host and network levels. Therefore, they are useless if any malicious script or listener is already installed on a server behind them because they do not prevent the installation of scripts at the application level (Aljawarneh, Alkhateeb, & Al Maghayreh, 2010).

Previously, the security developers claim that an adversary could only be on the outside. Currently, with mobile environment, an attack might originate from the inside as well, where a firewall can offer no protection (Aljawarneh, 2011a).

As a consequence of these improvements, several solutions have appeared to provide data validation in online banking applications. The present chapter presents a survey of the different technologies that have appeared over the recent years to provide data validation. The survey describes them and analyzes them from the security point of view. Thus, this survey will allow us to know what the most mature tools and systems are and develop non-repudiation-based applications or services to the commerce. Furthermore, the survey allows the developer of security solutions to decide, based on the advantages and disadvantages of each solution, which is best suited to develop his/her online banking application. This analysis is summed up at the end of the chapter where we compare the different solutions.

MAIN FOCUS OF THIS STUDY

In an application security, data validation is the process of ensuring that a web application operates on clean, correct and meaningful data (Mocean, 2007). It uses validation rules that check for correctness, meaningfulness, and security of data that are input to the online banking system. The rules may be deployed through the automated validation facilities of a data dictionary, or by the inclusion of explicit program validation logic.There are two key approaches of data validation:

1. Data should be checked in the data model, where the validation rules have maximum scope for interpreting the context; and
2. Escaping of harmful meta-characters should be performed just before the data is processed, typically in the data access components.

Criminals might be able to manipulate the SQL query and modify with data, retrieve banking database information or control of the banking database server by embedding characters that have special meaning or special commands to database. Thus, the key issue in this chapter is that a user input might be invalidated on a bank server that processes SQL queries. Many web developers rely on client-side validation to protect against escape characters being entered by customers (Lam et al., 2008), (Brabrand et al., 2002). For example, most banks adopt the client-side data validation for protection purposes.

Another penetration method is a script manipulation. A criminal removes the client-side data validation modules from a web browser to submit illegal data to a bank's web server. A web server accepts the request and then the data is saved in a backend database (Offutt et al., 2004).

In attempt to solve the poor data validation in the online banking applications, important step should be taken to ensure that the online banking application processes data in a secure manner. A number of approaches can be adopted when implementing data validation mechanisms within an application each of which has its own advantages and disadvantages.

Al-Nakib (Al-Nakib, 2007) clarified that the Arab Bank (AB) faces the largest risk which is the automation validation. Therefore, officers need enhanced IT solutions and software which are based on their policies, procedures and services to help their customers reach compliance.

Preservation of information is one of the most important and rapidly changing fundamental roles of the ICT banks (Al-Nakib, 2007). Therefore, ICT banks are required to support the research in information security area because the regulations of cyber-crimes are not properly activated. Indeed, three key challenges should be taken into account in order to preserve customer information (B. Al-Nakib, 2007):

1. Ensuring the quality, and integrity of digital information;
2. Bridging and connecting business worlds, disciplines, and paradigms for knowing and understanding; and
3. Archiving digital data in virtual world.

Another challenge is the clients of ICT banks, which are required by law to have policies, practices, and procedures in place to protect the privacy of the data they store, process, and transmit.

One of the applications in the client's portfolio transmits private data across the Internet. An organization engages to help them meet appropriate security and validation measures ensuring that only authorized users could access private data. Therefore, the assessment primarily consists of the following activities:

- Checking the ICT application environment for any sever-level vulnerabilities.
- Ensuring roles and privilege levels were respected.
- Evaluating use of cryptography for data at rest and in transit.
- Validating user input for malicious data that could result in loss of integrity or confidentiality of data.

DISCUSSION AND SOLUTIONS

In this section, we present the recent approaches that attempt to address the lack of data validation.

The current approaches include application-level gateway approach, WAVES approach, Pixy, Saner and Semantic Data Validation (SDV). Therefore, the administrators of ICT banks can adopt and use one of those approaches to minimize the security issues that facing the customers and banks. Note that we deeply describe the technical operations and components for each approach in order to ease the understanding for each approach process.

Scott and Sharp (Scott & Sharp, 2003) proposed a gateway model which is an application-level firewall on a server for checking invalid user inputs and detecting malicious script (e.g. SQL injection attack and cross-site scripting attack). They developed a security policy description language (SPDL) based on XML to describe a set of validation constraints and transformation rules. This language is translated into code by a policy compiler, which sent to a security gateway on a server. The gateway analyzes the request and augments it with a Message Authentication Code (MAC)[1].

However, the policies of validation constraints and transformation rules are enforced manually and need an engineer to write and check them by hand. Further limitations of this approach are that it is difficult to define all the policies and rules of a legacy web application for every single data entry point, URL entry, and cookie unit because these can consist of complex structures of multiple programming languages and imported binary components with little or no documentation. Therefore, it is not practical for a web administrator or publisher to be familiar with all of data entry points for existing web applications.

Offutt et al. (Offutt, Wu, Du et al., 2004) used behavior monitoring to detect malicious content before it reaches users. They have developed WAVES (Web application security assessment system) that performs behavior stimulation to induce malicious behavior in the monitored components.

Offutt et al. (Offutt, Wu, Du et al., 2004) were the first who attempt to address data validation issue in the context of PHP (n. d.) applications. They used a lattice-based analysis algorithm derived from type systems and type-state systems. The type of analysis in this algorithm is static analysis. WAVES approach is targeted for mitigating threats to web application at the server-side.

Jovanovic et al. (Jovanovic et al, 2006) developed Pixy, which is the first open source tool for statically detecting XSS vulnerabilities in PHP code by means of data follow analysis, which is based on a static analysis technique. They adopted PHP as target language since it is commonly used for developing web applications (Andreessen, 2005) and a substantial number of security advisories refer to PHP programs. Although the Pixy is aimed at the detection of XSS vulnerabilities, it can be equally applied to other taint-style vulnerabilities such as SQL injection or command injection.

However, Pixy does not support object-oriented features of PHP. Each use of object member variables and methods is treated in an optimistic way, meaning that malicious data can never arise from such constructs. Further limitation is that they have focused on the problem of identifying vulnerabilities, in which external input is used without any prior sanitization (e.g. a particular type of input validation). It should be noted that a sanitization is performed to remove possibly malicious elements from the user input. These vulnerability detectors are typically based on data flow analysis that tracks the flow of information from the inputs of application's (called sources) to points in the program that represent security-relevant operations (called sinks). However, the assumption of this approach is that if a sanitization operation is performed on all paths from sources to sinks, then the application is secure.

Balzarotti et al (Balzarotti, 2008) presented approach to the analysis of the sanitization. They combine static and dynamic analysis techniques to identify faulty sanitization procedures that can be bypassed by the criminal. This approach is implemented as a tool, called Saner, and applied on a number of real-world web applications.

The static analysis technique has been described, in Balzarotti et al's approach, to characterize the sanitization process by modeling the way in which a web application processes input values. This permits us to define the cases where the sanitization is incorrect or incomplete. Furthermore, they introduced a dynamic analysis technique that is able to reconstruct the code that is responsible for the sanitization of application inputs, and then execute this code on malicious inputs to identify faulty sanitization procedures.

Aljawarneh, Alkhateeb, & Al Maghayreh (2010) developed a Semantic Data Validation (SDV) service to stop the security vulnerabilities at the application level and to secure the web system such as online banking system even when the input validation modules are bypassed. The SDV architecture consists of the following components: RDFa annotation for elements of web pages, interceptor, RDF extractor, RDF parser, and data validator.

The developed SDV service has a number of advantages over other existing solutions such as (i) the SDV is the first solution that provides a semantic component to process the data validation, (ii) the solution has intercepting interface to manage all HTTP requests and responses and (iii) it does not require modifications to existing web application (banking) architectures.

The most important comparison criterion between different input validation solutions is whether the web application vulnerabilities can be prevented without modification on the structure of the existing web applications. In order to satisfy this criterion, we have to employ other criteria such as:

1. The solution should be based on dynamic analysis for every HTTP request and HTTP response from/to a web server and a client.
2. The solution should take into account the client and server validation routines for every (X)HTML form hosted on a web server.
3. The solution should protect the dynamic web pages that are generated on the fly.
4. The solution should be based on semantic technologies to meet the existing web application requirements rather than syntax technologies.
5. The solution should ensure the survivability of a web system in case of any illegal operation on a backend database using provision of a recovery.

Generally, in this section we have compared the above mentioned data validation solutions from several points of view: based on type of data, technologies implied, and features supported. As shown in Table 1, we have classified the current solutions in relations to the type of data that can be solved. All current solution supports static data validation either on the client side or server side.

As shown in Table 1, the SDV is the only solution which is able to address the validation of dynamic data. The dynamic data that generated on the fly is a real-time issue because the generation of dynamic data depends on user interaction. This means that different user information leads to different generated web content. Note that it is very difficult to automatically and even manually analyze the requested page of dynamic data before processing on a web server. The dynamic data of

Table 1. Type of data-based comparison

Solutions	Type of Data			
	Static User Data	Dynamic Data	Cookies	Session Values
Client-side validation	X			
Server-side validation	X			
Double checking validation	X			
Application-Level Gateway	X		X	X
WAVES	X			
Pixy	X			
Saner	X			
SDV	X	X		

server programming languages needs to be processed on a web server before returning the response to a web browser. The SDV uses the RDFa annotation for analyzing the elements of the web page and this makes the data validation possible for dynamic data.

As illustration in Table 2, the solutions are classified according to the features. Saner and SDV only are the solutions that use the static analysis and dynamic analysis. Using client-side data validation could cause code transparency. This means that the code can be viewed on a web browser, and hence, this could be vulnerable to security risks on web system.

From point of view, we recommend that these validation modules should be operated on the client and server because if the client validation modules are subverted, the server validation modules can still work. Some developers suppose that if user information has been properly validated, the static data will be secure. However, malicious code might be installed on a server either inside or outside the organization. Furthermore, as seen above, the data validation modules can be bypassed.

Another point is that even if the client validation modules are enhanced by an encryption approach, the data can be bypassed, because moving the encryption to a client-side is vulnerable to security risks. The encryption can be exposed through applying penetration strategies such as reverse engineering techniques.

After this analysis, the ICT banks should acquire the knowledge about the data validation issues and the suggested approaches, strengths, weaknesses and limitations. In addition, the suggested recommendations could raise the integrity and security of the online banking.

Table 2. Features-based comparison

Solutions	**Feature**				
	Online	**Free Browsers**	**Static Analysis**	**Dynamic analysis**	**Code Transparency**
Client-side validation	X	X			X
Server-side validation	X	X			
Double checking validation	X	X			X
Application-Level Gateway	X	X			X
WAVES			X		n/a
Pixy			X		n/a
Saner			X	X	n/a
SDV	X	X		X	

CONCLUSION AND FUTURE WORK

In this chapter, the effects of security issues on ICT banks were discussed. We have attempted to introduce a systematic summary to banking environment in the world. As mentioned in the analysis, a significant challenge that facing the ICT banks, including the customers of ICT banks require by law to have policies, practices, and procedures in place to protect the privacy of the data it stores, processes, and transmits. It should be noted that the law of cyber crimes is not activated in the world and this might give bad impression for using the online banking services, and customers will be worried about their data and money.

Therefore, we have presented the recent approaches that can minimize or prevent the security vulnerabilities in the ICT banks that come from the lack of data validation. Based on the advantages and disadvantages of each approach, IT developer then could decide which is best suited to develop a systematic online banking application.

To overcome such challenges, the collaboration among the countries in this area, is needed. This can take place by holding a number of forums, conferences and workshops. For example, the Jordan ICT Forum2 with different years (2003, 2004, 2006, etc.) discussed the information security track and other related issues, network, and established business ties and contacts. During these forums, Jordan presented its plans to develop its ICT industry to the audience, and solicited feedback and input. The Jordan ICT Forum 2006 presented the future of information and communication technologies and their impact on business and society, brought together global analysts and decision makers to uncover the latest in technologies. Moreover, the forum discussed the impact of the most important ICT trends and ideas affecting enterprises. The outcome of the forum had a number of recommendations need to be implemented to convert Jordanian ICT companies from “users of existing technologies” into creators of “new technologies”, especially in information security area (Jordan ICT Forum 2006, 2006).

REFERENCES

Abukhzam, M., & Lee, A. (2010). Factors Affecting Bank Staff Attitude Towards E-Banking Adoption In Libya. *EJISDC*, *42*(2), 1–15.

Al-Nakib, B. (2007). Challenges Facing Compliance Occupation. Retrieved from http://74.125.77.132/search?q=cache:t63v4nSO55cJ:www.uabonline.org/event/event-presentationdownload.php%3Fid%3D162%26eventid%3D58+the+CHALLENGES+FACING+THE+ORGANIZATION+by+using+data+or+input+validation&cd=8&hl=en&ct=clnk&gl=jo

Alhaj, A., Aljawarneh, S., Masadeh, S., & Abu-Taieh, E. (2013). A Secure Data Transmission Mechanism for Cloud Outsourced Data. *International Journal of Cloud Applications and Computing*, *3*(1), 34–43. doi:10.4018/ijcac.2013010104

Aljawarneh, S. (2011a). Cloud security engineering: Avoiding security threats the right way. *International Journal of Cloud Applications and Computing*, *1*(2), 64–70. doi:10.4018/ijcac.2011040105

Aljawarneh, S. (2011b). A web engineering security methodology for e-learning systems. *Network Security*, *2011*(3), 12–15. doi:10.1016/S1353-4858(11)70026-5

Aljawarneh, S., Al-Rousan, T., Maatuk, A. M., & Akour, M. (2014). Usage of data validation techniques in online banking: A perspective and case study. *Security Journal*, *27*(1), 27–35. doi:10.1057/sj.2012.10

Aljawarneh, S., Alkhateeb, F., & Al Maghayreh, E. (2010). A semantic data validation service for web applications. *Journal of Theoretical and Applied Electronic Commerce Research*, *5*(1), 39–55. doi:10.4067/S0718-18762010000100005

Aljawarneh, S., Dababneh, M., Hosseny, H., & Alwadi, E. (2010). A web client authentication system using smart card for e-systems: initial testing and evaluation. *Proceedings of the Fourth International Conference on Digital Society ICDS'10* (pp. 192–197). IEEE. doi:10.1109/ICDS.2010.40

Aljawarneh, S., Laing, C., & Vickers, P. (2008). Design and experimental evaluation of Web Content Verification and Recovery (WCVR) system: A survivable security system.*Proceedings of ACSF* (pp. 1–7).

Aljawarneh, S., Laing, C., & Vickers, P. (n. d.). Security policy framework and algorithms for web server content protection. *Proceedings of the ACSF'07.*

Aljawarneh, S. A., Moftah, R. A., & Maatuk, A. M. (2016). Investigations of automatic methods for detecting the polymorphic worms signatures. *Future Generation Computer Systems*, *60*, 67–77. doi:10.1016/j.future.2016.01.020

Alkatheeb, M., Wakileh, M., & Agha, O. (2006). ICT for Banking. *Proceedings of the Jordan ICT Forum 2006*. Retrieved from http://www.tagorg-theinstitution.com/Files/2006/Events/Dec_6_2006_The_Fourth_Jordan_ICT_Forum_exhibition.pdf

Andreessen, S. S. (2005). PHP succeeding where Java is not. Retrieved from http://www.zdnet.com.au

Balzarotti, D., Cova, M., Felmetsger, V., Jovanovic, N., Kirda, E., Kruegel, C., & Vigna, G. (2008). Saner: Composing Static and Dynamic Analysis to Validate Sanitization in Web Applications.*Proceedings of the 2008 IEEE Symposium on Security and Privacy* (pp. 387-401). DC, USA. doi:10.1109/SP.2008.22

Ben-Jadeed, M. & Molina, A. (2004). The Emergence and Evolution of e-Banking in Saudi Arabia: The Case of Samba Financial Group. *Chapter invited to conference of Frontier of E-Business Research.*

Brabrand, C., Moller, A., & Schwartzbach, M. (2002). The bigwig project. *ACM Transactions on Internet Technology*, *2*(2), 79–114. doi:10.1145/514183.514184

Dutta, S., & Coury, M. E. (2003). ICT challenges for the Arab world. The Global Information In *Technology Report 2002-2003* (pp. 116-131). Retrieved from http://old.developmentgateway.org/download/170136/Chapter_08_ICT_Challenges_for_the_Arab_World.pdf

Hamed, A. (2010). E-commerce and Economic Development in Libya [PhD Thesis]. University of Wales.

IBM. (2010). Mid-Year Trend and Risk Report. Retrieved from http://www-304.ibm.com/businesscenter/cpe/download0/207480/2010_XForce_Midyear_Report.pdf

Internet Security.ca. (n. d.). United Arab Emirates hit with massive bank fraud. Retrieved from http://www.internet-security.ca/internet-security-news-020/united-arab-emirates-hit-with-massive-bank-fraud.html

Jovanovic, N., Kruegel, C., & Kirda, E. (2006). Pixy: A Static Analysis Tool for Detecting Web Application Vulnerabilities (Short Chapter*).Proceedings of the 2006 IEEE Symposium on Security and Privacy*Washington, DC, USA (pp. 258-263).

Lam, M. S., Martin, M., Livshits, B., & Whaley, J. (2008). Securing web applications with static and dynamic information flow tracking.*Proceedings of the 2008 ACM SIGPLAN Symposium on Partial Evaluation and Semantics-Based Program Manipulation* (pp. 3-12). New York, NY. doi:10.1145/1328408.1328410

Libya Investment. (2007). General News. Retrieved from http://www.libyaninvestment.com/libya_news.php

Mocean. (2007). Internet Data Validation. *Journal of Economy Informatics*, 2007, 96-99. Retrieved from http://revistaie.ase.ro/content/EN7/Mocean.pdf

MySQL. (n. d.) Retrieved from: www.mysql.com

Offutt, J., Wu, Y., Du, X., & Huang, H. (2004). Bypass testing of web applications. *Proceedings the 5th International Symposium on Software Reliability Engineering,* Los Alamitos, CA (pp. 187–197).

Payment Card Industry (PCI). (n. d.). Data Security Standard, Security Audit Procedures. Retrieved from https://www.pcisecuritystandards.org/pdfs/pci_audit_procedures_v1-1.pdf

PHP. (n. d.) Retrieved from: http://www.php.net

Scott, D., & Sharp, R. (2003). Specifying and enforcing application-level web security policies. *IEEE Transactions on Knowledge and Data Engineering*, *15*(4), 771–783. doi:10.1109/TKDE.2003.1208998

ENDNOTES

1. Is used to protect the data integrity. For example, The MAC is used to secure session information in a cookie at the client-side. There are many ways to compute a MAC such as one-way hash algorithms (MD5, SHA-1) to create a unique fingerprint for data within the cookie.
2. Is a bi-annual international ICT industry event held in Jordan under the patronage of His Majesty King Abdullah II, and is the platform to showcase Jordan's efforts and achievements to position the country as a major player in the Information revolution.

Chapter 9
Anytime Anywhere Any-Amount Anybody to Anybody Real-Time Payment (5A-RTP):
With High Level Banking Security

Ranjit Biswas
Jamia Hamdard University, India

ABSTRACT

This chapter introduces about a Proposal to any bank of any country for fast but secured transfer of money anytime anywhere any-amount by anybody to anybody on the spot with confirmation from the payee on the spot. The work here is on a new method of real time payment system, which is highly secured and fast, and 100% technology-based without any paper format or paper work of the bank. This breaking scheme is entitled as "5A-RTP scheme" where '5A' stands for Anytime Anywhere Any-amount Anybody to Anybody and 'RTP' stands for Real-Time Payment. There is no paper-work at all. It is completely secured, realization of payment (debit + credit) happens immediately very fast, without any man-hour or manpower of the bank. It is claimed that 5A-RTP scheme, if incorporated in all the banks in any country, will give the country a huge momentum of customers' satisfaction, huge momentum in country's growth and economic progress. The revolutionary breakthrough in 5A-RTP scheme is that it dominates each of the existing banking instruments and facilities like Cheque, Pay-order, Draft, ATM machine, Credit Card, Debit Card, Internet Banking, Mobile Banking, Traveller's Cheque, etc. The 5A-RTP scheme may even slowly cause a natural death of the existing Cheque and Draft facilities from the country because of its huge application potential, in particular in vast countries like China, India, Brazil, USA, UK, etc.

DOI: 10.4018/978-1-5225-0864-9.ch009

INTRODUCTION

The present banking world of big data are expanding very fast in 4Vs: Volume, Varity, Velocity and Veracity, and also in many more directions (Biswas, 2013; Biswas 2015). It is because of the reason that presently most of the customers enjoy banking facilities sitting at home or at their working places or at their business station at real instant of time 24 hours a day, 7 days in a week, day and night whenever the customers need to do, without physically visiting the concerned bank or branch office.

How to deal with explosive momentum of big data of customers, how to process big data in an efficient way within limited resources but at real instant of demand, with all possible securities, etc. are of major concern to the world banks now-a-days. Besides that, banking law and practices are different in different countries (Mishra, 2010; Rajesh, 2010).

Instead of taking instance of any particular country, we consider a purely hypothetical country named by "World Country" (WC). Throughout in this chapter we will name "World Country" which is a country in the world having a good coverage of banking network. The method can be well customized with local constraints by any bank in any country in this world for implementation in its worldwide branches. For the sake of presentation of our method, let us consider a hypothetical organizational structures as shown in Figure 1.

There are many banks in the country WC under the 'Government of WC'. The central monitoring bank for the Govt. of WC (Ministry of Finance of WC) is Reserve Bank of World Country (RBWC). Thus Reserve Bank of World Country (RBWC)

Figure 1. Organizational structure of government monitoring the banks

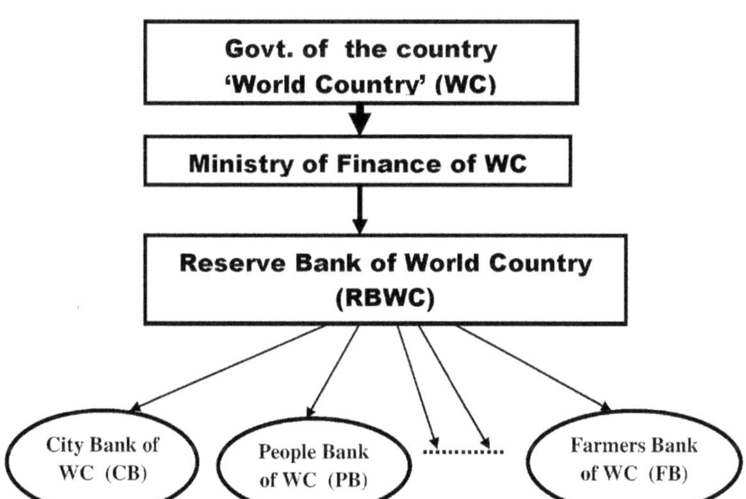

is the WC's central bank, the leader of all the banks in WC. It is not just officially, but by its huge statistics, by the amount of depth inside the heart of every WC customer it has penetrated in, by its strong philosophy behind its varieties of services it extends to all the customers of the banks in WC; by its mission, vision, quantity & quality of services, commitment, trust etc. to list a few only out of many. All the banks in WC are directly controlled by RBWC. Out of so many banks in WC like: "City Bank of WC" (CB), "People Bank of WC" (PB), … "Farmers Bank of WC" (FB) etc., the "People Bank of WC" is very popular to the customers and people of WC by the short-name "PB". In fact many of the customers in WC may not recognize what is the bank "People Bank of WC", but will immediately recognize what is PB, because of its excellent service and wide spread branches all over WC (Figure 2) and also all over the world in the name of PB.

In this research article the author submits a proposal for a new type of banking service called by "5A-RTP Scheme" for the customers, which can make a revolutionary change by a huge momentum in banking industry and customers satisfactions in WC, if adopted by Reserve Bank of World Country (RBWC). In "5A-RTP scheme", the part-phrase '5A' stands for Anytime Anywhere Any-amount Anybody to Anybody and 'RTP' stands for Real-Time Payment. There is no paper-work at all in this breaking scheme entitled "5A-RTP scheme. With no loss of generality, we will use transaction of US dollar in our presentation in this chapter (but in reality it is supposed to be the actual currency of the country concerned, here it is the country WC).

Figure 2. Branches of people bank (PB)

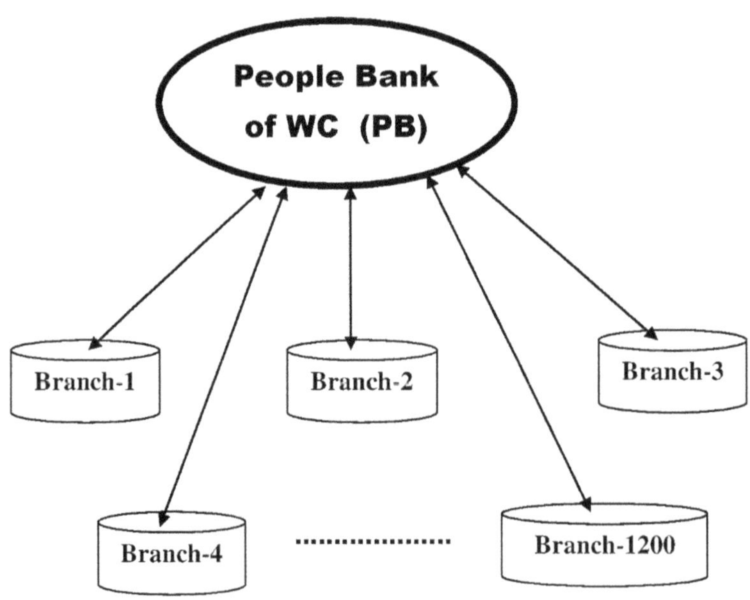

MANY "UNSOLVED PROBLEMS" OF PRESENT DAYS CUSTOMERS IN WC TO MAKE REAL TIME PAYMENT

Many "unsolved problems" of present day customers in wc is making real time payment. The Reserve Bank of World Country (RBWC) does not have real time solutions.

We show by a Real Life Example of Major Failures of Cheque facility, DD (Demand Draft), Pay Order, ATM withdrawal, Internet Banking, Mobile Banking, Credit Card, Debit Card, Travelers Cheque, etc. to satisfy the customers of PB bank in WC (with respect to the various domains of the customers' demand arising at ground level). There is no RBWC instrument which can support all the five distinct A of '5A' with a "real time solution" for instant, on the spot, guaranteed and secured payment.

Example:

The 'WC Central University' (hypothetical name) is a renowned university in the country WC. Prof. B. Sen of 'WC Central University' is now for few days travel for a work in a small village town 'WC-village' of his country WC, which is at about 1000 kilometer away from his working place 'WC Central University'. It is now 10 P.M. there in 'WC-village'. He wants right now to buy an important medical equipment from a shop there. Prof. Sen understands that the equipment is very costly, the price of it could be in between 6-10 thousand USD.

Prof. Sen does not know 'in ADVANCE':

1. From which shop he will finally buy it now at this town of 'WC-village'? But he will surely buy it making a good choice out of many varieties, and also by trying in few number of good shops in that town, and right now!
2. How much is the actual price of it? (Amount)?
3. Whom to pay? (Payee' Name A/C No.)?
4. How to pay?
5. Payable at? And also a Guaranteed payment system on the spot, as both the payer and payee are mutually unknown to each other!

All the RBWC instruments fail here:

1. The DD (Demand Draft) facility fails here to solve this 'real time payment' of Prof. Sen in WC-village.
2. The Cheque facility fails here. (Narayana, 2010; Swaroop, 2010).
3. The ATM facility fails here.
4. Credit Card or Debit Card fails here.
5. Travelers Cheque fails here.

6. Network connection may not be OK at that time in that small town in WC-village. Even if the network connection be active, Internet banking facility too fails here to help Prof. Sen!

Problem: What Prof. Sen will do now? Reserve Bank of World Country (RBWC) cannot provide Prof. Sen right now 'any bank' within Zero metre of his transaction location (shop). In this case the location is a small town at WC-village.

No support of real time banking facility available to Prof. Sen from Reserve Bank of World Country (RBWC) of such "LOCAL" nature, neither Physically nor Virtually, at this time of 10 P.M. there. Just imagine that, due to Non-Availability of a "real-time solution" of these type of real-life problems faced very frequently by the WC citizens every day, how much amount of Delays (even Failures) are frequently happening in the different kind of Business & Transactions in the country WC, at the ground level of the customers? Real Time Problems, NOT rare, rather of most frequent demand in the everyday life in WC to all the people and customers. A major portion of these huge torque of daily business & transactions in WC face the Non-availability of a 'Guaranteed Payment System' in Reserve Bank of World Country (RBWC) Banking, because of the genuine reasons that for many of such cases:

It is not known in advance to the payer:

1. Whom to pay (Payee Name)?
2. How much to pay (Amount)?
3. Where to pay (business-location)?
4. Payable at?
5. When to pay (Day and Night)?
6. How to pay (which instrument)?

About 'No. of Payments' (X) vs 'No. of Receipts' (Y) Made by Me in Every Month

Consider my personal case for an Example:

Every month I receive once only (which is my salary). But, every month I make a relatively large number of payments (for various purposes, small or big) to other people.

No.(X) of Payments >> No.(Y) of Receipts.

i.e. X >> Y

This inequation is fact for almost all the WC people.

And, for my case Y = 1, X = more than 100.

Few of the Limitations of ATM:

1. Using ATM, one cannot withdraw money on a day beyond a certain limit which may not be a high or reasonable figure to serve the actual need of a customer at real instant of time This is a major drawback.
2. ATM facility may not be available at any location (or nearby), where the customer physically has to make the transaction and payment.
3. Even if ATM facility exists, network may not have connectivity.
4. ATM machine may be out of order temporarily for that day.
5. Availing ATM means 'carrying cash amount' at least for few meters, which is having an element of insecurity.

Why Credit Card Facility Cannot Be Thought as a Parallel Meritorious Service of 5A-RTP Scheme

See, there are many constraints and limitations of Credit Card facility although it has enormous potential. It has a daily upper limit, it needs internet connection, it needs a machine, etc. which is not available at any arbitrary geographical locations in WC for 24 hours.

With the advent of advanced communications techniques, e-commerce as well as online payment transactions are popularly increasing day by day. With rapid growth in the number of credit card transactions or ATM card transactions, the fraudulent activities are also increased in the world. It is known to us that the Credit card fraud can be defined as the illegal use of any system or, criminal activity through the use of physical card or card information without the knowledge of the cardholder. The credit card is basically a small plastic card, which is issued to a customer as a system of payment. The credit card may be physical or may be virtual too. The practice is that in a physical-card, the cardholder presents his card physically to a merchant for making a real time payment. To carry out a fraud in this kind of transaction, an attacker has to steal the credit card. In the second kind of purchase, only some important information about a card such as name, card number, expiration date, secure code etc. are required to make the payment. Such purchases are normally done on the Internet or over the telephone. Most of the time, the genuine cardholder is not aware that someone else has stolen his card information. Credit card fraud is increasing considerably with the development of modern technologies and the global superhighways of advanced communication.

The financial frauds associated with these transactions are also intensifying which results in loss of billions of dollars every year globally. Among the various financial frauds, credit card fraud is the common, worldwide and dangerous one due to its widespread usage. It is mainly because of the convenience it offers to the customers. Also the various types of benefits like cash back, reward points, interest-free credit, discount offers on purchases made at selected stores, etc. tempt the customers to use credit card instead of cash for their purchases. One of the top five fraud detection consultants revealed by Top Credit Card Processors (n. d.) in the month of August 2013 says that 40% of the total financial fraud is related to credit card and the loss of amount due to credit card fraud worldwide is $5.55 billion. The fraud by credit card costs the consumers and the financial companies billions of dollars annually, and fraudsters continuously try to find new rules and tactics to commit illegal actions. Fraud detection systems have become essential for banks and financial institution, to minimize their losses. Fraudster gets access to credit card information in many ways, it is not an impossible task. According to a latest report by CBC News (Larsen, 2013), smart phones are used to skim credit cards data easily with a free Google application.

However, it is also fact that fraud is becoming increasingly more complex and financial institutions are under increasing regulatory and compliance pressures. In order to combat these type of frauds, the banks need more sophisticated techniques of fraud detection. The major problem for e-commerce business in the world today is that almost all the fraudulent transactions appear more and more like legitimate ones.

The individual merits of DD (Demand Draft), Cheque, Pay Order, Credit Card, Debit Card, ATM Machine, Travelers Cheque, Internet Banking, etc. are AVAILABLE in a single scheme "5A-RTP Scheme". The individual DEMERITS of DD (Demand Draft), Credit Card, Debit Card, Cheque, ATM Machine, Travellers Cheque, Internet Banking, etc. are eradicated in a single scheme "5A-RTP Scheme". The major advantage in this scheme is that it is highly secured.

When a bank's system is connected to the internet or intranet, an attack could originate anytime, anywhere, from any outside or inside source. Some essential level of security must be established and incorporated in the transaction system before business on the internet can be reliably conducted. An attack might be in the form of unauthorized access, destruction, corruption or alteration of data or any type of malicious procedure to cause network failure, reboot or hang, hacking, stealing, etc. Although the modern security techniques have made cracking very tedious but it can never be made impossible too. Furthermore, if the system is not configured properly or the updated patches are not installed then hackers may crack the system using security holes from any geographical location. A wide array of information regarding security holes and their fixes is freely available on the web, at just one click. We propose a secured and guaranteed payment system. In Internet banking as with traditional banking methods, security is a primary concern, and any innovative new idea must be developed in compliance with the security aspects. The 5A-RTP Scheme for real time payment provides to the customer a huge satisfaction because of the following exclusive reasons:

1. Immediate payment to the payee on the spot (money will be credited in the account immediately on the spot) which the payee can confirm the payer on the spot (face to face).
2. Genuine payment at real time of business.
3. At any time, day & night, 24x7 hours.
4. At any business location of the country, which even may not be known by the customer in advance; because it is not happening in a seriously planned way.
5. Payment to any person who may not be known by the customer in advance.
6. Without any "Payable at".
7. Without internet connectivity, without ATM machine.
8. Provides a feeling to the customers that bank is at a distance of Zero metre from them. Most LOCAL bank.

If the Reserve Bank of World Country (RBWC) Experts implements '5A-RTP System' across all the banks in WC, then the existing "DD (Demand Draft)-System" and "Cheque-System" both will have their 'Natural Discontinuation' in few years next.

5A-RTP SCHEME: A REVOLUTIONARY SCHEME PROPOSED FOR RBWC FOR ALL THE BANKS IN WC

For the sake of presentation of the 5A-RTP scheme and its Work-Flow Diagram, let us initially consider a payment case using 5A-RTP scheme from PEOPLE BANK OF WC (PB)-Account of Mr. A to the PEOPLE BANK OF WC (PB)-Account of Mr. B. Consider that Mr. A will make a real-time payment of amount USD R (say) by 5A-RTP scheme to Mr. B at some location in WC. The 5A-RTP scheme can be implemented using a small size physical machine (like a mobile phone) called by RTP Machine which is explained below.

RTP Machine

Banking fraud cannot be eliminated without a dedicated, trusted and secured machine for transaction. Common forms of e-banking fraud are not sufficient to protect against the criminal's avenues of attack. There is need of a robust scheme for authentication and authorization of online transactions by using a trusted device or machine to create a trusted computing base, enabling secure communication with the concerned banks. The device forms a trusted path from anybody to anybody for real time transaction of any amount at any time, and anywhere. The proposed device negates all such problems providing a trusted, authenticated path for transactions. Payment in 5A-RTP scheme can only be done using an electronic device called by

"RTP Machine". This machine allows payment of minimum USD 10, not less. It looks like a Mobile phone. Every customer interested to enjoy the 5A-RTP scheme will have his own RTP-machine whose ID No. is the mobile number of the customer (the mobile number which is registered with the PEOPLE BANK OF WC (PB) bank for this customer). The RBWC provides this machine to the bank-customers on demand. There is a "DIS" button pressing which the RTP-machine can be disabled too. This "DIS" button is physically well covered and well-protected in the RTP-machine so that the owner of the RTP-machine cannot by mistake press it, except by his own decision. However, if disabled by a decision, the owner has to contact the bank authority to enable it again. The 5A-RTP scheme is highly secured by its own algorithm. Nevertheless, the "DIS" button facility adds higher amount of security. Even the "DIS" button can be activated (i.e. RTP-machine can be disabled) using its remote-sensor too, from any distance.

Codes Used in 5A-RTP Scheme

The following codes are used for a successful payment using 5A-RTP scheme from PEOPLE BANK OF WC (PB)-Account of Mr. A to the PEOPLE BANK OF WC (PB)-Account of Mr. B.

1. **RP Code:** 4-digited Receive-Payment code (RP Code) of the customer A who wants to make payment to B: AAAA (a fixed unique secret Code for Mr. A provided by PEOPLE BANK to Mr. A for lifetime use).
2. **RP Code:** 4-digited Receive-Payment code (RP Code) of the customer B who will receive payment from A: BBBB (a fixed unique secret Code for Mr. B provided by PEOPLE BANK to Mr. B for lifetime use).
3. **Bank Code:** 3-digited bank code of the bank (a fixed 'Bank Code' provided by RBWC to all its banks across WC, one for each bank, and it is not secret): ZZZ
4. 11-digited code of the Customer's A/C No. in PEOPLE BANK (A/C. No. of A): XXX…XX
5. 11-digited code of the Payee's A/C No. in PEOPLE BANK (A/C. No. of B): YYY…YY
6. 6-digited OTP (One Time Password) which remains valid for a short period of time.

Below find the 8-steps algorithm which are executed for transfer of money in 5A-RTP method with implementations of all the five A of '5A'. Let us name the algorithm by "5A-RTP Algorithm".

"5A-RTP Algorithm": (How to Make Real-Time Payment of USD R by Mr. A to Mr. B using RTP-Machine?)

Step 1: Mr. A unlocks his RTP-machine using his own maintained password.

Step 2: Mr. A then types his own RP code on RP-machine (for every customer RP-code is a secret code and so not displayed on the RTP-machine except four dots) and then Mr. A will press OK button. Message comes to his RTP-machine "Please type Bank Code and Your A/C No."

Step 3: Mr. A then types bank code (of PEOPLE BANK OF WC (PB)) and types his own A/C. No. which is to be debited, and then Mr. A will press OK button.

- Message comes to his RTP-machine "Please type the payment-amount only, without using any other character except integers".

Step 4: Mr. A types the amount and then Mr. A will press OK button. Message comes to his RTP-machine "Please type Bank Code and A/C No. of Payee".

Step 5: Mr. B types bank code (of PEOPLE BANK OF WC (PB)) and types his own A/C. No. which is to be credited, and then Mr. A (or Mr. B) will press OK button. Message comes "Please type RP code of Payee".

Step 6: Mr. B types his RP code and then Mr. A (or Mr. B) will press OK button. Both A and B now receive OTP in their respective registered mobile phones.

- Message also comes to the RTP-machine "Type OTP of Payee first and then OTP of A, and then press OK button". (OTP is secret and so not displayed except dots).

Step 7: Mr. B types his OTP and then Mr. A types his OTP. Then Mr. A will press OK button.

Step 8: Mr. A receives message in his RTP-machine "USD R will be debited from your account. Is it OK?". Mr. A will press OK button to confirm the payment.

Step 9: (this step is not for any action for transfer of money)

- Mr. A receives SMS in his mobile that USD R has been debited from his account XXX…XX and credited in the A/C No. YYY…YY.
- And also Mr. B receives SMS in his mobile that USD R has been credited in his account YYY…YY from the A/C XXX…XX.

"WORK-FLOW Diagram" With a Hypothetical Case-Study On: "How Does Mr. A Make Real-Time Payment of USD 5000 From his Own PB Account to the PB Account of Mr. B using His RTP-Machine?"

Here payer is Mr. A and the payee is Mr. B. Money transfer is to be made on the spot with the support of 5A facility, and Mr. A has to get on the spot confirmation from Mr. B. The event is to be a face to face successful event.

Let us suppose that (all data are hypothetical):

1. Password of the RTP-machine of Mr. A is 1111.
2. RP code of Mr. A is 2222.
3. RP code of Mr. B is 3333.
4. Bank Code for PEOPLE BANK OF WC (PB) is 444.
5. PB A/C No. of Mr. A is 55555555555.
6. PB A/C No. of Mr. B is 66666666666.
7. The OTP received by A is 777777, and the OTP received by B is 888888.

The steps of "5A-RTP Algorithm" executed by the RTP-machine of Mr. A can be viewed in Figure 3.

Figure 3. Work flow diagram

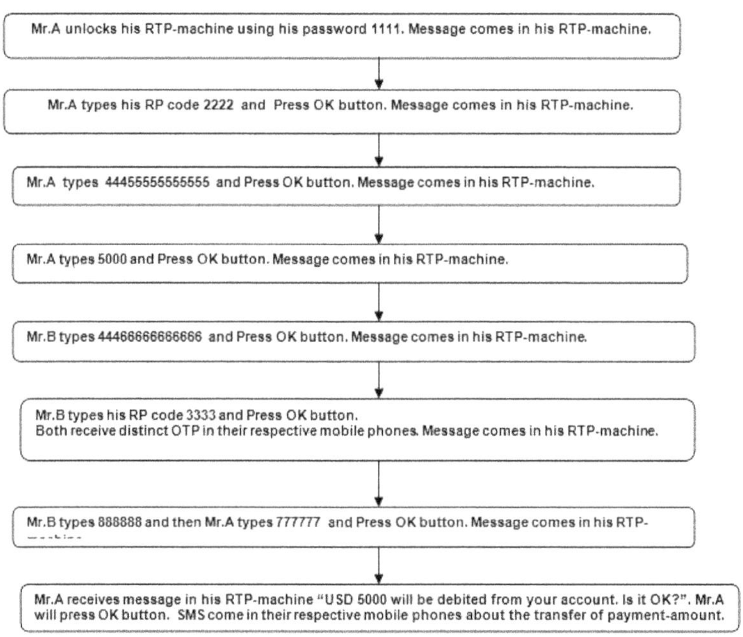

CONCLUSION

The authors in (Aljawarneh, et. el., 2010) proposed data validation service which might provide a detection, and prevention of some web application attacks. Several reports have shown a sharp increase in the number of web-based attacks. Assessing the security of internet banking applications requires specialized knowledge on vulnerabilities, attacks and countermeasures, to gain an understanding of all kind of possible threats, how they are realized and how to properly address them. Aljawarneh, et. el. focused the security vulnerabilities that result at the application level, considering the importance of the difference between the vulnerabilities at the network level and at the application level. But some web organizations use firewalls to solve this problem. The firewalls are necessary, but they are not sufficient to ensure data integrity at the application level because fundamentally they are designed to provide protection at the host and network levels. Therefore, they are useless if any malicious script or listener is already installed on a server behind them because they do not prevent the installation of scripts at the application level. In earlier days, a firewall could suppose that an adversary could only be on the outside. Currently, with mobile environment, an attack might originate from the inside as well, where a firewall can offer no protection. But later in another pioneer work in (Aljawarneh, et. el., 2014) the authors have rightly reported that owing to information security concerns, most Arab small and medium enterprises depend on traditional interactions and have not moved their operations online. The insufficient preparation for the information and communication technologies revolution led to few offering online transaction platforms, information security features and credit facilities. One of the security concerns is a lack of data validation. Data that are not validated or not properly validated is the main issue for serious security vulnerabilities affecting online banking applications. The present series of security issues are: Credit Cards get cloned; ATM Cards get cloned; online bank accounts get phished; bank staff embezzle money; banks rip off their own customers. Both cardholders and merchants rip off banks. Bank fraud is a multibillion dollar industry, and getting more complex all the time. Most of the bad things that happen on the Internet end up with money vanishing from someone's account. The real increased risks to an e-banking have to do with ways in which traditional risk management mechanisms don't scale properly from a world of local physical transactions to one of worldwide, dematerialized ones. Credit card transaction repudiation is the main example at present. There are also significant risks to rapidly growing companies that have hired a lot of new staff but that don't have the traditional internal controls in place. Fraud detection is generally viewed as a data mining classification problem, where the objective is to correctly classify the Credit card or ATM card transactions as legitimate or fraudulent. Even though fraud detection has a long past history, not that much research has appeared in this area. The reason is the unavailability of real world data on which researchers can perform real time experiments, since banks are not ready to disclose their customer transaction data due to privacy reasons as well as business policy. Due to this scarcity of real dataset, not many fraud detection models have been developed and described in the academic literature, and even fewer are known to have been implemented in actual detection systems. In (Adam Ali.Zare Hudaib, 2014), the author has reviewed different payment protocols and security methods that are being used to run banking systems. He has surveyed some of the popular systems that are being used nowadays, with a deeper focus on the Chips, cards, NFC, authentication etc.

Needing to meet consumers' rising expectations around payments, the banking industry around the world is facing rising pressure from governments to create ubiquitous nationwide and regional immediate payments systems that can be used by all financial institutions (Gray, 1993; Schoenmakers, 1995; Summers, 1994; Zhu, 2001, 2002). Across the world, immediate payments systems and infrastructures are being planned or rolled out in more and more countries. The sweeping nature of the global migration to immediate payments is the todays unique demand of the customers. Using the 5A-RTP scheme, a person can make successful payment within one second or less without any paper work, without any signature, but at any place at any time by any person to any person of any amount. The actual payment immediately materializes from one account to another account, and the other party can confirm it too face to face. It is a highly secured scheme, and for real-time payment. Very easy to use the RTP-machine by any person, all the 8-steps are simple steps. The "DIS" button provides additional security-help to the owner of the RTP-machine pressing which he can disable his RTP-machine in case of any security threat (the "DIS" button can also be activated i.e. pressed from distance using its remote-sensor in case of lost or robbed or steal case or in case of any confusion about security).

The 5A-RTP scheme is not to be compared with the existing "Mobile Banking System". Rather, all the facilities of the "Mobile Banking System" can be incorporated in 5A-RTP scheme, but not conversely. For the sake of initial presentation, the transfer of payment-amount is considered here from PEOPLE BANK to PEOPLE BANK, but the method can be easily generalized for transfer of payment-amount from any RBWC bank to any RBWC bank. The algorithm for execution of this method presented here is called by "5A-RTP Algorithm". A Work-Flow Diagram of the "5A-RTP Algorithm" is presented with a hypothetical case study. The 5A-RTP scheme needs the requirement of RTP-machine which can be designed easily by any good hardware manufacturer of communication devices.

Some common characteristics of 5A-RTP payments are as below:

- **24x7 Availability:** Consumers should be able to make or receive a payment at any time of day or night, in compliance with the 5A commitment.
- **Immediacy:** The funds being transferred should be available in the recipient's account in real-time, which the payee can confirm himself.
- **Irrevocability:** Once a payment has been received, it cannot be revoked.
- **Certainty:** Both payer and payee must be notified in real-time that the 5A-RTP payment has been accepted or rejected by the recipient's bank.
- **Alias/Proxy/Tokens:** In parallel to the demand for immediate real time payments, there is demand to proliferate ways to connect and transfer funds at real-time between parties in the digital economy too. This requires the use of addressing databases linking aliases such as mobile phone numbers, email addresses, social media ids, or virtual account numbers, etc. to bank account information, but subject to secured path.

The 5A-RTP scheme will not trigger Big Data Problem (in any of 4Vs) to Reserve Bank of World Country (RBWC) banks, will not make the communication-network congested, there will be no traffic jam issue. It is claimed that the 5A-RTP scheme will play as a revolutionary scheme in the banking industries leading to a fast economic growth of the country WC in a huge momentum if adopted by RESERVE BANK OF WC (RBWC) for all its banks and branches across the country.

REFERENCES

Adam Ali.Zare Hudaib. (2014). Banking and Modern Payments System Security Analysis. *International Journal of Computer Science and Security*, *8*(2), 38–62.

Aljawarneh, S., Al-Rousan, T., Maatuk, A. M., & Akour, M. (2014). Usage of data validation techniques in online banking: A perspective and case study. *Security Journal*, *27*(1), 27–35. doi:10.1057/sj.2012.10

Aljawarneh, S., Alkhateeb, F., & Al Maghayreh, E. (2010). A Semantic Data Validation Service for Web Applications. *Journal of Theoretical and Applied Electronic Commerce Research*, *5*(1), 39–55. doi:10.4067/S0718-18762010000100005

Biswas, R. (2013). Heterogeneous Data Structure "r-Atrain". In B. K. Tripathy & D. P. Acharjya (Eds.), *Global Trends in Knowledge Representation and Computational Intelligence*. Hershey, PA, USA: IGI Global.

Biswas, R. (2015). Atrain Distributed System: An Infinitely Scalable Architecture for Processing Big Data of Any 4Vs. In D.P. Acharjya, Satchidananda Dehuri & Sugata Sanyal (Eds.), Computational Intelligence for Big Data Analysis Frontier Advances and Applications. Switzerland: Springer International Publishing.

Gray, J., & Reuter, A. (1993). *Transaction Processing: Concepts and Techniques*. San Francisco, CA: Morgan Kaufmann Publishers.

Kalakota, R., & Whinston, A. (1996). *Frontiers of Electronic Commerce*. MA: Addision Wesley.

Larsen, L. (2013) Smartphones Easily Skim Credit Card Information: CBC Investigation. Huffington Post. Retrieved from www.huffingtonpost.ca/2013/04/24/smartphones-steal-credit-card-%20data_n_3148170.html

Mishra, S. (2010). *Banking Law And Practice*. New Delhi: S.Chand.

Narayana, J. P. S. (2010). *Law of Negotiable Instruments and Dishonor of Cheques*. Hyderabad: Asia Law House.

Rajesh, R., & Sivagnanasithi, T. (2009). *Banking Theory: Law and Practice*. New Delhi: Tata Mcgraw Hill Education Private Limited.

Schoenmakers, B. (1995). An efficient electronic payment system withstanding parallel attacks (Report CS-R9522). Centrum voor Wiskunde en Informatica.

Summers, B. J. (1994). *The Payment System: Design, Management, and Supervision*. Washington, D.C.: International Monetary Fund.

Swaroop, R. (2010). *A Case Book on Dishonor of Cheques*. Hyderabad: ALT Publications.

Top Credit Card Processors. (n. d.). Retrieved from www.topcreditcardprocessors.com

Zhu, D. (2002). Security Control in Inter-Bank Fund Transfer. *Journal of Electronic Commerce Research*, *3*(1), 15–22.

Zhu, D., Premkumar, G. X., Zhang, X., & Chu, C.-H. (2001). Data Mining for Network Intrusion Detection, A Comparison of Alternative Methods. Decision Sciences Journal, 32(4), 635–660. doi:10.1111/j.1540-5915.2001.tb00975.x

KEY TERMS AND DEFINITIONS

5A: '5A' stands for Anytime Anywhere Any-amount Anybody to Anybody.

5A-RTP: A breaking scheme entitled as "5A-RTP scheme" for a secured Anytime Anywhere Any-amount Anybody to Anybody real time money transfer by self with instant confirmation.

Bank Code: 3-digited bank code of the bank (a fixed 'Bank Code' provided by RBWC to all its banks across WC, one for each bank, and it is not secret).

DIS Button: There is a "DIS" button pressing which the RTP-machine can be disabled. This "DIS" button is physically well covered and well-protected in the RTP-machine so that the owner of the RTP-machine cannot by mistake press it, except by his own decision. However, if disabled by a decision, the owner has to contact the bank authority to enable it again. The 5A-RTP scheme is highly secured by its own algorithm. Nevertheless, the "DIS" button facility adds higher amount of security. Even the "DIS" button can be activated (i.e. RTP-machine can be disabled) using its remote-sensor too, from any distance.

PB: People Bank (a very popular bank in WC) under RBWC.

RBWC: Reserve Bank of WC which is the overall authority of all the banks in WC, under the Government of WC (Ministry of Finance of FC).

RP Code (Of Customer): 4-digited Receive-Payment code (RP Code) of the customer B who will receive payment from A.

RTP: 'RTP' stands for Real-Time Payment.

RTP-Machine: The 5A-RTP scheme can be implemented using a small size physical machine (like a mobile phone) called by RTP Machine.

WC: Short name of a country (hypothetical) named by 'World Country'.

Chapter 10
An Algorithm for Securing Hybrid Cloud Outsourced Data in the Banking Sector

Abdullah Alhaj
The University of Jordan, Jordan

Shadi A Aljawarneh
Jordan University of Science and Technology, Jordan

ABSTRACT

The Cloud has become a significant topic in the banking computing; however, the trend has established a new range of security issues that need to be addressed. In Cloud, the banking data and associated software are not under their control. In addition, with the growing demands for Cloud networks communication, it becomes increasingly important to secure the data flow path. The existing research related to security mechanisms only focuses on securing the flow of information in the communication banking networks. There is a lack of work on improving the performance of networks to meet quality of service (QoS) constrains for various services. The security mechanisms work by encryption and decryption of the information, but do not consider the optimised use of the network resources. In this chapter the authors propose a Secure Data Transmission Mechanism (SDTM) with Preemption Algorithm that combines between security and quality of service for the banking sector. Their developed SDTM enhanced with Malicious Packets Detection System (MPDS) which is a set of technologies and solutions.

DOI: 10.4018/978-1-5225-0864-9.ch010

INTRODUCTION

The concept of cloud computing offers new methods and approaches for information processing and data transmission and however, the Federal CIO Vivek Kundra has emphasized that information security is still a top concern about cloud computing (Worthen, 2009). For instance, In Cloud, the data and associated software are not under their control (Aljawarneh, 2011a). Aljawarneh, Al-Rousan, & Maatuk et al. (2014) addresses the security threats that effect on the online banking services. A number of policies are suggested to face this kind of application vulnerabilities (Aljawarneh et al, 2014).

In Devargas (1993) an overview of multi-processor scheduling algorithm is given without exploiting the two characteristics which are typical in IPsec packet processing (see Section 3). There is also the discussion of the problem of load balancing on multiple processors which could cause many problems in data transmission for the banking services (Aljawarneh, Dababneh, Hosseny et al., 2010).

The SDTA presented in this paper allows scheduling packets to be processed either by the CPU or by the accelerators among the online banking services. This also enhances scalability: one may use an accelerator tailored for the bandwidth normally required for VPNs and use the CPU to have a further processing capability when a higher bandwidth is required. In this paper a SDTA in heterogeneous net-works IPSec-based is presented. Our goal is: to maximize the security to communications at the IP level, to minimize latency and, possibly, maximize throughput.

It is explained in Raghuram and Chakrabarti (2000) that how to obtain data independency among packets for AES. Our approach fully exploits these characteristics to achieve high security and better performance.

Wang and others (Wang, Li, Owens, & Bhargava, 2009) developed a mechanism to solve this issue in owner- write-users-read applications. They proposed to encrypt every data block with a different key so that flexible cryptography-based access control might be achieved. Through the adoption of key derivation methods, the owner needs to maintain only a few secrets. In this mechanism, the data can be updated only by the original owner through authentication way. At the same stage, clients with various access rights need to read the information in an efficient and secure manner. Both banking data and client dynamics should be properly processed to preserve the performance and safety of the outsourced storage system.

Section 2 will explain the system architecture; in Section 3 the Data Transmission Mechanism will be explained. The simulations and its result analysis will be explained in Section 4 and in Section 5 includes the conclusion and the future work.

SYSTEM ARCHITECTURE

The architecture of the developed SDTM is com-posed of generator computers, N cryptographic accelerators connected to the normal system bus of the gateway and distributed bandwidth negotiator as shown in Figure 1. We consider heterogeneous accelerators, i.e., accelerators implementing different cryptographic algorithms and allowing different processing speeds. CPU-memory communication is performed on a faster bus, as in most modern personal computers. The network card is also connected to the faster CPU bus. Only cryptography-related operations are offloaded to the accelerator(s). This means that all the IPSec header processing is done by the CPU.

The SDTM

The main goal of this research is to secure the data flow in heterogeneous networks in the Cloud. This can be achieved by detecting and preventing malicious packets, implementing various security strategies and investigating various security algorithms. The developed protocol provides security services and tries to treat the vulnerabilities in the previously used protocols as well as minimizes the hackers' and crackers' threats. The next stage of this research will look at secure data transmission mechanism in heterogeneous networks and to study a range of scenarios to see the impact of the developed scheme on network performance and behaviour.

Figure 1. Secure data transmission mechanism based on distributed bandwidth negotiator

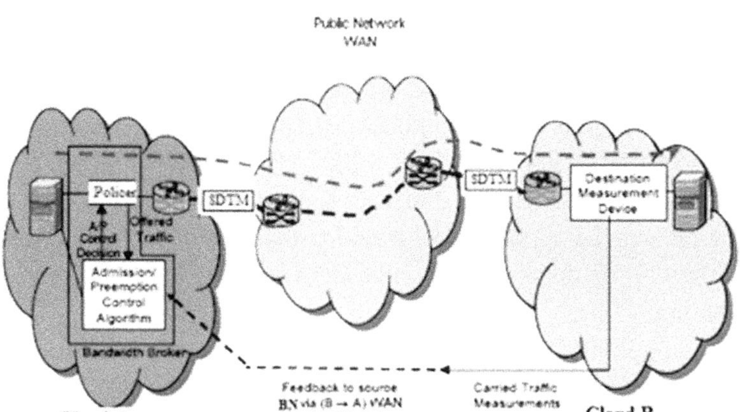

As shown in Figure 1 presenting the SDTM architecture, which uses preemption control algorithm, each accelerator can support different sets of cryptographic algorithms (DES, 3DES, and AES…) and different processing speeds. A common application interface is needed to allow for uniformly accessing all the cryptographic accelerators. This common application interface should also provide software implementations of the cryptographic algorithms, as it is possible in AES.

In this section we present the assumptions made for the developed SDTM and their motivations, the description of our system and the MPDS.

Assumptions

Our algorithm is based on two fundamental assumptions: the first one is that the processing time for packets is known (at least approximately) in advance. This is true for symmetric-key cryptographic algorithms, which are normally used within the IPSec context: their processing time only depends on the number of data blocks to be processed. The only exception is for the software implementations of these algorithms. In this case the computation time may vary depending on the current CPU load. The second assumption is that each packet can be processed independently from the others (i.e., there are no data dependencies between different packets). This comes from IPSec specifications is that each packet must carry any data required for its processing (Anderson,2001). In Devargas (1993) it is explained how to obtain data independency among packets for AES. Our approach fully exploits these assumptions to achieve high security and QoS.

Description of the SDTM

The main goal of our SDTM is to secure data transmission mechanism in heterogeneous networks and providing QoS data transmission such as maximising throughput, minimizing delay and lost packets by implementing the strongest security strategy and investigating various security algorithms. The main features of the SDTM:

- When SDTM is implemented in a firewall or gateway, it provides strong security that can be applied to all traffic crossing the perimeter. Traffic within a workgroup or company does not incur the overhead of security–related processing.
- SDTM in a firewall is resistant to bypass if all the external traffic must use IP, and the firewall is the only means of entrance from the Internet into the organization.

SDTM as it investigates the IPsec is be-low the transport layer (TCP, UDP) and so is transparent to application. There is no need to change software on a user or server system when it is implemented in the firewall or gateway. SDTM can be transparent to end-users. There is no need to train users on security mechanisms, issue keying material on a per-user basis, or revoke keying material when users leave the organization.

SDTM can provide security for individual users if needed. This is useful for off site workers and for setting up a secure virtual sub network within an organization for sensitive application. SDTM can provide a quality of service data flow by possibly increasing throughput, decreasing delay and lost packets.

The main idea underlying the developed SDTM is to receive the packets generated by the host computers to be processed on the gateway (i.e., either one of the accelerators or the CPU) which can provide the shortest processing time. The developed SDTM processes each packet as follows:

- SDTM, implemented in a firewall or gateway, has a Malicious Packet Detection System (MPDS), which will analyze all the incoming packets and will decide to deny or pass the packets through the gateway.
- For the passed packets from MPDS, accelerators will be able to perform the cryptographic algorithm(s) required by the considered packet is selected.

The main goal of this research is to pro-vide the more secure path to data transmission through the network, and so SDTM will investigate the IPsec as the future standard security protocol with Advanced Encryption Security (AES), which was already improved and chosen by National Institute of Security and Technology in USA as the more secure encryption algorithm.

The Malicious Packet Detection System (MPDS)

With the rapidly increasing threat to the network resources, it becomes very important to detect unauthorised packets on a network and estimate the damage they can cause to the legitimate users. As the main goal of the developed SDTM is to secure data transmission mechanism in heterogeneous networks, so MPDS will analyse all the incoming packets and try to pass only the trusted packets whilst discarding the malicious ones.

There are a number of commercial IDS's available. The description of some IDS's lists the types of unusual packets they captured during continuous operation (Lough & Krizman, 2003). And others give description of attacks based on individual malicious packets that can cause harm (Baghaei & Hunt, 2004). IEEE Std 802.11-1999 (1999) presents a statistical analysis of network packets characteristics, to enhance detecting network intrusions. After a global analysis of the nature of malicious packets, the fundamental assumption is that malicious packets tend to display UPD-like traffic behaviour and maintain a high flow rate without alerting the flow identification (i.e., the source and destination addresses and port numbers) during the attack. On the other hand, legitimate flows such as TCP traffic are bursty in nature (IEEE Std 802.11-1999, 1999).The main idea of our developed MPDS is characterised as follows:

- As the security is the main goal of our SDTM the MPDS is turned on with the operating of the gateway and will start analyzing the kind of each packet.
- The MPDS will secure the data flow at the gateway against possible attacks that used invalid values of IP and TCP headers fields through proper gateway configuration and filter out at least the following packets:
    - Packets carrying zero port number
    - Packets with private source or private destination IP address.
    - Packets carrying zero IP source address or destination address.

MPDS will be modified in the future to detect all types of unauthorised packets.

SECURE DATA TRANSMISSION ALGORITHM WITH PREEMPTION CONTROL ALGORITHM

This Data transmission algorithm (DTA) assumes a distributed Bandwidth Negotiator (Barnet et al., 2000; Dasarathy et al., 2005) architecture, as depicted in the Figure 1. A Bandwidth Negotiator (BN) is located in each of the LANs interconnected by the public network backbone: BN is responsible for regulating traffic going into the public network. Suppose a host in Cloud A has a flow of traffic that needs to be sent to Cloud B, the requesting host in Cloud A would first make a request to the BN by sending the amount of requested bandwidth to BN. BN would run the CAC algorithm (to be described below) based on real-time measurements made on the existing traffic at the destination side. If an admit decision is made, the requesting host starts sending traffic, and the Policer is also informed to police the traffic.

If a reject decision is made, the requesting host is notified about the decision. In addition, Policer is informed to prevent the rejected flow from entering into the public network (Dasarathy et al., 2005). In order for the source to quickly make an admission/preemption decision, we believe the most valuable piece of information is the amount of carried traffic, i.e. the amount of traffic that is successfully sent through the WAN backbone. Therefore, at Cloud B, a measurement device measures the amount carried traffic. Such measurements are done on a per Differentiated Services Code Point (DSCP) basis.

The measurements are periodically sent back to Cloud A, which are used for the CAC and preemption algorithm. Suppose due to congestion in the public network, the bandwidth of a link along the path in the public network suddenly decreases to the extent that the link bandwidth is no longer able to support the amount of offered traffic. After "congested" state is declared by the measurement device in Cloud B and the BN at Cloud A is notified, the preemption algorithm is triggered and a fraction of the ongoing traffic flows are preempted. Then both the affected hosts and Policer are notified by BN. Determination of the traffic flows to be preempted upon congestion or blockage is based on the carried traffic measurements, per-call requested bandwidth and a set of pre-defined policy (e.g. a policy based on MLPP described in Developed draft strawman DSCP mapping for GIG enterprise IP networks (n. d.)). Compared to the conventional Bandwidth Broker (BB), such as the one described in Soltwisch, Hogrefe, Bericht, and Gottingen (2004); IPSec Develop-ers Forum, n.d.), in which BB is assumed to have global knowledge about the network, this CAC utilizes a distributed architecture. Namely, each BN makes admission and preemption decision solely based on the feedback from the destination, and there is no other inter BN information exchanged. In addition, BN is consulted only when a call needs to traverse through the public network. If a call originated from Cloud A does not need to go through the public network, BN will not be consulted. The detailed description of this algorithm is shown in the Figure 2 adopted from (IPSec Developers Forum, n. d.).

For UDP flow, the requested bandwidth is assumed to be the encoding rate of the codec. For TCP flows, the requested bandwidth is calculated as file size/speed of service requirement. The result is then sent to PSM, where a leaky bucket algorithm is used to regulate the traffic. An alternative way to determine the requested bandwidth for TCP flows would be to deterministically assign a fixed value. We also note that the Preemption Algorithm is run as part of the data transmission mechanism. Suppose a high priority flow (e.g. a Flash Overwrite flow) requests for admission and the congested flag is on, lower priority flows may need to be preempted to accommodate the higher priority call, as mandated by the preemption policy. When the "congested" flag is set by the measurement device, the preemption algorithm is triggered to preempt existing flows. Preemption algorithm is shown in

Figure 2. Secure data transmission algorithm

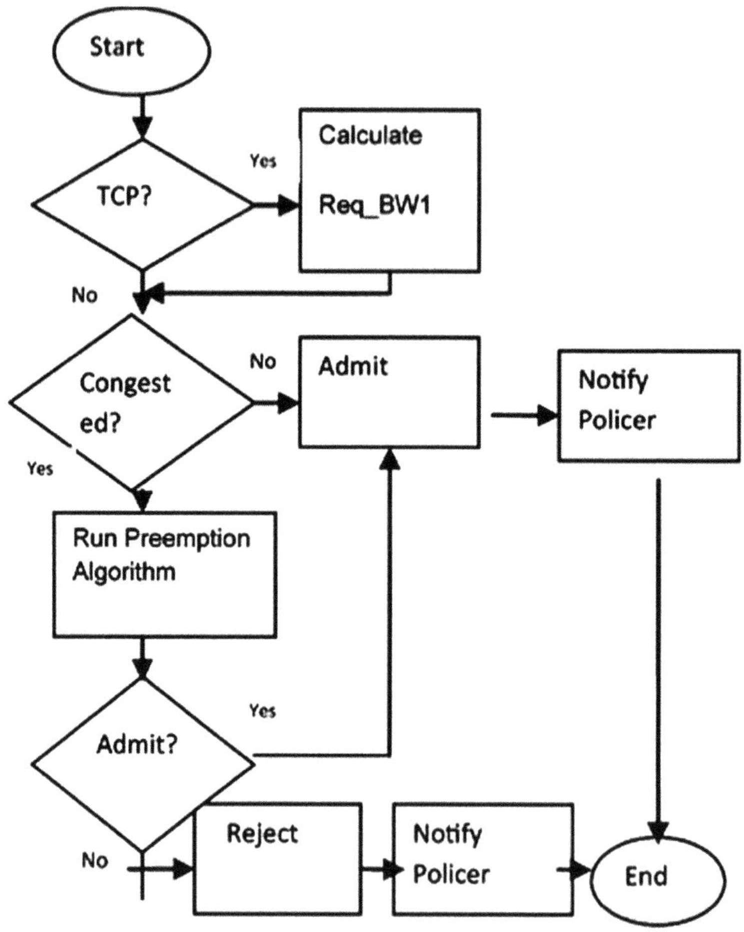

Figure 3, in which two examples of preemption policy are presented. We note that the preemption policy can be set by the network operator dynamically, according to the need of the underlying mission.

By carefully observing Figure 2, we note that the data transmission algorithm shows a strong "reactive" nature, i.e. traffic will be admitted until congested state is declared. If the "available bandwidth" can be determined through bandwidth estimation techniques, the data transmission algorithm can be made more "proactive"; namely, traffic flows are rejected before congestion is observed. In a companion paper (Sucec, Samtani, & Bereschinsky, 2005), powerful bandwidth estimation techniques are presented such that the bottleneck link bandwidth (defined as the link with the smallest amount of bandwidth along the path) and avail-able

Figure 3. Preemption algorithm

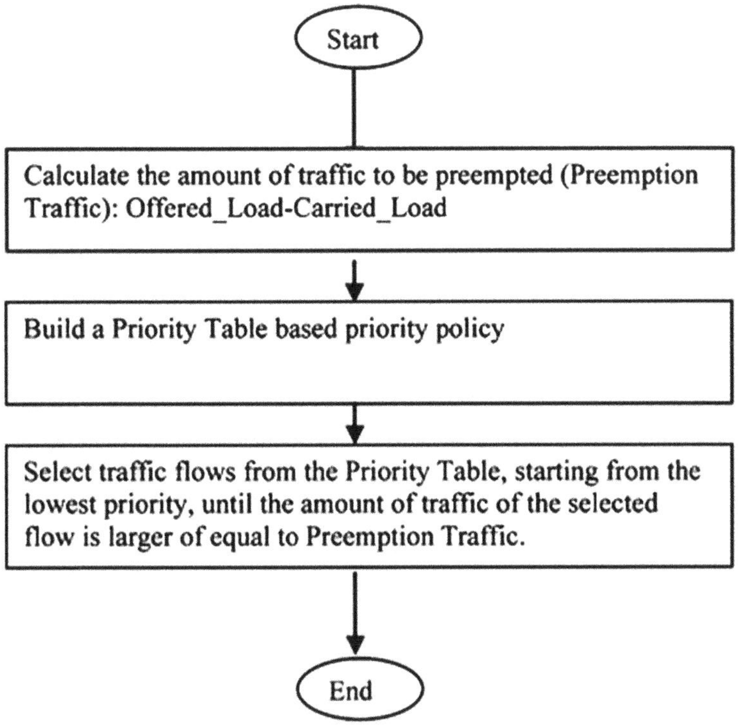

bandwidth (defined as how much band-width "headroom" along the path for new traffic) are estimated. They can then be used in the data transmission, as shown in Figure 4. Our analysis showed that using bandwidth estimation; congestion avoidance can be effectively achieved.

SIMULATION

To investigate the effectiveness of the data transmission /preemption algorithm, OMNET++ simulator was used to compare two different QoS setups, one with data transmission /preemption algorithm and the other without. We used the same components of the model in Figure 1 to validate the SDTM, but with implementing data transmission algorithm/preemption algorithm and without data transmission/ preemption algorithm to study the behaviour of the system in both experiments.

Figure 4. Data transmission algorithm when available bandwidth can be obtained through bandwidth estimation techniques

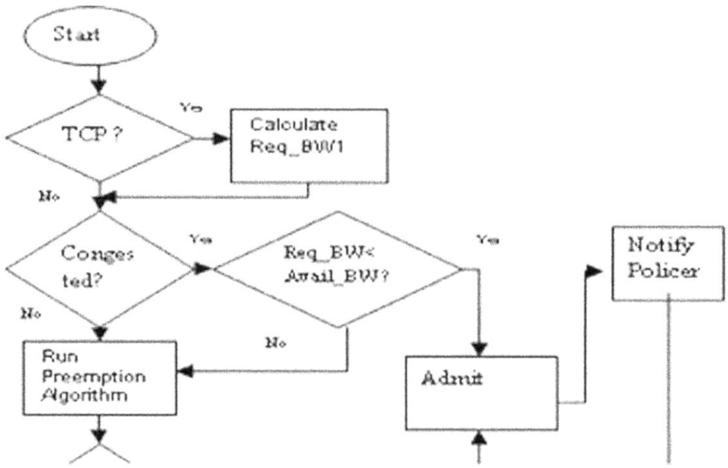

Simulation Results

Queuing Delay

Figure 5 shows the queuing delays as function of simulation time, with Data Transmission Algorithm (DTA) in red and without DTA in green. Figure 5. indicate that, as flow arrival rate increases over time, the queuing delay for the QoS scheme without DTA increases significantly, while as the average queuing delay with DTA stays low.

Throughput

Figure 6 compares the throughput performance between the two experiments with DTA in red and without DTA in green; one interesting observation is that with DTA, the network throughput is slightly less than without DTA.

Figure 6 shows that the simulation experiment with DTA yields a small network throughput decrease, especially when the network is heavily overloaded.

Packet Loss

Figure 7 shows once admitted, first-rate flows have a high chance of being delivered to their destination with DTA in red and without DTA in green. As we see from Figure 7. the packet loss performance without DTA is better than with DTA.

Figure 5. Queuing delay

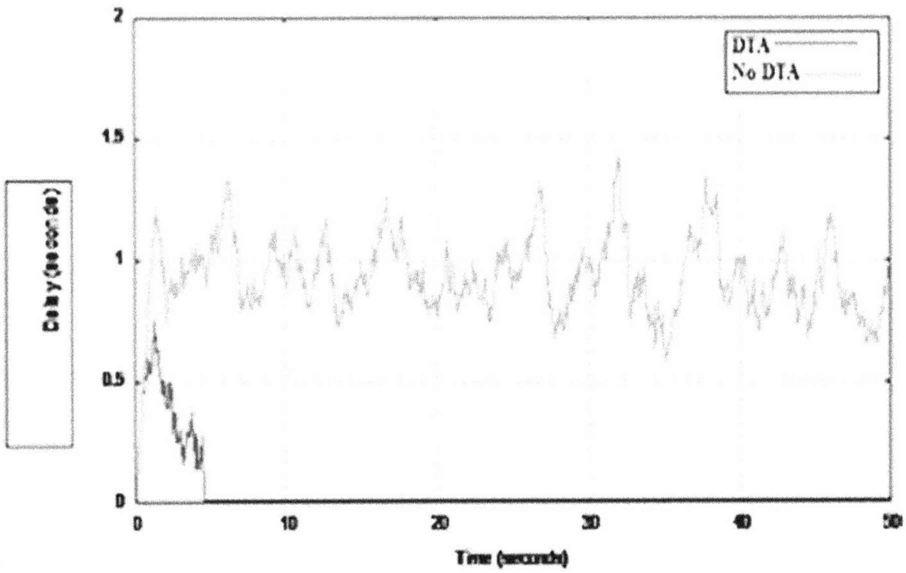

Figure 6. Throughput

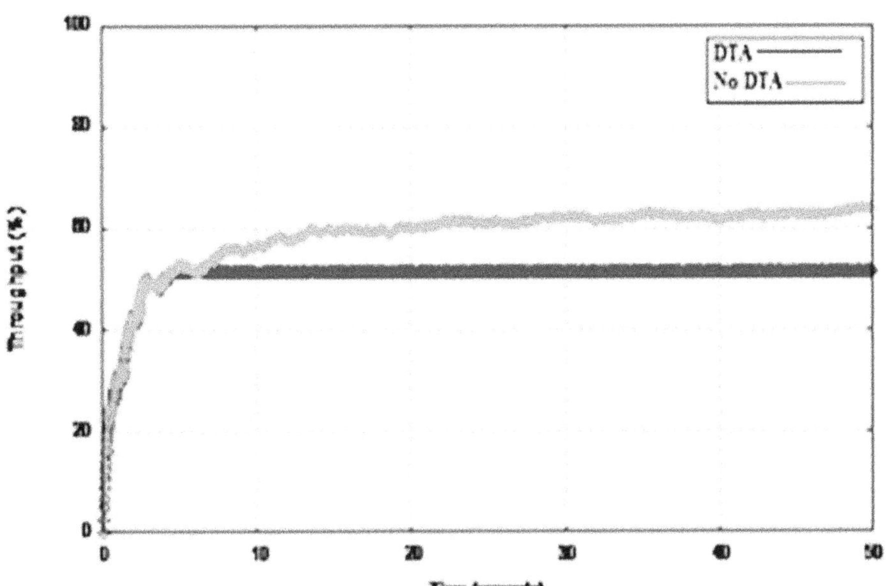

Figure 7. Packet loss

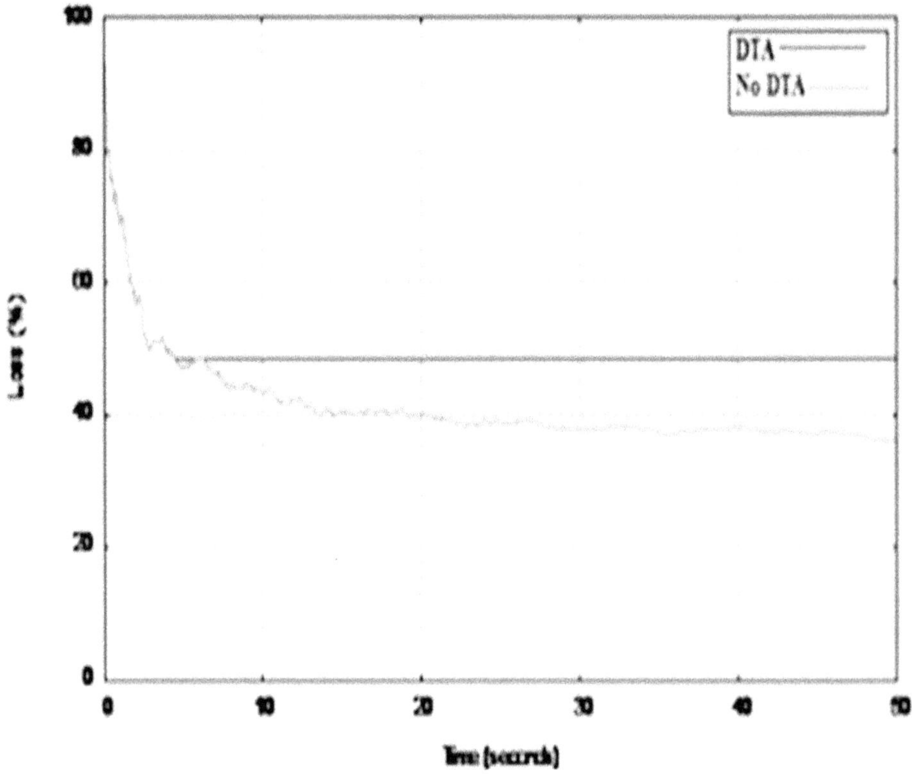

CONCLUSION AND FUTURE WORK

This paper has presented an investigation into the more secure protocols and security mechanisms to develop a Secure Data Transmission Mechanism (SDTM) with preemption control algorithm for online banking services. Such mechanism is to combine between security and quality of service to improve the performance of networks to meet quality of service (QoS) constrains for various applications in the Cloud environment. We also provide some high-level simulation to prove that the SDTM works as desired and that it can provide good security and enhanced network performance. A comparison between the SDTM we presented here with one or multiple queues and other suitable security protocols will also be carried out.

REFERENCES

Alhaj, A., Aljawarneh, S., Masadeh, S., & Abu-Taieh, E. (2013). A Secure Data Transmission Mechanism for Cloud Outsourced Data. *International Journal of Cloud Applications and Computing*, *3*(1), 34–43.

Alhaj, A., Mellor, J., & Awan, I. (2009). Performance evaluation of secure call admission control for multiclass internet services.*Proceedings of the 23rd IEEE-AINA'09,*Bradford, UK.

Aljawarneh, S. (2011a). Cloud security engineering: Avoiding security threats the right way. *International Journal of Cloud Applications and Computing*, *1*(2), 64–70. doi:10.4018/ijcac.2011040105

Aljawarneh, S. (2011b). A web engineering security methodology for e-learning systems. *Network Security*, *2011*(3), 12–15. doi:10.1016/S1353-4858(11)70026-5

Aljawarneh, S., Al-Rousan, T., Maatuk, A. M., & Akour, M. (2014). Usage of data validation techniques in online banking: A perspective and case study. *Security Journal*, *27*(1), 27–35. doi:10.1057/sj.2012.10

Aljawarneh, S., Alkhateeb, F., & Al Maghayreh, E. (2010). A semantic data validation service for web applications. *Journal of Theoretical and Applied Electronic Commerce Research*, *5*(1), 39–55. doi:10.4067/S0718-18762010000100005

Aljawarneh, S., Dababneh, M., Hosseny, H., & Alwadi, E. (2010). A web client authentication system using smart card for e-systems: initial testing and evaluation. *Proceedings of the Fourth International Conference on Digital Society ICDS'10* (pp. 192–197). IEEE. doi:10.1109/ICDS.2010.40

Aljawarneh, S., Laing, C., & Vickers, P. (2008). Design and experimental evaluation of Web Content Verification and Recovery (WCVR) system: A survivable security system.*Proceedings of ACSF.*

Aljawarneh, S., Laing, C., & Vickers, P. (n. d.). Security policy framework and algorithms for web server content protection. *Proceedings of ACSF'07.*

Aljawarneh, S. A., Moftah, R. A., & Maatuk, A. M. (2016). Investigations of automatic methods for detecting the polymorphic worms signatures. *Future Generation Computer Systems*, *60*, 67–77. doi:10.1016/j.future.2016.01.020

Anderson, R. (2001). *Security engineering: A guide to building dependable distributed systems*. John Wiley & Sons.

Baghaei, N., & Hunt, R. (2004). IEEE 802.11 wireless LAN security performance using multiple clients. *Proceedings of the 12th IEEE International Conference on Networks* (ICON '04).

Barnet, Y., Ford, P., Yavatkar, R., Baker, F., Zhang, L., Speer, M., . . . Felstaine, E. (2000). A framework for integrated services operation over diffserv networks. Retrieved from http://tools.ietf.org/html/rfc2998

Chang, K., Kim, G. T., Samtani, S., Staikos, A., Muzzelo, L., & Palumbo, J. (2006). A study on the call admission and preemption control algorithms for secure wireless ad hoc networks using IPSec tunneling.*Proceedings of the MILCOM '06*. doi:10.1109/MILCOM.2006.302177

Dasarathy, B., Gadgil, S., Vaidyanathan, R., Par-meswaran, K., Coan, B. A., Conarty, M., & Bhanot, V. (2005). Network QoS assurance in a multi-layer adaptive resource management scheme for mission-critical application using CORBA middleware framework.*Proceedings of the 11th Real Time and Embedded Technology and Applications Symposium*. doi:10.1109/RTAS.2005.34

Devargas, M. (1993). *Network security*. Manchester, UK: NCC Blackwell.

Developed draft strawman DSCP mapping for GIG enterprise IP networks. (n. d.).

Hendry, M. (1995). *Practical computer network security*. Norwood, MA: Artech House.

IPSec Developers Forum. (n. d.). Retrieved from http://www-ip-sec.com5PSecinfo.html

Lough, D. L., & Krizman, K. J. (2003). A short tutorial on wireless LANs and IEEE802.11.

Moore, G. E. (1997). *An update on Moore's law*. Santa Clara, CA: Intel Corporation.

Raghuram, S. S., & Chakrabarti, C. (2000). A programmable processor for cryptography.*Proceedings of the IEEE International Symposium on Circuits and Systems (ISCAS '00)*, Geneva, Switzerland (pp. 685–688).

Soltwisch, R., Hogrefe, D., Bericht, T., & Gottingen, G.-a.-u. (2004). Survey on network security - 2004. IEEE Std 802.11-1999 (1999). Part II: Wireless LAN medium access control (MAC) and physical layer (PHY) specifications.

Sucec, J., Samtani, S., & Bereschinsky, M. A. (2005, October 17-20). Resource friendly approach for estimating available bandwidth in secure IP networks.*Proceedings of the Military Communications Conference (MILCOM '05)*. doi:10.1109/MILCOM.2005.1605660

Wang, W., Li, Z., Owens, R., & Bhargava, B. (2009). Secure and efficient access to outsourced data. Proceedings of the ACM Workshop on Cloud Computing Security (CCSW '09) (pp. 55-66). doi:10.1145/1655008.1655016

Worthen, B. (2009). Inside the head of Obama's CIO. *The Wall Street Journal Digits*.

Chapter 11
Prevention, Detection, and Recovery of CSRF Attack in Online Banking System

Nitin Nagar
DAVV, India

Ugrasen Suman
SCSIT, India

ABSTRACT

Online banking system has created an enormous impact on IT, Individuals, and networking worlds. Online banking systems and its exclusive architecture have numerous features and advantages over traditional banking system. However, these new uniqueness create new vulnerabilities and attacks on an online banking system. Cross-site scripting request forgery or XSS attack is among the top vulnerabilities, according to recent studies. This exposure occurs, when a user uses the input from an online banking application without properly looking into them which allows an attacker to execute malicious scripts into the application. Current approaches use to mitigate this problem, especially on effective detection of XSS vulnerabilities in the application or prevention of real-time XSS attacks. To address this problem, the survey of different vulnerability attacks on online banking system performed and also presents a concept for the prevention, detection, removal and recovery of XSS vulnerabilities to secure the banking application.

DOI: 10.4018/978-1-5225-0864-9.ch011

INTRODUCTION

Online banking (Internet banking or e-banking) offers benefits such as, fast transaction, data accuracy, and data consistency, for both banks and its customers. Online banking has enabled traditional banking work with lower operational cost through the reduction of physical facilities and staffing resources needed. It reduces the waiting times in branches leading to potential increase in sales performance. (Sarel & Mamorstein, 2003). Online banking permits customers to perform banking transactions electronically via bank's website anytime and anyplace. Additionally, customers is not area restricted to the gap hours of banks, travel and waiting times aren't any longer necessary in online banking (Hamlet, 2000). The delivery channels/ services are the primarily represent the domain of on-line banking which include ATM Machines (ATMs), Net Banking, Phone Banking, Mobile Banking, TV Banking and Non-Cash Retail Payments (e.g., Debit Cards, Credit Cards, ECS, NEFT, and RTGS).

Online banking involves different facilities for the banking customers. The provision of facilities is include accessing accounts, transferring funds, and shopping for monetary product or services on-line. Furthermore, new banking services such as, electronic bill generation and payment, also involve in online banking which permit the purchasers to pay and receive the bills on a banks web site. This mechanism is often referred to as transactional on-line banking (Abha& Vinita, 2010). Online banking can be series of processes within which a bank customer login on to the web site of the bank through the browser that's installed on client laptop, desktop, palmtop, and smartphone. It is useful to carries out numerous transactions such as, account transfers, bill submissions, account inquiries etc. Online banking comprise of four major stages such as, PC booting and OS execution, banking services, cloud or internet and banking websites. Figure 1 shows the working of online banking system.

Online banking threats and vulnerabilities are a foremost challenge in the field of research. The rest of the chapter is organized as follows. Section 2 includes an online banking mechanism. The section 3 states that online banking security issues along with case study of online banking system with CSRF attack impact. In Section

Figure 1. Working of online banking system

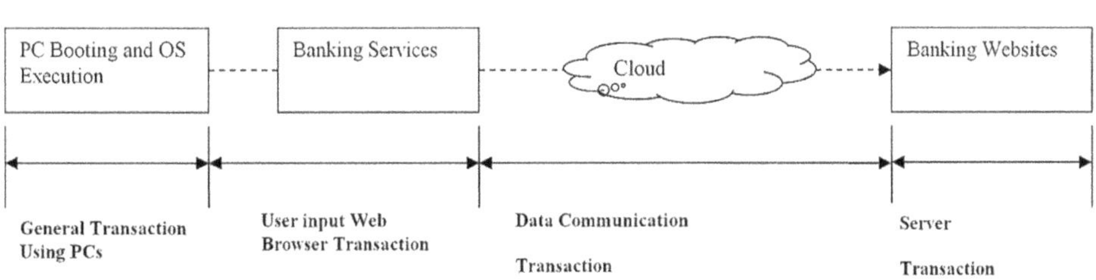

4, the proposed work focuses on XSS detection and recovery in the DOM. We also discuss the implementation of work with performance evaluation of different aspects. In section 5, we state the conclusion and final.

ONLINE BANKING SYSTEM MECHANISMS

Online banking has basically transformed the manner in which banks traditionally conduct their businesses and therefore the customers can perform their banking activities through online banking (Eriksson et al., 2008; Sathye, 1999). Nowadays, on-line banking has full-fledged extraordinary growth in the market and has become one of the most sources of avenues for banks is to deliver their product and services to customer (Amato-McCoy, 2005).

Online banking is defined as automated delivery of latest and traditional banking product and services to the customers through electronically and interactive communication channels (Sathye, 1999). Online banking includes the systems that enable financial organization customers, individuals or businesses, to access accounts, interaction of business, or acquire data on money product and services through a public or personal network, as well as the web or cloud. The five basic services related to on-line banking are such as, view account balances and dealing histories, paying bills, transferring funds between accounts, requesting MasterCard advances, and ordering checks for quicker services which will be offer by domestic and foreign bank (Chou & Chou, 2000). The mechanism of online banking can be subdivided in component such as, user and delivery channels, core business processes, data and information and technology enabler. The enterprise view of online banking shows in Figure 2 shows different users to access the banking applications over various delivery channels. The details descriptions of these components are as follows:

Users and Delivery Channels

User will access applications over the Internet or cloud using browser. Employees, including administrators or call center personnel, can access the banking applications through an intranet via browser. They can also access the applications through VPN. Each channel can use to provide the user with access to a subset of the banking applications. The capabilities and the presentation style may differ depending upon the user and the channel. For example, employees might have access more functions than customers, which might have different, more robust and scalable presentation capabilities.

Figure 2. Users accessibility to the banking applications over various delivery channels

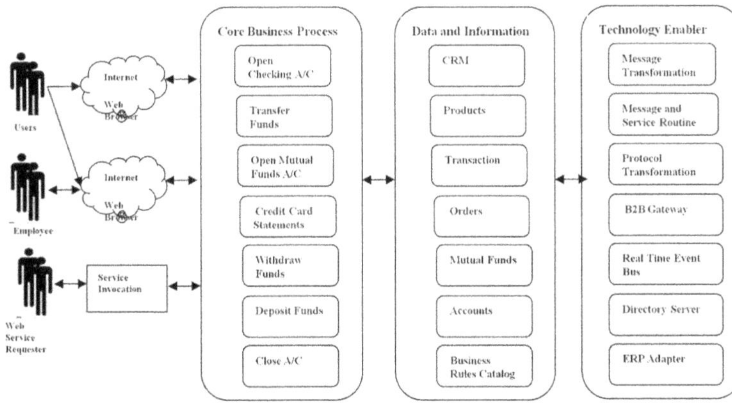

Core Business Processes

It is a core business processes that represents the operation processes in which user focuses on in order to excel in the preferred functional model. The business processes that promote operational excellence for the customers are open checking account, transfer funds, open mutual funds account, pay credit card settlement, withdrawal funds, deposit funds and close account. The details descriptions of these components are as follows:

- **Open Checking Account**: The customer can open a checking account in less than a determined minute. The process can be invoked at the branch office or banking server through a cashier counter and through a self-service online banking gateway.
- **Transfer Funds**: The process offers the capability to transfer funds from one account type to another within the bank at domestic level and also use to transfer funds between other national or international bank.
- **Open Mutual Funds Account**: Employee and customers can open a mutual funds account within a bank and access the banks most trusted and highest performing funds and can analyze them.
- **Pay Credit Card Settlement:** Customer can have online credit card settlement capabilities to overdraft protection facilitate through credit card payments and direct debit from the account.
- **Withdrawal Funds:** Customer and employee can withdrawal funds from the respective accounts.

- **Deposit Funds:** Customer and employee can deposit funds to their respective account.
- **Close Account:** Customer and Employee can close the respective account.

Data and Information

The core conceptual data and information are required to understand the core set of business processes. Data and information subcomponents are fundamental business units that include CRM, products, transaction, order, mutual funds, account and business rules catalog. The detail description of data and information subcomponents are as follows:

- **CRM**: The CRM (Customer Relationship Management) system is the subcomponent that manages all customers' information, subscribed product list, and information regarding account.
- **Products**: The product subcomponent represents the products which the bank offers to customers and employees. The banks provided products are include checking accounts, savings accounts, mutual funds, and credit cards.
- **Transaction**: Transaction represents the transformation of funds from one account to another via employee or customer. The transformation must require the account of both the sender and receiver.
- **Order**: The order subcomponent represents the orders placed by customer to the bank. The orders place by customers includes payments, funds transfers, and mutual funds transactions.
- **Mutual Funds**: It is the facility provided by online banking which consist a pool of money from numerous investors who wish to save or make money.
- **Account**: The account such as, checking accounts, savings accounts, and current account.
- **Business Rules Catalog:** The business rules catalog is used for the implementations of the business processes. Each business rule uses information elements and enforces certain conditional logic upon them.

Technology Enablers

Technology enablers can comprise element of the IT infrastructure which require supporting implementation of core business processes. The conceptual technology subcomponents are message transformation, message and service routing, protocol transformation, business-to-business (B2B) gateway, real-time event bus, directory server, and ERP adapter:

- **Message Transformation**: Message transformation provides the ability to transform different forms of message formats used by customers and access the enterprise business processes. It also enables transformation of the standard message format into the specific message format that the requesting customers expects or supports.
- **Message and Service Routing:** Message and service routing provides essential and advance message and service routing potentials. It also provides the intelligence mechanism to discover the correct service provider for a specified service request and route the service request accordingly.
- **Protocol Transformation:** Protocol transformation is a banking application where the identity of attacker is known by the protocol initiator. It also reduces the number of potential attackers and hence it builds the protocol transformation feasible.
- **Business-to-Business (B2B) Gateway:** B2B receives requests from third parties via service invocations. The gateway provides a central point for handling requests that originate from external components of web services.
- **Real-Time Event Bus:** It provides the basic and advanced features for simple and complex event processing. The bus features facilitate asynchronous processing of funds transfer within and outside of the enterprise in close to real-time speed.
- **Directory Server:** It manages customer profiles required to validate customer credentials, identity and roles. Customers profiles are also used to perform authorize access.
- **ERP Adapter:** ERP adapter used for bank's treasury systems to support payments automation. The gateway is responsible for receiving requests from external systems, which invoke the necessary adapters to perform the business logics, and composing a response and sending it back to the requesting system in the case of incoming traffic. For outgoing traffic requests, the gateway is responsible for sending credit card settlement requests and international funds transfer requests.

Secure and safe surroundings of banking are the most vital concern for all monetary service of organizations. The responsibility of secure online banking isn't solely depends upon banks however, it is also responsibility of customers to control the net banking, need to have aware about particular level of information and technical ability (Zakaria, Karim, & Aliar, 2009). This chapter aims to clarify about the rationale behind the security breaches and therefore the participation of each customer and the banks to change the hackers or crackers or trespasser to access banking network. In spite of these, the employment of on-line banking is increasing and can be increase within the future. The present study aims to seek out numerous sorts of flaws within the security of on-line banking those leads to loss of cash of account holders at the side of leak of their personal data to unauthorized persons. Security breaches aren't solely gratitude to banks faults and banks inadequate polices however customers are equally accountable for it, as a result of customer's awareness regarding security is equally necessary and important.

ONLINE BANKING SECURITY ISSUES AND CASE STUDY OF ONLINE BANK ACCOUNT ATTACK

Billions of financial data transactions occur online every day, at the same time banking information is also compromised by hackers to manipulate a financial institution's online information system. These causes huge financial loses to the banks and customers. The evolution history of attacks began more than ten years ago and quickly became known as phishing. Its sophistication has increased on par with the new security technologies adopted by the bank industry intended to mitigate the problem. This means there are some flaws in the security of online banking that result in loss of money of many account holders along with leakage of their personal information to unauthorized persons.

Security-sensitive information such as SSN or passwords or account statements provided through email that is passes through insecure channel of communication. Some banks send passwords or user IDs through email, if user request that information incase user forget it and most of banks provide account statements monthly through email. But if mail server is insecure, an attacker could be view unencrypted traffic on the network and obtain the sensitive information and accounts of users can be compromised. Some banking sites have IP addresses that match with other lot of unsightly sites that can result in easy hacking. An example of it is Jammu and Kashmir Bank's website. A reverse IP check shows this jkbank.net has the IP address: 68.178.156.75 and 53 sites found with the IP 68.178.156.75, a shared host with 53 unsightly sites (webDEViL, 2008). ICICI bank recently done mistake in contents of the CAPTCHA image was being sent in the response header. This happened on the form where you enter your credit card details. It definitely made no sense having the CAPTCHA.

Case Study: Bank Account Attack

This case study focuses the concern on online banking applications that use the authentication through user name and password. According to a recent study by University of Michigan, in an examination of 214 bank websites, more than 75 percent of bank websites have at least one design issues that could lead to the theft of customer information. The defects are so much dangerous that even an expert individual would find difficulties to detect and unlike bugs, cannot be fixed with a patch. It was recommended to use SSL throughout the entire website and to avoid using links to third-party sites. Secure banking websites have become an integral part of our routine life from our personal to our job-related business. A survey conducted by pew Internet states that 42% of all Internet users bank online (Sue, 2008). With 24/7 access from around the world users can view balances, transfer funds and lots more at their convenience using online banking. Due to the sensitive nature of these sites, security is a top priority. Hackers are increasingly launching targeted attacks against weak websites, as opposed to automated attacks against tens of thousands of sites at once. A report from White Hat Security Council (WHSC) finds that nearly half of all applications (47.9 percent) are vulnerable to XSS attacks (IBM Security Intelligence, 2014). If the targeted end users have an administrator account then it can be exploited banking application through CSRF or XSS attack. XSS is based on the following subsection.

Cross Site Request Forgery (CSRF) or XSS Attack

Cross-site request forgery is a category of attack that occurs when a malicious web site, email, blog, instant message, or program causes a user's browser to perform an unwanted action on a trusted site or banking site for which the user is currently authenticated (Johns, 2011). The impacts of successful CSRF exploits vary based on the role of the victim. When it targets a normal user, a successful CSRF attack can compromise user data and their related functions. If the targeted user is an administrator account, a CSRF attack can compromise the entire Web application or cloud application (Kieyzun, Guo, Jayaraman et al., 2009). The websites that are more likely to be attacked are community websites such as social networking, email or websites that have high financial value accounts associated with them (e.g., banks, stock brokerages, and bill pay services). This attack can happen even if; the user is logged into a web site using strong encryption such as HTTPS. XSS attack can be classified into three categories such as, non-persistent XSS, persistent XSS and DOM-based XSS. Description of XSS attack categories are discussed in following subsections:

- **Non-Persistent XSS:** Non-persistent XSS is also experienced as a reflected XSS vulnerability. It is the common example of XSS. In which the injected by the attacker data are reflected in the reaction. A typical non-persistent XSS contains a link with XSS vector.
- **Persistent XSS:** Persistent XSS is also known as stored XSS or cross site scripting. These scripts occur when XSS vectors are stored in database and cloud application is run with unfolded pages by the user. Persistent XSS is more harmful, than the non-persistent XSS because the script is performed automatically when the user uses the cloud application. Orkut was vulnerable to XSS persistent, which ruined the name of the website.
- **DOM-based XSS:** Document object model (DOM) based XSS is a cross-site scripting vulnerability that is part of the HTML and seems to be transmitted in the DOM. In reflection and stored cross-site scripting attacks, users can find out the vulnerability of payload on the response side, but in the DOM-based cross-site scripting is the HTML source code of the response to the attack exactly the same browser and the payload cannot be initiated in the browser. DOM-based XSS is sometimes referred to as "Type 0 XSS". It occurs when the vector results XSS as a result of a DOM modification of a cloud application through a user's browser. On the user side of the HTTP response will not vary, but the script in a malicious manner. It is sited on the user side browser only. DOM based XSS attack occurs when users provided un-desired data in JavaScript using methods such as eval (), document write () or innerHTML (). The main culprit for this part of the attack is JavaScript code. This is the most advanced and least known type of XSS attack on cloud virtual environment. Most of the time, this vulnerability occurs because the developer does not determine how it works (Nagar & Suman, 2016).

In banking application, XSS attacks are not similar to other attacks. Attacks use an injecting code, usually through client-side scripting such as JavaScript as a output to an application. The application has numerous injection areas such as search areas, feedback, forums, and cookies that can be vulnerable to cross-site scripting. The purpose of XSS attacks is to gather all cookie data, as cookies are common and regularly used to store information such as session IDs and login details. Figure 3 show the various attack areas in the banking application. Although, client-side scripts cannot directly affect the server-side information even if they manipulate in DOM to alter form values or change the build action to send the submitted data to the attacker's browser to gain information (IBM Security-Intelligence, 2012).

Figure 3. Attacks area in banking applications

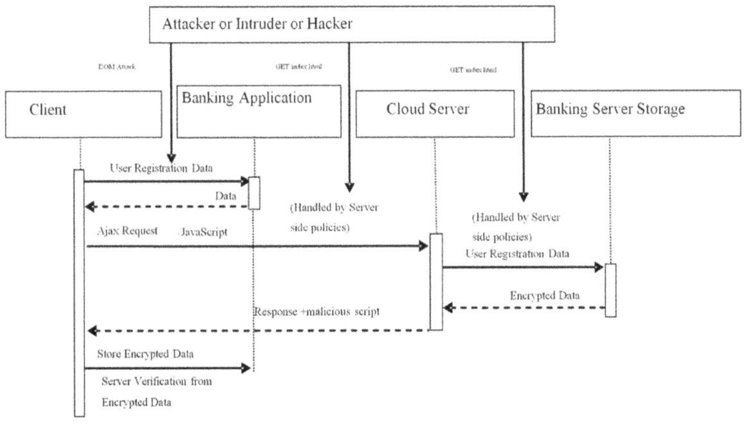

XSS attacks work, even if the site has an SSL connection and a script is run as a part of the secure site. Browsers cannot distinguish between legal and malicious cloud environment. Phishing email then injected into a display page for giving the attacker to full access of application through URL. This type of attack is known as non-persistent XSS attack. Cloud service providers are focused on reducing the response time of the application. The proposed solution is not widely applied in existing response time. Thus, in this respect to attained security, we compromise between response time and security.

XSS DETECTION AND RECOVERY IN DOM

The existing solutions are implemented as an input filter mechanism to avoid XSS attack. But to deliver user's data as an input is not a good idea since we do not know how that data used by the applications (Bates, Barth, & Jackson, 2010). Filtering is the response from the server to the user request which also holds inserted data that is supplied by the user agent in the cloud virtualized environment. Hence the response from the server is filtered in the presence of malicious scripts. The proposed modified cloud applications, we first extract user data inserted from the response and if it is used for malicious scripts then we apply a filter on it. After straining it again payload embedded in the user's response. Our proposed solution uses DOM-based filtering mechanism for the spotting and removal of malicious scripts. This filtering mechanism uses an HTML parser to parse user data provided in DOM after filtering malicious script from the reaction and then result sends to the user's browser. The filter works with a white list based filtering mechanism. In this work, we have also incorporated 'post' method instead of the 'get' method to avoid other attacks (Nagar and Suman, Oct-2014). Figure 4 shows the attack through malicious script.

Implementation

We set up a functional sample where the concepts identified in this paper are placed into practice. The purpose of this section is to monitor the proposed working with filter scripts to control DOM-based XSS attacks. So, we demonstrate the feasibility and effectiveness of the integration models. For functional test on OpenStack, we use several virtual machines with M-pin authentication server and application to perform the analysis (Nagar & Suman, 2014). The OpenStack identity service, known as the keystone which provide services for authentication and management of user accounts and role information in a private cloud computing environment (Report, Jan-2014). It is an important service that transmits the authentication and verification between OpenStack and cloud services. Authentication mechanism ensures that the only legal user can access the other services such as storage and computing from (Nagar & Suman, 2014):

- **Parsing of HTML:** HTML parser is a used to analyze HTML in either a linear or nested manner in the Java library. Primarily, it is used for transformation or extraction. It also content filters, record of visitors, custom tags and it is easily used with Java. HTML parser is fast, robust as well as tested software. There are a number of implementations done in the Java HTML parser. We compare them to upgrade to the bottom of the HTML parsing capabilities, handling of malformed HTML, clean HTML and support for HTML5 features. Table 1 shows the comparison between different from HTML parser.

Figure 4. Attacks through malicious scripts

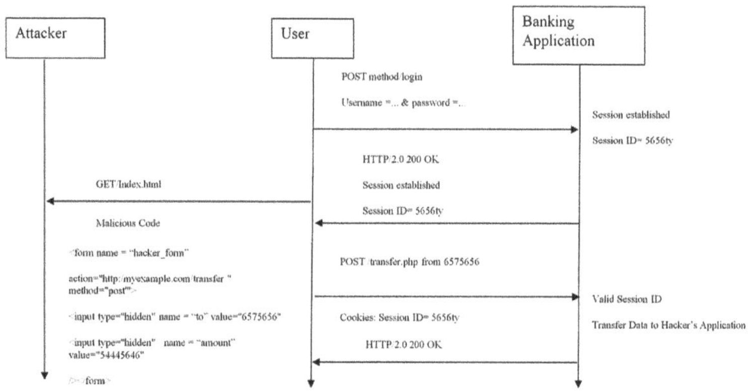

Table 1. Comparison of different HTML parser

Parser	Implementation Language	HTML Update	Clean HTML	HTML Parsing
HTML Cleanser	JAVA	Unknown	Yes	No
Jaunt API	JAVA	Yes	Yes	No
Jericcho HTML Parser	JAVA	No	Unknown	Unknown
Jsoup	JAVA	Yes	Yes	Yes
JTidy	JAVA	Yes	Yes	No

- **Modification of HTML Parsing:** We modify the comments handling mechanism of the original Jsoup parser. Since there are many attack comment parsing quirks. We concentrate the Jsoup escapes the every ‘ (single-quotes), “(double-quotes) and \ with a backslash automatically. For example script>alert (“N”) </script> will be filtered as <script>alert (\N\) </script>. So the attacker will not be able to attack on the script. With this we also integrate a hex coding, bypassing using obfuscation and closing tag to build Jsoup more robust.
- **Deployment of Filter:** Java Filter Interface (JFI) is uses for filtering the server response from user (Java response Filter, 2014). For implementation of the filter we created a class named as FailedRequestFilter.java which will implement through Java Interface ’Filter’. In doFilter () method of this class we will chain the response to another class named ‘LoginResponse.java’ which extends by ’HttpServletResponse Wrapper’. In this we call Java program extract user provided contents of the response and calling the filter API. The filtered output from the API is embedded in response and it is sent back to the user. In order to implicitly call the filter for every application request, we need to change in the ’Web.xml’.
- **Performance Evaluation of Proposed Work with Different Aspects:** The M-pin provides two factor authentication server used to design a secure a cloud environment. M-pin authentication server and the cloud filter authentication server worked together. Figure 5 shows the filter between user and cloud server browser. The equipments used to obtain the measurements are an Intel (R)

Figure 5. The filter between user and cloud server browser

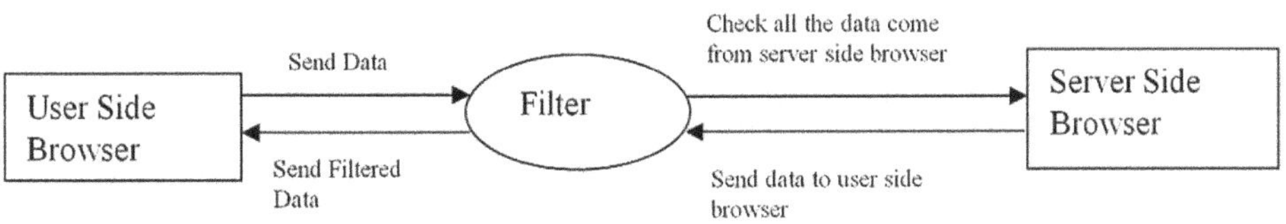

Pentium (R) Core 2 Duo i3 processor (Virtual Technology enables machine), with 8 GB of RAM, running on Ubuntu 14.04 (i.e., LTS). For testing we have created on XSS vulnerable cloud application using JSP and Servlet deployed on Apache Tomcat 8.0 web server. It has enough resources to work. We have tested our filter on around 160 attack vectors from XSS cheat sheet, HTML5 security cheat sheet and other sources (Boganatham, 2009). Out of 160 attack vector some of them are not effective due changes in modern browsers. We have tested on 3 majorly used web browsers.

- **Response Time Analysis:** For response time analysis, we used Firefox 37.0 and Apache Tomcat 8.0 as a cloud server deployed on OpenStack. We used firebug extension in Firefox for calculation of response time. For each request of mentioned size, we have performed 20 reloads and the average time is used for analysis. The results are shown in Figure 6 and Table 2 represents the data analysis.

Figure 6. Analysis of response time without filter and response time with filter

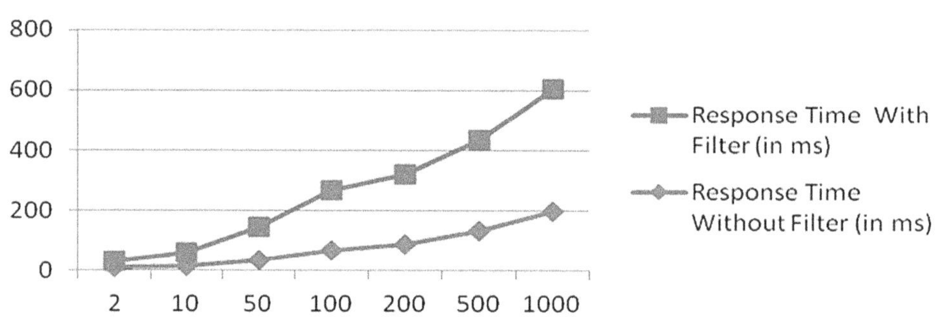

Table 2. Response time without filter and response time with filter

Size (in KB)	Response Time without Filter (in ms)	Response Time with Filter (in ms)
2	9.9034	23.0034
10	13.5675	45.9056
50	35.8989	107.9087
100	69.9094	198.8737
200	89.0939	232.2312
500	134.3545	299.2134
1000	198.4657	405.9034

Testing for XSS Vulnerabilities in Banking Authentication System

A full security testing in online banking systems usually not only involves identification of XSS vulnerabilities; it also involves testing for overflows, threat modeling, error handling, information disclosure, SQL injection, authentication, and authorization bugs. In our work, we only focus to find out security loop wholes in cross site scripting. For this purpose, we identify every single query string parameter, cookies value, and POST data value in the banking application. Testing can be done automatically with different online available tools, but we include some require tools for testing which involves, Paros proxy, TamperIE and Fiddler. For each page, we list out all of the query string parameters, cookie values, custom HTTP headers, POST data values, and other forms of user supplied input into application. We also search out Web services and similar SOAP requests, and identify all fields that allow user input. We list every input parameter separately because we need to test each of them independently. Query string values such as, forwardURL and lang. POST data values such as, name, password, msgBox, msgTitle, and even some cookie values. All of these values are essential and important to test. For example, test case of <script>alert('IIPS')</script> isn't producing the alert box user is expecting. We also can adjust our tests to encode those characters and try again, or find other ways to inject. Figure 7 shows the testing of success and failure of various scripts with different parameters.

CONCLUSION

Banking applications are very fast and growing technology for the last few years. Banking environment cannot be visualized without cloud. Cloud is also very popular and well known technology since last few decades. Cloud based banking application creates a new dimension to organization to think forward apart from traditional approaches because they are less effective and costly. But with these new features, banking application also faces new security challenges for the organizations. The banking components and environment cannot be protected by existing security mechanisms. Additional considerations and protections must be kept in place to ensure a strong security mechanism, planning and preparation as well as training need to be implemented in advance. Our proposed filtering API will filter the cloud server response rather that user input, which will ensure the more insight in attack mitigation. The proposed mechanism employs the API for detection of malicious scripts rather than using a modified browser, which will result in low overhead as discussed in result section, and also it will block attacks vectors targeted to almost

Figure 7. Testing of success and failure of various scripts with different parameters

Area	Page or Cloud Application	OBJECTIVE	Input Type	Field Parameter	(Boundary test) SQL Injection	Test	SUCCESS / FAILED
List of Major Area	List of Pages and Cloud Applications	Attack Possibilities on Login Page	Cookie, query string, HTTP header, hidden field,POST data	List Values	XSS Overflow	Details of the Test	
Login	Login.php		Query String	ForwardURL	XSS	<script>alert("IIPSDAVV")</script>	SUCCESS
Login	Login.php		Query String	ForwardURL	XSS	& ! alert("IIPSDAVV")	FAILED
Login	Login.php		Query String	lang	XSS	22%27><img%20src%3d%22javascript:alert(%27XSS%27)%22>	FAILED
Login	Login.php		Post Data	name	XSS	& ! alert("IIPSDAVV")	FAILED
Login	Login.php		Post Data	name	XSS	<script>alert("IIPSDAVV")</script>	SUCCESS
Login	Login.php		Post Data	password	XSS	22%27><img%20src%3d%22javascript:alert(%27XSS%27)%22>	
Login	Login.php		Post Data	password	XSS		
Message Box	Message.php		Query String	ForwardURL	XSS	<script>alert("IIPSDAVV")</script>	
Message Box	Message.php		Query String	ForwardURL	XSS	22%27><img%20src%3d%22javascript:alert(%27XSS%27)%22>	
Message Box	Message.php		Query String	lang	XSS	& ! alert("IIPSDAVV")	
Message Box	Message.php		Post Data	MsgBoDY	XSS	<script>alert("IIPSDAVV")</script>	
Message Box	Message.php		Post Data	MsgBoDY	XSS	22%27><img%20src%3d%22javascript:alert(%27XSS%27)%22>	
Message Box	Message.php		Post Data	MsgID	XSS	& ! alert("IIPSDAVV")	
Message Box	Message.php		Cookie	UserAuth	XSS	<script>alert("IIPSDAVV")</script>	
Message Box	Message.php		Cookie	UserAuth	XSS	22%27><img%20src%3d%22javascript:alert(%27XSS%27)%22>	
Message Box	Message.php		Cookie	UserAuth	XSS	& ! alert("IIPSDAVV")	

all popularly used web browser rather than for one which was used for malicious script detection.

REFERENCES

Abha C., & Vinita S. (2010). Analytical Research on Indian Online Banking and Users'Privacy. *Global Journal of Enterprise Information System*, 2(1).

Amato-McCoy,, D.M. (2005). Creating virtual value. Bank Systems and Technology, 1(22).

Bates, D., Barth, A., & Jackson, C. (2010, April). Regular expressions considered harmful in client-side XSS filters.*Proceedings of the 19th international conference on World wide web* (pp. 91-100). ACM. doi:10.1145/1772690.1772701

Boganatham, K. K. (2009). Server Side API to Secure XSS [Doctoral Dissertation]. National Institute of Technology Karnataka, Surathkal.

Chou, D., & Chou, A. Y. (2000). A Guide to the Internet Revolution in Banking. *Information Systems Management*, *17*(2), 51–57. doi:10.1201/1078/43191.17.2.20000301/31227.6

Eriksson, K., Kerem, K., & Nilsson, D. (2008). The adoption of commercial innovations in the former Central and Eastern European markets: The case of internet banking in Estonia. *International Journal of Bank Marketing*, *26*(3), 154–169. doi:10.1108/02652320810864634

Hamlet, C. (2000). Community Banks Go Online. *ABA Journal*, *92*(3).

Java response filter. (2014). Retrieved from http://docs.oracle.com/javaee/5/tutorial/doc/bnagb.html

Johns, M. (2011). Code-injection Vulnerabilities in Web Applications Exemplified at Cross-site Scripting. IT Information technology, and innovative, 53(5), 256-260.

Kieyzun, A., Guo, P. J., Jayaraman, K., & Ernst, M. D. (2009, May), Automatic creation of SQL injection and cross-site scripting attacks. *Proceedings of the IEEE 31st International Conference on Software Engineering ICSE '09* (pp. 199-209). IEEE. doi:10.1109/ICSE.2009.5070521

Nagar, N., & Suman, U. (2014, October). A Secure Cloud Environment through Location Signature and HTML5 WebDB.*Proc. of the 3rd International conference on Advances in Cloud Computing* (pp. 31-36). CSI.

Nagar, N., & Suman, U. (2014, October). Two Factor Authentication using M-pin Server for Secure Cloud Computing Environment. *International Journal of Cloud Applications and Computing*, *4*(4), 42–54. doi:10.4018/ijcac.2014100104

Nagar, N., & Suman, U. (2016). Analyzing Virtualization Vulnerabilities and Design a Secure Cloud Environment to Prevent from XSS Attack. *International Journal of Cloud Applications and Computing*, *6*(1), 1–14. doi:10.4018/IJCAC.2016010101

webDEViL. (2008, October 20). Report on Internet Banking Flaws in India Banking.

Sarel, D., & Marmorstein, H. (2003). Marketing online banking services: The voice of the customer. *Journal of Financial Services Marketing*, *8*(2), 106–118. doi:10.1057/palgrave.fsm.4770111

Sathye, M. (1999). Adoption of Internet banking by Australian consumers: An empirical investigation. *International Journal of Bank Marketing*, *17*(7), 324–334. doi:10.1108/02652329910305689

IBM Security Intelligence. (n. d.) Retrieved from: http://securityintelligence.com/cross-site-scripting-attacks-pose-ongoing-threat

Sue, M.P. (2008, July 28). Study: Security flaws threaten online banking. Retrieved from http://www.scmagazine.com/study-security-flaws-threaten-online-banking/article/113010/

Zakaria, K., Karim, M. R., & Aliar, H. (2009). Towards Secure Information Systems in Online Banking. *Proceedings of the 2nd International Conference on Internet Technology and Secured Transactions.*

Chapter 12
Ransomware:
A Rising Threat of new age Digital Extortion

Akashdeep Bhardwaj
UPES Dehradun, India

ABSTRACT

Compared to the last five to six years, the massive scale by which innocent users are being subjected to a new age threat in form of digital extortion has never been seen before. With the rise of Internet, use of personal computers and devices has mushroomed to immense scale, with cyber criminals subjecting innocent users to extortion using malware. The primary victim to be hit the most has been online banking, impacting the security and reputation of banking and financial transactions along with social interactions. Online security revolves around three critical aspects – starting with the use of digital data and files, next with the use of computer systems and finally the internet as an unsecure medium. This is where Ransomware has become one of the most malicious form of malware for digital extortion threats to home and corporate user alike.

DOI: 10.4018/978-1-5225-0864-9.ch012

INTRODUCTION TO RANSOMWARE

With the recent explosion of internet and use of personal computers, has led to cyber criminals' subject internet users to widespread and damaging threats leading to extortion focused on making profits at such a massive scale that has never been seen before. Apart from facing virus, worms, spyware, phishing, Ransomware has now become the new form of malware threat entering the user systems from various infection aiding vectors like browser exploit kits, drive-by freeware apps, malicious email attachments, links offering free software or advertisements offering free cash and incentives through a downloaded file or an unpatched vulnerability in the operating system with a malicious program running a payload that compromises and encrypts the user data files or even hijacking the system itself forcing the innocent user into paying up to the ransom demands before having the data files and system restored and released.

According to NIST, "Malware refers to a program that is inserted into a system, usually covertly, with the intent of compromising the confidentiality, integrity, or availability of the victim's data, applications, or operating system (OS) or of otherwise annoying or disrupting the victim."

The malware injects a malicious code into the user system that installs randomly in the system location as an executable. This code then takes the user system hostage by preventing users from accessing their computer systems normally, stopping certain applications or input devices from running or encrypting user data files and using scare tactics like asking the user to either do something like pay a ransom amount in form of Bitcoin or fill in surveys before releasing the system or data. Ransomware uses different psychological, social-engineering, coercing, behavior-economic techniques to convince the users to pay the ransom to regain control of their systems.

Malware is an umbrella term that represents malicious software whose sole purpose is intentionally malicious in nature operating with different actions and concealment technologies for attacking end users. Some of the common malware are virus, worms, Trojans, backdoors, rootkits, bots and spyware as

- Virus one of the most commonly available globally, represents multiple subcategories of the malware versions. This malware is parasitic in nature, unable to survive alone and generally found replicating itself by copying onto other application programs.
- Worm comprise of malicious code causing maximum damage to data and user information. It has the capability of replicating itself via networks, using inbuilt email or scan engines to identify and spread to other hosts. Worms tend to exploit OS vulnerabilities, executing other malware as payload.

- Backdoors are standalone alternative entrance to user systems bypassing the existing security mechanisms built into OS and application systems. Usually created by programmers and accidently left behind when testing specific code functionality at the last moment, however, these are planted and utilized by attackers in order to enjoy continued privileged access of an application or the server system.
- Trojans are programs that resemble a legitimate code or application, however have some malicious code inbuilt. These are based on Homer's Iliad on the concept of the Trojan horse and are non-replicating parasitic in nature, requiring a legitimate application program to hide and execute.
- Spyware are the most popular tools used for Identity thefts, comprising of malicious code to spy on victim's activities and system and then for stealing sensitive information. Identity theft has become a major risk for users accessing their data from unsecured or public systems.
- Rootkits are a set of programs to alter the standard functionality of operating systems in order to hide any malicious activity done by it. These replace common operating utilities like kernel, net stat, ls, ps with their own set of programs with the intention of any malicious activity gets filtered before displaying results on screen.
- Bot is a program that performs action based on instructions received from the master controller system. These are mostly autonomous programs residing on unsuspecting end user systems, used majorly in the 'dark community' to accomplish malicious tasks as dictated by the controllers. A network of such bots is called a botnet. IRC is an example of bot that is used to communicate with other botnets.

Ransomware started with misleading applications and free software programs around 2005 as the use and acceptance of Internet grew (Savage, Coogan, & Lau, 2015). These free and fake applications came across as system enhancement tools (Registry Care or Perf Optimizer), fake spyware removal tools (Spy Sherriff) hidden with add-ons or hidden bundles of browser hijackers, spyware apps, ad libraries which mainly impacted the Windows OS. Typically, such applications exaggerated performance or spyware issues and promised to remove those after a payment was made when in fact these applications did not do anything at all.

The first Crypto Ransomware appeared in form of Trojan.GPcoder in late 2005 using weak symmetric algorithm custom encryption techniques having same key for encryption as well as for decryption. Around mid-2006, the Crypto Ransomware (Kotov & Rajpal, 2015) concept took off with emergence of Trojan.Cyzip which after copying the original data into password protected encrypted files, deleted the original data and files. Another password protected file archiver called Trojan.

Figure 1. Misleading apps, fake antivirus, lockers and crypto ransomware from 2005-2015

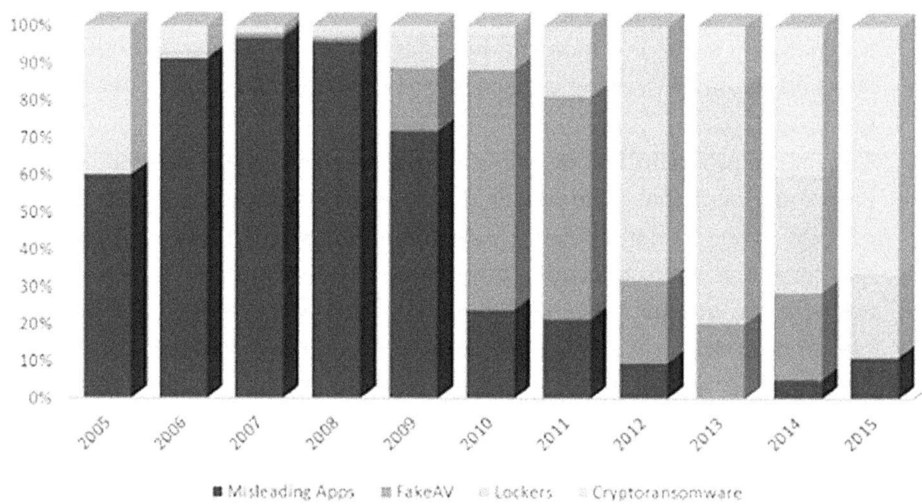

Archiveus made the attacked victims buy medicines online instead of asking for a ransom payment.

Around 2008-2009 fake and misleading applications came up which simulated the features and functionalities of antivirus or performance enhancement applications which performed fake scans and displayed large number of security and virus issues on the system. The end user was coerced to pay a certain amount after which another fake scan was rerun apparently fixing the earlier issues and viruses. These malwares even had annual and offered annual support services on payment.

The years from 2010 to 2012 saw the attackers move from fake applications to more sophisticated ransomware in form of Locker Ransomware in which access and control of the user systems was compromised. Trojan.Randsom.C mimicked Windows Security Center update message that locked the user system display a screen message and forcing the user to call a high rate premium number in order to activate the license and access the system. These reformed from reporting misleading or fake issues to actually introducing errors and faults into the systems and posing as law enforcement notices instead of anti-virus or performance optimizers.

Since 2013, the last few years (Wyke & Ajjan, 2015) have seen the cyber attackers going back to using Crypto Ransomware techniques using social engineering as their tool to propagate their malicious intents and seeking ransom demands. However, these new age Crypto Malware are a lot more advanced, capable, stronger in their encryption operations and wiping out session keys from memory after usage making it difficult to get the decryption key as compared to the legacy Crypto apps. The attackers enhanced their approach by using better key management and choosing the right encryption algorithm like RSA, 3DES and AES.

Ransomware malware have two major variants – the most common version is Crypto Ransomware or data locker that encrypts the files and data while the other version is Locker Ransomware that locks down the user systems, applications or input devices, thereby preventing the users from performing normal operations. Both of them are designed to deny access to what rightfully belongs to the end user and a ransom asked in return yet the approach for each ransomware is different. As recently as January 2016, Emisof Malware engineers found a new ransomware package (Wyke & Ajjan, 2015) that encrypts user files before releasing and restoring the files after accepting a ransom demand. This worked in a different manner as compared to other ransomware variants as the code was purely java script and the package was being offered online as a service. This has been named Ransomw32 and effectively meant that ransomware has now evolved to become Ransomware as a Service.

Crypto Ransomware

Crypto ransomware or Data locker once injected into user system, works in stealth mode to search for files and data with such extensions as FLV, RTF, PPT, CHM, TXT, DOC, CPP, ASM, XLS, JPG, MP3, MP4, CGI, KEY, MDB, PGP, PDF and acts as a data locker.

During this time the system continues to work normally as critical OS and system files are not targeted or the system's functionality is not tempered to raise any suspicion. Then the malware encrypts the user files and data. This makes the files and data unusable to the user forcing them to pay in order to obtain the decryption key.

Figure 2. Crypto ransomware demand screens

Unlike traditional malware, Crypto ransomware does not steal any user information, it just compromises their access and does not try to be stealthy after data has been encrypted, since detecting the malware does not help decrypt and recover the data.

Locker Ransomware

Locker ransomware or computer locker locks out the compute resources and input interface devices like mouse or keyboard, denying access to computer systems itself.

The malware then asks user to pay a fee in order to restore normal access and even ensures limited functionality to just interact with the Ransomware like keeping mouse and limited numeric keyboard keys enabled to input ransom amount and code.

This malware keeps the system and files untouched and can be removed to restore a system to its original state relatively easily as compared to the data locker malware.

Figure 3. Crypto ransomware demand

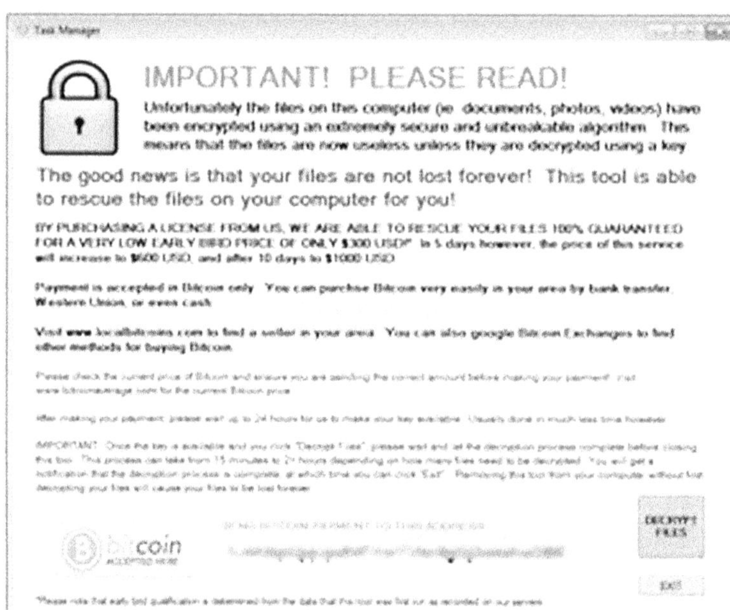

Figure 4. Locker Ransomware demand notifications

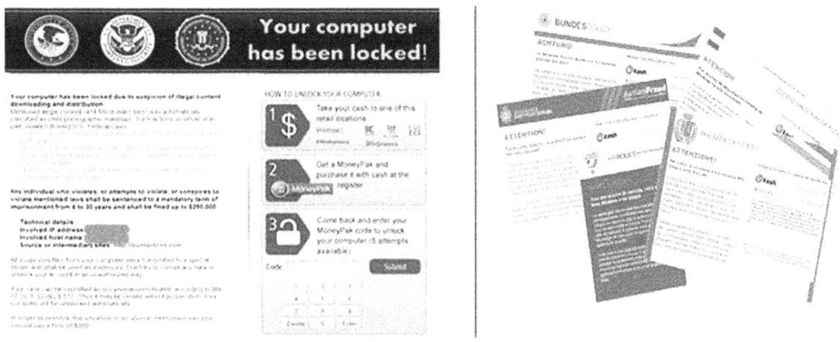

Figure 5. Locker ransomware demand notifications

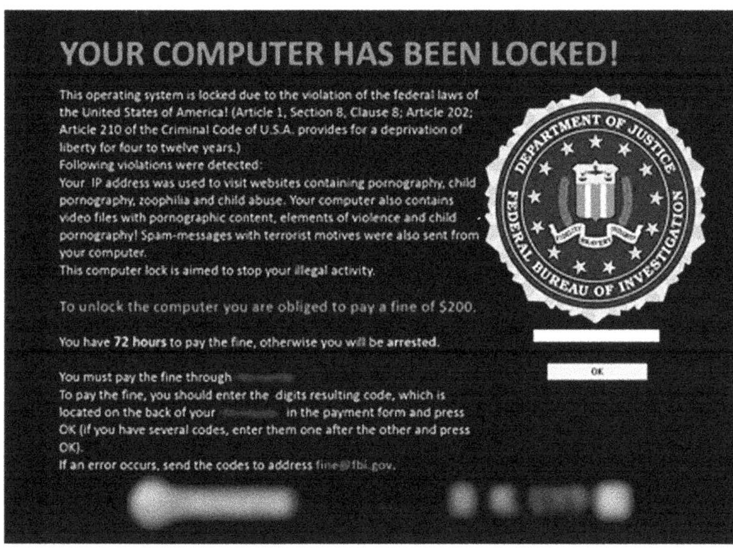

INTRODUCTION TO BITCOINS

Bitcoins started in 2008 by MIT under open source credential, Bitcoin is a network that consists of a new form of commercial payment and an exchange medium and virtually Digital Cash. Any individual can purchase Bitcoins or Crypto Currency (Baek & Lebeck, 2015) from online exchanges, direct sellers or in person with hard cash or credit cards. Bitcoin transactions are stored in a public worldwide ledger known as Block Chain, where in money exchange is seen by the entire network almost immediately and recorded making it difficult to identify the owners, however the system is not anonymous.

Bitcoin is not actually owned by any single company and are more like email exchanges where no one can block two entities from exchanging emails, details or Bitcoins among themselves. Bitcoins are used for sending or receiving money with anyone, anywhere globally at a very small transaction cost. The payments cannot be blocked or frozen. Short of turning off the Internet, and keeping the Bitcoin network switched off, Bitcoin seems to be seemingly unstoppable.

Bitcoin $ price has been making headlines in 2015-16 and has jumped past $450, almost reaching $500. The rise in Bitcoin value has been phenomenal; about 25 Bitcoins are created every 10 minutes globally. In 2011 1 Bitcoin was under $1, currently 1 Bitcoin is worth 100s of US$. As Bitcoin's demand and popularity increases, 1 Bitcoin might well be worth hundreds of thousands of dollars. For the user, Bitcoin is nothing more than a mobile application or computer software providing a wallet through which the user can send or receive bitcoins.

As Cyber Security experts battle against malware infections and Ransomware extortions, the financial losses for innocent user and corporate keep increasing as recently in August 2015 FBI announced US $18 million as "stolen" due to Ransomware. India ranks 9th for Ransomware attacks worldwide even as US, UK, Japan, Australia and Germany are others. These type of extortion attacks are usually done by infecting the user systems with a malware as a rouge malicious code. The top Ransomware malware abound globally is Crowti.Here is how the Bitcoin transactions work:

Figure 6. Bitcoin price over the years

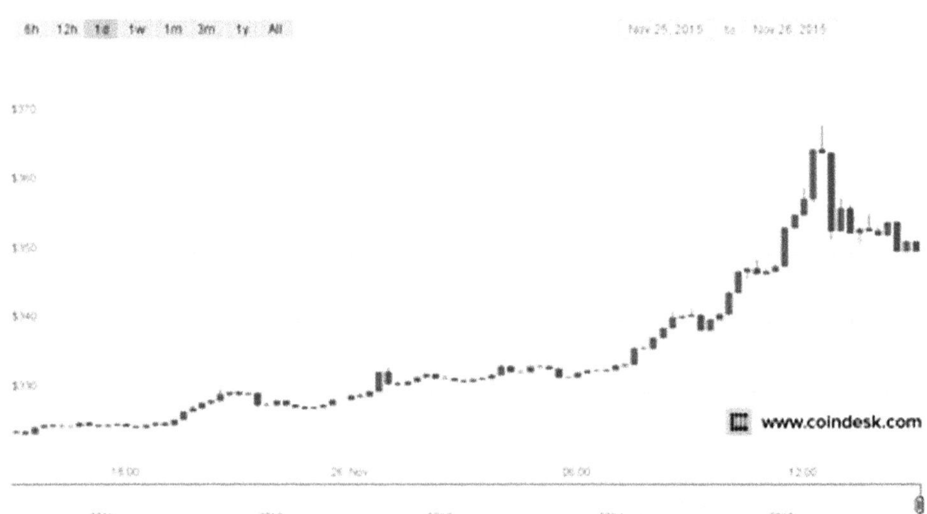

Figure 7. Bitcoin notification

- The user downloads a wallet software to their systems or phones are initiate Bitcoin payment
- This is broadcasted on the worldwide Bitcoin network or the World Ledger
- Every 10-15 minutes, groups of computers (or miners) collect few hundred transactions, combining them into a block or transaction
- This block is validated by a hash function and re-broadcasted to the Bitcoin network
- The miners keep performing checks for the validity of such transactions and blocks
- In this process, the miners are awarded 25 bitcoins per transaction. This is the incentive for providing compute power to the Bitcoin network
- The validated blocks are added to a block chain that serves as live record for the Bitcoin network
- The payee can then use his wallet software to see their own ledger, having coins received or sent

MALWARE AND ONLINE BANKING SECURITY

Internet users, large Corporates or small enterprises and most home users are increasingly moving to the usage of online banking and use of mobile applications when performing online banking transactions rising from 30% in 2007 to over 70% in 2015. Online banking is convenient, faster and simplifies life working from home or office instead of going over to a bank and then standing in a long queue.

However, a significant percentage of these online banking consumers are at a major security risk of fraud from malware attacks infecting their handhelds or user systems. While banks and commercial institutions have been bolstering their online banking web portals and mobile apps working overtime to reassure customers by bolstering the security of their online banking portals and banking mobile apps. With malware payloads that can seek 16-digit credit card numbers or user passwords, the online banking security is always doubted just as mobile banking apps can be compromised as smart phones and android OS are known to have security flaws causing any online transaction from an infected desktop or mobile to be deliberately seeking danger. The "It-Will-Not-Happen-To-Me" mindset usually gets attacked first. Only the fools reckon that malware would not infect their systems or mobiles (Davis, Bodmer & LeMasters, 2014). The main reason why malware has been able to survive despite several attempts to mitigate is due to its unpredictability with the ethical teams always a step behind the cyber attackers. UK has online banking fraud as the fastest growing crime going from £ 60 million in 2014 to over £ 150 million in 2015. RBS revealed 5000 of their customers fell victim to online scams and fraud.Online banking security fraud is typically done in the following ways:

- **Malware**: Infected user systems can steal end user credentials and password being entered on the bank portal by recording anything being typed for accessing a particular bank URL.
- **Remote Purchase**: Stealing user credentials and card via malware or unsolicited email or phone call.
- **Phishing**: Cyber criminals posing as genuine bank portals, elicit unsuspecting users who logon with their credentials and passwords. Malware can affect user systems, modifying DNS redirecting them to the malicious bank site posing as the user's bank.
- **Cloned**: Cyber criminals clone cards from magnetic strips on a card and use for online purchases
- **Identity Theft**: Infiltrating user account, taking over the account and requesting a new card and pin

Tips for safe online banking

- **Use Unique Account ID and Passwords**: User Id and password should be unique and never be the same.
- **Regular Malware Scan**: Use of antimalware scanner is a must for those performing online transactions
- **No Online in Public Wi-Fi**: Shops and establishments offering free Wi-Fi have a risk of the network traffic being snooped using sniffers that can decipher logon credentials and passwords.
- Never give your banking and personal details on phone to someone claiming to be from a bank.
- Banks need to perform Behavioral patterns analysis, Web signature Injects detection, User Input analysis as well as inbound/outbound traffic analysis.

The authors reviewed Online Banking Malwares targeting customers (Aljawarneh, Al-Rousan, Maatuk, A. & Akour, 2014) of financial and banking institutions. The study found several banking malware being sold as software apps 'off-the-shelf'. Dridex and Dyre were identified as the top online banking malwares which can bypass regular user authorization methods like TAN Codes, Hardware Token Numbers and SMS. Dridex malware steals customer information or modifying information on the fly using HTML injections, sent to an unsuspecting user as a word or excel document attachment from a bank. On opening the attachment, the payload copying itself to mapped and removable drives and opening a backdoor to download malicious payload on the victim's systems. This malware also features novel routines and techniques to bypass detection. Dyre steals financial data by hiding in email attachments posing as an email from a tax consultant. The proposed anti-malware solution discussed in this chapter holds enough promise to mitigate and block malware from being detected and spreading.

RANSOMWARE PROPAGATION

Ransomware infects user systems from various factors and there are several way that help propagate malware into user systems and lead to Ransomware infection (Aljawarneh, Alkhateeb, & Al Maghayreh, 2010).

Some of those are discussed here.

Table 1. Lists recent ransomware attack methodologies

Ransomware	Attack Method	Ransomware Payment
Trojan.Punder.A	Copy different types of files to hidden folders	Remit $10 to designated Chinese Industrial and Commercial Bank
Arhiveus	• Link all original files in the 'My Documents' folder to point to a single file named EncryptedFiles.als • Deletes all original files • Creates a HOW-TO-GET-YOUR-FILES-BACK. TXT ransom demand text file directing the victim to receive decryption keys, which exists in malicious codes	• Suggests victims purchase some products from Russian pharmaceutical websites and send the order ID. • The attacker validates the order ID and then emails the decryption key.
Trojan.Randsom.A	A distracting notification window displays over other application windows on the screen with a bluff that every 30 minutes a file is being deleted.	Remit $10.99 through Western Union
Trojan.PGPCode	Encrypts all files using RSA algorithm	Notify victims to remit $200 to a designated E-Gold account.
Trojan.Cryzip	• Compress document files (txt, doc, rft, etc.), data base files or multimedia files → password-protected ZIP. • The decryption key used for the ZIP file is stored in file Cryzip.	Notify victims to remit $300 to a designated E-Gold account. Specific instructions are given.
Onion	Encrypts files with 72-hour deadline using TOR network	Requires bitcoin payment to release

- **Traffic Redirection**: This is the most common method to entice the user and redirect the web traffic to other site hosting the malware as an exploit kit. Usually the redirected traffic originates from porn sites to a portal offering free games or upgrade for user applications. If the user accepts and downloads the freeware, malware payload exploits vulnerabilities in the user computer leading to lock or encryption of their systems and files.
- **Malvertisements and Spam**: This involves using a drive–by-download process making the user click a malicious advertisement flashing on the screen for freebies or money on web site being browsed or opening emails with attachments or link to entice users to access web portals having the Ransomware malware. The email on first look seem to have legitimate senders like the user's energy bill, tax returns, legal notifications or even job seekers asking to open the attachment or clicking a link and updating it with the user's latest information. While the user opens the attachment or browses the web site, in the background the malware sets about infecting users.

- **Ransomware as a Service**: With the growing trend of digital extortion, cybercriminals have started providing Ransomware as a service or RaaS (in cloud computing terms) offering to carry out malware attacks on payment or from the profits and running the attacks like a business service from the cloud.
- **Botnets**: These are distributed by way of downloaders compromising user systems and then downloading the malware as a second step process. The downloaders are legitimate software like free games or tools which don't have the malware themselves; they download the malicious code and infect the user system later.
- **Social Engineering**: At times Ransomware has an inbuilt functionality of self-propagation to spread to other systems by either sending emails to user's Outlook address book or from their phone list sending out SMS. This method is effective for malware to spread as it comes from a legitimate source and gets accepted easily. W32.Ransomlock.AO is a screen locker malware that infects a user system and also spreads to others.

Figure 8. Ransomware propagation

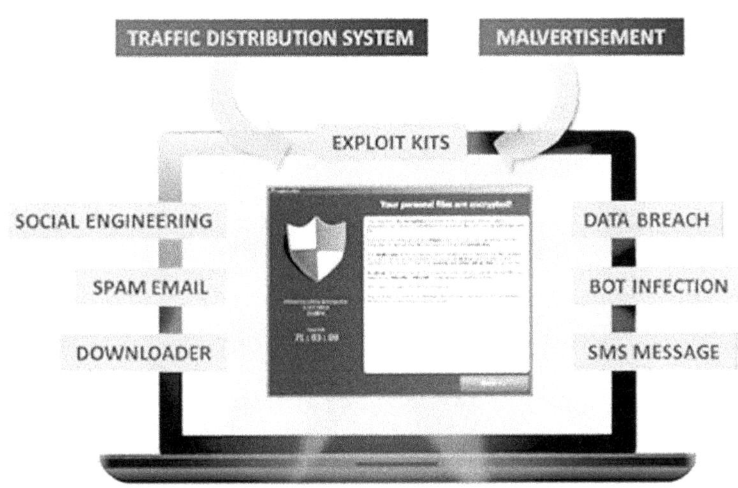

RANSOMWARE TECHNIQUES

While Ransomware is devised for extortion of money from innocent users making them victims of malware attack, the manner in which this is performed can be varied from operational and technical aspects. Most malware hide and the below mentioned folders to execute and propagate.Few Windows registry settings are also modified to enable the malware to manifest and stay 'alive':

- HKEY_LOCAL_MACHINE\SYSTEM\CurrentControlSet\Services\
- HKEY_LOCAL_MACHINE\SOFTWARE\Microsoft\Windows\CurrentVersion\
- HKEY_LOCAL_MACHINE\SOFTWARE\Microsoft\WindowsNT\CurrentVersion\

Figure 9. Spam email containing CHM file as a RAR payload

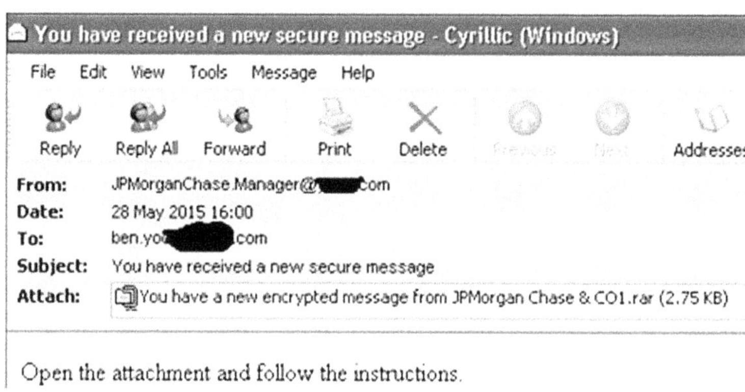

Table 2. Impact factors in Windows operating systems

Folder Locations	OS Process	Services Stopped
• ApplicationData%\Microsoft\ • %Temp%\File.dll • %System%\File.tmp • %Temp%\File.tmp • %System%\File.dll • %Program Files%\Movie Maker\File.dll • %All Users Application Data%\File.dll • %Program Files%\Internet Explorer\File.dll	• svchost.exe • services.exe • explorer.exe	• Windows Defender Service (WinDefend) • Windows Error Reporting Service (ERSvc) • Windows Error Reporting Service (WerSvc) • Windows Automatic Update Service (Wauserv) • Background Intelligent Transfer Service (BITS) • Windows Security Center Service (Wscsvc)

- HKEY_CURRENT_USER\SOFTWARE\Microsoft\Windows\CurrentVersion\

Recent crypto Ransomware use symmetric as well as asymmetric encryption methods. Here we take a look at few file encrypting ransomware.

CryptoWall 4.0

CryptoWall 4.0 has been released recently which displays a new redesigned ransom note, new filenames, and encrypts name of the files along with the file data. Initially the cyber world was alerted to this new malware variant by blog postings about being infected by what was originally called as 'Help your files' ransomware. After sample analysis, it was in fact determined to be a new version of CryptoWall.

The most significant change in the new CryptoWall version 4.0 is the ability to encrypt file names of the encrypted files. Typically file names get changed to a unique encrypted name similar to 68p7k6037z.x1nep or 9102on67c.63a8. The encryption on files is done to make it seemingly difficult in order to gain any information about the files to be recovered, making it all the more frustrating for the impacted victim. The second feature change in CryptoWall 4.0 is a redesigned HTML ransom note

Table 3. Impact factors in Unix and Linux operating systems

Folder locations	OS Process
• /bin/login /bin/ps /bin/.login /tmp/ /etc/rc.d/ /usr/scr/ • /usr/bin/.ps /etc/ /usr/sbin/ /usr/spool/ /usr/lib/	• Apached ftpd lpd • rpc.statd zssld

Figure 10. Folder displaying encrypted files after CryptoWall 4.0 impact

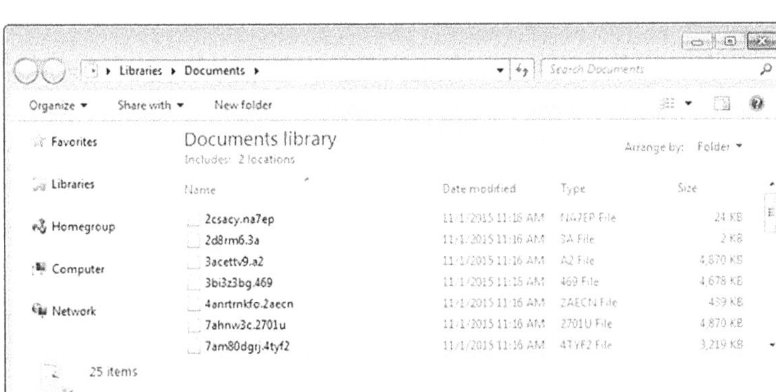

displaying names to help_your_files.html as well as displaying ransom quotes with annoying arrogance to impact the victim further as:

- Cannot find the files you need?
- Are you now unable to read the contents of the files?
- Do you know the data and your files have been encrypted?

The new CryptoWall version continues to use the traditional email distribution methods with the payloads analyzed coming in form of a email attachment having a zipped word document resume. The resume files are actually Java Scripts, which when executed download an executable to the Windows %Temp% folder, and executing it.

In this new version, CryptoWall 4.0 has similar installation characteristics and communication methods as the previous versions. During the communication phase with the Command Control Servers, RC4 encryption is used creating the victim's unique ID from the MD5 hash of the computer name, volume serial, processor information, and OS version details. Much like the previous versions:

- 4.0 injects itself into the Explorer.exe
- Disables System Restore, deletes all the Shadow Volume Copies, and turns off Windows Startup Repair using BCDEdit.

Figure 11. Resume having JavaScript file sample

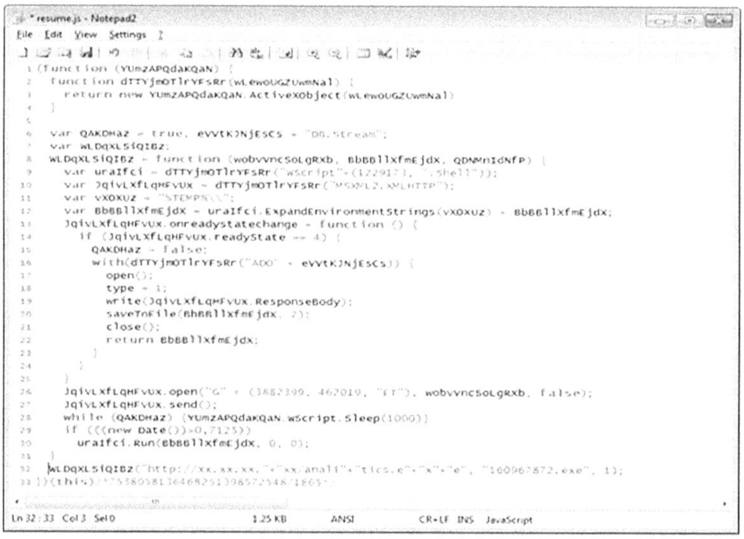

- Then injects itself into svchost.exe and encrypts data on all the local, removable and mapped drives.
- After encryption is completed, the ransom notes that explain the mishap, impact and purchase information is launched and displayed.

CryptoWall 3.0

This ransomware uses AES Symmetric and RSA asymmetric encryption techniques by encrypting user files with a common 256-bit AES key, however using a different RSA private key to decrypt for each infection. However, access to internet and server is required for communicating with the live central command control system of the attacker and Tor networks for the ransom demand payments.

Crypto Wall typically downloads the CHM payload into the system's TEMP folder where its contents in form of interactive HTML files that are usually compressed holding java scripts and other image files. When the Crypto Wall starts its execution, it opens up a new explorer.exe instance, injects and executes its malicious payload and more critically ensures there is no back track to recover the encrypted data and files by deleting the volume shadow copy using VSSADMIN tool (command: Vssadmin.exe Delete Shadows /ALL /QUIET). The malware then launches a new SVCHOST.exe process with user privilege and injects it script code into that new process. This then tries to connect to proxies to find a live central command control system of the attacker which generates and supplies the public key specifically for the victim displaying ransom notes and instructions to follow. This starts the file encryption for all folders and file and copies the ransom notes into them. Finally, the user's internet explorer is started displaying the ransom demand.

Crypto Wall typically encrypts the following mentioned file extensions with Symmetric AES 256 key as xls, wpd, wb2, txt, tex, avi, ava, ass, asp, js, py, odt, obj, msg, mpg, mp3, lua, key, jpg, hpp, gif, pl, db, c, h, ps, cs, m, rm, swf, sql, rtf, RAW, ppt, png, pem, pdf, pdb, PAS, eps, DTD, doc, der, crt, cpp, cer, bmp, bay. Once encryption is done for a file, the Crpto Wall copies the file with an additional random character encrypting the file contents and deletes the original file. After all the files are encrypted, Crypto Wall flashes the ransom content on the system screen which has instructions about the ransom demand to be met.

Torrent Locker or Tor

This malware spreads exclusively through spam email campaigns and localized to specific geographical regions. This ransomware uses AES to encrypt file and demands their release in Bitcoin and goes a step further by accessing email addresses of the victim and further advancing its spread.

Figure 12. Ransomware payment demand note

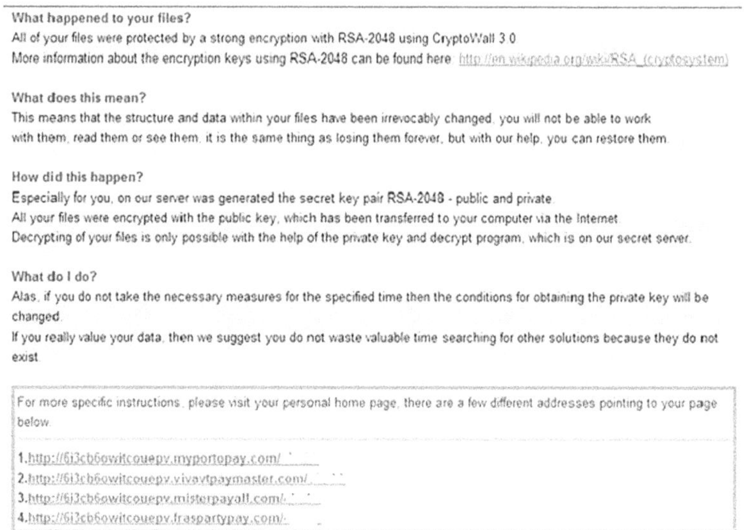
What happened to your files?
All of your files were protected by a strong encryption with RSA-2048 using CryptoWall 3.0
More information about the encryption keys using RSA-2048 can be found here: http://en.wikipedia.org/wiki/RSA_(cryptosystem)

What does this mean?
This means that the structure and data within your files have been irrevocably changed, you will not be able to work with them, read them or see them, it is the same thing as losing them forever, but with our help, you can restore them.

How did this happen?
Especially for you, on our server was generated the secret key pair RSA-2048 - public and private.
All your files were encrypted with the public key, which has been transferred to your computer via the Internet.
Decrypting of your files is only possible with the help of the private key and decrypt program, which is on our secret server.

What do I do?
Alas, if you do not take the necessary measures for the specified time then the conditions for obtaining the private key will be changed.
If you really value your data, then we suggest you do not waste valuable time searching for other solutions because they do not exist.

For more specific instructions, please visit your personal home page, there are a few different addresses pointing to your page below:

1.http://6i3cb6owitcouepv.myportopay.com/
2.http://6i3cb6owitcouepv.vivavtpaymaster.com/
3.http://6i3cb6owitcouepv.misterpayall.com/
4.http://6i3cb6owitcouepv.fraspartypay.com/

Tor infections spread with spam email which typically have Microsoft Office document with macro embedded to download the payload and execute the torrent locker file. “Process Howling” technique is used by Tor where initially a legitimate windows system process is launched, then suspended so the malicious code can be injected and then the process resumed. Tor uses Explorer.exe to further its activities and deletes the volume shadow copies using the VSSAdmin tool to reduce the chances of encrypted files to be recovered from a previous system restore point as also Tor disables the internet browser’s Phishing filter so as to disable any future warnings when the ransom page is displayed to the victim.

Tor usually resides in the C:\Windows folder with a strange random name (like ycizsrqlys.exe) and has a registry key entry for runtime persistence. Tor then contacts the central command control system with a POST request over HTTPS. The command system responds with the ransom demand to be displayed and Tor generates the encryption key which is sent back to the command system before the data and files are encrypted.

Tor Locker harvests email addresses of the victim, sends them to the central command control system for further spreading the Tor malware. The new Tor variants have become smart and enhanced their encryption process, where in the use of AES in CBC mode and part encryption of files is now being followed. AES in CBC mode results in a unique alphanumeric key stream for each file being encrypted, which actually means the files cannot be decrypted without the original key.

Figure 13. Ransomware payment demand note

Part encryption manages to encrypt only the first 1MB of the file (instead of the 2MB sized originally), rendering the file to be useless. Tor communicates with the central command control system using POST over HTTPS sending the Encrypted AES key, Encrypted file numbers and the victim's friends email addresses.

After the files were encrypted, the ransom demand is displayed with instructions to follow to be paid in Bitcoins. Tor also offers a single file decryption option which gave the victim some sort of confidence that using the instructions, they could actually get back their encrypted data after payment was made. After the payment was made, the user would typically receive a link and access a personalized decryption tool and the AES decryption key.

Ransom32

This is the latest variant in the malicious world of ransomware, making Ransomware available as a service. Initially this was a malware campaign with signups being managed with a hidden Tor network server seeking a simple Bitcoin address to send the funds generated to that worked based on Java Script which disables java script execution in browsers which do not stop this malware from infecting.

After the Bitcoin address was provided, access to the administration panel is allowed which provide various attack statistics about number of people who have paid or number of infected systems at that point of time or change the ransom amount

Figure 14. Ransom32 Bitcoin address to send the funds to

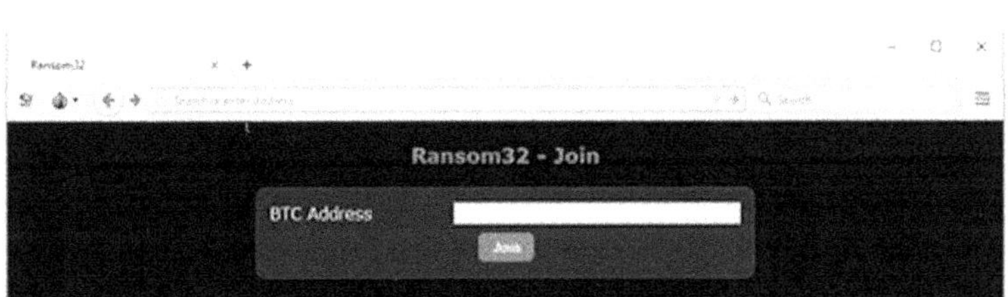

of Bitcoins as well as create the message boxes or ransom notes the malware is supposed to display.

On clicking the download button, a 22MB sized malware file "client.scr" gets generated (previous variants rarely exceeded 1MB). The Client.scr was infract a self-extracting RAR with automated script that unpacked the contents to a temp folder and executed an application (Chrome.exe) that contained the malicious malware code. The malware code turned out to be a windows applications framework development code using script to create a "Chrome service" and establish Tor network access to its command control system to negotiate the Bitcoin address and send the ransom to as well as interchange the cryptographic encryption keys before displaying the ransom note.

Figure 15. Ransom32 Admin Panel to check status of the malware attack

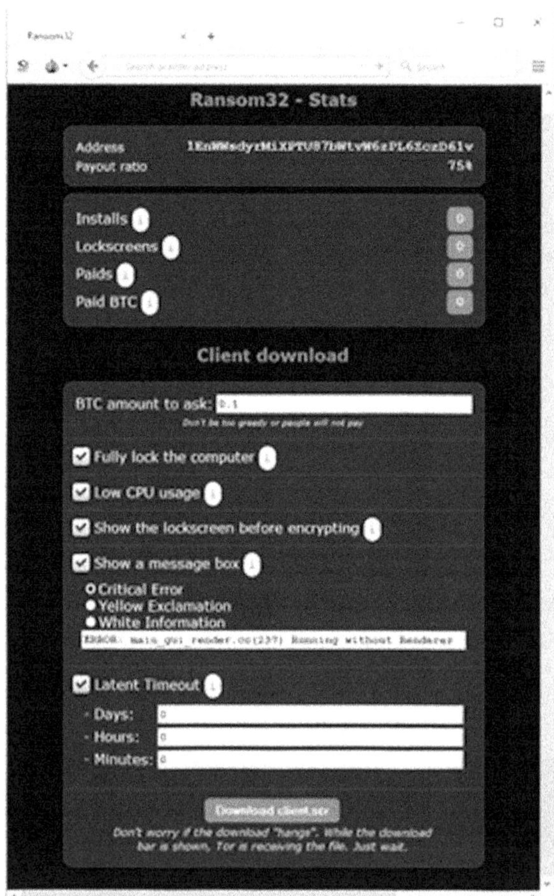

The malware goes about encrypting the victim files using AES 128bit with CTR as a Block mode – so a new hey got generated for each file, making it a lot more difficult to restore.

Screen Lock Ransomware

This ransomware displays a message on the user system screen with the malware Trojan constantly getting the locker window to foreground in a continuous loop and even android mobiles changing the lock screen PIN utilizing APIs from the operating system itself to perform this task. The ransomware infects the OS locking the user screen and covers the entire desktop displaying only the ransom demand windows. On android mobiles, this ransomware tricks the mobile user into granting admin privileges, allowing the malicious app to make changes in the Android configuration, resetting the screen lock PIN.

Windows and Browser Lock

This ransomware executes entirely within the web browser, displaying the ransom message on the system screen or browser controlling the background threads and applications ensuring the message is active. The malware is not executable and the ransom message page contains just images and HTML code running JavaScript executing within the web browser like other variants which have binary executables. This is propagated mainly using “client side” web technology by the attackers. The

Figure 16. Ransom32 demand ransom note

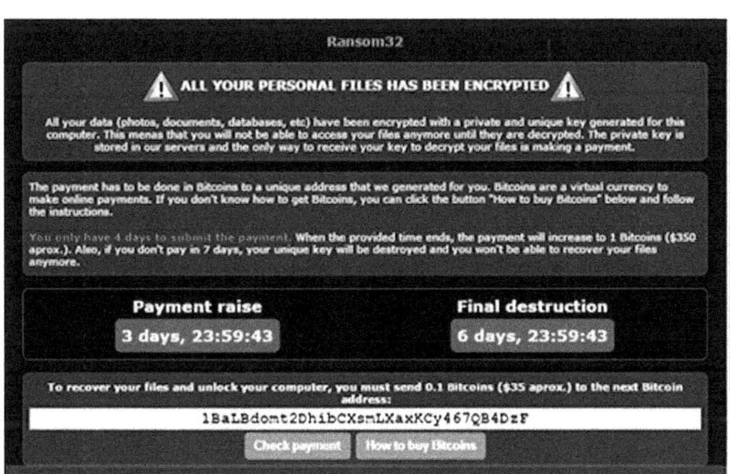

Figure 17. Screen lock ransomware

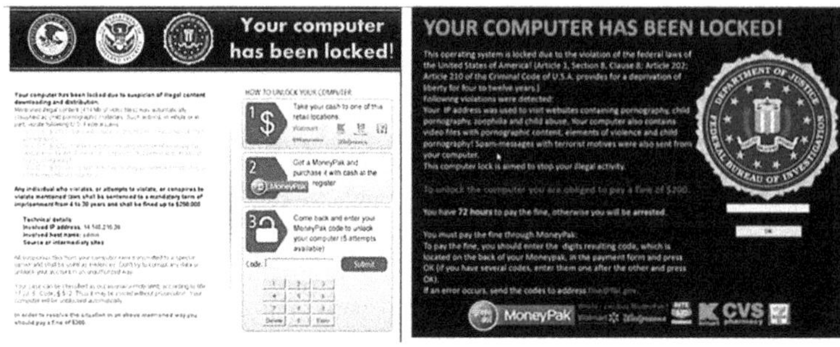

ransom page has HTML code, images and iframes and point to other ransom pages that are called whenever the user attempts to exit the page.

POPUP Advertisements

As POPUP advertisement get displayed when accessing web sites, the main concept and goal behind popup malware is to get the end user to click the pop up at least once. The malware attacker gets paid for each click by having a unique ID for its malware application.

Once clicked, another web window opens that takes the end user to another URL that has malware waiting to be pushed by using java or flash. Initially web browsers had pop up blockers but those blocked even useful popup windows and attacker methods improved to bypass the web browser popup blockers using a simple Java script as below that bypassed the traditional user's web browser pop-up blocker:

```
<HEAD>
<SCRIPT LANGUAGE="JavaScript">
<!-- Begin
function popUp(URL)
{
day = new Date();
id = day.getTime();
eval("page" + id + " = window.open(URL, '" + id + "', 'tool-
bar=0, scrollbars=0, location=0, statusbar=0, menubar=0, resiz-
able=0, width=200, height=300,left = 740,top = 375');");
}
// End -->
</script>
```

```
<form>
<input type=button value="Open the Popup Window"
onClick="javascript:
popUp('http://mailicious.url.net/expl01tu')">
</form>
```

Detecting Pop-Ups

Mozilla web browser released a popup blocker patch update in 2005 that prevented Java and Flash pop ups and using a simple function we can detect a popup blocker and work to bypass the blocker as:

```
function DetectBlocker() {
var oWin = window.open ("","detectblocker","width=100,height=10
0, top=5000,left=5000");
if (oWin==null || typeof(oWin)=="undefined")
{
return true;
}
else
{
oWin.close();
return false;
}
}
```

In recent times, Adobe Flash is being used for pop up advertisements making the pop up being virtually not getting detected as no popup s are displayed and the advertisement run from the web landing page itself or the current window. Then they push the ransomware script and execute it on the fly.

The main reason for using popups by malware creators is to redirect the unsuspecting end user to another location with hardly any alarming change in the URL such as GOOGLE.com or icic.com or icicic.com instead of the correct URLs. Such malicious redirects give an opportunity to the attackers to a copy of the site they wanted to browse (say a bank site) that is in fact filled with multiple attack vector injection points where after the user clicks anywhere on the page and becomes infected with malware leading to ransomware executable files to be pushed to their systems (even asking for their bank logon and password).

A more sinister method being employed by the attackers for planning Ransomware attacks is to push scripts and get access to user trace logs for servers and sites. This method is used to detect which sites are accessed regularly by the user and collect his/her browsing pattern and plan an advanced intelligence method by the attackers against those sites and push their malicious malware applications to those sites for ransomware attacks. By modifying the metadata of internet search engines for specific keywords, user are misguided and attackers target those end users who regularly first search for a word and then access the web site from a search engine, instead of typing the web site name.

RANSOMWARE PROTECTION

For any security process to be successful, end user awareness and education is most critical. The average user accessing the internet are in fact the first and last line of defense. There is a critical need to ensure the end users are kept aware of data security, possible impact should ransomware or other malwares attack them and most importantly, the process end users need to follow. This can preempt loss of data and minimize damage and no amount of high end technology or security tools and protection can protect an organization from one simple mistake of an end user. However, it must be accepted that to have end users keep up with each and every potential threats and new attack vectors and perform their bit is asking for too much.

Minimizing Ransomware Impact

The impact of Ransomware can be minimized by ensuring end user follow the steps mentioned below:

- **Security Awareness Training and Procedures:** Are essential and mandatory to ensure the end users in an organization are well informed about computer and internet usage. Awareness needs to be generated about topics such as those mentioned below:
  - **Security Policy:** should cover the enterprise policies, procedures and SLAs including the dos and don'ts to remind the end user about their role and responsibilities
  - **Clear Desk:** ensuring all sensitive and confidential material, records, papers or documents are kept secure and locked away by the end user on the work space when leaving the office for the day, clearing.

- **Access Passwords:** Defining authentication factors (single, two or three), code length, complexity, use of alphanumeric, manner of storing passwords is the single most important aspect
- **Viruses:** end users need to be aware about the approved process procedures to follow in case of malware or virus outbreak occurs and what the end users looks out to prevent further infection.
- **Email:** emphasizing spam and mail attachments so users understand this vector where many malware samples enter the network. Users should also be aware of your organization's email usage and abuse policies.
- **Internet Usage:** Ensure users understand that when working access to the Internet is a privilege and not a right. End users must be made to understand "Dos and Don'ts" when accessing Internet and what to be aware of and what to avoid.
- Computer Theft Instructions and User Awareness for users help in ensuring computing and portable electronic devices and corporate data.
- Social engineering awareness ensures users understand how to verify someone's identity and what information they should and should not share about the organization. The human tendency to be helpful with information is the biggest downfall of any organization.

- Always have an updated Antivirus, Anti Malware and Web browser monitoring software with a personal firewall running on each user system. While strong personal firewall enforcing rules for what goes out or comes into the system and having an Anti-Malware application blocks most malicious code from infecting the user systems, ensuring the security applications are up to date is most critical.
- Maintaining a regular back as often as possible or after a major project to either an external hard disk or an online cloud backup service reduces the threats, as the user can simply wipe and reimage the system to default starting afresh and restoring data.
- Popup blockers should always be kept enabled as these are the main tactic used by the attackers to display luring advertisements and offers. Users need to simply close the popup if finding them suspicious.
- Never open links and attachments inside spam emails or from unknown senders. Attackers create fake sites, trying to entice users to enter their user id and passwords.
- Not all the time depends upon security controls, organization should have expert team to handle such situations
- Input of threat Intel feeds so that proactively block can be placed for highlighted Ransomware URL & IP addresses.

- Weekly/monthly scanning of network with the newly/available Ransomware IOC's(Indicator of compromise)
- Removal of non-reputational applications
- Always keep updated applications such as Java & Flash players.

Malware Prevention for Home Users

- Always be wary of web sites that prompt for software installations.
- Do not install new software from your browser unless you absolutely understand and trust both the web page and the software provider.
- Scan every item and any program downloaded through the Internet prior to installation with updated antivirus and anti-spyware software.
- Be aware of unexpected emails attachments even if they are from known sources.
- Always enable the automatic updating feature for your operating system and apply new updates as soon as they are available.
- Always use an antivirus real-time scan service.

Malware Prevention for IT Administrators

- Deploy HTTP-scanning and content management systems.
- Do not allow unneeded protocols to enter the corporate network.
- Deploy vulnerability scanning software on the network and perform frequent audits.
- Restrict user privileges for all network users.
- Deploy corporate anti-spyware, anti-malware and Data loss prevention solutions.

In case the system does actually get infected and the screen displays the Ransomware note, immediately disconnect from Internet. This would deny any personal data from being sent back to the attackers, then shutting down the computer would stop encryption process to continue. By reimaging and reinstalling the OS and application software and restoring data from back, the user would be to normal operations.

RESEARCH REVIEW

The authors reviewed existing solutions and threat vectors for online malware detection, blocking and removal. Some of the existing options for detecting and blocking malware, spyware, viruses are as

- **Dynamic Analysis**: Automated analysis of suspicious files which are scanned and analyzed for signatures or impact using tools. Reports are produced at the end of analysis with information like registry keys used by malware, configuration changes done, device, file or network activity trend. However, an automated scan do not necessarily provide detailed insight. These are signature based scans comparing and matching against a database of known malware,
- **Static Analysis**: Manual analysis taking a deep dive look at the malicious file's activities looking at file headers, embedded resources, payload, hashes, signature, meta data among host of other properties that are analyzed. Heuristic scans are done here that do not need a signature analysis. Rules algorithms, commands or which point to its malicious properties are evaluated to detect the malware.
- **Cloud Services**: Using IaaS to build virtualized environment, record and analyze behavior of malicious files and predict the next action or occurrence event. This is a real-time protection and system are updated several times a day to mitigate zero-day attack vectors. The system integrates with antivirus engines with a lightweight agent running on user devices (laptop, desktop, mobiles) to monitor any deviation or new files in the user devices.

Identifying threat Vectors

Behavioral Malware analysis used the below mentioned threat vector end points to monitor as:

- User Outbox generates thousands of emails in a very short period of time
- Sudden generation of new programs with executable capability
- Modified Auto run registry keys
- Modification of the end user "hosts" file.
- Creation of "autorun.inf" file on a USB or removable disk or on a network folder.

Proposed Solution

The authors implemented Malware Detection as a Service (MDaaS) which provides malware detection, analysis and reporting services (Hasan Mahmoud Kanakar, Madihah Modh Saudi & Modh Fadzli Marhusin, 2015). Testing the malware in this manner requires the malicious code be run and observe its behavior, even as this results in infect the sandbox system making it potentially unsafe. Hence the authors performed the tests on isolated system environments.

In this solution, three environments are implemented having virtual machines with malware tools. User device snapshot is taken to determine any changes to OS, Registry, processes or files and lightweight agent installed that constantly pushes user system and device snapshot and status is sent to Monitoring servers. The agent can also send the malicious file from the user devices to the test bed environment for analysis, detecting and blocking.

Figure 18. Registry keys showing unwanted programs (malware apps) in startup

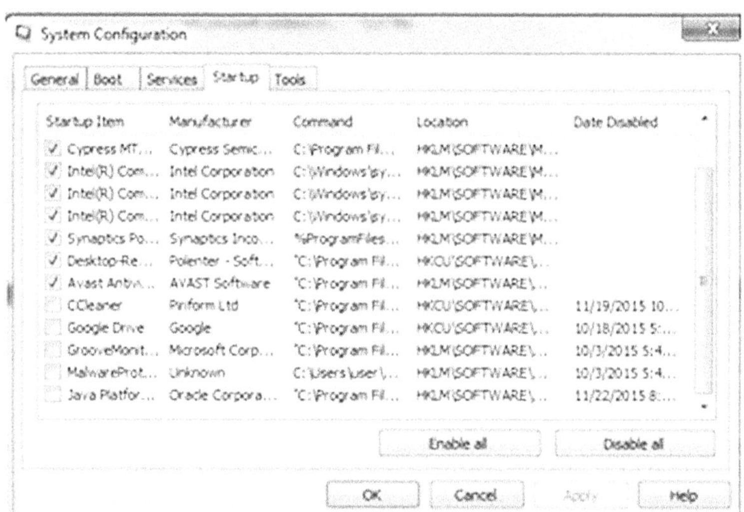

Figure 19. Hosts file

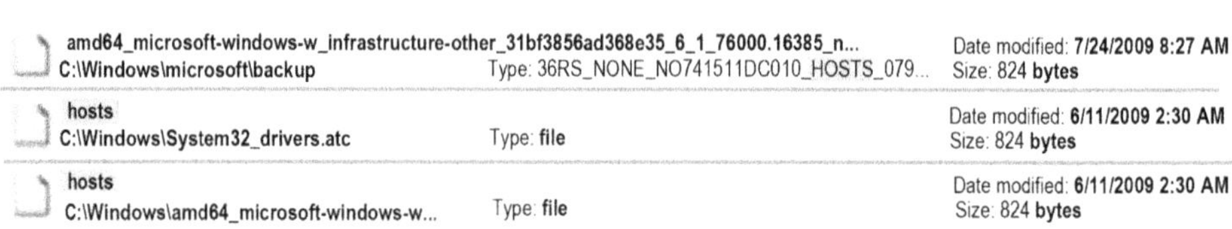

Figure 20. Autorun file with malware payload

- The servers are commissioned and decommissioned each time a new malware analysis is completed. This is done to avoid any chance of the malware polymorphic features get into action and potentially infecting the analysis servers, leaking data or payload to other systems, contacting the attacker for new action to perform or even upgrading themselves. The malware detection service environments are implemented using virtual machines running VMware Servers with Windows 2008 Server hosts in three lab environments.

Environment Setup

Malware Behavior Analysis Environment

The first environment is configured for Malware Behavior Analysis, with server snapshots taken before and after receiving malware payload files and logs from user devices that may have got infected.

Infrastructure tools implemented:

Figure 21. Malware detection environments

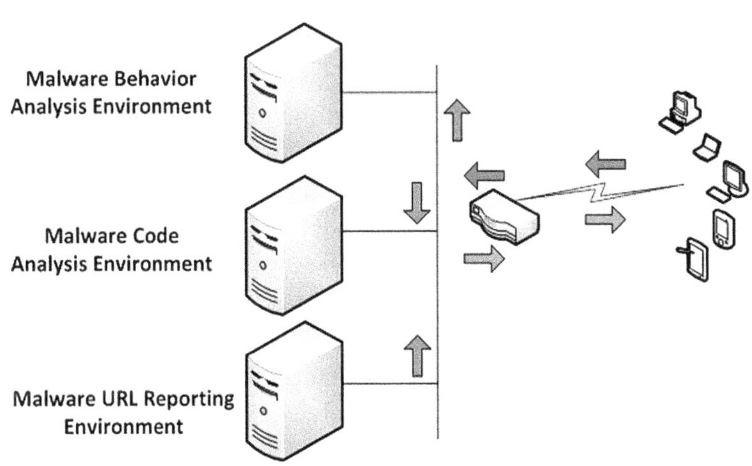

- Process Monitor with Proc DOT tool to determine the manner in which the malware starts to infect and way in which the processes then interact with the system, infecting OS, Files and Registry.
- Wireshark sniffer for Network Bandwidth Monitoring and observing the malware payload attempts to contact the attacker, DNS or other external sources (P2P servers) for engaging bot traffic and trying to download the payload binaries or java scripts.
- Process Explorer and Process Hacker tools to observe malware behavior processes like opening of new ports, contacting attacker IP addresses.
- Lightweight agent combined with Regshot tool to take user system and device snapshot for before and after state comparison.

Malware Code Analysis Environment

The second environment is setup with Malware Code Analysis tools analyzing instructions in their assembly code and memory dumps from memory.

Infrastructure and tools implemented:

- IDA Pro tool used as disassembler to parse Windows OS executable files
- Scyalla a Memory Dump tool used to obtain code from system memory. This is a novel way of code analysis since executable payload instructions are mostly encoded, getting extracted in RAM only during execution time.

Malware Reporting Environment

This environment acts as the reporting system for Internet, analyzing Web URL proactively for sites hosting malware code or payloads. This also checked the user system and devices taking snapshots for before and after analysis.

Infrastructure and tools implemented:

- MalWr, Threat Expert tools used to perform automated behavior analysis of payload executables.
- WebInspector MxToolKit for real time threat assessment and reputation of Web URL hosting suspected malware payloads and codes.
- Process Monitor with ProcDOT – analyze processes read-write, update or delete registry entries. This helped the authors ascertain the manner in which malware attempts their actions and attacks.
- File and System Registry analyzers for collecting the user data and checks for presence of suspicious malware. Basic dynamic analysis method is done for analysis and the behavior observed.

RESULTS

The approach to follow include identifying suspicious codes and applications based on their heuristic characteristics, code and behaviors. As compared to signature based antivirus scanning systems, this process can have its own advantages. The Anti Malware scanning security is shown here that it can be offered as a cloud service with the scanners operating from a secure cloud platform. When the above suspicious actions were observed on the endpoint system, the MDaaS would detect and help block malicious or infected application programs and report the incident to the cloud sandbox system. In this way, other users of the same application program get benefited from the experience of other users.

Apart from having the advantages of being a cloud based services which offers user driven implementation, elasticity and pay-as-you-use model. This even helps save huge costs and promotes the concept of BYOD (Bring your own Device). MDaaS approach also has few more advantages:

Figure 22. Before and after malware detection as a service results

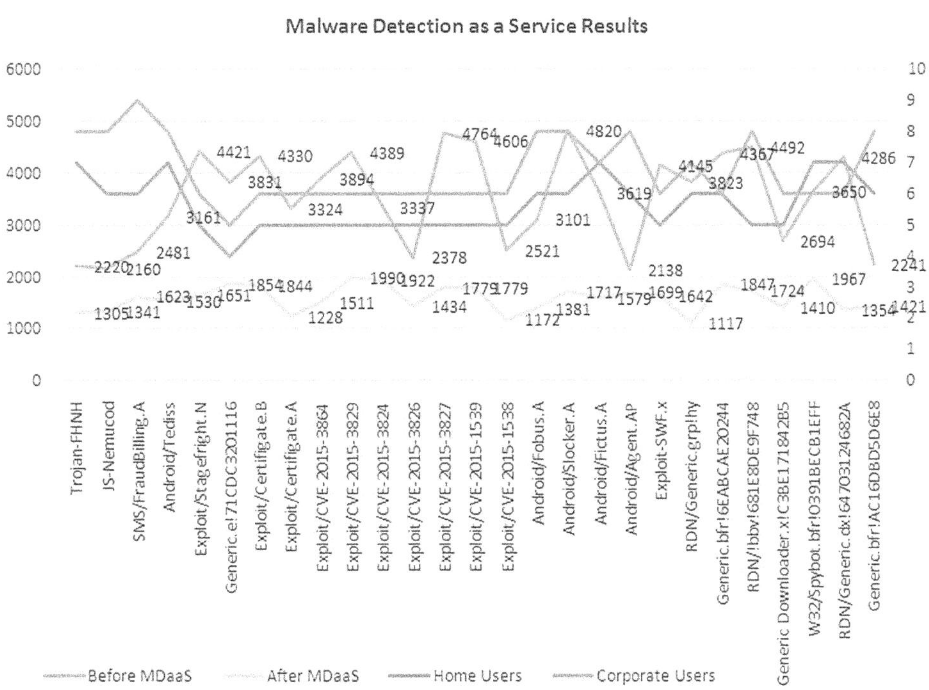

- Public Cloud Scanners are not limited by hardware infrastructure, making them highly scalable and elastic. Thus tracking malware over long periods, searching in huge anti-malware database and have robust malware profiles of targeted threats is not confined to lack of computing power.
- Cloud Service is customizable, having the ability of being updated thru any method, OS type or version apart from the default set of images. In fact, organizations can upload their preferred images, signatures or even a custom environment configured for scanning their employee systems.
- Being a Cloud based sandbox, the service is not limited by geography. When attackers target office employees located in remote regions than on premise sandbox is running (usually organization's IT Data center), the cloud service will quickly update employee systems globally and help avoid and block the attack.

CONCLUSION

In this chapter we reviewed the origins and subsequent evolution of ransomware and can easily conclude that Ransomware is increasingly being used for ransomware demands to victims seeking to create an alternative source of direct income. Starting from less persuasive forms of direct revenue generation using misleading applications such as PC performance tools, cybercriminals learned and iterated over the years and with each step, ratcheted up the levels of aggression. Online banking industry has been hit hard as many cyber threats due to malware have risen immensely.

Malware attacks progressed from misleading apps to fake antivirus scams and then later moved onto pure Ransomware in the form of locker and crypto Ransomware threats that are so prevalent today. The Bitcoin can change the financial landscape we see today and the growing demand of this digital currency application might just be the beginning for a new world order. Malicious code is seen as the primary enabler for any attacker to help gain access and maintain a foothold on the end user system. The probability of finding malware programs and malicious codes during detection is useful when used with the proposed cloud based sandbox environment.

REFERENCES

Aljawarneh, S., Al-Rousan, T., Maatuk, A. M., & Akour, M. (2014). Usage of Data Validation Techniques in Online Banking: A Perspective and Case Study. *Security Journal*, *27*(1), 27–35. doi:10.1057/sj.2012.10

Aljawarneh, S., Alkhateeb, F., & Al Maghayreh, E. (2010). A Semantic Data Validation Service for Web Applications. *Journal of Theoretical and Applied Electronic Commerce Research*, *5*(1), 39–55. doi:10.4067/S0718-18762010000100005

Baek, R., & Elbeck, E. (2015). Bitcoin as an Investment or Speculative Vehicle? A First Look. *Applied Economics Letters*, *22*(1), 30–34. doi:10.1080/13504851.2014.916379

Davis, M. A., Bodmer, S. M., & LeMasters, A. (2014). *Hacking Malware and Rootkits Exposed*. New York: McGraw-Hill.

Kanakar, H. M., Saudi, M. M., & Marhusin, M. F. (2015). *A Systematic Analysis on Worm Detection in Cloud Based Systems*. Asian Research Publishing Network.

Kotov, V., & Rajpal, M. S. (2015). Understanding Crypto Ransomware: In-Depth Analysis of the Most Popular Malware Families. *Bromium*. Retrieved from https://www.bromium.com/sites/default/files/bromium-report-ransomware.pdf

Savage, K., Coogan, P., & Lau, H. (2015). The Evolution of Ransomware. *Symantec*. Retrieved from http://www.symantec.com/content/en/us/enterprise/media/security_response/whitepapers/the-evolution-of-ransomware.pdf

Wyke, J., & Ajjan, A. (2015). The Current State of Ransomware. Sophos. Retrieved from https://www.sophos.com/en-us/medialibrary/PDFs/technical%20papers/sophos-current-state-of-ransomware.pdf

Chapter 13
Insider Threat in Banking Systems

Qussai Yaseen
Jordan University of Science and Technology, Jordan

ABSTRACT

Insider threat poses huge loss to organizations since malicious insiders have enough knowledge to attack high sensitive information. Moreover, preventing and detecting insider attacks is a hard job because malicious insiders follow legal paths to launch attacks. This threat leads all kinds of attacks in banking systems in the amount of loss it causes. Insider threat in banking systems poses huge harm to banks due to the importance and attractiveness of assets that banks have. This chapter discusses insider threat problem in banking sector, and introduces important surveys and case studies that show the severeness of this threat in this sector. Moreover, the chapter demonstrates some policies, technologies and tools that may prevent and detect insider threat in banking systems.

DOI: 10.4018/978-1-5225-0864-9.ch013

INTRODUCTION

Insider threat is one of the riskiest threats that worry individuals and organizations. A malicious insider is a trusted insider who misuses his/her privileges in a system to hinder the system's operations, damage data, or disclose sensitive information which causes damage to the system. According to different surveys, such as the CSI survey (Richardson, 2010), Forrester Research (Forrester Research, 2010) and the ISBS survey (InfoSecurity Europe, 2010), insider threat causes huge harm to individuals and organizations. The CSI survey (Richardson, 2010) stated that the cost of data records lost to insider attacks is greater than the cost of those lost to outsiders. This is because insiders are familiar with the system, and attack the valuable records, while outsiders steal what they can access.

Financial institutions are especially subject to insider threats due to the highly sensitive stored information and their highly dependence on information technologies. According to CERT (Cappelli, Moore & Trzeciak, 2012), the financial sector suffers from the most cases of fraud, and the second most in IT sabotage and theft of intellectual property carried out by malicious insiders. Furthermore, there are non-malicious insiders who may pose risks unintentionally, through mistakes or bad behaviors that may be exploited by external parties. Non-malicious insiders may be fooled by some attackers to click on URL that contains malware, or may mistakenly send corporate materials to unauthorized recipients.

This chapter discusses the problem of insider threat in banking systems. It introduces the problem of insider threat in information systems and its growing threat. Furthermore, the chapter presents some survey results that show how risky is the insider threat. Next, the problem of insider threat in banking systems is introduced. Basically, the chapter discusses the special sensitivity of this problem in banking systems, and how insider threat poses high risk in this sector. Surveys results and case studies that show the increasing risk and loss posed by insider threat and threaten this sector are introduced. In addition, the chapter discusses how recent exposure of technologies such as Cloud Computing increased the threat and maximized the vulnerabilities that may be used by insiders to harm banking systems. Next, the technologies and tools used to fight insider threat in banking systems are introduced.

INSIDER THREAT

Insider threat is a critical security problem. The threat of insiders can be posed unintentionally or intentionally by malicious insiders. Malicious insider threat is defined as the threat that is caused by a person who has authorized access privileges and knowledge of the computer systems of an organization, and is inspired to antagonistically influence the organization (Brackney & Anderson, 2004). Insiders could be employees, contractors, or business partners. They have the capabilities, which outsiders do not have, that enable them to launch complicated attacks.

According to different surveys (Gordon, Loeb, Lucyshyn & Richardson, 2005; CERT, 2011), insider threat is as risky as outsiders' threat (hackers) due to the extreme harm that it may pose. The FBI Computer Crime Survey (Gordon, Loeb, Lucyshyn & Richardson, 2005) reported that trusted insiders were responsible of about 33% of all security breaches in 2005. Similarly, the Cyber Security Watch Survey (CERT, 2011) showed that 58% of attacks are caused by outsiders, whereas 21% of attacks are caused by insiders. Moreover, the survey shows that insider threat is as costly as outsider threat. However, Forrester Research (Forrester Research, 2010) showed that insider threat is the costliest type of incident. In addition, after analyzing the security practices of more than 300 European, American, and Australian enterprises, Forrester estimated that insiders were responsible for 75% of data security incidents in those enterprises in 2010. Similarly, Verizon Business breach report (Cooper, 2008; Subashini & Kavitha, 2010) stated that outsiders exposed about 30,000 records, whereas insiders exposed about 375,000 records indicating that the cost of insider threat is greatly more than the cost of outsider threat.

Obviously, many surveys have shown that insider threat is an immense and urgent security problem. Yet, organizations are investing very little to defend their systems against insider threat. Most organizations' investments are focused on protecting their assets from outsiders' threat. Organizations rely on insiders' morals and ethics not to violate systems security. Nonetheless, surveys show that this assumption is incorrect. Mechanisms that have been proposed for protecting data from outside attacks are inappropriate to secure systems from authorized users who may misuse their privileges. Therefore, the development of mechanisms that protect sensitive data from insiders has become a key demand due to the amount of harm that can be caused by malicious insiders.

Researchers in insider threat mitigation proposed some techniques for fighting insider threat at system level or application level such as relational databases. Many approaches focused on visualizing the capabilities an insider has through using graph based models. The purpose of this representation is to discover how knowledgeable an insider is and what risk s/he poses through his knowledge. The knowledgebase of insider may have the values of data items s/he recently accessed and read, or the information s/he gets when s/he read an object. In addition, the knowledgebase may contain the access rights s/he has on data items and the type of accesses such as read, write, etc. Furthermore, the knowledgebase may contain the dependencies among objects or data items that the insider knows.

Insiders may attack systems directly using their access privileges to attack systems components. They may rely on some techniques to hide their footprints, which enable them to harm the systems with small probability of discovering their attacks. Moreover, insiders may discover some vulnerabilities in the organization laws or installed countermeasures. They may use these flaws with their knowledge about other systems components to attack the systems.

Serious attacks may be launched by insiders using dependencies among data items or objects. Therefore, determining dependencies among data items or objects is a major part in handling insider threat. A dependency between two data item, components or objects A and B is defined as the existence of a relationship between their values. That is, we say that B depends on A, denoted by A→B, when the value of B depends on the value of A, and any change in the value of A will result in the B's value (Yaseen & Panda, 2012, 2009). Dependencies could be direct, as in the later example, or transitive. A transitive dependency among the data items, components or objects A, B and C, denoted by A→B→C exist when a change in A's value will result in a change in B's value, and in turn, this will result in a change in C's value. In this example, we say that C depends transitively on A, or there is a transitive dependency between A and C (Yaseen & Panda, 2012; 2009). Insiders may use these dependencies to launch attacks. For example, suppose that an insider, say Alice, has a read access to a data item A, where A is regular information. In addition, that the underlying system has the dependency A→B, where B is sensitive information that Alice should not access. Alice can infer information about B using the dependency A→B and her authorized access to A.

Dependencies among data items or objects could be naïve or complex. Naïve dependencies are easily detectable by systems designers or security officers. Therefore, they can take those dependencies into account when distributing access privileges to prevent insiders' attacks. However, some dependencies are complex, especially transitive dependencies, and may be discovered and used by malicious insiders. Therefore, security officers should pay too much attention to dependencies and what information insiders can get using these dependencies (Yaseen & Panda, 2012, 2009).

Insiders get knowledge about dependencies during their work in organizations' systems. They can get a part of the knowledge through their activities and transactions in systems. This accumulated knowledge enables insiders to discover the strengths and weaknesses of the defense mechanisms and the systems' structure. Nonetheless, outsiders have little information (in comparison to insiders) about the structure of the systems they attack. Moreover, insiders use legal paths to breach the systems' security throughout legal access, whereas outsiders rely on violating systems security using different methods such as bogus URLs in phishing attacks, SQL injection, Man-in-the Middle attacks, etc.

Insiders may launch standalone or collaborative attacks. Standalone attacks mean that an insider launch attacks alone using his knowledge and access privileges only. Meanwhile, collaborative attacks are launched by two or more insiders. In this type of attacks, insiders share their knowledge about the victim system, including dependencies, and use their access privileges to harm the system. Collaborative attacks may greatly harm organizations more than standalone attacks since the capabilities of collaborative insiders together are much more than the capabilities of individual insiders. However, most discovered insider attacks were launched by individual insiders. Obviously, collaborative attacks are harder to form since insiders need to talk together and agree about the attack. This process includes some risk that some insiders may need not to take.

INSIDER THREAT IN BANKING SYSTEMS

The world of banking has been changed dramatically in the last few years. The immense growth of information technology tools forms a major cause of this continuous change. Smart credit cards, online services, the spread of E-commerce applications, the outsourcing of information and applications, the cloud computing and the rapid growth of the number of third parties are few examples of this change. The fast speed networks and internet have made many networked applications applicable, and increased the spread of such applications among clients. Banks are in a race to provide a friendly and easy access services to clients. They invest large amount of money in building a technological infrastructure to achieve their goals. One aspect of technological change in how organizations dealing with their information is the increasingly relying on third party systems for storing information and providing many of digital services. Many banks find themselves in need to adapt such cloud services because of cost reduction, scalability and resources availability in the huge infrastructures of cloud providers. However, the technological evolution has brought major security concerns, especially in banking systems due to the high sensitive information that is processed in such sector.

The type of information is a major factor of its attractiveness to attacks. Information in banks such as credit card numbers, account numbers and budgets are targets for different types of attacks due to its high sensitivity. Outside attacks form the larger percentage of attacks of information in banking systems. The evolution of internet and networking has led to an immense growth on the number of attackers who can attack information systems in banks. Hackers around the world costs banking sector huge amount of money yearly due to credit cards stealing, money movements and financial compensations for clients. Therefore, highly cost countermeasures should be purchased, installed and updated to prevent, detect and mitigate cyber security attacks. In banking systems, the tradeoff between the costs of defense mechanisms and information leakage always pushes towards buying expensive security tools to mitigate security attacks and prevent information leakage.

Banks have to adapt new security policies and countermeasures because of the continuous change in attack tactics followed by intruders. According to the report issued by the New York Department of Financial Services (Cuomo & Lawsky, 2014), the cyber-attacks against banks are becoming more complicated, wide spreading quickly and increasing immensely. The report demonstrated that banks face different types of intrusions. Account takeovers forms 46% of cyber intrusions. Identity theft intrusions formed about 18% of cyber intrusions in the surveyed institutions. Telecommunication network disruptions and data integrity breaches were reported by 15% and 9.3% respectively. Breaches caused by third-party partners formed about 18% and 15% of small and large institutions, respectively. ATM skimming/point-of-sale schemes were reported by 23%, mobile banking exploitation (in large institutions) formed 15%, and insider access breaches were reported by 8% of intrusion incidents.

The stream of attacks costs financial sector a huge loss. According to US Government Accountability Office (United States Government Accountability Office USGA, 2015), information about the losses by U.S. depository institutions because of cyber-attacks is limited. The report demonstrated that some sources estimate the losses for about $23 millions of dollars in 2013. Moreover, the report says that the loss is increasing dramatically. However, the report assures that the loss is much more than this number because many institutions do not report their actual loss. Outside attacks by hackers forms a huge loss to financial sector. However, insiders form more harm to banks and the loss an insider causes to banking sector is much greater than a harm caused by a hacker.

The Risk of Insider Threat in Banking Systems: Surveys and Case Studies

Hackers are not the only threat to information systems in banking sector. Insider threat poses much more harm than outsiders. Insiders attacking banking systems costs banks a huge loss since insiders usually attack highly valuable information, while outsiders steal what they can access. The reason behind this result is that insiders are familiar with the technological infrastructure of banks. Moreover, they usually know where the valuable information is stored and how they can access it. In addition, insiders follow legal paths that are hardly traceable or detectable. Meanwhile, outsiders follow random paths and scan many ports before they succeed in attacking systems. These attempts can be detectable before a breach happens, and in most cases, they are easily detectable because of the footprints left.

Banking and financial sector leads all other sectors in insider threat, and has the greatest loss because of this problem. Many surveys showed the risk of insider threat in banking systems. A study by Carnegie Mellon University (Cummings, Lewellen, McIntire et al., 2012) examined 23 incidents of insider activity in the banking and finance sector. The study found that 91 percent of victim organizations suffered financial loss ranges from hundreds of dollars to hundreds of millions of dollars. According to a recent RSA presentation (Richards, 2013), in 10 years, the average loss per industry is $15 million, and the average cost per incident is $412,000. Moreover, the damage in many instances was more than $1 billion. However, many insider threat cases showed that the loss caused by insiders is terrifying and it is much greater than what was found in those surveys as will be discussed shortly.

The history of banking system is full of insiders' cases that have caused too much damage to banks. For example, Kweku Adoboli caused $2.3 billion in losses for UBS, Switzerland's biggest and most error-prone bank (Walker, 2012). In 2011, Adoboli used his knowledge of the bank system and infrastructure to create fake trades to hide his track. He bet the bank's money on the future price of various stock indices. To hide his crime, he created offsetting fictitious transactions. His knowledge as an insider helped him in taking advantages of some vulnerabilities of the securities law, and in using them for exchange-traded funds (ETFs) to book these factious transactions. As an employee in the front disk, he knew that ETFs rules do not require brokers to produce the confirmation of trades immediately. This rich information gave him the advantage to attack the system. Obviously, outsiders may not have this kind of information to launch this type of attacks.

The case of trader Bruno Iksil is another example about how insiders in banking sector could cause catastrophic loss to banks. In May 2012, Jamie Dimon, the CEO of JP Morgan Chase & Co, announced that the bank lost about $2 billion because of bad trades in London. After this announcement, the bank lost about $14 billion of its share price. This catastrophic loss was caused by the trader Bruno lksil or "the London Whale" as he is nicknamed. The "London Whale" took bad bets on a credit derivatives index. Later, Dimon discovered that this process caused the bank a loss of about $6.2 billion, not $2 billion as estimated early (Childs, 2013).

The cases discussed in the previous paragraphs are few examples of the risk of insider threat. Obviously, one insider threat case may cause loss greater than the loss caused by too many outsiders' attacks. Definitely, insider threat may be intentional or unintentional. However, in both cases, the loss in banks because of this threat is catastrophic. Therefore, suitable mechanisms are needed to mitigate this threat. To design, install and update insider threat countermeasures, security officers in banking sector should have a detailed knowledge about the approaches that insiders follow to attack systems.

Approaches of Insider Attacks in Banking Systems

Insider attacks are becoming frequent, more sophisticated and more harmful. Continuously, insiders develop new types of attacks to bypass countermeasures. Moreover, some organizations do not invest enough money to defend their systems against insider threat. Most investments focused on protecting organizations systems against hackers. They usually rely on insiders' ethics and morals to not harm systems, which is a wrong assumption and proved by many surveys and insider attacks cases.

The method of attack may be determined by the type of target. Some attacks used insider privileges to get unauthorized benefit without harming clients' accounts. Other attacks target clients' accounts. The most prominent target in banking systems is the attacking of Personally Identifiable Information (PII) of clients (Cummings, Lewellen, McIntire et al., 2012), which is account number, credit or debit card number, in addition to any required security code, access code, or password. However, some attacks do not involve PII. This section discusses some approaches that were used by insiders to attack banking systems.

Attacking Banking Policies

The first type of attack discussed here does not target clients, and is performed by a high privileged insider. The insider in this type targets banks using the loans policy. In this attack, an insider, say Alice, has an access to loans database. She has the read and write privileges in this access. Alice applies for a loan in her bank, which approves her request according to the bank policy. Alice gets an amount of X money as a loan. Later, Alice uses her privileges several times to maliciously increase her personal loan amounts, and withdraws the resulting difference and removes essential loan documentation to hide the fraud.

An example of this attack is the case discussed in an interesting study conducted by CERT program in Carnegie Mellon University. In that case, an insider working at the loan department at a bank applied for two legitimate loans of $39000 in total. The bank approved her loans according to the bank policy. Later, she used her full privilege in reading and modifying loans to increase her loans amount several times and withdrew the difference. To hide her crime, she removed essential loans documentation. Totally, the insider stole $112,000 using this approach. Fortunately, her crime was discovered during a routine audit, which found missing loan documents from her account.

Attacking Personally Identifiable Information (PII)

The second type of attacks targets the Personally Identifiable Information (PII) as described previously. In this attack, the insider uses his/her privileges in viewing clients PII to copy and use it fraudulently. The insider can exploit his/her access to the PII of clients in various malicious ways. For example, s/he can use the information in purchasing items on internet, or s/he can change the address of a client and issue a new credit card and send it to the new address and use it later. Moreover, the insider can use an outsider and give him/her the PII of some client. Next, the outsider can make fake identification using the PII information and withdraws fund from the victim account. Real stories about this type of attack are provided next.

The first example took place in New York, where an insider in a bank printed the account information of several clients and gave it to her boyfriend. Using his friends, her boyfriend talked with a homeless man who agreed to enter some of the bank branches posing as legitimate account holders and withdraw fund from their accounts. The total losses because of this crime exceeded $235,000.

The second example is about criminals who were ordinary customer service employees at a bank call center. Surprisingly, the employees had access to customer information including PII. Using their legitimate access, they printed customer records and gave them to an outsider who used them to make purchases. In some cases, the insiders changed the address of some customers and issued credit cards which were sent to the new incorrect address. Later, they used the new credit cards to perform some purchases. The estimate loss that was caused by this fraud was about $2.2 million.

The last example about this type was conducted by a branch manager of a national bank. The father of the manager branch, which had a criminal history, persuaded his son to conduct identity theft scheme in collaboration with the father's friend (outsider). The outsider asked the manager to steal the account information of some customers using his privileges, and offered him $1,000 for each account information. Using a team of complicit cashiers, the outsider made fake identifications using the account information to fraudulently withdraw funds. The total losses because of this fraud in a period of three months were $228,000.

Non-Technical Attacks

Banks may suffer insider threat in non-technical cases. Although the focus of this chapter is on technical attacks, non-technical attacks are discussed briefly in this chapter. This type of attacks spans many attack areas such as stealing cash from drawers. A good example of this type is what demonstrated in CERT study about insider threat in financial sector. In this example, a temporary employee was responsible for placing large cash deposits in the vault in bank-issued deposit bags. The insider created fake bags using the bank system, and put them in place of legal deposit bags, and stole the money from the legal bags. During a period of three months, the insider succeeded to steal about $92,000 (Cummings, 2012).

Insider Threat Mitigation in Banking Systems

Defending banks information systems against insider threat require robust prevention, detection and recovery countermeasures. Preventive countermeasures should raise alerts and prevent insiders before committing a crime. Despite the fact that the concept of prevention is clear in information security, designing and applying these controls is not an easy job in insider threat mitigation. The majority of insiders are employees who perform normal daily tasks in the system. An insider threat prevention countermeasure should take into account the tradeoff between allowing insiders to perform their tasks and stopping insiders' tasks that are considered attacks to the underlying system.

Insider Threat Prevention

Adopting good access control models in banking systems is crucial to prevent insider threat. Insiders, despite the job level they have, should be allowed to access authorized information. Moreover, insiders should get access to the minimum number of data items needed to perform his/her task. The aforementioned principle is called the *Least Privilege*. Applying this rule limited or prevented the damage of insider threat cases in many financial organizations. Another important rule in insider threat prevention is called *Separation of Duties*. An insider who has too much access and privileges is a high risky insider. For example, consider an insider, say John, who has write access to loans and can modify the log file in a bank. John can fraudulently change the amount of loans and remove his record from the log file, or modify it to trap other insiders. The rule Separation of Duties is a very important rule, which reduce the probability of insider attacks by removing or mitigating the capability of one insider to harm the system. Moreover, restricting access to PII and applying good monitoring system on PII or other sensitive information increase the probability of preventing insider attacks or reduce the damage that may occur in systems because of attacking such valuable information. Furthermore, good sanction policies may reduce the probability of insider attacks.

Preventing insider threat requires removing or reducing the capabilities or factors that facilitate launching insider attacks. Adopting strong authentication techniques, strong passwords, laptop theft tracking decreases the probability of insider identity theft. Moreover, preventing employees from downloading or printing emails help in preventing insider threat.

SANS survey (SANS Institute, 2015) showed some factors that may limit preventing insider threat. Lack of training, lack of budget, lack of internal staff, lack of technology solutions are examples of these limitations. They survey demonstrated the most important tools and technologies used to prevent or deter insider threat. These tools are as follows.

- Content Filtering and Sandboxing of executables
- Inbound and outbound proxies
- Web filtering and content blocking
- Data Loss Prevention (DLP) with data flow analysis
- Data classification
- Net flow analysis to detect data exfiltration
- SIEM systems or other log-focused tools for detecting anomalies in user patterns
- User activity monitoring

Using these tools and technologies may reduce the risk of insider threat. However, advanced insider attacks may bypass these tools. Thus, implementing another level of security in insider threat mitigation is compulsory. Insider threat detection phase form the second layer that should by adopted by organization, especially banks, to mitigate insider threat.

Insider Threat Detection

Prevention controls do not always succeed in preventing insider attacks. Therefore, detection controls are needed to defend systems against insider threat. Auditing activities of insiders, especially accountants and managers, is a very crucial job in insider threat detection process. Most insider attacks were discovered during normal auditing activities.

Technical solutions must be correctly designed, implemented and configured to detect insider threat. According to the SANS survey (SANS Institute, 2015), the following solutions lead the pack for potential tools in insider threat detection.

- Internal audits
- Internal network monitoring
- Centralized log management
- SIEM tools
- External monitoring
- Employee monitoring
- Data Loss Prevention (DLP)

Most insider threat incidents were discovered during normal auditing activities. Therefore, checking log files and the activities of insiders are crucial in insider threat detection. Building patterns of insider threat incidents and using them for early threat alerting help in detection insider attacks in early stages. For example, some insiders follow specific steps when they intend to attack the banking system. These steps form a pattern of that kind of attack. Therefore, monitoring insiders' activities and checking them against this pattern (or a database of patterns in general), enable security officers to shed light on potential malicious insiders and stop them before the damage becomes sever. Hence, technical details behind these solutions are behind the scope of this chapter.

Damage Assessment and Recovery

Insiders can cause huge loss in banking systems due to the expensive value that this sector has. Financial loss is the major loss that banking sector suffers. However, bank reputation and reliability are major elements that may be harmed by insider threat. Reducing the damage caused by insider threat starts by early detection of attacks and fast assessment and recovery. Training incident response team is a major step towards having rapid assessment and recovery after insider attacks. Creating attack models to train and evaluate the incident response team may help in reducing the losses after attacks. Moreover, implementing secure backup and recovery processes, and testing them periodically is crucial in fast recovery.

SUMMARY

Insider threat is a major concern in banking sector. According to many surveys, the losses that are caused by an insider are greatly more than the losses caused by a hacker. Despite the aforementioned fact, banks still invest much more money in mitigating outsider attacks than mitigating insider threat. Therefore, banks should pay more attention to this threat, and should invest more money in developing tools to mitigate this threat.

The insider threat cases that have been discussed in this chapter shows that insiders may launch different types of attacks, such as technical and non-technical attacks, attacks on banking systems and attacks on the Personally Identifiable Information (PII). The later type of attacks is the most common one in insider threat in banking systems. Therefore, banks should pay more attention to the PII, and limit the access to this important information using high secure access controls, and implementing good auditing and monitoring tools.

Securing banking systems may not guarantee the block of insider threat door. However, multiple levels of security help in greatly reducing the probability of insider attacks. Good tools and security policies should be used to prevent insider threat. However, advanced insider attacks that succeed in bypassing insider threat prevention tools should be detected. Adopting reliable insider threat detection countermeasures is crucial in reducing the damage caused by malicious insiders. Moreover, training incident response team about fast assessment and recovery after attacks is very important in controlling the insider attacks and reducing the damage.

REFERENCES

Brackney, R., & Anderson, R. (2004). *Understanding the insider threat(technical report).*Santa Monica, CA, USA: RAND Corporation.

Cappelli, D., Moore, A., & Trzeciak, R. (2012). *The CERT Guide to Insider Threats: How to Prevent, Detect, and Respond to Information Technology Crimes (Theft, Sabotage, Fraud).* Addison-Wesley Professional.

CERT. (2011). *The 2011 CyberSecurity Watch Survey*. Retrieved from www.cert.org/

Childs, M. (2013). *JPMorgan Whale Pushed for 'Young' Trader Who Later Took His Job*. Retrieved from http://www.bloomberg.com/news/articles/2013-03-18/jpmorgan-s-whale-advocated-young-trader-who-later-took-his-job

Cooper, R. (2008). *Verizon Business Data Breach Security Blog*. Retrieved from http://www.securityblog.verizonbusiness.com/2008/

Cummings, A., Lewellen, T., McIntire, D., Moore, A., & Trzeciak, R. (2012). *Insider Threat Study: Illicit Cyber Activity Involving Fraud in the U.S. Financial Services Sector* (Special Report CMU/SEI-2012-SR-004). CERT Program. Retrieved from www.sei.cmu.edu/reports/12sr004.pdf

Cuomo, A., & Lawsky, B. (2014). *Report on Cyber Security in the Banking Sector*, New York State Department of Financial Services. Retrieved from http://www.dfs.ny.gov/reportpub/dfs_cyber_banking_report_052014.pdf

Forrester Research. (2010). *The Value of Corporate Secrets*. Retrieved from https://www.nsi.org/pdf/reports/The%20Value%20of%20Corporate%20Secrets.pdf

Gordon, L., Loeb, M., Lucyshyn, W., & Richardson, R. (2005). *Computer Crime and Security Survey*. Retrieved from http://www.cpppe.umd.edu/

InfoSecurity Europe. (2010). *Information Security Breaches Survey*. Retrieved from http://www.pwc.co.uk/eng/publications/isbs survey 2010.html

Mario, S. (2013). *17 Proven Currency Trading Strategies: How to Profit in the Forex Market*. Wiley.

Richards, K. (2013). *FBI Offers Lessons Learned on Insider Threat Detection*. Retrieved from http://searchsecurity.techtarget.com/news/2240179082/RSA-2013-FBI-offers-lessons-learned-on-insider-threat-detection

Richardson, R. (2010). *15th Annual 2010/2011 Computer Crime and Security Survey*. Retrieved from http://gatton.uky.edu/faculty/payne/acc324/CSISurvey2010.pdf

SANS Institute. (2015). *Insider Threats and the Need for Fast and Directed Response, A SANS Survey*. Retrieved from https://www.sans.org/reading-room/whitepapers/analyst/insider-threats-fast-directed-response-35892

Subashini, S., & Kavitha, V. (2010). A Survey on Security Issues in Service Delivery Models of Cloud Computing. *Journal of Network and Computer Applications*, *34*(1), 1–11. doi:10.1016/j.jnca.2010.07.006

United States Government Accountability Office USGA. (2015). *Bank and Other Depository Regulators Need Better Data Analytics and Depository Institutions Want More Usable Threat Information*. Report to Congressional Requesters. Retrieved from http://www.gao.gov/assets/680/671105.pdf

Walker, P. (2012). UBS rogue trader Kweku Adoboli jailed over 'UK's biggest fraud'. *The Guardian*. Retrieved from http://www.theguardian.com/uk/2012/nov/20/ubs-trader-kweku-adoboli-jailed-fraud

Wang, J., Gupta, M., & Raghav, H. (2015). Insider Threat in a Financial Institution: Analysis of Attack-Proneness of Information Systems Applications. *Journal of MIS Quarterly*, *39*(1), 91–112.

Yaseen, Q., & Panda, B. (2009). Knowledge Acquisition and Insider Threat Prediction in Relational Database Systems.*Proceedings of the 2009 International Conference on Computational Science and Engineering*, Vancouver, Canada. doi:10.1109/CSE.2009.159

Yaseen, Q., & Panda, B. (2012). Insider Threat Mitigation: Preventing Unauthorized Knowledge Acquisition. *International Journal of Information Security, 11*(4), 269–280. doi:10.1007/s10207-012-0165-6

Chapter 14
Achieving Security to Overcome Attacks and Vulnerabilities in Mobile Banking Security

Balamurugan Balusamy
VIT University, India

Saranya Nandagopal
VIT University, India

Malathi Velu
VIT University, India

Shirley Jothi Mano
VIT University, India

ABSTRACT

Mobile Banking is a means of connectivity between bank and its customers. It would be impractical to expect customers to regularly visit banks or connect to a web site for regular upgrade of their mobile banking application. Mobile Banking is a provision and availability of both banking and financial services with the help of mobile telecommunication devices as an Application. It would be expected that the mobile application itself check the upgrades and updates and download necessary patches. Mobile banking has brought the advantage to have an alternate to debit and credit card usage. Mobile banking has the below three inter-related concepts: Mobile accounting, Mobile brokerage, Mobile financial information services. Mobile banking services are Account information provision, Monetary Transaction, Investment facilitation, Support and Content services. The threats involved in Mobile Banking are categorized as, Threats against end user and end user device, Threats against communication network, Threats against remote banking service. The impact of various threats is discussed below.

DOI: 10.4018/978-1-5225-0864-9.ch014

INTRODUCTION TO MOBILE BANKING

The recent technology that had major impact on bank services is Internet banking. Customers can access the banks anytime by means of Internet Banking. With Internet banking, customers can perform various operations like getting bank statements, performing transactions and paying bills without the need of going to bank every time.

Though there are number of advantages, the limitation of Internet banking is that it requires a device like computer and an Internet connection. This may not be an issue in developed countries like US or Europe but in developing countries like India and China this is a major drawback. This limitation has been overcome by means of Mobile Banking since it requires a simple mobile instead of computers and laptops.

The term Mobile Banking can be defined as 'A system that helps bank users/customers to access bank services such as transactions by means of a mobile device such as a mobile phone or tablet.

The sales and usage rate of mobile phones is increasing rapidly everyday even in developing economies like India. It is estimated that there are 207 million users in India alone in the year of 2014. This proves the fact that mobile devices have become an integral part of our life.

In recent days, providing mobile banking service has become compulsory for all the banks, in order to enhance the comfort of their customers. The mobile banking applications provided by banks these days are optimized, that they can run smoothly and efficiently on various mobile platforms. Mobile Banking provides greater advantage for customers who frequently use smart phones. The main advantage of mobile banking is that mobile banking enables "Anywhere Banking". Customers can access bank services even during their regular activities such as travelling, while waiting for buses or during break times in work.

Mobile Banking faces several threats and attacks like Phishing is an attack that targets vulnerabilities that exists in the system due to human factor. Phishing attack is an attempt to acquire sensitive information like username, passwords and credit card details, by masquerading as a trustworthy entity in an electronic communication via HTTP link which links to threat. Several cyber attacks are spread via mechanisms that express weakness found in end users, and make the user existing to vulnerability (Worring, et al., 2012). This problem is broad and thus multiple techniques are often implemented to mitigate specific attacks. A high level over-viewing of categories of phishing techniques are detection, offensive defense, correction and prevention. The hacker may use some trusted authorities Id, make the user to believe and steal the information from the user. User education or training is an attempt to increase the technical level awareness of users to reduce their susceptibility to phishing attacks. A detection method termed Intrusion Detection System (IDS) promises to detect the phishing attack based on Natural Language Processing(NLP). This method uses blacklists for eliminating the fake websites. Based on blacklists websites are authenticated (Khonji, et al., 2013).

Normalized Compression Distance (NCD) is a reasonable approach to overcome phishing attack. This approach works by comparing the legitimate website with the fake one. Compression algorithm is used for comparing the websites (Chen, et al., 2014).

SQL injection is a code injection technique, used to attack data-driven (Alnabulsi, et al., 2014) technique applications, in which malicious SQL statements are inserted into an entry field for execution. This attack poses a serious security threat among the Internet community nowadays and it continues to increase exploding flaws found in internet applications. The attackers take the advantage of poorly developed web applications and introduce malicious code to the system and retrieve sensible information. So, additional information must be processed to enhance the security of the data and integrity of the applications. There is a technique that filters the SQL injection attacks by SNORT IDS. SNORT is nothing but network intrusion prevention system which is capable of performing real-time traffic control analysis and packet-logging techniques. SQL injection uses some signature techniques to inject the SQL data and creates threat to user information.

Security of Vehicular Ad Hoc networks plays a major role in strengthening critical life. VANET is a type of MANET (Mobile Ad hoc Networks) which plays role in secure communication of wireless network for data exchange- to domain of vehicles. They are the key component of ITS (Intelligent Transportation Systems). The above VANET technology is exposed to several types of attacks like Sybil attack (reputation system is subverted by forging identities in peer-to-peer networks), misbehaving nodes generate false information, jamming attacks, sending false information, etc., Among these attacks, DOS (Denial of Service) attack is a major threat to information technology. DOS attack in vehicle is caused by network insiders and outsiders that stops giving network information to real users. Jamming attack is one, where the network is being jammed and reduces the performance of the network. By introducing Malicious and Irrelevant Packet Detection Algorithm (MIPDA), which is used to analyze and detect the DOS attack. By this, we can avoid wasteful attack traffic overloading the network. (Katkar, & Kulkarni, 2013) This algorithm overall reduces the overhead delay in information processing, thus increasing the security in VANET technology. MIPDA algorithm detects position of vehicle that sends unwanted data or packets and ignores the vehicle data. This algorithm deals with correct packet generation.

MOBILE BANKING SERVICES

There are a number of services provided by mobile banking. The services include:

- Account Balance Enquiry.
- Account Statement Enquiries.
- Cheque Status Enquiry.
- Cheque Book Requests.
- Fund Transfer between Accounts.
- Credit/Debit Alerts.
- Minimum Balance Alerts.
- Bill Payment Alerts.
- Bill Payment.
- Recent Transaction History Requests.
- Information Requests like Interest Rates/Exchange Rates.

These services can be classified into a number of different types. Based on the originator of a service session, the services can be classified into two types:

- Push,
- Pull.

Push

In case of push, the originator of service session is the bank. Based on a set of instructions, the bank starts the session. This includes services such as alert message sent by the bank when the account balance reaches the minimum level.

Pull

In case of pull, the originator of the service session is the customer. The customer requests for service or information from the bank. This includes services such as, the customer requesting for statement of last five transactions performed.

Based on the nature of the service, mobile banking services can be classified into two types.

- Transaction based service,
- Enquiry based service.

Transaction Based Service

Requesting for fund transfer to another account is transaction based service. This service requires secured channel between the bank data servers and mobile phone.

Enquiry Based Service

Requesting the bank for a bank statement is an enquiry based service. This does not require much security. Based upon the above classifications, we arrive at the following taxonomy of the services listed before. Push Based, Pull Based, Transaction Base, Fund Transfer, Bill Payment, Other financial services like share trading, Enquiry Based, Credit/Debit Alerts, Minimum Balance Alerts, Bill Payment Alerts, Account Balance Enquiry, Account Statement Enquiry, Cheque Status Enquiry, Cheque Book Requests, Recent Transaction History.

TECHNOLOGIES ENABLING MOBILE BANKING

There are a number of channels on which mobile banking is deployed. Following are the channels on which mobile banking applications are developed:

- **IVR**: Interactive Voice Response.
- **SMS**: Short Messaging Service.
- **WAP**: Wireless Access Protocol.
- Standalone Mobile Application Clients.

More than one of these channels can be used for deployment of mobile banking services.

Interactive Voice Response

IVR or Interactive Voice Response service is where the customers can call specific IVR numbers. These IVR numbers are advertised by the bank to the customers. The customers who call these numbers are provided with a stored electronic message that consists of a menu of different options. Customers are asked to select an option by pressing a key in the device keypad. Based on the selected option customers are provided with information they choose for, using a text to speech program.

The major drawback of Mobile banking based on IVR is, it can be used only for Enquiry based services. Another drawback is that it is more expensive compared to SMS, WAP and Standalone Mobile Application Clients.

IVR can be implemented by deploying PBX system that can host IVR dial plans. One of the best available PBX system is Asterisk. It is an open source Linux PBX system that takes only low cost for banks to implement it.

The major drawback with using Asterisk is the noise on multiple Asterisk related forums over the stability of Asterisk based systems.

Short Messaging Service

Short message service is a process of conveyance of short messages over the portable systems. It is a store and forward method for transmitting messages to and from mobiles. The message just from the sending portable is put away in a focal short message focus (SMS) which then advances it to the destination versatile. This implies for the situation that the beneficiary is not accessible, the short message is put away and can be sent later. Every short message can be no more than 160 characters. These characters can be content (alphanumeric) or twofold Non-Text Short messages. An intriguing element of SMS is return receipts. This implies the sender, if wishes, can get a little message telling if the short message was conveyed to the expected beneficiary. Since SMS utilized flagging channel instead of devoted channels, these messages can be sent/received at the same time with the voice/information/fax administration over a GSM system. SMS bolsters national and global wandering. This implies you can send short messages to some other GSM portable client around the globe. With the PCS systems in light of all the three advances, GSM, CDMA and TDMA supporting SMS, SMS is pretty much an all-inclusive versatile information administration.

Figure 1. Short messaging service

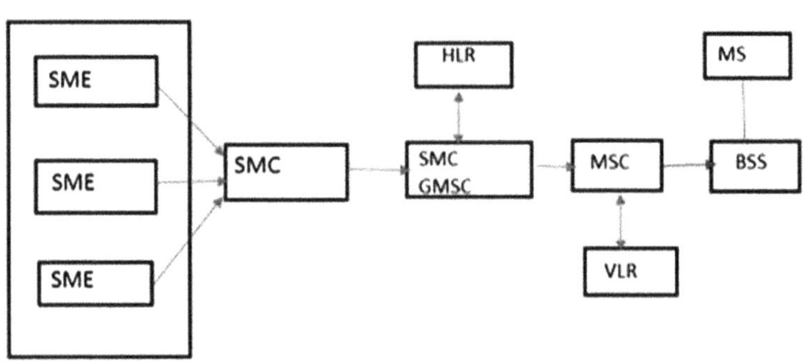

SMS Function

The figure above demonstrates a run of the mill association of system components in a GSM system supporting SMS. The SMC (Short Message Centre) is the substance which does the occupation of store and forward of messages to and from the versatile station. The SME (Short Message Entity) which can be situated in the settled system or a portable station, sends and receives short messages. The SMS GWMS (SMS door MSC) is an entryway MSC that can likewise get short messages. The portal MSC is a versatile system's purpose of contact with different systems. On getting the short message from the short message focus, GMSC utilizes the SS7 system to grill the present position of the portable station shape the HLR i.e., Home Area Register. HLR is the fundamental database in a versatile system. It holds data of the membership profile of the portable furthermore about the steering data for the supporter, i.e. the zone (secured by a MSC) where the versatile is as of now arranged. The GMSC is in this way ready to go on the message to the right MSC. MSC (Mobile Switching Centre) is the substance in a GSM system which does the employment of exchanging associations between versatile stations or between portable stations and the settled system.

A VLR (Visitor Location Register) compares to every MSC and contains provisional data about the versatile, data like portable distinguishing proof and the cell (or a gathering of cells) were the portable is as of now arranged. Utilizing data frame both the VLR and MSC can switch the data (short message) to the corresponding BSS (Base Station System, BSC + BTSs), which transmits the short message to the portable. The BSS comprises of handsets, which send and get data over the air interface, to and from the portable station. This data is disregarded the flagging channels so the versatile can get messages regardless of the possibility that a voice or information call is going on.

Wireless Access Protocol

Wireless Access Protocol (WAP) is an industry determination that permits propelled informing and data administrations to be conveyed to remote gadgets free of which remote innovation they utilize. A WAP server is a PC that can get, process, and react to an end client's (client's) solicitation for data or data handling. WAP gadget asking for information through the Internet to a WAP Server. To begin with, the WAP use select substance (a record) on their handset that they yearning to get. This makes a solicitation message that is sent to the IP location of the WAP server. The WAP server forms this solicitation and returns the asked for record to the IP address relegated to the WAP gadget. At the point when the WAP gadget gets the information (record), it can show the report on the screen.

Secure Mobile Payment

Mobile payments are carried out by mobile devices in wireless environment. The accelerator of the payment is e-commerce and m-commerce. Nowadays mobile payment faces several problems, to improve the requirement of e-commerce such as: The payment process need to be simplified, we need to provide security payment during transaction. In this paper, Mobile Banking services aimed at J2ME enabled mobile phones over Bluetooth communication. The scope of the above designed model is combination of J2EE and J2ME capabilities. It is a secure transaction between the mobile client and payment server.

JAVA TECHNOLOGY

Sun has introduced Java™ 2 Platform, Micro Edition (J2ME™). The user can download the application from the network if his/her smart phone has J2ME (Manvi, et al., 2009). J2ME runs on constrained memory devices like Smart Phones and Personal Digital Assistant (PDA). J2ME plays a vital role in fast growing marketplace. The advantage of J2ME over the wireless world is:

1. The J2ME code should be portable from one device to another device.
2. The network security is safe and secure over the network.
3. The interactive application that runs on the environment DOS not utilize extensive bandwidth.
4. Even though the mobile network is in offline mode, the application can run on the mobile devices since the service code is written in java technology, the cost consumption for running the mobile application has been reduced.
5. Platform, Enterprise Edition (J2EE™) (Katkar, & Kulkarni, 2013) is an open, standard-based, development and deployment platform for building n-tier, web-based and server-centric, and component-based enterprise applications.

Algorithm:

num = number of clients,
acno =account number,
pwd =password,
CB = Current Balance,
FT = Fund Transaction,
CP = Change Password,
DC = DD Clearance,

CC = Cheque Clearance,
op = old password,
np = new password,
cp = confirm password,
amt =amount,
Ddt = DDdate, Dno= DD number,
Cno = Cheque number,
Cdt = Chequedate,
M = number oftransaction,
P = 3. Begin

Enter the accno and pwd, it will check in database.

Step 1: For k=1 to P do//Maximum limit for checking authenticated user. Begin If it is correct will go to process list (step 2) otherwise screen shows the tried once message, try again, gotostep1. In second attempt if data is wrong it displays last chance to attempt otherwise will go to process list (step2). In third attempt if data is wrong, whole application is closed otherwise will go to process list (step2). End

Step 2: For i=1 to m do//Process list Begin. The process list shows the mobile authenticated user choices such as:

- Current Balance,
- Fund Transaction,
- Change Password,
- DD Clearance and
- Cheque Clearance.

If mobile authenticated user choice is (less than or equal) <=5otherwise gotostep3. Choice 1: Current Balance Form Begin. Click on Find button to find current balance of the account. Click on Back to go back to the process list (step 2). End// End of Current Balance form Choice 2: Fund Transaction Form Begin. Enter the accno (account number) and amt (amount), which is provided in fund transfer form for transferring the amount. Click on submit button after successful entering otherwise goto process list (step2). Click on Exit. End// End of Fund Transaction form Choice 3: Change Password Form Begin Enter the op (old password), np (new password) and cp (confirm password). Click on submit button. Click on exit, if screen displays passwords changed successfully otherwise go to process list (step 2). End//End of Change Password form Choice 4: DD Clearance Form Begin

Enter the Dno(DD number) and Ddt(DD Date) issued. Click on submit button. If screen displays successful clearance click on exit otherwise goto the process list (step 2). End//End of DD Clearance form Choice 5: Cheque Clearance Form Begin Enter the Cno(Cheque number) and Cdt (Cheque Date)issued. Click on submit button. If screen displays successful clearance click on exit otherwise goto the process list(step2). End//End of Cheque Clearance form.

The recreation results are taken around 20 meters range from the server area. We watched the diminishing in time required to hack secret word from 50 to 20 minutes for 10 customers (Hackers) in Bluetooth correspondence. Figure 3 shows that as the quantity of customers or programmers expands, the time (minutes) required to secret word hack likewise diminishes in different length of characters i.e. either in lower case letters and additionally in blended case letters and this is very regular in remote systems or computational environment. In blended case letters, time (minutes) required to secret word hack is higher than the time (minutes) required to watchword hack in lower case letters as appeared.

INFORMATION SECURITY AND PROTECTION METHODS

Mobile banking faces various issues in various technologies like Encryption technology, identity authentication, digital signature, WPKI technology. The operation of mobile banking system embraces data processing centre and mobile banking unit. All the customer's information is stored in the mainframe computer, it is responsible for banking transaction and data storage. The terminologies in mobile banking such as ATM's, deposit machines and multimedia enquiry stations (Nie, & Hu, 2008). Versatile saving money framework has given a decent establishment to giving customized, client situated, new model of budgetary administrations, which joins various remote correspondence channels; coordinate the benefits of various innovations.

Mobile banking zones are Hand set user's zone and mobile operator zone; Mobile operators and bank system zones. In mobile banking, customer observes various issues like hackers, virus attacks, etc., Mostly all the information are transferred through wireless network. All the transmitted (analog) information are converted in to digital signal i.e., zeros and ones, and in another end demodulation process is done, all the zero's and one's are converted back to analog signal. Analog signal is the only signal known to the user.

The arcane banking information may be hacked, lost or warp in the mobile devices. The attackers can interrupt sentinel information on the smart phone device network communication, and then the intruder may steal, modify or rewrite the original information, without the knowledge of the user/customer.(Nie, & Hu, 2008) At the point when a user utilizing cellular telephone, enter a zone with poor scope

Figure 2. Secure zone of mobile banking

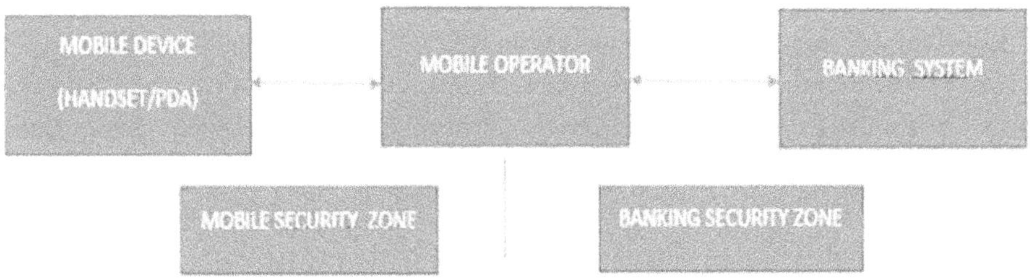

from the district with great remote signs, or the correspondence is bothered by different signs, data will happen frequently postpone or disappointment so exchanges could without much of a stretch lead to inadequate information or information misfortune.

The attackers send continuous messages to the smart phone by controlling the gateway. Gateway outlet to complete SMS Denial of Service Attack. The intruder uses the specific devices to attack the mobile banking service and change the process of its regular maintenance as well as it slow down the response of the server system. This process leads to consistent users not able to utilize the services provided by the bank.

Virus assaults Despite the present infection on versatile operations discovered for the most part destruct cellular telephone capacity, devour power of telephones and uproot records of cellular telephone and other data, the potential risk of portable managing an account is far more prominent than that of the system saving money. Possibly the followings can clarify the reasons: firstly, the virus carried on versatile terminals cannot just contaminate working arrangement of remote system terminals additionally taint that of the altered system terminal; furthermore, it is exceptionally hard to utilize antivirus programming for cell phones registering power imperatives; thirdly, many remote systems don't have hostile to virus measures. As of late, Russia interestingly found a PC virus, which spread by means of portable systems. The virus cannot just taint working arrangement of cell telephones with the Symbian through remote systems, additionally can spread through Bluetooth innovation, that is, Mobile telephones with virus will be initiated, then pass on a protected record including virus to close other Bluetooth-empowered cellular telephones. 3 The Mobile Banking Information Security Protection Methods From the above examination of data wellbeing issues of versatile saving money, (Nie, & Hu, 2008) we can see the contrast between data security issues of portable managing an account and system keeping money. Portable managing an account confronts more mind boggling security issues.

Authentication

Online banking authentication plays a vital role in the online banking security. The existing system includes password token, short message password, and USB token has been established for online banking transaction. In this paper we have introduced a new authentication for net banking (Fuglerud, & Dale, 2011). In this approach, we have improved the security and performance of the system by using smart phones to store the client's digital signature. The strength of the protocol is increased.

In online banking authentication, the widely used protocol is HTTP (HYPER TEXT TRANSFER PROTOCOL). HTTPS is a composite of Hypertext Transfer Protocol (HTTP) and Secure Socket Layer (Fang, & Zhan, 2010). In SSL's handshake the authentication process is deployed. DC is send by the bank for proving its identity, issued by a Certificate Authority(CA) like VeriSign, to one customer. The CA includes the following information such as issuer's name, certification validation period, version number, serial number and subject. Once the certificate has been issued by the bank, then client need to validate the certificate and provide his credential to the bank.

The Symmetric encryption algorithm is used. In symmetric encryption algorithm same key is used in both client and server side. At last bank identifies the customer. The initial two security issues have been settled entirely well with the usage of SSL (Fang, & Zhan, 2010). A digital certificate contains CA's digital signature which makes difficult for the intruder to hack the credential information. The bank's public key is used to encrypt the client's crediential information, the encrypted information is decrypted in the bank side. Financial institutions Examination Council proposed multi-factor Authentication which is capable of third security issues as well as internet environment. We can say, mobile phone OTP is a one authentication factor.

Biometrics is another variable embroiling 'Something a man is'. These two elements alongside the first secret key plan, something a man knows, make up three conventional online verification elements. Be that as it may, individuals regularly lose, break, or overlook their token gadgets as though they can't safely deal with their passwords (Fang, & Zhan, 2010). Additionally, cell telephone OTP is liable to spillage since SMS message is transmitted in plaintext which leaves assailants to listen in. In addition, ID gadgets for biometrics are costly and capacity of individuals' interesting biometrics information additionally turned into a dubious issue that might bargain individual security.

VANET

VANET (Vehicular Ad Hoc Networks is a subtitle of MANET. For the safe communication of basic life related data, system must be accessible to user at all the times. The system accessibility is presented to a few sorts of assaults and strings conceivable in VANET (Quyoom, et al., 2015). These security assaults and dangers incorporate Sybil assaults, getting out of hand hubs create false data, sticking assaults, selfish driver assault and wrongs vehicle position data. DOS (Denial Of Service) attack is a major threat occurs in communication network. Malicious and Irrelevant Packet Detection Algorithm (MIPDA) which is used to analyze and detect the Denial-of-Service (DOS) (Quyoom, et al., 2015). Accordingly, the assault is in the long run confined inside of its source spaces, along these lines staying away from inefficient assault traffic over-burdening the system base. It additionally decreases the overhead postpone in the data handling, which builds the correspondence speed furthermore improves the security in VANET.

VANET Model

Generally, VANET consist of two environments such as infrastructure and Ad Hoc environment.

Infrastructure Environment

This environment includes various entities such as manufacture and trusted third party.

These substances are forever associated with each other and used to keep up traffic as well as external services in the network (Quyoom, et al., 2015). Manufacturer identify each vehicle uniquely; legal authority is mostly present in vehicular system.

Figure 3. VANET model

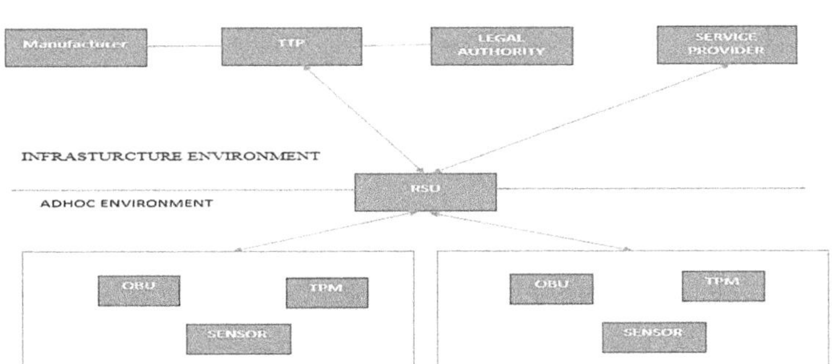

Each nation has diverse principle and regulations; here it is identified with two fundamental assignments which are offense reporting and vehicle enlistment. In the wake of assembling of vehicle, the reason for legitimate power is to issue tag and procedures traffic reports. Trusted Third Parties (TTP) offers different administrations, for example, time stamping and qualification administration. Administration supplier offer administrations, for example, Location Based Services or Digital Video Broadcasting. TTP and Service supplier are trading the data with the RSU.

Ad-Hoc Environment

In this environment correspondence is built up, vehicle is furnished with three distinct gadgets. Firstly, they are outfitted with correspondence unit, second they have an arrangement of sensor put which are utilized to gauge the status of their own and finally Trusted Platform module is mounted on the vehicle. (Quyoom, et al., 2015). These gadgets are utilized to give the dependable stockpiling and calculation. The capacity of switch Roadside unit (RSU) is to make association with the moving vehicles on the streets furthermore interfaces the various dynamic gadgets in the system.

POSSIBLE ATTACKS IN VANET

Broadcast Tempering

An inside ambush might infuse wrong heading related message, rub which incorporate data with respect to the blockage of streets, false wellbeing messages, inaccurate and unlawful dictation, message giving data of colossal jam on the streets into the system to bring about harm, for example, bringing on a mishap by stifling traffic manages or controlling the flow of traffic around a picked course and by making misconception for alternate vehicles around it in the system additionally.

DOS Attack

Denial Of Service (DOS) assaults target blocking accessibility of PC frameworks, administrations, systems, and flood them with over the top traffic through the channel with high stable of actually produced messages so that it is possible that they crash or they can't work precisely which viably denies the support of real clients from its legitimate working. Also, rather than appropriate working it is performing some other and superfluous capacities which are not should be finished (Quyoom, et al., 2015). DOS assaults should be possible by the system insiders and outcasts and quit flooding so as to give system availability to genuine clients the control channel with fast of normally produced unlawful and malevolent message. The key assets which are affected in DOS assault incorporate data transmission, CPU and memory. This assault can diminish the rate and volume of honest to goodness system by devouring transmission capacity assets (Tan, et al., 2014). It avoids handling bundles or a system gadget from reacting to administration demands and viably consuming so as to bolt up the gadget memory and CPU assets. Edge gadgets are utilized to configure the ordinary DOS assaults.

SYBIL Attack

In this kind of assault, assailant hub manufactures the character of different vehicles for their own beneficial purposes. Directly or in a roundabout way they cheat the other accessible vehicle in the system, later on it characters can be utilized to cast any sort of assault on the framework. (Quyoom, et al., 2015) The message imparted in this sort of assault incorporate sending of false position and additionally wrong bearing data, these false characters likewise make a hallucination that there are some extra vehicles out and about and parody the positions of all other vehicle hubs which are accessible in the system.

Message Suppression Attack

An aggressor at first sniff the bundles traveling through the channels and select a percentage of the parcel among them which are beneficial for it and after that specifically drops bundles from the system and these bundles might hold vital and basic (Quyoom, et al., 2015) data for the beneficiary. The assailant smothers these parcels, take a duplicate of it and might utilize them again when required (Quyoom, et al., 2015). The target of this assault is to keep enrollment and protection powers from finding out about assaults and crashes about the vehicle, to change the position of impact and/or to abstain from conveying crash reports to RSU.

Alteration Attack

This sort of assault happens when an assailant modifies an existing information. It sniffs the data from the divert roll out the improvements in the header and body of the data, later on utilize this changed data for its benefits as and when needed (Quyoom, et al., 2015). An alternative attack includes delaying the transmission of the data, replaying prior transmission, furthermore adjusting the genuine section of the information transmitted.

Jamming Attack

This is an abnormal state of DOS assault in which assailant sticks the channel, the principle objective of jammer is to play with authentic remote correspondence and to decrease or debase the general system execution. What's more, does not allow different clients to get to the system administrations. Primary target of jammer is to drop the bundles so that required data does not achieve the destination. Conceivable systems in the sticking assaults are beguiling jammer, responsive jammer arbitrary jammer and steady jammer, Deceptive jammer transmits semi-substantial parcels. Here, the parcel header is substantial yet payload is not utilized. Steady jammer consistently transmits radio signs. Responsive jammer squanders assets by trying so as to stick and also focus on the collector to info more clamor in the parcel. Irregular jammer is in two modes; at first mode the jammer sticks the traffic for an arbitrary timeframe and in second mode jammer stop transmission of sign for another arbitrary timeframe (Quyoom, et al., 2015). The two primary ordinarily utilized procedures that overcome sticking assaults are recurrence bouncing spread range (FHSS) and direct succession spread range (DSSP).

Sending False Information

In this kind of assault, wrong or fake data was intentionally sent by a hub to different hubs in the system to make a tumult traffic situation, which it might prompt error of the genuine circumstance. With the falsie data, the clients would be liable to leave the street; along these lines it makes the street free for the assailant to utilize it for his own particular purposes. Some aggressor imparts through the spam messages and builds the danger of assault. To control spam message is difficult in view of absence of concentrated organization and framework.

MIPDA Algorithm

MIPDA calculation is distinguishing the position of the vehicle and recognizes the malignant and invalid packet sent through that vehicle (Quyoom, et al., 2015). If the packet is not invalid, malevolent or assaulted, then the message creating vehicle won't be followed else track the specific vehicle.

This algorithm based on continuous position changing requirements of a vehicle along the road. Malicious and irrelevant packets are analyzed and identified by the following parameters which include Frequency (f), Velocity (v), α is Coefficient which is determined by the road characteristics and VMax is the maximum speed (s), frequency (f) is the numbers of broadcast packets (Khonji, et al., 2013) per second in the network, malicious attack, irrelevant, and invalid packets are identified by the following conditions. F and V are high because the position will change quickly as the vehicle is continuously changing its positions. F and V are low because the vehicle positions will not change much, if the F and V both are lie in the specified range between low and high, then the packet received are the real packets. Our main aim is to detect the malicious packet generated by the vehicle moving on the road, which cause the danger for other in the network. Our proposed algorithm based on the change in position and change frequency f, velocity v. $f=\alpha * | v - VMax / 2 |$ INPUT: Changing position of the moving vehicle along the road requires velocity of the moving vehicle V, maximum speed attained by the vehicle VMax, α Coefficient and request R. On the basis of all these factors frequency is calculated.

ALGORITHM

1. Identifies (Malicious packet)
2. Begin
3. Find $f = \alpha * | v- VMax / 2 |$
4. If (f ≥high && v≥ high)
5. Identify (Malicious Packet or Invalid Request)
6. Apply MIPDetAlg(R)
7. Begin if Verify (Request)
8. Return true
9. Else if (f ≤ low&&V ≤ low)
10. Return irrelevant packet or invalid Request
11. Else if (low<f<high && low <v<high)
12. Return real packets
13. Else
14. Received packets are not real
15. Apply MIPDetAlg(R) again
16. End if
17. End if
18. End if
19. End
20. End

MIPDA calculation is utilized to guarantee about the vindictive and insignificant bundles produced. It likewise manages the right bundle era; upgrade the security of VANET framework and to maintain a strategic distance from the deferral overhead in early time. The calculation can be connected before the verification time with a specific end goal to investigate quality of parcel era and to decrease the likelihood of postponement overhead and upgrade the security parts of VANET.

PHISHING ATTACK

Phishing is a confidence trick that used for collecting private information fraudulently, system access by taking advantage of the weakness caused by the system user in the system process. It acquires confidential information like username, password and other personal details in an electronic communication often for malicious purpose. Phishing is a type of identity thieving that happens once a malicious internet web site impersonates a legitimate one in order to acquire sensitive data such as passwords, account details, or credit card numbers. Though there square measure many anti-phishing computer code and techniques for detection potential phishing makes an attempt in emails and detection phishing contents on websites, phishers come back up with new and hybrid techniques Avoid} the available computer code and techniques (Khonji, et al., 2013).Phishing may be a deception technique that utilizes a mix of social engineering and technology to gather sensitive and personal data, such as passwords and credit card details by masquerading as a trustworthy person or business in associate electronic communication. Phishing makes use of spoofed emails that square measure created to look authentic and reputed to be coming back from legitimate sources like monetary Institution, ecommerce sites etc., to lure users to visit deceitful websites through links provided in the phishing email. The fraudulent websites are designed to mimic the look of a real company webpage. The phishing attacker's trick users by employing different social engineering tactics such as threatening to suspend user accounts if they do not complete the account update process, provide other information to validate their accounts or some other reasons to get the users to visit their spoofed web pages. PHISHING MOTIVES. The primary motives behind phishing attacks, from Associate in Nursing attacker's perspective, are: money Gain: phishers will use purloined banking credentials to their financial benefits (Khonji, et al., 2013). Identity Hiding: rather than victimization purloined identities directly, phishers may sell the identities to others whom may well be criminals seeking ways that to cover their identities and activities Fame and Notoriety: phishers may attack victims for the sake of peer recognition.

A whole phishing attack entails three roles of phishers. First off, mailers ship out a large quantity of fraudulent emails (usually through botnets), which direct users to fraudulent web sites. Secondly, creditors set up fraudulent web sites (commonly hosted on compromised machines), actively set off customers to offer private facts. Ultimately, cashers use the confidential information to obtain a pay-out. Economic exchanges regularly occur among those phishers.

Types of Phishing

- Clone Phishing,
- Spear Phishing,
- Phone Phishing.

Clone Phishing

In this type phisher creates a cloned electronic mail. He does this by way of getting data together with content material and recipient addresses from a legitimate electronic mail which changed into added formerly, then he sends the same e mail with links changed by means of malicious ones. He also employs address spoofing in order that the electronic mail seems to be from the authentic sender. The email can declare to be a re-ship of the unique or an updated model as a trapping strategy.

This form of phishing refers to messages that declare to be from a bank asking users to dial a telephone quantity regarding issues with their financial institution bills. Conventional smartphone device has dedicated traces, so Voice over IP, being easy to manipulate, turns into an excellent choice for the phisher. Once the telephone number, owned by using the phisher and provided by a VoIP provider, is dialed, voice prompts inform the caller to enter her account numbers and PIN. Caller identification spoofing, which isn't prohibited by way of law, may be used together with this so that the decision appears to be from a relied on source.

Spear Phishing

Spear phishing objectives at a specific institution. So in place of casting out lots of emails randomly, spear phishers target selected corporations of people with something in commonplace, for instance people from the identical corporation. Spear phishing is likewise being used against high-level goals, in a type of attack called "whaling". For example, in 2008, several CEOs within the U.S. Were dispatched a faux subpoena at the side of an attachment that might installation malware while viewed. Victims of spear phishing attacks in overdue 2010 and early 2011 include the Australian high Minister's workplace, the Canadian government, the Epsilon mailing list service, HBGary Federal, and o.K.Ridge countrywide Laboratory.

PHISHING TECHNIQUES AND COUNTER MEASURES

Numerous techniques are advanced to behavior phishing attacks and lead them to much less suspicious. Electronic mail spoofing is used to make fraudulent emails look like from valid senders, so that recipients are much more likely to believe inside the message and take moves in keeping with its commands. Web spoofing makes cast web sites look similar to valid ones, so that users would enter personal information into it. Pharming draws site visitors to those solid websites. Malware are hooked up into victims' computer systems to accumulate statistics immediately or useful resource different strategies. PDF documents, which helps scripting and fillable bureaucracy, also are used for phishing.

Email Spoofing

A spoofed email is one that claims to be originating from one source when it was actually sent from another. Email spoofing is a common phishing technique in which a phisher sends spoofed emails, with the sender address and other parts of the email header altered, in order to deceive recipients. Spoofed emails usually appear to be from a website or financial institution that the recipient may have business with, so that an unsuspecting recipient would probably take actions as instructed by the email contents, such as:

- Reply the email with their credit card number
- Click on the link labelled as "view my statement", and enter the password when the (forged) website prompts for it
- Open an attached PDF form, and enter confidential information into the form

Sending a Spoofing

On a mail-enabled UNIX device, one line of command is all you need to ship a spoofed e-mail that looks to be from Twitter

Other Detection Method

Microsoft's Sender ID validates the sending server's IP addresses towards a TXT record posted in the originator deal with DNS sector Heuristic-primarily based detection strategies are proposed to become aware of phishing emails. As an instance, an easy heuristic is the commentary that emails generated by the equal toolkit show a high degree of similarity. As soon as the heuristic identifies a form of phishing emails, it is able to be entered right into a blacist, and in addition emails may be blocked.

Web Spoofing

A phisher ought to forge a internet site that looks just like a legitimate internet site, in order that sufferers may think this is the genuine website and input their passwords and personal facts, that's accumulated by the phisher. Present day internet browsers have positive built-in safety indicators that can guard users from phishing scams, consisting of area name highlighting and https indicators. However, they're frequently unnoticed through careless customers. Growing a solid website, It's trivial to clone the appearance of an internet site with the aid of copying the front-give up code; a touch bit of web programming is essential to redirect user information into a record or database, then display a "website beneath renovation" observe. Proxy software inclusive of squid or Fiddler2 could be prolonged to create a fully practical clone. Users can successfully sign in and use all the services furnished by means of the original website, whilst all the inputs are accrued with the aid of the server, and all the pages can be changed by the server.

- Attracting traffic to forged website
- Browser Security Indicator: Domain Name Highlight
- Browser Security Indicator: HTTPS padlock

EFFECTIVENESS OF BROWSER SECURITY INDICATOR AND HTTP

Browser security indicators are not as effective as one might think. A survey reports that 23% of participants used only the content of a webpage to determine legitimacy; an identical-looking clone under any domain name without https is enough to deceive them. Many users cannot distinguish between a padlock icon in the browser chrome and a padlock icon as the favicon or in the page contents. Relying on HTTPS is also not sufficient. Malware can install the public key of a phisher's CA to local computer's trusted root CA list, so that certificate signed by this CA would be trusted. When the phishing website is using a similar-looking domain that is registered by the phisher, a real certificate can be requested after domain ownership verification. CAs could be hacked to issue fraudulent certificates. Moreover, if a government is involved in phishing, it can order a CA under its control to issue a certificate for the phishing server.

Anti-Phishing Group

PhishTank, released in October 2006, is a collaborative clearing house for facts and information about phishing on the net. PhishTank employs a complicated vote casting device that calls for the network to vote "phish" or "now not phish", decreasing the opportunity of false positives and enhancing the overall breadth and coverage of the phishing facts (Khonji, et al., 2013). It also affords an open API for builders and researchers to combine anti-phishing records into their packages at no rate. PhishTank is backed by Open DNS, a public DNS resolver; Open DNS makes use of PhishTank records to prevent phishing assaults for his or her customers. Shaped in 2003, the Anti-Phishing running organization (APWG) is an international consortium that brings together companies affected by phishing assaults, protection products and services groups, law enforcement organizations, authorities' groups, trade association, nearby international treaty agencies, and communications agencies. FraudWatch worldwide, a privately owned net protection corporation mounted in 2003, affords a spread of anti-phishing products and services to shield economic provider, e-commerce, and net web hosting businesses from phishing.

Mitigation of Phishing Attacks

Once the phishing attack is detected, several actions can be applied against the campaign. The following are the different categories of approaches that exist in the phishing attack.

- Detection Approach
- Offensive Detection Approach
- Correction Approach
- Prevention Approach

Detection Approach

User training Approaches - end-users will be educated to higher perceive the character of phishing attacks, phishing and non-phishing messages. Package classification approaches — these mitigation approaches aim at classifying phishing and legit messages on behalf of the user in an effort to bridge the gap that's left attributable to the human error or content.

Offensive Detection Approach

Offensive defense Approach aim to render phishing cam- pains vain for the attackers with the aid of disrupting the phishing campaigns, which is often carried out by flooding phishing net- websites with fake credentials in order that the attacker could have a difficult time to find the actual credentials. Instantly, BogusBiter: A browser toolbar that submits faux statistics in HTML forms whenever a phishing internet site is encountered.

Correction Approach

Correction is the act of taking the phishing assets down. This is frequently completed via reporting attacks to service providers. Phishing campaigns frequently depend upon sources, inclusive of websites, e-mail messages and Social Networking services to be able to correct such tries

- Removal of phishing content material from web sites, or suspension of website hosting services.
- Suspension of email accounts, SMTP relays, VoIP services.
- Trace lower back and shutdown of botnets.

Prevention Approach

The “prevention” of phishing attacks may be perplexing, as it can suggest different things depending on its context: Prevention of customers from falling victim — in this situation, phishing strategies can also be taken into consideration prevention strategies. Prevention of attackers from beginning phishing campaigns — law fits and consequences towards attackers via law Enforcement corporations (LEAs) are taken into consideration as prevention strategies.

Passive Warning

The warning does now not block the content-region and permits the consumer to view each the content and the warning.

Active Warning

The caution blocks the content material- information, which prohibits the consumer from viewing the content- records whilst the warning is displayed.

CONCLUSION

The contours of banking business have been changing across the globe and the rippling effect of the same can be expressed in the Indian banking sector as well. The process of liberalization, privatization, globalization and deregulation has opened new vistas for banks to increase their revenues by diversifying in to universal banking, investment banking, bank assurance, mortgage financing, depository services, securitization, personal banking etc. An inevitable result of globalization is that it increases the soundness of financial system as a whole and facilitates global competition. To survive in this competition, the information and communication technology significantly contributed to the exponential growth and profit of financial institutions worldwide. Technology is the key to move towards providing integrated banking services to customers. Indian banks have been late starter in the adoption of technology for automation of processes and the integrated banking services. Further the banking sector reforms and introduction of mobile banking has made very structural changes in service quality, managerial decisions, operational performance, profitability and productivity of the banks. Mobile banking is one of the emerging trends in the Indian banking and is playing a unique role in strengthening the banking sector and improving service quality. Foreign banks are the pioneers in Mobile banking, private banks introduced it in a big way and public sector banks are in the process of transformation from traditional banking to Mobile banking. Mobile banking impinges on operations of banking in a number of different ways. Nowadays, mobile phones are used widely all around the world. Every good thing has both its pros and cons. Mobile Banking has several pros like banking can be done at any place and at any time and cons are like it is subjected to several attacks like Phishing, DOS, SQL Injection, etc., Now Mobile Banking provides a boost to the economy. Thus in the above chapter, we have discussed various threats and how to overcome those threats by using security algorithms i.e., for DOS – MIPDA algorithm.

REFERENCES

Aljawarneh, S. (2011). A web engineering security methodology for e-learning systems. *Network Security*, *2011*(3), 12–15. doi:10.1016/S1353-4858(11)70026-5

Aljawarneh, S., Al-Rousan, T., Maatuk, A. M., & Akour, M. (2014). Usage of data validation techniques in online banking: A perspective and case study. *Security Journal*, *27*(1), 27–35. doi:10.1057/sj.2012.10

Aljawarneh, S., Alkhateeb, F., & Al Maghayreh, E. (2010). A semantic data validation service for web applications. *Journal of Theoretical and Applied Electronic Commerce Research*, *5*(1), 39–55. doi:10.4067/S0718-18762010000100005

Alnabulsi, H., Islam, M. R., & Mamun, Q. (2014, November). Detecting SQL injection attacks using SNORT IDS. *Proceedings of the2014 Asia-Pacific World Congress onComputer Science and Engineering (APWC on CSE)* (pp. 1-7). IEEE. doi:10.1109/APWCCSE.2014.7053873

Chen, T. C., Stepan, T., Dick, S., & Miller, J. (2014). An anti-phishing system employing diffused information. *ACM Transactions on Information and System Security*, *16*(4), 16. doi:10.1145/2584680

Fang, X., & Zhan, J. (2010, May). Online banking authentication using mobile phones. *Proceedings of the2010 5th International Conference onFuture Information Technology (FutureTech)* (pp. 1-5). IEEE. doi:10.1109/FUTURETECH.2010.5482634

Fuglerud, K. S., & Dale, Ø. (2011). Secure and inclusive authentication with a talking mobile one-time-password client. *Security & Privacy*, *9*(2), 27–34. doi:10.1109/MSP.2010.204

Katkar, V. D., & Kulkarni, S. V. (2013, December). Experiments on detection of Denial of Service attacks using ensemble of classifiers. *Proceedings of the2013 International Conference onGreen Computing, Communication and Conservation of Energy (ICGCE)* (pp. 837-842). IEEE. doi:10.1109/ICGCE.2013.6823550

Khonji, M., Iraqi, Y., & Jones, A. (2013). Phishing detection: A literature survey. *IEEE Communications Surveys and Tutorials*, *15*(4), 2091–2121. doi:10.1109/SURV.2013.032213.00009

Manvi, S. S., Bhajantri, L. B., & Vijayakumar, M. A. (2009, April). Secure mobile payment system in wireless environment. *Proceedings of theInternational Conference onFuture Computer and Communication ICFCC 09* (pp. 31-35). IEEE. doi:10.1109/ICFCC.2009.125

Nie, J., & Hu, X. (2008, December). Mobile banking information security and protection methods. *Proceedings of the2008 International Conference onComputer Science and Software Engineering* (Vol. 3, pp. 587-590). IEEE. doi:10.1109/CSSE.2008.1422

Quyoom, A., Ali, R., Gouttam, D. N., & Sharma, H. (2015, May). A novel mechanism of detection of denial of service attack (DoS) in VANET using Malicious and Irrelevant Packet Detection Algorithm (MIPDA). *Proceedings of the2015 International Conference onComputing, Communication & Automation (ICCCA)* (pp. 414-419). IEEE.

Tan, Z., Jamdagni, A., He, X., Nanda, P., & Liu, R. P. (2014). A system for denial-of-service attack detection based on multivariate correlation analysis. *IEEE Transactions on* Parallel and Distributed Systems, *25*(2), 447–456.

Worring, M., Engl, A., & Smeria, C. (2012, October). A multimedia analytics framework for browsing image collections in digital forensics.*Proceedings of the 20th ACM international conference on Multimedia* (pp. 289-298). ACM. doi:10.1145/2393347.2393392

Chapter 15
Credit Card Fraud:
Behind the Scenes

Dan DeFilippi
Independent Researcher, USA

Katina Michael
University of Wollongong, Australia

ABSTRACT

This chapter provides a single person case study of Mr. Dan DeFilippi who was arrested for credit card fraud by the US Secret Service in December 2004. The chapter delves into the psychology of a cybercriminal and the inner workings of credit card fraud. A background context of credit card fraud is presented to frame the primary interview. A section on the identification of issues and controversies with respect to carding is then given. Finally, recommendations are made by the convicted cybercriminal turned key informant on how to decrease the rising incidence of cybercrime. A major finding is that credit card fraud is all too easy to enact and merchants need to conduct better staff training to catch fraudsters early. With increases in global online purchasing, international carding networks are proliferating, making it difficult for law enforcement agencies to be "policing" unauthorized transactions. Big data may well have a role to play in analyzing behaviors that expose cybercrime.

DOI: 10.4018/978-1-5225-0864-9.ch015

INTRODUCTION

Fraud is about exploiting weaknesses. They could be weaknesses in a system, such as a lack of controls in a company's accounting department or a computer security hole, or a weakness in human thinking such as misplaced trust. A cybercriminal finds a weakness with an expected payout high enough to offset the risk and chooses to become involved in the endeavor. This is very much like a traditional business venture except the outcome is the opposite. A business will profit by providing goods or services that its customers value. Fraud takes value away from its victims and only enriches those committing it.

Counterfeit documents rarely need to be perfect. They only need to be good enough to serve their purpose, fooling a system or a person in a given transaction. For example, a counterfeit ID card will be scrutinized more closely by the bouncer at a bar than by a minimum wage cashier at a large department store. Bouncers have incentive to detect fakes since allowing in underage drinkers could have dire consequences for the bar. There is much less incentive to properly train cashiers since fraud makes up a small percentage of retail sales. This is sometimes referred to as the *risk appetite and tolerance* of an organization (Levi, 2008).

Lack of knowledge and training of store staff is by far the biggest weakness exploited when counterfeit or fraudulent documents are utilized by cybercriminals. If the victim does not know the security features of a legitimate document, they will not know how to spot a fake. For example, Visa and MasterCard are the most widely recognized credit card brands. Their dove and globe holograms are well known. A card without one would be very suspicious. However, there are other less known credit card networks such as Discover and American Express. Their security features are not as well recognized which can be exploited. If a counterfeit credit card has an appearance of legitimacy it will be accepted.

BACKGROUND

Dan DeFilippi was a black hat hacker in his teens and early twenties. In college he sold fake IDs, and later committed various scams, including phishing, credit card fraud, and identity theft. He was caught in December 2004. In order to avoid a significant jail sentence, DeFilippi decided to become an informant and work for the secret service for two years, providing training and consulting and helping them understand how hackers and fraudsters think. This chapter has been written through his eyes, his practices and learnings. Cybercriminals do not necessarily have to be perfect at counterfeiting, but they do have to be superior social engineers not to get caught. While most of the cybercrime now occurs remotely over the Internet,

DeFilippi exploited the human factor. A lot of the time, he would walk into a large electronics department store with a fake credit card, buy high-end items like laptops, and then proceed to sell them online for a reduced price. He could make thousands of dollars like this in a single week.

In credit card fraud, the expected payout is so much higher than traditional crimes and the risk of being caught is often much lower making it a crime of choice. Banks often write off fraud with little or no investigation until it reaches value thresholds. It is considered a cost of doing business and additional investigation is considered to cost more than it is worth. Banks in Australia, for instance, used to charge about $250 to investigate an illegal transaction, usually passing the cost onto the customer before 2002. Today they usually do not spend effort on investigating such low-value transactions but rather redirect attention on how to uphold their brand. Since about the mid-2000s, banks also have openly shared more security breaches with one another which have acted to aid law enforcement task forces to respond in a timely manner to aid in investigating cybercrime. Yet, local law enforcement continues to struggle with the investigation of electronic fraud due to lack of resources, education, or jurisdictional issues. Fraud cases may span across multiple countries requiring complex cooperation and coordination between law enforcement agencies. A criminal may buy stolen credit cards from someone living on another continent, use them to purchase goods online in state 1, have the goods shipped to state 2 while living in state 3, with the card stolen from someone in state 4.

Online criminal communities and networks, or the online underground, are often structured similarly to a loose gang. New members (newbies) have to earn the community's trust. Items offered for sale have to be reviewed by a senior member or approved reviewer before being offered to the public. Even when people are considered "trustworthy" there is a high level of distrust between community members due to a significant level of law enforcement and paranoia from past crackdowns. Very few people know anyone by their real identity. Everyone tries to stay as anonymous as possible. Many people use multiple handles and pseudonyms for different online activities, such as one for buying, one or more for selling, and one for online discussion through asynchronous text-based chat. This dilutes their reputation but adds an additional layer of protection.

The most desirable types of fraud in these communities, and for monetary crime in general, involves directly receiving cash instead of goods. Jobs, such as "cashing out" stolen debit cards at ATMs, are sought after by everyone and are handled by the most trusted community members. Due to their desirability the proceeds are often split unequally, with the card provider taking a majority share of the reward and the "runner" taking a majority of the risk. The types of people in these communities vary from teens looking to get a new computer for free to members of organized crime syndicates. With high unemployment rates, low wages, and low levels of literacy particularly in developing nations, it is no surprise that a large number of credit card fraud players are eastern European or Russian with suspected ties to organized crime. It is a quick and easy way of making money if you know what you are doing.

Of course, things have changed a little since DeFilippi was conducting his credit card fraud between 2001 and 2004. Law enforcement agencies now have whole task forces dedicated to online fraud. Bilateral and multilateral treaties are in place with respect to cybercrime, although this still lacks the buy-in of major state players and even states where cybercrime is flourishing (Broadhurst, 2006). In terms of how technology has been used to combat credit card fraud, the Falcon system has been able to help in fraud that would have otherwise gone unnoticed. If the Falcon system identifies any transaction as suspect or unusual, the bank will attempt to get in touch with the cardholder to ascertain whether or not it is an authentic transaction. If individuals cannot be reached directly, then their card is blocked until further confirmation of a given transaction. Banks continue to encourage travelers to contact them when their pattern of credit card use changes, e.g. when travelling abroad. Software platforms nowadays do much of the analytical processing with respect to fraud detection. Predictive analytics methods, not rule-based methods, are changing the way fraud is discovered (Riordan et al., 2012). Additionally, banks have introduced two factor (also known as multifactor) authentication requirements which means an online site requires more than just a cardholder's username and password. Commonly this takes the form of a SMS or a phone call to a predesignated number containing a randomized code. Single factor authentication is now considered inadequate in the case of high-risk transactions, or movement of funds to other parties (Aguilar, 2015).

MAIN FOCUS OF THE CHAPTER

Issues, Controversies, Problems

Katina Michael: *Dan, let's start at the end of your story which was the beginning of your reformation. What happened the day you got caught for credit card fraud?*

Dan DeFilippi: *It was December 2004 in Rochester, New York. I was sitting in my windowless office getting work done, and all of a sudden the door burst open, and this rush of people came flying in. "Get down under your desks. Show your hands. Hands where I can see them." And before I could tell what was going on, my hands were cuffed behind my back and it was over. That was the end of that chapter of my life.*

Katina Michael: *Can you tell us what cybercrimes you committed and for how long?*

Dan DeFilippi: *I had been running credit card fraud, identity theft, document forgery pretty much as my fulltime job for about three years, and before that I had been a hacker.*

Katina Michael: *Why fraud? What led you into that life?*

Dan DeFilippi: *Everybody has failures. Not everybody makes great decisions in life. So why fraud? What led me to this? I mean, I had great parents, a great upbringing, a great family life. I did okay in school, and you know, not to stroke my ego too much, but I know I am intelligent and I could succeed at whatever I chose to do. But when I was growing up, one of the things that I'm really thankful for is my parents taught me to think for myself. They didn't just focus on remembering knowledge. They taught me to learn, to think, to understand. And this is really what the hacker mentality is all about. And when I say hacker, I mean it in the traditional sense. I don't mean it as somebody in there stealing from your company. I mean it as somebody out there seeking knowledge, testing the edges, testing the boundaries, pushing the limits, and seeing how things work. So growing up, I disassembled little broken electronics and things like that, and as time went on this slowly progressed into, you know, a so-called hacker.*

Katina Michael: *Do you remember when you actually earned your first dollar by conducting cybercrime?*

Dan DeFilippi: *My first experience with money in this field was towards the end of my high school. And I realized that my electronics skills could be put to use to do something beyond work. I got involved with a small group of hackers that were trying to cheat advertising systems out of money, and I didn't even make that much. I made a couple of hundred dollars over, like, a year or something. It was pretty much insignificant. But it was that experience, that first step, that kind of showed me that there was something else out there. And at that time I knew theft and fraud was wrong. I mean, I thought it was stealing. I knew it was stealing. But it spiraled downwards after that point.*

Katina Michael: *Can you elaborate on how your thinking developed towards earning money through cybercrime?*

Dan DeFilippi: *I started out with these little things and they slowly, slowly built up and built up and built up, and it was this easy money. So this initial taste of being able to make small amounts, and eventually large amounts of money with almost no work, and doing things that I really enjoyed doing was what did it for me. So from there, I went to college and I didn't get involved with credit card fraud right away. What I did was, I tried to find a market. And I've always been an entrepreneur and very business-minded, and I was at school and I said, "What do people here need? ... I need money, I don't really want to* *work for somebody else, I don't like that." I realized people needed fake IDs. So I started selling fake IDs to college students. And that again was a taste of easy money. It was work but it wasn't hard work. And from there, there's a cross-over here between forged documents and fraud. So that cross-over is what drew me in. I saw these other people doing credit card fraud and making money. I mean, we're talking about serious money. We're talking about thousands of dollars a day with only a few hours of work and up.*

Katina Michael: *You strike me as someone who is very ethical. I almost cannot imagine you committing fraud. I'm trying to understand what went wrong?*

Dan DeFilippi: *And where were my ethics and morals? Well, the problem is when you do something like this, you need to rationalize it, okay? You can't worry about it. You have to rationalize it to yourself. So everybody out there committing fraud rationalizes what they're doing. They justify it. And that's just how our brains work. Okay? And this is something that comes up a lot on these online fraud forums where people discuss this stuff openly. And the question is posed: "Well, why do you do this? What motivates you? Why, why is this fine with you? Why are you not, you know, opposed to this?" And often, and the biggest thing I see, is like, you know, the Robin Hood scenario- "I'm just stealing from a faceless corporation. It's victimless." Of course, all of us know that's just not true. It impacts the consumers. But everybody comes up with their own reason. Everybody comes up with an explanation for why they're doing it, and how it's okay with them, and how they can actually get away with doing it.*

Katina Michael: *But how does a sensitive young man like you just not realize the impact they were having on others during the time of committing the crimes?*

Dan DeFilippi: *I've never really talked about that too much before... Look the average person when they know they've acted against their morals feels they have done wrong; it's an emotional connection with their failure and emotionally it feels negative. You feel that you did something wrong no one has to tell you the crime type, you just know it is bad. Well, when you start doing these kinds of crimes, you lose that discerning voice in your head. I was completely disconnected from my emotions when it came to these types of fraud. I knew that they were ethically wrong, morally wrong, and you know, I have no interest in committing them ever again, but I did not have that visceral reaction to this type of crime. I did not have that guilty feeling of actually stealing something. I would just rationalize it.*

Katina Michael: *Ok. Could I ask you whether the process of rationalization has much to do with making money? And perhaps, how much money did you actually make in conducting these crimes?*

Dan DeFilippi: *This is a pretty common question and honestly I don't have an answer. I can tell you how much I owe the government and that's ... well, I suppose I owe Discover Card ... I owed $209,000 to Discover Card Credit Card Company in the US. Beyond that, I mean, I didn't keep track. One of the things I did was, and this is kind of why I got away with it for so long, is I didn't go crazy. I wasn't out there every day buying ten laptops. I could have but chose not to. I could've worked myself to the bone and made millions of dollars, but I knew if I did that the risk would be significantly higher. So I took it easy. I was going out and doing this stuff one or two days a week, and just living comfortably but not really in major luxury. So honestly, I don't have a real figure for that. I can just tell you what the government said.*

Katina Michael: *There is a perception among the community that credit card fraud is sort of a non-violent crime because the "actor" being defrauded is not a person but an organization. Is this why so many people lie to the tax office, for instance?*

Dan DeFilippi: *Yeah, I do think that's absolutely true. If we are honest about it, everyone has lied about something in their lifetime. And people... you're right, you're absolutely right, that people observe this, and they don't see it in the big picture. They think of it on the individual level, like I said, and people see this as a faceless corporation, "Oh, they can afford it." You know, "no big deal". You know, "Whatever, they're ripping off the little guy." You know. People see it that way, and they explain it away much easier than, you know, somebody going off and punching someone in the face and then proceeding to steal their wallet. Even if the dollar figure of the financial fraud is much higher, people are generally less concerned. And I think that's a real problem because it might entice some people into committing these crimes because they are considered "soft". And if you're willing to do small things, it's going to, as in my case, eventually spiral you downwards. I started with very small fraud, and then got larger. Not that everybody would do that. Not that the police officer taking the burger for free from Burger King is going to step up to, you know, to extortion or something, but certainly it could, could definitely snowball and lead to something.*

Katina Michael: *It has been about 6 years since you were arrested. Has much has changed in the banking sector regarding triggers or detection of cybercriminal acts?*

Dan DeFilippi: *Yeah. What credit card companies are doing now is pattern matching and using software to find and root out these kind of things. I think that's really key. You know, they recognize patterns of fraud and they flag it and they bring it out. I think using technology to your advantage to identify these* *patterns of fraud and investigate, report and root them out is probably, you know, one of the best techniques for dollar returns.*

Katina Michael: *How long were you actually working for the US Secret Service, as a matter of interest? Was it the length of your alleged, or so-called prison term, or how did that work?*

Dan DeFilippi: *No. So I was arrested early December 2004. I started working with the Secret Service in April 2005, so about six months later. And I worked with them fulltime almost for two years. I cut back on the hours a little bit towards the end, because I went back to university. But it was, it was almost exactly two years, and most of it was fulltime.*

Katina Michael: *I've heard that the US is tougher on cybercrime relative to other crimes. Is this true?*

Dan DeFilippi: *The punishment for credit card fraud is eight-and-a-half years in the US.*

Katina Michael: *Do these sentences reduce the likelihood that someone might get caught up in this kind of fraud?*

Dan DeFilippi: *It's a contested topic that's been hotly debated for a long time. And also in ethics, you know, it's certainly an interesting topic as well. But I think it depends on the type of person. I wasn't a hardened criminal, I wasn't the fella down on the street, I was just a kid playing around at first that just got more serious and serious as time went on. You know, I had a great upbringing, I had good morals. And I think to that type of person, it does have an impact. I think that somebody who has a bright future, or could have a bright future, and could throw it all away for a couple of hundred thousand dollars, or whatever, they recognize that, I think. At least the more intelligent people recognize it in that ... you know, "This is going to ruin my life or potentially ruin a large portion of my life." So, I think it's obviously not the only deterrent but it can certainly be useful.*

Katina Michael: *You note that you worked alone. Was this always the case? Did you recruit people to assist you with the fraud and where did you go to find these people?*

Dan DeFilippi: *Okay. So I mainly worked alone but I did also work with other people, like I said. I was very careful to protect myself. I knew that if I had partners that I worked with regularly it was high risk. So what I did was on these discussion forums, I often chatted with people beyond just doing the credit card fraud, I did other things as well. I sold fake IDs online. I sold the printed cards online. And because I was doing this, I networked with people, and there were a few cases where I worked with other people. For example, I met somebody online. Could have been law enforcement, I don't know. I would print them a card, send it to them, they would buy something in the store, they* *would mail back the item, the thing they bought, and then I would sell them online and we would split the money 50/50.*

Katina Michael: *Was this the manner you engaged others? An equal split?*

Dan DeFilippi: *Yes, actually, exactly the same deal for instance, with the person I was working with in person, and that person I met through my fake IDs. When I had been selling the fake IDs, I had a network of people that resold for me at the schools. He was one of the people that had been doing that. And then when he found out that I was going to stop selling IDs, I sort of sold him my equipment and he kind of took over. And then he realized I must have something else going on, because why would I stop doing it, it must be pretty lucrative. So when he knew that, you know, he kept pushing me. "What are you doing? Hey, I want to get involved." And this and that. So it was that person that I happened to meet in person that in the end was my downfall, so to speak.*

Katina Michael: *Did anyone, say a close family or friend, know what you were doing?*

Dan DeFilippi: *Absolutely not. No. And I, I made it a point to not let anyone know what I was doing. I almost made it a game, because I just didn't tell anybody anything. Well, my family I told I had a job, you know, they didn't know... but all my friends, I just told them nothing. They would always ask me, you know, "Where do you get your money? Where do you get all this stuff?" and I would just say, "Well, you know, doing stuff." So it was a mystery. And I kind of enjoyed having this mysterious aura about me. You know. What does this guy do? And nobody ever thought it would be anything illegitimate. Everybody thought I was doing something, you know, my own websites, or maybe thought I was doing something like pornography or something. I don't know. But yeah, I definitely did not tell anybody else. I didn't want anybody to know.*

Katina Michael: *What was the most outrageous thing you bought with the money you earned from stolen credit cards?*

Dan DeFilippi: *More than the money, the outrageous things that I did with the cards is probably the matter. In my case the main motivation was not the money alone, the money was almost valueless to a degree. Anything that anyone could buy with a card in a store, I could get for free. So, this is a mind-set change a fraudster goes through that I didn't really highlight yet. But money had very little value to me, directly, just because there was so much I could just go out and get for free. So I would just buy stupid random things with these stolen cards. You know, for example, the case where I actually ended up leading to my arrest, we had gone out and we had purchased a laptop before that one that failed, and we bought pizza. You know? So you know, a $10 charge on a stolen credit card for pizza, risking arrest, you know, for, for a pizza. And I would buy stupid stuff like that all the time. And just because I knew it, I had that experience, I could just get away with it mostly.*

Katina Michael: *You've been pretty open with interviews you've given. Why?*

Dan DeFilippi: *It helped me move on and not to keep secrets.*

Katina Michael: *And on that line of thinking, had you ever met one of your victims? And I don't mean the credit card company. I actually mean the individual whose credit card you defrauded?*

Dan DeFilippi: *So I haven't personally met anyone but I have read statements. So as part of sentencing, the prosecutor solicited statements from victims. And the mind-set is always, "Big faceless corporation, you know, you just call your bank and they just, you know, reverse the charges and no big deal. It takes a little bit of time, but you know, whatever." And the prosecutor ended up getting three or four statements from individuals who actually were impacted by this, and honestly, you know, I felt very upset after reading them. And I do, I still go back and I read them every once in a while. I get this great sinking feeling, that these people were affected by it. So I haven't actually personally met anyone but just those statements.*

Katina Michael: *How much of hacking do you think is acting? To me traditional hacking is someone sort of hacking into a website and perhaps downloading some data. However, in your case, there was a physical presence, you walked into the store and confronted real people. It wasn't all card-not-present fraud where you could be completely anonymous in appearance.*

Dan DeFilippi: *It was absolutely acting. You know, I haven't gone into great detail in this interview, but I did hack credit card information and stuff, that's where I got some of my info. And I did online fraud too. I mean, I would order stuff off websites and things like that. But yeah, the being in the store and playing that role, it was totally acting. It was, like I mentioned, you are playing the part of a normal person. And that normal person can be anybody. You know. You could be a high-roller, or you could just be some college student going to buy a laptop. So it was pure acting. And I like to think that I got reasonably good at it. And I would come up with scenarios. You know, ahead of time. I would think of scenarios. And answers to situations. I came up with techniques that I thought worked pretty well to talk my way out of bad situations. For example, if I was going to go up and purchase something, I might say to the cashier, before they swiped the card, I'd say, "Oh, that came to a lot more than I thought it would be. I hope my card works." So that way, if something happened where the card was declined or it came up call for authorization, I could say, "Oh yeah, I must not have gotten my payment" or something like that. So, yeah, it was definitely acting.*

RECOMMENDATIONS

Katina Michael: *You've mentioned this idea of downward spiraling. Could you elaborate?*

Dan DeFilippi: *I think this is partially something that happens and it happens if you're in this and do this too much. So catching people early on, before this takes effect is important. Now, when you're trying to catch people involved in this, you have to really think about these kinds of things. Like, why are they doing this? Why are they motivated? And the thought process, like I was saying, is definitely very different. In my case, because I had this hacker background, and I wasn't, you know, like some street thug who just found a computer. I did it for more than just the money. I mean, it was certainly because of the challenge. It was because I was doing things I knew other people weren't doing. I was kind of this rogue figure, this rebel. And I was learning at the edge. And especially, if I could learn something, or discover something, some technique, that I thought nobody else was using or very few people were using it, to me that was a rush. I mean, it's almost like a drug. Except with a drug, with an addict, you're chasing that "first high" but can't get back to it, and with credit card fraud, your "high" is always going up. The more money you make, the better it feels. The more challenges you complete, the better you feel.*

Katina Michael: *You make it sound so easy. That anyone could get into cybercrime. What makes it so easy?*

Dan DeFilippi: *So really, you've got to fill the holes in the systems so they can't be exploited. What happens is crackers, i.e. criminal hackers, and fraudsters, look for easy access. If there are ten companies that they can target, and your company has weak security, and the other nine have strong security, they're going after you. Okay? Also, in the reverse. So if your company has strong security and nine others have weak security, well, they're going to have a field-day with the others and they're just going to walk past you. You know, they're just going to skip you and move on to the next target. So you need to patch the holes in your technology and in your organization. I don't know if you've noticed recently, but there's been all kinds of hacking in the news. The PlayStation network was hacked and a lot of US targets. These are basic things that would have been discovered had they had proper controls in place, or proper security auditing happening.*

Katina Michael: *Okay, so there is the systems focus of weaknesses. But what about human factor issues?*

Dan DeFilippi: *So another step to the personnel is training. Training really is key. And I'm going to give you two stories, very similar but with totally different outcomes, that happened to me. So a little bit more about what I used to do frequently. I would mainly print fake credit cards, put stolen data on those cards and use them in store to go and purchase items. Electronics, and things like that, to go and re-sell them. So ... and in these two stories, I was at a big-box well-known electronics retailer, with a card with a matching fake ID. I also made the driver's licenses to go along with the credit cards. And I was at this first location to purchase a laptop. So pick up your laptop and then go through the standard process. And when committing this type of crime you have to have a certain mindset. So you have to think, "I am not committing a crime. I am not stealing here. I am just a normal consumer purchasing things. So I am just buying a laptop, just like any other person would go into the store and buy a laptop." So in this first story, I'm in the store, purchasing a laptop. Picked it out, you know, went through the standard process, they went and swiped my card. And it came up with a 'CFA' – call for authorization. Now, a call for authorization is a case where it's flagged on the computer and you actually have to call in and talk to an operator that will then verify additional information to make sure it's not fraud. If you're trying to commit fraud, it's a bad thing. You can't verify this, right? Right? So this is a case where it's very possible that you could get caught, so you try to talk your way out of the situation. You try to walk away, you try to get out of it. Well, in this case, I was unable to escape. I was unable to talk my way out of it, and they did the call for authorization. They called in. We had to go up to the front of the store, there was a customer service desk, and they had somebody up there call it in and discuss this with them. And I didn't overhear what they were saying. I had to stand to the side. About five or ten minutes later, I don't know, I pretty much lost track of time at that point, they come back to me and they said, "I'm sorry, we can't complete this transaction because your information doesn't match the information on the credit card account." That should have raised red flags. That should have meant the worse alarm bells possible.*

Katina Michael: *Indeed.*

Dan DeFilippi: *There should have been security coming up to me immediately. They should have notified higher people in the organization to look into the matter. But rather than doing that, they just came up to me, handed me back my cards and apologized. Poor training. So just like a normal consumer, I act surprised and alarmed and amused. You know, and I kind of talked my way out of this too, "You know, what are you talking about? I have my ID and here's my card. Obviously this is the real information." Whatever. They just let me walk out of the store. And I got out of there as quickly as possible. And* *you know, basically walked away and drove away. Poor training. Had that person had the proper training to understand what was going on and what the situation was, I probably would have been arrested that day. At the very least, there would have been a foot-chase.*

Katina Michael: *Unbelievable. That was very poor on the side of the cashier. And the other story you were going to share?*

Dan DeFilippi: *The second story was the opposite experience. The personnel had proper training. Same situation. Different store. Same big-box electronic store at a different place. Go in. And this time I was actually with somebody else, who was working with me at the time. We go in together. I was posing as his friend and he was just purchasing a computer. And this time we, we didn't really approach it like we normally did. We kind of rushed because we'd been out for a while and we just wanted to leave, so we kind of rushed it faster than a normal person would purchase a computer. Which was unusual, but not a big deal. The person handling the transaction tried to upsell, upsell some things, warranties, accessories, software, and all that stuff, and we just, "No, no, no, we don't ... we just want to, you know, kind of rush it through." Which is kind of weird, but okay, it happens.*

Katina Michael: *I'm sure this would have raised even a little suspicion however.*

Dan DeFilippi: *So when he went to process the transaction, he asked for the ID with the credit card, which happens at times. But at this point the person I was with started getting a little nervous. He wasn't as used to it as I was. My biggest thing was I never panicked, no matter what the situation. I always tried to not show nervousness. And so he's getting nervous. The guy's checking his ID, swipes the card, okay, finally going to go through this, and call for authorization. Same situation. Except for this time, you have somebody here who's trying to do the transaction and he is really, really getting nervous. He's shifting back and forth. He's in a cold sweat. He's fidgeting. Something's clearly wrong with this transaction. Now, the person who was handling this transaction, the person who was trying to take the card payment and everything, it happened to be the manager of this department store. He happened to be well-trained. He happened to know and realize that something was very wrong here. Something was not right with this transaction. So the call for authorization came up. Now, again, he had to go to the front of the store. He, he never let that credit card and fake ID out of his hands. He held on to them tight the whole time. There was no way we could have gotten them back. So he goes up to the front and he says, "All right, well, we're going to do this." And we said, "Okay, well, we'll go and look at the stock while you're doing it." You know. I just sort of tried to play off, and as soon as he walked away, I said, "We need to get out of here." And we left; leaving behind the ID and card. Some may not realize* *it as I am retelling the story, but this is what ended up leading to my arrest. They ran his photo off his ID on the local news network, somebody recognized him, turned him in, and he turned me in. So this was an obvious case of good, proper training. This guy knew how to handle the situation, and he not only prevented that fraud from happening, he prevented that laptop from leaving the store. But he also helped to catch me, and somebody else, and shot down what I was doing. So clearly, you know, failing to train people leads to failure. Okay? You need to have proper training. And you need to be able to handle the situation.*

Katina Michael: *What did you learn from your time at the Secret Service?*

Dan DeFilippi: *So a little bit more in-depth on what I observed of cybercriminals when I was working with the Secret Service. Now, this is going to be a little aside here, but it's relevant. So people are arrogant. You have to be arrogant to commit a crime, at some level. You have to think you can get away with it. You're not going to do it if you can't, you know, if you think you're going to get caught. So there's arrogance there. And this same arrogance can be used against them. Up until the point where I got caught in the story I just told you that led to my arrest, I was arrogant. I actually wasn't protecting myself as well as I had been, should have been. Had I been investigated closer, had law enforcement being monitoring me, they could have caught me a lot earlier. I left traces back to my office. I wasn't very careful with protecting my office, and they could have come back and found me. So you can play off arrogance but also ignorance, obviously. They go hand-in-hand. So the more arrogant somebody is, the more risk they're willing to take. One of the things we found frequently works to catch people was email. Most people don't realize that email actually contains the IP address of your computer. This is the identifier on the Internet to distinguish who you are. Even a lot of criminals who are very intelligent, who are involved in this stuff, do not realize that email shows this. And it's very easy. You just look at the source of the email and boom, there you go. You've got somebody's location. This was used countless times, over and over, to catch people. Now, obviously the real big fish, the people who are really intelligent and really in this, take steps to protect themselves with that, but then those are the people who are supremely arrogant.*

Katina Michael: *Can you give us a specific example?*

Dan DeFilippi: *One case that happened a few years ago, let's call the individual "Ted". He actually ran a number of these online forums. These are "carding" forums, online discussion boards, where people commit these crimes. And he was extremely arrogant. He was extremely, let's say, egotistical as well. He was very good at what he did. He was a good cracker, though he got caught multiple times. So he actually ran one of these sites, and it was a large site,* *and in the process, he even hacked law enforcement computers and found out information about some of these other operations that were going on. Actually outed some, some informants, but the people didn't believe him. A lot of people didn't believe him. And his arrogance is really what led to his downfall. Because he was so arrogant he thought that he could get away with everything. He thought that he was protecting himself. And the fact of the matter was, law enforcement knew who he was almost the whole time. They tracked him back using basic techniques just like using email. Actually email was used as part of the evidence, but they actually found him before that. And it was his arrogance that really led to his getting arrested again, because he just didn't protect himself well enough. And this really I cannot emphasize it enough, but this can really be used against people.*

Katina Michael: *Do you think that cybercrimes will increase in size and number and impact?*

Dan DeFilippi: *Financial crime is going up and up. And everybody knows this. The reality is that technology works for criminals as much as it works for businesses. Large organizations just can't evolve fast enough. They're slow in comparison to cybercriminals.*

Katina Michael: *How so?*

Dan DeFilippi: *A criminal's going to use any tools they can to commit their crimes. They're going to stay on top of their game. They're going to be at the forefront of technology. They're going to be the ones out there pioneering new techniques, finding the holes before anybody else, in new systems to get access to your data. They're going to be the ones out there, and combining that with the availability of information. When I started hacking back in the '90s, it was not easy to learn. You really pretty much had to go into these chat-rooms and become kind of like an apprentice. You had to have people teach you.*

Katina Michael: *And today?*

Dan DeFilippi: *Well after the 2000s, when I started doing the identification stuff, there was easier access to data. There were more discussion boards, places where you could learn about these things, and then today it's super easy to find any of this information. Myself, I actually wrote some tutorials on how to conduct credit card fraud. I wrote, like, a guide to in-store carding. I included how to go about it, what equipment to use, what to purchase, and it's all out there in the public domain. You don't even have to understand any of this. You know, you could know nothing about technology, spend a few hours online searching for this stuff, learn how to do it, and order the stuff overnight and the next day you could be out there going and doing this stuff. That's how easy it is. And that's why it's really going up, in my opinion.*

Katina Michael: *Do you think credit card fraudsters realize the negative consequences of their actions?*

Dan DeFilippi: *People don't realize that there is a real negative consequence to this nowadays. I'm not sure what the laws are in Australia about identity theft and credit card fraud, but in the United States, it used to be very, very easy to get away with. If you were caught, it would be a slap on the wrist. You would get almost nothing happening to you. It was more like give the money back, and possibly serve jail time if it was a repeat offence, but really that was no deterrent. Then it exploded post dot com crash, then a few years ago, we passed a new law that it's a mandatory two years in prison if you commit identity theft. And credit card fraud is considered identity theft in the United States. So you're guaranteed of some time in jail if caught.*

Katina Michael: *Do you think people are aware of the penalties?*

Dan DeFilippi: *People don't realize it. And they think, "Oh, it's nothing, you know, a slap on the wrist." There is a need for more awareness, and campaigning on this matter. People need to be aware of the consequences of their actions. Had I realized how much time I could serve for this kind of crime, I probably would have stopped sooner. Long story short, because I worked with the Secret Service and trained them for a few years, I managed to keep myself out of prison. Had I not done that, I would have actually been facing eight-and-a-half years. That's serious, especially for somebody who's in their early 20s. And really had that happened, my future would have been ruined, I think. I probably would have become a lifelong criminal because prisons are basically teaching institutions for crime. So really I, had I known, had I realized it, I wouldn't have done it. And I think especially younger people, if they realize that the major consequences to these actions, that they can be caught nowadays, that there are people out there looking to catch them, that really would help cut back on this. Also catching people earlier of course is more ideal. Had I been caught early on, before my mind-set had changed and the emotional ties had been broken, I think I would have definitely stopped before it got this far. It would have made a much bigger impact on me. And that's it.*

FUTURE RESEARCH DIRECTIONS

Due to the availability of information over the Internet, non-technical people can easily commit "technical" crimes. The internet has many tutorials and guides to committing fraud, ranging from counterfeit documents to credit card fraud. Many of the most successful are hackers turned carders, those who understand and know how to exploit technology to commit their crimes (Turgeman-Goldschmidt, 2008). They progress from breaking into computers to committing fraud when they discover how much money there is to be made. All humans rationalize their actions. The primary rationalization, criminals use when committing fraud, is blaming the victim. They claim that the victim should have been more knowledgeable, should have taken more steps to protect themselves, or taken some action to avoid the fraud. Confidence scams were legal in the US until a decade ago due to the mindset that it was the victim's fault for falling for the fraud. There needs to be a lot more research conducted into the psychology of the cybercriminal. Of course technological solutions abound in the market, but it is less of a technology problem, than a human factor problem. Technology solution patents for making credit cards more secure abound. But with near field communication (NFC) cards now on the market, fraud is being propelled as investment continues in insecure devices. One has to wonder why these technologies are being chosen when they just increase the risk appetite. There also has to be more campaigning in schools, informing young people of the consequences of cybercrime, especially given so many schools are now mandating the adoption of tablets and other mobile devices in high school.

CONCLUSION

Avoiding detection, investigation, and arrest for committing identity theft or electronic fraud is, in most cases, fairly simple when compared to other types of crime. When using the correct tools, the internet allows the perpetrator to maintain complete anonymity through much of the crime (Wall, 2015). In the case of electronic fraud, the only risk to the perpetrator is when receiving the stolen money or goods. In some cases, such as those involving online currencies designed to be untraceable, it may be impossible for authorities to investigate due to anonymity built into the system. The internet and broad reach of information is a two-way street and can also work in law enforcement's favor. Camera footage of a crime, such as someone using a stolen credit card at a department store, can now be easily and inexpensively distributed for the public to see. The same tools that keep criminals anonymous can be used by law enforcement to avoid detection during investigations. As with "traditional" crimes, catching a fraudster comes down to mistakes. A single mistake can unravel the target's identity. One technique used by the US Secret Service is to check emails sent by a target for the originating IP address. This is often overlooked. Engaging a target in online chat and subpoenaing IP records from the service provider is often successful as well. Even the most technologically savvy criminal may slip up once and let their true IP address through.

Many types of fraud can be prevented through education. The general population becomes less vulnerable and law enforcement is more likely to find the perpetrator. A store clerk who is trained to recognize the security features of credit cards, checks, and IDs will be able to catch a criminal in the act. The problem with education is its cost. A store may not find a positive return on investment for the time spent training minimum wage employees. Law enforcement may not have the budget for additional training or the personnel available to investigate the crime. Added security can also prevent certain types of crime. Switching from magnetic stripe to chip and PIN-based payment cards reduced card present fraud in Europe but then we have seen the introduction more recently of NFC cards that do not require a PIN for a transaction less than $100. Consumers may be reluctant to adopt new technologies due to the added process or learning curve. Chip and PIN have not been adopted in the USA due to reluctance of merchants and banks. The cost of the change is seen as higher than the cost of fraud. NFC cards on the other hand allegedly add to convenience of conducting transactions and have seen a higher uptake in Australia. However, some merchants refuse to accept NFC transactions, as usually fraudsters go undetected and the merchant is left to with problems to address.

Human exploitation is the largest factor of fraud and can make or break a scam (Hadnagy, 2011). Social engineering can play an important role when exploiting a system. Take using a stolen credit card to purchase an item in a store. If the fraudster appears nervous and distracted employees may become suspicious. Confidence goes a long way. When purchasing a large ticket item, the fraudster may suggest to the cashier that he hopes the total is not over his limit or that he hopes his recent payment has cleared. When presented with an explanation for failure before a failure happens, the employee is less likely to expect fraud. However, if there is more training invested when new employees start at an organization, the likelihood that basic frauds will be detected is very high. There is also the incidence of insider attack which is growing, where an employee, knowingly accepts an illegitimate card from a known individual, and then splits the profits. Loss prevention strategies need to be implemented by organizations and the sector as a whole need to address the credit card fraud problem in a holistic manner with all the relevant stakeholders engaged and working together to crack down on cybercrime.

REFERENCES

Aguilar, M. (2015). Here's Why Your Bank Account Is Less Secure Than Your Gmail. *Gizmodo.* Retrieved from http://gizmodo.com/heres-why-your-bank-account-is-less-secure-than-your-gm-1683777281

Broadhurst, R. (2006). Developments in the global law enforcement of cyber-crime. *Policing: An International Journal of Police Strategies & Management*, *29*(3), 408–433. doi:10.1108/13639510610684674

Hadnagy, C. (2011). *Social Engineering: The Art of Human Hacking*. Indiana: John Wiley.

Herley, C., van Ooirschot, P.C., & Patrick, A.S. (20). Passwords: If We're So Smart, Why Are We Still Using Them? *Financial Cryptography and Data Security, LNCS* (Vol. 5628, pp. 230-237).

Levi, M. (2008). Organized fraud and organizing frauds: Unpacking research on networks and organization. *Criminology & Criminal Justice*, *8*(4), 389–419. doi:10.1177/1748895808096470

Reardon, B., Nance, K., & McCombie, S. (2012). Visualization of ATM Usage Patterns to Detect Counterfeit Cards Usage. *Proceedings of the45th Hawaii International Conference on System Science (HICSS)*. Hawaii (pp. 3081-3088). doi:10.1109/HICSS.2012.638

Turgeman-Goldschmidt, O. (2008). Meanings that hackers assign to their being a hacker. *International Journal of Cyber Criminology*, *2*(2), 382–396.

Wall, D. S. (2015). The Internet as a conduit for criminal activity. In A. Pattavina (Ed.), Information Technology and the Criminal Justice System (pp. 77-98). London: Sage Publications.

KEY TERMS AND DEFINITIONS

Authorization: Authorizing electronic transactions done with a credit card and holding this balance as unavailable until either the merchant clears the transaction or the hold ceases.

Call for Authorization: Also known as CFA. A message that may come up when attempting to purchase something using a credit card. Requires the store to call in and verify the transaction.

Carding: Illegal use of a credit card. When criminals use carding to verify the validity of stolen card data, they test it the card by presenting it to make a small online purchase on a website that has real-time transaction processes. If the card is processed successfully, the thief knows the card is still good to use.

Card-Not-Present Fraud: Card-not-present fraud is when you make purchases over the phone or internet using card details without the card being physically presented.

Credit Card Fraud: Defined as the fraudulent acquisition and/or use of credit cards or card details for financial gain.

Cybercrime: Either crimes where computers or other information technologies are an integral part of an offence or crimes directed at computers or other information technologies (such as hacking or unauthorized access to data).

Hacking: Criminals can hack into databases of account details held by banks that hold customer information, or intercept account details that travel in unencrypted form. Hacking bank computers can lead to the withdrawal of sums of money in excess of account credit balances.

Identity Document Forgery: The process by which identity documents issued by banks are copied and/or modified by unauthorized persons for the purpose of deceiving those who would view the documents about the identity of the bearer.

Merchant: Account that allows businesses to process credit card transactions.

Risk Appetite and Tolerance: Can be defined as 'the amount and type of risk that an organization is willing to absorb in order to meet their strategic objectives.

Compilation of References

Aarts, J., & Gorman, P. (2007). IT in health care: Sociotechnical approaches to err is system. *International Journal of Medical Informatics*, *76*(1), s1–s3. doi:10.1016/S1386-5056(07)00078-0 PMID:17466251

Abha C., & Vinita S. (2010). Analytical Research on Indian Online Banking and Users'Privacy. *Global Journal of Enterprise Information System*, 2(1).

Abukhzam, M., & Lee, A. (2010). Factors Affecting Bank Staff Attitude Towards E-Banking Adoption In Libya. *EJISDC*, *42*(2), 1–15.

Adam Ali.Zare Hudaib. (2014). Banking and Modern Payments System Security Analysis. *International Journal of Computer Science and Security*, *8*(2), 38–62.

Aguilar, M. (2015). Here's Why Your Bank Account Is Less Secure Than Your Gmail. *Gizmodo*. Retrieved from http://gizmodo.com/heres-why-your-bank-account-is-less-secure-than-your-gm-1683777281

Ainin, S., Lim, C. H., & Wee, A. (2005). Prospects and challenges of E-Banking in Malaysia. *The Electronic Journal of Information Systems in Developing Countries*, *22*, 1–11.

Ajzen, I. (1991). The theory of planned behavior. *Organizational Behavior and Human Decision Processes*, *50*(2), 179–211. doi:10.1016/0749-5978(91)90020-T

Akın, F., & Karaboğa, K. (2011). Bireysel Müşterilerin Şubesiz Bankacılık Hizmetlerini Kullanma Kararına Etki Eden Faktörlerin Belirlenmesi Üzerine Bir Araştırma: Bilecik Örneği, Marmara Üniversitesi İ.İ.B.F Dergisi, Cilt XXX. *Sayı*, *I*, 301–320.

Aksoy, T. (2000). *Elektronik Ticaret*. Ankara: Sistem Yayınları.

Al Eroud, A., & Karabatis, G. (2012). Discovering Unknown Cyber Attacks using Contextual Misuse and Anomaly Detection. The ASE science Journal.

Aladwani, A. M. (2001). Online banking: A field study of drivers, development challenges, and expectations. *International Journal of Information Management*, *21*(3), 213–225. doi:10.1016/S0268-4012(01)00011-1

Alawadhi, S., & Morris, A. (2008). The use of the utaut model in the adoption of e-government services in Kuwait.*Proceedings of the 41st Hawaii International Conference on System Sciences* (p. 219). doi:10.1109/HICSS.2008.452

AlEroud, A., & Karabatis, G. (2012). Contextual Anomaly Detection Approach to Discover Zero-Day Attacks. Proceedings of the ASE/IEEE international conference on cyber security, Washington DC. doi:10.1109/CyberSecurity.2012.12

Alhaj, A., Aljawarneh, S., Masadeh, S., & Abu-Taieh, E. (2013). A Secure Data Transmission Mechanism for Cloud Outsourced Data. *International Journal of Cloud Applications and Computing*, *3*(1), 34–43. doi:10.4018/ijcac.2013010104

Alhaj, A., Mellor, J., & Awan, I. (2009). Performance evaluation of secure call admission control for multiclass internet services.*Proceedings of the 23rd IEEE-AINA'09,*Bradford, UK.

Aljawarneh, S. A. (2012). Survivability of Web Content: Theoretical and Practical Approaches Protection of static and dynamic data against tampering.

Aljawarneh, S., Dababneh, M., Hosseny, H., & Alwadi, E. (2010b). A web client authentication system using smart card for e-systems: initial testing and evaluation. *Proceedings of the Fourth International Conference on Digital Society ICDS '10* (pp. 192–197). IEEE. doi:10.1109/ICDS.2010.40

Aljawarneh, S., Laing, C., & Vickers, P. (n. d.). Security policy framework and algorithms for web server content protection. *Proceedings of ACSF'07.*

Aljawarneh, S., Laing, C., & Vickers, P. (n. d.). Security policy framework and algorithms for web server content protection. *Proceedings of the ACSF'07.*

Aljawarneh, S. (2011a). Cloud security engineering: Avoiding security threats the right way. *International Journal of Cloud Applications and Computing*, *1*(2), 64–70. doi:10.4018/ijcac.2011040105

Aljawarneh, S. (2011b). A web engineering security methodology for e-learning systems. *Network Security*, *2011*(3), 12–15. doi:10.1016/S1353-4858(11)70026-5

Aljawarneh, S. A., Moftah, R. A., & Maatuk, A. M. (2016). Investigations of automatic methods for detecting the polymorphic worms signatures. *Future Generation Computer Systems*, *60*, 67–77.

Aljawarneh, S., Alkhateeb, F., & Al Maghayreh, E. (2010). A Semantic Data Validation Service for Web Applications. *Journal of Theoretical and Applied Electronic Commerce Research*, *5*(1), 39–55. doi:10.4067/S0718-18762010000100005

Aljawarneh, S., Alkhateeb, F., & Al Maghayreh, E. (2010a). A semantic data validation service for web applications. *Journal of Theoretical and Applied Electronic Commerce Research*, *5*(1), 39–55. doi:10.4067/S0718-18762010000100005

Aljawarneh, S., Al-Rousan, T., Maatuk, A. M., & Akour, M. (2014). Usage of data validation techniques in online banking: A perspective and case study. *Security Journal*, *27*(1), 27–35. doi:10.1057/sj.2012.10

Aljawarneh, S., Laing, C., & Vickers, P. (2007). Security policy framework and algorithms for web server content protection.*Proceedings of ACSF'07.*

Aljawarneh, S., Laing, C., & Vickers, P. (2008). Design and experimental evaluation of Web Content Verification and Recovery (WCVR) system: A survivable security system.*Proceedings of ACSF* (pp. 1–7).

Alkatheeb, M., Wakileh, M., & Agha, O. (2006). ICT for Banking. *Proceedings of the Jordan ICT Forum 2006.* Retrieved from http://www.tagorg-theinstitution.com/Files/2006/Events/Dec_6_2006_The_Fourth_Jordan_ICT_Forum_exhibition.pdf

Alnabulsi, H., Islam, M. R., & Mamun, Q. (2014, November). Detecting SQL injection attacks using SNORT IDS. *Proceedings of the2014 Asia-Pacific World Congress onComputer Science and Engineering (APWC on CSE)* (pp. 1-7). IEEE. doi:10.1109/APWCCSE.2014.7053873

Al-Nakib, B. (2007). Challenges Facing Compliance Occupation. Retrieved from http://74.125.77.132/search?q=cache:t63v4nSO55cJ:www.uabonline.org/event/event-presentationdownload.php%3Fid%3D162%26eventid%3D58+the+CHALLENGES+FACING+THE+ORGANIZATION+by+using+data+or+input+validation&cd=8&hl=en&ct=clnk&gl=jo

Alsajjan, B., & Dennis, C. (2010). Internet Banking Acceptance Model: Cross-Market Examination. *Journal of Business Research, 63*(9-10), 957–963. doi:10.1016/j.jbusres.2008.12.014

Alshehri, M., Drew, S., Alhussain, T., & Alghamdi, R. (2012, December 3-5). The effects of website quality on adoption of E-government service: An empirical study applying UTAUT model using SEM. *Proceedings of the23rd Australasian Conference on Information Systems.*

Al-Somali, S. A., Gholami, R., & Clegg, B. (2009). An investigation into the acceptance of online banking in Saudi Arabia. *Technovation, 29*(2), 130–141. doi:10.1016/j.technovation.2008.07.004

Alzahrani M, & Goodwin R. (2012) Towards a UTAUT-based Model for the study of E-government citizen acceptance in Saudi Arabia. *International Journal of Economics and Management Sciences.* 64, 109-115.

Amato-McCoy,, D.M. (2005). Creating virtual value. Bank Systems and Technology, 1(22).

Anderson, R. (2001). *Security engineering: A guide to building dependable distributed systems.* John Wiley & Sons.

Andreessen, S. S. (2005). PHP succeeding where Java is not. Retrieved from http://www.zdnet.com.au

Aparikyan, B. (2000). Bankacılıkta Teknoloji Kullanımı. *Banka ve Para Teknolojileri Dergisi,* 6(2).

Appei, M. (2009). *Investing with exchange trade funds made easy: A start to finish plan to reduce costs and achieve higher returns* (2nd ed.). Upper Saddle River, NJ: Pearson Education Inc.

Arasli, H., Smadi, S. M., & Katircioglu, S. T. (2005). Customer service quality in the Greek Cypriot banking industry. *Managing Service Quality, 15*(1), 41–56. doi:10.1108/09604520510575254

Baek, R., & Elbeck, E. (2015). Bitcoin as an Investment or Speculative Vehicle? A First Look. *Applied Economics Letters*, *22*(1), 30–34. doi:10.1080/13504851.2014.916379

Baghaei, N., & Hunt, R. (2004). IEEE 802.11 wireless LAN security performance using multiple clients. *Proceedings of the 12th IEEE International Conference on Networks* (ICON '04).

Balzarotti, D., Cova, M., Felmetsger, V., Jovanovic, N., Kirda, E., Kruegel, C., & Vigna, G. (2008). Saner: Composing Static and Dynamic Analysis to Validate Sanitization in Web Applications. *Proceedings of the 2008 IEEE Symposium on Security and Privacy* (pp. 387-401). DC, USA. doi:10.1109/SP.2008.22

Barnet, Y., Ford, P., Yavatkar, R., Baker, F., Zhang, L., Speer, M., . . . Felstaine, E. (2000). A framework for integrated services operation over diffserv networks. Retrieved from http://tools.ietf.org/html/rfc2998

Batchelor, B. (2010). The History of Internet Banking. *Ehow.com.* Retrieved 0 from http://www.ehow.com/about_5109945_history-ebanking.html

Bates, D., Barth, A., & Jackson, C. (2010, April). Regular expressions considered harmful in client-side XSS filters.*Proceedings of the 19th international conference on World wide web* (pp. 91-100). ACM. doi:10.1145/1772690.1772701

Ben-Jadeed, M. & Molina, A. (2004). The Emergence and Evolution of e-Banking in Saudi Arabia: The Case of Samba Financial Group. *Chapter invited to conference of Frontier of E-Business Research.*

Benklifa, M., & Olmstead, W. (2013). *Learn how to trade options (Collection).* Upper Saddle River, NJ: Pearson Education.

Berg, M., Aarts, J., & Van Der Lei, J. (2013). ICT in health care: Sociotechnical approaches. *Methods of Information in Medicine*, *4*(42), 297–301. PMID:14534625

Biswas, R. (2015). Atrain Distributed System: An Infinitely Scalable Architecture for Processing Big Data of Any 4Vs. In D.P. Acharjya, Satchidananda Dehuri & Sugata Sanyal (Eds.), Computational Intelligence for Big Data Analysis Frontier Advances and Applications. Switzerland: Springer International Publishing.

Biswas, R. (2013). Heterogeneous Data Structure "r-Atrain". In B. K. Tripathy & D. P. Acharjya (Eds.), *Global Trends in Knowledge Representation and Computational Intelligence.* Hershey, PA, USA: IGI Global.

Boganatham, K. K. (2009). Server Side API to Secure XSS [Doctoral Dissertation]. National Institute of Technology Karnataka, Surathkal.

Bonn, M. A., Furr, H. L., & Susskind, A. M. (1999). Predicting a behavioural profile for pleasure travellers on the basis of interne use segmentation. *Journal of Travel Research*, *37*(4), 330–340. doi:10.1177/004728759903700403

Booth, K., Whicker, L., Wyman, T., Pugh, D., & Thompson, S. (2009). *Medical assisting: administrative and clinical procedures* (3rd ed.). McGraw-Hill.

Brabrand, C., Moller, A., Ricky, M., & Scwartzbach, M. I. (2000). Powerforms: Declarative client-side form field validation. *World Wide Web (Bussum)*, *3*(4), 205–214. doi:10.1023/A:1018772405468

Brabrand, C., Moller, A., & Schwartzbach, M. (2002). The bigwig project. *ACM Transactions on Internet Technology*, *2*(2), 79–114. doi:10.1145/514183.514184

Brackney, R., & Anderson, R. (2004). *Understanding the insider threat(technical report).*Santa Monica, CA, USA: RAND Corporation.

Bradley, L., & Stewart, K. (2002). A delphi study of the drivers and inhibitors of internet banking. *International Journal of Bank Marketing*, *20*(6), 250–260. doi:10.1108/02652320210446715

Bradley, L., & Stewart, K. (2003). The diffusion of online banking. *Journal of Marketing Management*, *19*(9-10), 1087–1109. doi:10.1080/0267257X.2003.9728252

Broadhurst, R. (2006). Developments in the global law enforcement of cyber-crime. *Policing: An International Journal of Police Strategies & Management*, *29*(3), 408–433. doi:10.1108/13639510610684674

Çabuk, S., & İnan, H. (2005). İnternet Aracılığıyla Bankacılık Hizmetlerinin Pazarlaması. *Marmara Üniversitesi Sosyal Bilimler Enstitüsü Dergisi*, *6*(23), 23–34.

Cappelli, D., Moore, A., & Trzeciak, R. (2012). *The CERT Guide to Insider Threats: How to Prevent, Detect, and Respond to Information Technology Crimes (Theft, Sabotage, Fraud).* Addison-Wesley Professional.

Cartwright, I.R. (2000). Mastering Customer Relations. London: McMillan.

Casalo, L. V., Flavian, C., & Guinaliu, M. (2007). The role of security, privacy, usability and reputation in the development of online banking. *Online Information Review*, *31*(5), 583–603. doi:10.1108/14684520710832315

CERT. (2011). *The 2011 CyberSecurity Watch Survey*. Retrieved from www.cert.org/

Chang, K., Kim, G. T., Samtani, S., Staikos, A., Muzzelo, L., & Palumbo, J. (2006). A study on the call admission and preemption control algorithms for secure wireless ad hoc networks using IPSec tunneling.*Proceedings of the MILCOM '06*. doi:10.1109/MILCOM.2006.302177

Chavan, J. (2013). Internet banking - Benefits and challenges in an emerging economy. *International Journal of Research in Business Management*, *1*, 19–26.

Cheng, T.C.E., Lam, D.Y.C., & Yeung, A.C.L. (2006). Adoption of Internet Banking: An Empirical Study in Hong Kong. *Decision Support Systems*, *42*(3), 1558–1572. doi:10.1016/j.dss.2006.01.002

Chen, T. C., Stepan, T., Dick, S., & Miller, J. (2014). An anti-phishing system employing diffused information. *ACM Transactions on Information and System Security*, *16*(4), 16. doi:10.1145/2584680

Chen, Y.-H., Lin, C.-Y., Sirakriengkrai, W., & Weng, I.-C. (2015). Repairable Image Authentication Scheme. *International Journal of Network Security*, *17*(4), 439–444.

Childs, M. (2013). *JPMorgan Whale Pushed for 'Young' Trader Who Later Took His Job.* Retrieved from http://www.bloomberg.com/news/articles/2013-03-18/jpmorgan-s-whale-advocated-young-trader-who-later-took-his-job

Chou, D., & Chou, A. Y. (2000). A Guide to the Internet Revolution in Banking. *Information Systems Management*, *17*(2), 51–57. doi:10.1201/1078/43191.17.2.20000301/31227.6

Chou, D., & Chou, A. Y. (2000). A guide to the internet revolution in banking. *Information Systems Management*, *25*, 352–360.

Churchill, G., & Surprenant, C. (1982). An investigation into the determinants of customer satisfaction. *JMR, Journal of Marketing Research*, *19*(4), 491–504. doi:10.2307/3151722

Clemes, M. D. (2008). An empirical analysis of customer satisfaction in international air travel. *Innovative Marketing*, *4*, 49–62.

Compeau, D. R., & Higgins, C. A. (1995). Computer self-efficacy: Development of a measure and initial test. *Management Information Systems Quarterly*, *19*(2), 189–211. doi:10.2307/249688

Cooper, R. (2008). *Verizon Business Data Breach Security Blog*. Retrieved from http://www.securityblog.verizonbusiness.com/2008/

Cummings, A., Lewellen, T., McIntire, D., Moore, A., & Trzeciak, R. (2012). *Insider Threat Study: Illicit Cyber Activity Involving Fraud in the U.S. Financial Services Sector* (Special Report CMU/SEI-2012-SR-004). CERT Program. Retrieved from www.sei.cmu.edu/reports/12sr004.pdf

Cuomo, A., & Lawsky, B. (2014). *Report on Cyber Security in the Banking Sector*, New York State Department of Financial Services. Retrieved from http://www.dfs.ny.gov/reportpub/dfs_cyber_banking_report_052014.pdf

D., Gefen,, & Straub, D. (2000). The Relative Importance of Perceived Ease-ofUse in IS Adoption: A Study of E-Commerce Adoption. *Journal of the Association for Information Systems*, *1*(8), 1–30.

Dasarathy, B., Gadgil, S., Vaidyanathan, R., Par-meswaran, K., Coan, B. A., Conarty, M., & Bhanot, V. (2005). Network QoS assurance in a multi-layer adaptive resource management scheme for mission-critical application using CORBA middleware framework.*Proceedings of the 11th Real Time and Embedded Technology and Applications Symposium*. doi:10.1109/RTAS.2005.34

Davis, F. D. (1989). Perceived usefulness, perceived ease of use, and user acceptance of information technology. *Management Information Systems Quarterly*, *13*(3), 319–339. doi:10.2307/249008

Davis, F. D., Bagozzi, R. P., & Warshaw, P. R. (1992). Extrinsic and intrinsic motivation to use computers in the workplace. *Journal of Applied Social Psychology*, *22*(14), 1111–1132. doi:10.1111/j.1559-1816.1992.tb00945.x

Davis, M. A., Bodmer, S. M., & LeMasters, A. (2014). *Hacking Malware and Rootkits Exposed.* New York: McGraw-Hill.

Dawes, J., & Rowley, J. (1998). Enhancing the customer experience: Contributions from information technology. *Management Decision*, *36*(6), 350–357. doi:10.1108/00251749810220568

Devargas, M. (1993). *Network security*. Manchester, UK: NCC Blackwell.

Developed draft strawman DSCP mapping for GIG enterprise IP networks. (n. d.).

Dickens, B., & Cook, R. (2006). Legal and ethical issues in telemedicine and robotics. *International Journal of Gynaecology and Obstetrics: the Official Organ of the International Federation of Gynaecology and Obstetrics*, *94*(1), 73–78. doi:10.1016/j.ijgo.2006.04.023 PMID:16777109

Dutta, S., & Coury, M. E. (2003). ICT challenges for the Arab world. The Global Information In *Technology Report 2002-2003* (pp. 116-131). Retrieved from http://old.developmentgateway.org/download/170136/Chapter_08_ICT_Challenges_for_the_Arab_World.pdf

Eriksson, K., Kerem, K., & Nilson, D. (2004). Customer Acceptance of Internet Banking in Estonia. *International Journal of Bank Marketing*, *23*(2), 200–216. doi:10.1108/02652320510584412

Eriksson, K., Kerem, K., & Nilsson, D. (2008). The adoption of commercial innovations in the former Central and Eastern European markets: The case of internet banking in Estonia. *International Journal of Bank Marketing*, *26*(3), 154–169. doi:10.1108/02652320810864634

Fang, X., & Zhan, J. (2010, May). Online banking authentication using mobile phones. *Proceedings of the2010 5th International Conference onFuture Information Technology (FutureTech)* (pp. 1-5). IEEE. doi:10.1109/FUTURETECH.2010.5482634

Financial Services Technology Consortium – FTSC. (1998). BIPS Specification V.1.0. Retrieved from http://www.echeck.org

Financial Services Technology Consortium – FTSC. (2015). FSML Version 2.0. Retrieved from http://echeck.org/echeck-specs-and-references-fsml-2-0-logging-proposal/

Fishbein, M., & Ajzen, L. (1975). *Belief, attitude, intention and behavior: An introduction to theory and research.* Reading, MA: Addison-Wesley.

Flavian, C., Guinaliu, M., & Torres, E. (2006). How Bricks and Mortar Attributes Affect Online Banking Adoption. *International Journal of Bank Marketing*, *24*(6), 406–423. doi:10.1108/02652320610701735

Fontanills, G., & Cawood, R. (2009). *Trade options online*. Hoboken, NJ: Wiley.

Forrester Research. (2010). *The Value of Corporate Secrets*. Retrieved from https://www.nsi.org/pdf/reports/The%20Value%20of%20Corporate%20Secrets.pdf

Friedman, B. M. (2000). Decoupling at the margin: The threat to monetary policy from the electronic revolution in banking. *International Finance*, *3*(2), 261–272. doi:10.1111/1468-2362.00051

Fuglerud, K. S., & Dale, Ø. (2011). Secure and inclusive authentication with a talking mobile one-time-password client. *Security & Privacy, 9*(2), 27–34. doi:10.1109/MSP.2010.204

Fysh, G. (1999, June 3). Customers Cash in on Increased Availability of Internet Banking. Knight-Ridder/Tribune Business News.

Gan, C., Clemes, M., Limsombunchai, V., & Weng, A. (2006). A Logit Analysis of Electronic Banking in New Zealand. *International Journal of Bank Marketing*, *24*(6), 360–383. doi:10.1108/02652320610701717

Gehling, B., & Stankard, D. (2005, September). eCommerce security.*Proceedings of the 2nd annual conference on Information security curriculum development* (pp. 32-37). ACM. doi:10.1145/1107622.1107631

Gerrard, P., Barton Cunningham, J., & Devlin, J. F. (2006). Why Consumers Are Not Using Internet Banking: A Qualitative Study. *Journal of Services Marketing*, *20*(3), 160–168. doi:10.1108/08876040610665616

Gerrard, P., & Cunningham, J. B. (2003). The diffusion of internet banking among Singapore consumers. *International Journal of Bank Marketing*, *21*(1), 16–28. doi:10.1108/02652320310457776

Gilbert, G. R., & Veloutsou, C. (2006). A Cross-Industry Comparison of Customer Satisfaction. *Journal of Services Marketing*, *20*(5), 298–308. doi:10.1108/08876040610679918

Gordon, L., Loeb, M., Lucyshyn, W., & Richardson, R. (2005). *Computer Crime and Security Survey*. Retrieved from http://www.cpppe.umd.edu/

Gray, J., & Reuter, A. (1993). *Transaction Processing: Concepts and Techniques*. San Francisco, CA: Morgan Kaufmann Publishers.

Gu, J., Lee, S., & Suh, Y. (2009). Determinants of Behavioral Intention to Mobile Banking. *Expert Systems with Applications*, *36*(9), 11605–11616. doi:10.1016/j.eswa.2009.03.024

Gurau, C. (2002). Online banking in transition economies: The implementation and development of online banking systems in Romania. *International Journal of Bank Marketing*, *20*(6), 285–296. doi:10.1108/02652320210446742

Hadnagy, C. (2011). *Social Engineering: The Art of Human Hacking*. Indiana: John Wiley.

Hamed, A. (2010). E-commerce and Economic Development in Libya [PhD Thesis]. University of Wales.

Hamlet, C. (2000). Community Banks Go Online. *ABA Journal*, *92*(3).

Hart, C. M. (2005). *I want to make money in the stock market: Learn to begin investing without losing your life savings*. Denver, CO: Outskirts Press.

Hashem Sherif, M. (2003). *Protocols for Secure Electronic Commerce* (2nd ed.). London, UK: CRC Press. doi:10.1201/9781420040012

Hassinen, M., & Mussalo, P. (2005, November). Client controlled security for web applications. *Proceedings of the 30th Anniversary IEEE Conference on Local Computer Networks* (p. 7). IEEE. doi:10.1109/LCN.2005.38

Hazlina. (2011). Impacts of service quality on customer satisfaction: Study of Online banking and ATM services in Malaysia. *International Journal of Trade Economics Finance*, 2(1).

Hedberg, A., & Taylor, N. (Eds.). (2001). *Net Banking Must Do Better*. Marketing Week. Retrieved from https://www.marketingweek.com/2001/02/08/net-banking-must-do-better/

Hendry, M. (1995). *Practical computer network security*. Norwood, MA: Artech House.

Herley, C., van Ooirschot, P.C., & Patrick, A.S. (20). Passwords: If We're So Smart, Why Are We Still Using Them? *Financial Cryptography and Data Security, LNCS* (Vol. 5628, pp. 230-237).

Hobson, R. (2012). *The dividend investor: A practical guide to building a share portfolio designed to maximise income*. Hampshire, United Kingdom: Harriman House Ltd.

Hodgson, G. (2015). Breaking Encryption and Gathering Data: International Law Applications. *Journal of Technology Law & Policy*.

Hossain, M., & Prybutok, V. (2008). Consumer acceptance of RFID technology: An exploratory Study. *IEEE Transactions on Engineering Management*, *55*(2), 316–328. doi:10.1109/TEM.2008.919728

IBM Security Intelligence. (n. d.) Retrieved from: http://securityintelligence.com/cross-site-scripting-attacks-pose-ongoing-threat

IBM. (2010). Mid-Year Trend and Risk Report. Retrieved from http://www-304.ibm.com/businesscenter/cpe/download0/207480/2010_XForce_Midyear_Report.pdf

İlter, B., Saatçıoğlu, Ö. Y., & Kuruoğlu, E. (2009). Who Uses Internet Banking in Turkey and Why? *Proceedings of theEuropean and Mediterranean Conference on Information Systems* (pp. 1-18).

InfoSecurity Europe. (2010). *Information Security Breaches Survey*. Retrieved from http://www.pwc.co.uk/eng/publications/isbs survey 2010.html

Internet Security.ca. (n. d.). United Arab Emirates hit with massive bank fraud. Retrieved from http://www.internet-security.ca/internet-security-news-020/united-arab-emirates-hit-with-massive-bank-fraud.html

Internet World Stats. (2006). Internet Usage Statistics, 2006. Retrieved from http://www.Internetworldstats.com/stats.htm

IPSec Developers Forum. (n. d.). Retrieved from http://www-ip-sec.com5PSecinfo.html

Jaffe, F., & Landry, S. Electronic checks: the best of both worlds (1997). *Electron. Commerce World*. Retrieved from http://www.echeck.org/kitprint/article.htm

Jahangir, N., & Begum, N. (2008). The role of perceived usefulness, perceived ease of use, security and privacy, and customer attitude to engender customer adaptation in the context of electronic banking. *African Journal of Business Management*, *2*(1), 32–40.

Java response filter. (2014). Retrieved from http://docs.oracle.com/javaee/5/tutorial/doc/bnagb.html

Jayawardhena, C., & Foley, P. (2000). Changes in the Banking Sector: The Case of Internet Banking in the UK. *Internet Research: Electronic Networking Applications and Policy*, *10*(1), 19–30. doi:10.1108/10662240010312048

Johns, M. (2011). Code-injection Vulnerabilities in Web Applications Exemplified at Cross-site Scripting. IT Information technology, and innovative, 53(5), 256-260.

Jovanovic, N., Kruegel, C., & Kirda, E. (2006). Pixy: A Static Analysis Tool for Detecting Web Application Vulnerabilities (Short Chapter*).Proceedings of the 2006 IEEE Symposium on Security and Privacy*Washington, DC, USA (pp. 258-263).

Kalakota, R., & Whinston, A. (1996). *Frontiers of Electronic Commerce*. MA: Addision Wesley.

Kanakar, H. M., Saudi, M. M., & Marhusin, M. F. (2015). *A Systematic Analysis on Worm Detection in Cloud Based Systems*. Asian Research Publishing Network.

Karjaluoto, H., Matilla, M., & Ve Pento, T. (2002). Electronic banking in Finland: Consumer beliefs and reactions to a new delivery channel. *Journal of Financial Services Marketing.*, *6*(4), 346–361. doi:10.1057/palgrave.fsm.4770064

Katkar, V. D., & Kulkarni, S. V. (2013, December). Experiments on detection of Denial of Service attacks using ensemble of classifiers. *Proceedings of the2013 International Conference onGreen Computing, Communication and Conservation of Energy (ICGCE)* (pp. 837-842). IEEE. doi:10.1109/ICGCE.2013.6823550

Khonji, M., Iraqi, Y., & Jones, A. (2013). Phishing detection: A literature survey. *IEEE Communications Surveys and Tutorials*, *15*(4), 2091–2121. doi:10.1109/SURV.2013.032213.00009

Kieyzun, A., Guo, P. J., Jayaraman, K., & Ernst, M. D. (2009, May), Automatic creation of SQL injection and cross-site scripting attacks. *Proceedings of the IEEE 31st International Conference on Software Engineering ICSE '09* (pp. 199-209). IEEE. doi:10.1109/ICSE.2009.5070521

Kijsanayotin, B., Pannarunothai, S., & Speedie, S. (2009). Factors influencing health information technology adoption in Thailand's community health centers: Applying the UTAUT model. *International Journal of Medical Informatics*, *78*(6), 404–416. doi:10.1016/j.ijmedinf.2008.12.005 PMID:19196548

Kotler, P., & Armstrong, G. (1999). *Principles of Marketing*. Upper Saddle River, NJ: Prentice Hall.

Kotov, V., & Rajpal, M. S. (2015). Understanding Crypto Ransomware: In-Depth Analysis of the Most Popular Malware Families. *Bromium.* Retrieved from https://www.bromium.com/sites/default/files/bromium-report-ransomware.pdf

Krantz, M. (2013). *Investing online for dummies*. Hoboken, NJ: Wiley.

Kumar Bhajantri, V., Sujatha, C., Yaligar, S., & Pawar, M. K. (2016). An Experiential Learning in Web Technology Course. *Journal of Engineering Education Transformations*.

Laforet, S., & Li, X. (2005). Consumers' attitudes towards online and mobile banking in China. *International Journal of Bank Marketing*, *23*(5), 362–380. doi:10.1108/02652320510629250

Lam, M. S., Martin, M., Livshits, B., & Whaley, J. (2008). Securing web applications with static and dynamic information flow tracking.*Proceedings of the 2008 ACM SIGPLAN Symposium on Partial Evaluation and Semantics-Based Program Manipulation* (pp. 3-12). New York, NY. doi:10.1145/1328408.1328410

Laopodis, N. (2013). *Understanding investments: Theories and strategies*. New York, NY: Routledge.

Larsen, L. (2013) Smartphones Easily Skim Credit Card Information: CBC Investigation. Huffington Post. Retrieved from www.huffingtonpost.ca/2013/04/24/smartphones-steal-credit-card-%20data_n_3148170.html

Lassar, P., Lambert, L., Woodford, C., & Moschovitis, C. J. P. (2005). *The internet: A historical encyclopedia*. Santa Barbara, CA: ABC-CLIO.

Lassar, W. M., Manolis, C., & Lassar, S. S. (2005). The relationship between consumer innovativeness, personal characteristics, and online banking adoption. *International Journal of Bank Marketing*, *23*(2), 176–199. doi:10.1108/02652320510584403

Lee, E., Kwon, K., & Schumann, D. (2005). Segmenting the non-adopter category in the diffusion of internet banking. *International Journal of Bank Marketing*, *23*(5), 414–437. doi:10.1108/02652320510612483

Lee, M. C., Lee, Y., & Yoo, D. (2000). The determinants of perceived service quality and its relationship with satisfaction. *Journal of Services Marketing*, *14*(3), 217–231. doi:10.1108/08876040010327220

Lee, W., Park, S. S., Lim, C., Kim, J., & Kang, S. (2015). Proxy Server Authentication for Blocking HTTP-Cache-Poisoning Attacks. *Applications of Mathematics*, *9*(2L), 483–492.

Levi, M. (2008). Organized fraud and organizing frauds: Unpacking research on networks and organization. *Criminology & Criminal Justice*, *8*(4), 389–419. doi:10.1177/1748895808096470

Li, S., Ekberg, P., & Morina, P. (2007). Online banking access system: Principles behind choices and further development, seen from a managerial perspective.

Liao, S., Shao, Y. P., Wang, H., & Chen, A. (1999). The adoption of virtual banking: An empirical study. *PERGAMON International Journal of Information Management*, *19*(1), 63–74. doi:10.1016/S0268-4012(98)00047-4

Liao, Z., & Cheung, M. T. (2002). Internet-based e-banking and consumer attitudes: An empirical study. *Information & Management*, *39*(4), 283–295. doi:10.1016/S0378-7206(01)00097-0

Libya Investment. (2007). General News. Retrieved from http://www.libyaninvestment.com/libya_news.php

Lin, F., Lu, L., & Hsieh, P. (2011). Understanding the adoption of wireless sensor network service in households.*Proceedings of 2011 International Joint Conference on Service Sciences* (pp. 218–222). doi:10.1109/IJCSS.2011.50

Lo, B., & Yang, G. (2005) key technical challenges and current implementations of body sensor network. *Proceedings of theInternational Workshop on Wearable and Implantable Body Sensor Networks.*

Lo, L. K., Osman, M., Ramayah, T., & Rahim, M. (2010). The impact of service quality on customer loyalty: A study of banks in Penang, Malaysia. *International Journal of Marketing Studies*, *2*(2), 57–66.

Lough, D. L., & Krizman, K. J. (2003). A short tutorial on wireless LANs and IEEE802.11.

Luarn, P., & Lin, H.-H. (2005). Toward an Understanding of the Behavioral Intention to Use Mobile Banking. *Computers in Human Behavior*, *21*(6), 873–891. doi:10.1016/j.chb.2004.03.003

Manvi, S. S., Bhajantri, L. B., & Vijayakumar, M. A. (2009, April). Secure mobile payment system in wireless environment. *Proceedings of theInternational Conference onFuture Computer and Communication ICFCC 09* (pp. 31-35). IEEE. doi:10.1109/ICFCC.2009.125

Mario, S. (2013). *17 Proven Currency Trading Strategies: How to Profit in the Forex Market*. Wiley.

Matilla, M., Karjaluoto, H., & Pento, T. (2003). Internet Banking Adoption among Mature Customer: Early Majority Or Laggards? *Journal of Services Marketing*, *17*(5), 514–528. doi:10.1108/08876040310486294

McGraw, G., & Morrisett, G. (2000). Attacking malicious code: A report to the Infosec Research Council. *IEEE Software*, *17*(5), 33–41. doi:10.1109/52.877857

Mengi, P. (2009). Customer satisfaction with service quality: An empirical study of public and private sector banks. *Journal of Management Research*, *8*(9), 7–17.

Mermod, A. Y. (2011). *Elektronik Bankacılık ve Riskler*. İstanbul: Beta Basım Yayım Dağıtım A.Ş.

Mishra, S. (2010). *Banking Law And Practice*. New Delhi: S.Chand.

Mocean. (2007). Internet Data Validation. *Journal of Economy Informatics*, 2007, 96-99. Retrieved from http://revistaie.ase.ro/content/EN7/Mocean.pdf

Moore, G. C., & Benbasat, I. (1991). Development of an instrument to measure the perceptions of adopting an information technology innovation. *Information Systems Research*, *2*(3), 192–222. doi:10.1287/isre.2.3.192

Moore, G. E. (1997). *An update on Moore's law*. Santa Clara, CA: Intel Corporation.

Mukherjee, A., & Nath, P. (2003). A model of trust in online relationship banking. *International Journal of Bank Marketing*, *21*(1), 5–15. doi:10.1108/02652320310457767

MySQL. (n. d.) Retrieved from: www.mysql.com

Nagar, N., & Suman, U. (2014, October). A Secure Cloud Environment through Location Signature and HTML5 WebDB.*Proc. of the 3rd International conference on Advances in Cloud Computing* (pp. 31-36). CSI.

Nagar, N., & Suman, U. (2014, October). Two Factor Authentication using M-pin Server for Secure Cloud Computing Environment. *International Journal of Cloud Applications and Computing*, *4*(4), 42–54. doi:10.4018/ijcac.2014100104

Nagar, N., & Suman, U. (2016). Analyzing Virtualization Vulnerabilities and Design a Secure Cloud Environment to Prevent from XSS Attack. *International Journal of Cloud Applications and Computing*, *6*(1), 1–14. doi:10.4018/IJCAC.2016010101

Narayana, J. P. S. (2010). *Law of Negotiable Instruments and Dishonor of Cheques*. Hyderabad: Asia Law House.

Nath, R., Schrick, P., & Parzinger, M. (2001, Fall). Bankers Perspectives on Internet Banking. *e-Service Journal*, *1*(1), 21–36. Retrieved from http://muse.jhu.edu/journals/eservice_journal/v001/1.1nath.pdf doi:10.2979/ESJ.2001.1.1.21

Neal, W. D. (1998). Satisfaction be damned, value drives loyalty. *Paper presented at the ARF Week of Workshops*, New York.

Neuman, B. C. (1993). Proxy-based authorization and accounting for distributed systems. *Proc. 13th Int. Conf. on Distributed Comput. Syst. 1993* (pp. 283–291). doi:10.1109/ICDCS.1993.287698

Nie, J., & Hu, X. (2008, December). Mobile banking information security and protection methods. *Proceedings of the2008 International Conference onComputer Science and Software Engineering* (Vol. 3, pp. 587-590). IEEE. doi:10.1109/CSSE.2008.1422

Nielsen Consult. (2002). China Online Banking Study. Retrieved from http://estore.chinaonline.com/chinonlbanstu.html

Nor, K.Md. & ve Pearson, J.M. (2007). The Influence of Trust on Internet Banking Acceptance. *Journal of Internet Banking and Commerce*, *12*(2), 1–10.

Offutt, J., Wu, Y., Du, X., & Huang, H. (2004). Bypass testing of web applications. *Proceedings the 5th International Symposium on Software Reliability Engineering,* Los Alamitos, CA (pp. 187–197).

Oppliger, R., & Gajek, S. (2005, September). Effective protection against phishing and web spoofing. In *Communications and Multimedia Security* (pp. 32–41). Springer Berlin Heidelberg. doi:10.1007/11552055_4

Packin, N. G., & Lev, A. Y. (2016). Big data and social netbanks: Are you ready to replace your bank? *Houston Law Review*.

Pala, E., & Kartal, B. (2010). Banka Müşterilerinin İnternet Bankacılığı ile İlgili Tutumlarına Yönelik Bir Pilot Araştırma. *Yönetim ve Ekonomi.*, *2*(17), 43–61.

Pala, E., & Kartal, B. (2010). Banka Müşterilerinin İnternet Bankacılığıyla ile İlgili Tutumlarına Yönelik Bir Araştırma. *Journal of Management and Economy*, *17*(2). Retrieved from http://www2.bayar.edu.tr/yonetimekonomi/dergi/pdf/C17S22010/43_61.pdf

Payment Card Industry (PCI). (n. d.). Data Security Standard, Security Audit Procedures. Retrieved from https://www.pcisecuritystandards.org/pdfs/pci_audit_procedures_v1-1.pdf

PHP. (n. d.) Retrieved from: http://www.php.net

Pikkarainen, T., Pikkarainen, K., Karjaluoto, H., & Pahnila, S. (2004). Consumer acceptance of online banking: An extension of the technology acceptance model. *Internet Research: Electronic Networking Applications and Policy*, *14*(3), 224–235. doi:10.1108/10662240410542652

Polasik, M., & Wisniewski, T.P. (2008). Empirical Analysis of Internet Banking Adoption in Poland. *International Journal of Bank Marketing*, *27*(1), 32–52. doi:10.1108/02652320910928227

Polatoğlu, V. N., & Ekin, S. (2001). An Empirical Investigation of Turkish Consumers' Acceptance of Internet Banking Services. *International Journal of Bank Marketing*, *19*(4), 156–165. doi:10.1108/02652320110392527

Quyoom, A., Ali, R., Gouttam, D. N., & Sharma, H. (2015, May). A novel mechanism of detection of denial of service attack (DoS) in VANET using Malicious and Irrelevant Packet Detection Algorithm (MIPDA). *Proceedings of the2015 International Conference onComputing, Communication & Automation (ICCCA)* (pp. 414-419). IEEE.

Raghuram, S. S., & Chakrabarti, C. (2000). A programmable processor for cryptography.*Proceedings of the IEEE International Symposium on Circuits and Systems (ISCAS '00)*, Geneva, Switzerland (pp. 685–688).

Rajesh, R., & Sivagnanasithi, T. (2009). *Banking Theory: Law and Practice*. New Delhi: Tata Mcgraw Hill Education Private Limited.

Ray, N., & Ghosh, D. (2014). Internet Service Quality (I-SQ) Dimensions and their Impact on Consumer Satisfaction: Case From Banking Industry. *Asian Journal of Research In Banking and Finance*, *4*(8), 212–221.

Reardon, B., Nance, K., & McCombie, S. (2012). Visualization of ATM Usage Patterns to Detect Counterfeit Cards Usage. *Proceedings of the45th Hawaii International Conference on System Science (HICSS)*. Hawaii (pp. 3081-3088). doi:10.1109/HICSS.2012.638

Reid, M. (2008). Integrating Trust and Computer Self-Efficacy with TAM: An Empirical Assessment of Customers' Acceptance of Banking Information Systems (BIS) in Jamaica. *Journal of Internet Banking and Commerce*, *12*(3).

Repubblica Italiana. (2011). *Decreto Legge 13 maggio 2011 n.70 "Prime disposizioni urgenti per l'economia"*. Retrieved from http://www.gazzettaufficiale.it/

Rexha, N., Kingshott, R. P. J., & Shang Shang Aw, A. (2003). The impact of the relational plan of adoption of electric backing. *Journal of Services Marketing*, *17*(1), 53–67. doi:10.1108/08876040310461273

Rezaie, H., & Abadi, D. (2012). Investigate the customers' behavioral intention to use mobile banking based on TPB, TAM and Perceived Risk (A case study in Meli bank). *International Journal of Academic Research in Business and Social Sciences*, *2*(10), 312–322.

Richards, K. (2013). *FBI Offers Lessons Learned on Insider Threat Detection*. Retrieved from http://searchsecurity.techtarget.com/news/2240179082/RSA-2013-FBI-offers-lessons-learned-on-insider-threat-detection

Richardson, R. (2010). *15th Annual 2010/2011 Computer Crime and Security Survey*. Retrieved from http://gatton.uky.edu/faculty/payne/acc324/CSISurvey2010.pdf

Rotchanakitumnuai, S., & Speece, M. (2003). Barriers to Internet Banking Adoption: A Qualitative Study Among Corporate Customers in Thailand. *International Journal of Bank Marketing*, *21*(6), 312–323. doi:10.1108/02652320310498465

Saffu, K., Walker, J. H., & Hinson, R. (2008). Strategic Value and Electronic Commerce Adoption Among Small and Medium-Sized Enterprises in A Transitional Economy. *Journal of Business and Industrial Marketing*, *23*(6), 396–404.

Sanayei, A., & Bahmani, E. (2012). Integrating TAM and TPB with perceived risk to measure customers acceptance of internet banking. *International Journal of Information Science and Management*, *2012*, 25–37.

Sanmugam, A. (2007). Factors Determining Consumer Adoption of Internet Banking. Retrieved from http://papers.ssrn.com/sol3/papers.cfm?abstract_id=1021484#

SANS Institute. (2015). *Insider Threats and the Need for Fast and Directed Response, A SANS Survey*. Retrieved from https://www.sans.org/reading-room/whitepapers/analyst/insider-threats-fast-directed-response-35892

Sarel, D., & Marmorstein, H. (2003). Marketing Online Banking Services: The Voice of The Customer. *Journal of Financial Services Marketing*, *8*(2), 106–118. doi:10.1057/palgrave.fsm.4770111

Sarlak, M. A., & Astiani, A. A. (2011). *E-banking and emerging multidisciplinary processes: Social, economical, and organizational models*. Hershey, PA: IGI Global. doi:10.4018/978-1-61520-635-3

Sathye, M. (1999). Adoption of internet banking by Australian consumer's an empirical investigation. *International Journal of Bank Marketing*, *17*(7), 324–334. doi:10.1108/02652329910305689

Savage, K., Coogan, P., & Lau, H. (2015). The Evolution of Ransomware. *Symantec.* Retrieved from http://www.symantec.com/content/en/us/enterprise/media/security_response/whitepapers/the-evolution-of-ransomware.pdf

Schoenmakers, B. (1995). An efficient electronic payment system withstanding parallel attacks (Report CS-R9522). Centrum voor Wiskunde en Informatica.

Schwartz, R. A. (2010). *Micro markets: A market structure approach to microeconomic analysis.* Hoboken, NJ: Wiley. doi:10.1002/9781118268131

Scott, D., & Sharp, R. (2003). Specifying and enforcing application-level web security policies. *IEEE Transactions on Knowledge and Data Engineering*, *15*(4), 771–783. doi:10.1109/TKDE.2003.1208998

Shergill, G. S., & Li, B. (2006). Internet Banking-An Empirical Investigation of a Trust and Loyalty Model for New Zealand Banks. *Journal of Internet Commerce*, *4*(4), 101–118. doi:10.1300/J179v04n04_07

Siddiqi, K. O. (2010). Interrelationships between service quality attributes, customer satisfaction and customer loyalty in the retail banking sector in Bangladesh. *Paper presented at theInternational Trade and Academic Research Conference*, London.

Singh, A. M. (2004). Trends in South African internet Banking. *Aslib Proceedings: New Information Perspectives*, *56*(3), 187–196. doi:10.1108/00012530410539368

Sohail, M. S., & Shanmugham, B. (2003). E-Banking and Customer Preferences in Malaysia: An Empirical Investigation. *Information Science*, *150*(3-4), 207–217. doi:10.1016/S0020-0255(02)00378-X

Soltwisch, R., Hogrefe, D., Bericht, T., & Gottingen, G.-a.-u. (2004). Survey on network security - 2004. IEEE Std 802.11-1999 (1999). Part II: Wireless LAN medium access control (MAC) and physical layer (PHY) specifications.

Spinellis, D. (2016, January). Addressing Threats and Security Issues in World Wide Web Technology. In Communications and Multimedia Security (Vol. 3, p. 33). Springer.

Standard Generalized Markup Language (SGML). (1986). ISO 8879 Information Processing Text and Office Systems. Retrieved from http://www.iso.org/cate/d16387.html

Statista, The Statistics Portal. (n. d.). Online Banking Penetration in Selected European Markets in 2014. Retrieved from http://www.statista.com/statistics/222286/online-banking-penetration-in-leading-european-countries/

Statista. (2012). Global Online Banking Penetration in April 2012, By region. Retrieved http://www.statista.com/statistics/233284/development-of-global-online-banking-penetration/

Subashini, S., & Kavitha, V. (2010). A Survey on Security Issues in Service Delivery Models of Cloud Computing. *Journal of Network and Computer Applications*, *34*(1), 1–11. doi:10.1016/j.jnca.2010.07.006

Sucec, J., Samtani, S., & Bereschinsky, M. A. (2005, October 17-20). Resource friendly approach for estimating available bandwidth in secure IP networks.*Proceedings of the Military Communications Conference (MILCOM '05)*. doi:10.1109/MILCOM.2005.1605660

Sue, M.P. (2008, July 28). Study: Security flaws threaten online banking. Retrieved from http://www.scmagazine.com/study-security-flaws-threaten-online-banking/article/113010/

Suh, B., & Han, I. (2002). Effect of trust on customer acceptance of Internet banking. *Electronic Commerce Research and Applications*, *1*(3-4), 247–263. doi:10.1016/S1567-4223(02)00017-0

Sulieman. (2011). Banking Service Quality Provided by Commercial Banks and Customer Satisfaction. *American Journal of Scientific Research*, 27(2), 68-83.

Summers, B. J. (1994). *The Payment System: Design, Management, and Supervision*. Washington, D.C.: International Monetary Fund.

Swaroop, R. (2010). *A Case Book on Dishonor of Cheques*. Hyderabad: ALT Publications.

Tan, Z., Jamdagni, A., He, X., Nanda, P., & Liu, R. P. (2014). A system for denial-of-service attack detection based on multivariate correlation analysis. *IEEE Transactions on* Parallel and Distributed Systems, *25*(2), 447–456.

Taylor, S., & Todd, P. A. (1995). Assessing IT usage: The role of prior experience. *Management Information Systems Quarterly*, *19*(2), 561–570. doi:10.2307/249633

The Banks Association of Turkey. (n. d.) Retrieved from http://www.tbb.org.tr/tr/banka-ve-sektor-bilgileri/istatistiki-raporlar/59

The Financial Brand. (n. d.). PEW Research Online Banking Users Demographic Trends. Retrieved from http://thefinancialbrand.com/32428/pew-research-online-banking-users-demographic-trends/

Thompson, R. L., Higgins, C. A., & Howell, J. M. (1991). Personal computing: Toward a conceptual model of utilization. *Management Information Systems Quarterly*, *15*(1), 124–143. doi:10.2307/249443

Ting, D. H. (2004). Service Quality and Satisfaction Perceptions: Curvilinear and Interaction Effect. *International Journal of Bank Marketing*, *22*(6), 407–420. doi:10.1108/02652320410559330

Top Credit Card Processors. (n. d.). Retrieved from www.topcreditcardprocessors.com

Turban, E., King, D., Lee, J., Warkentin, M., & Chung, M. H. (2008). *E-Commerce: A Managerial Perspective*. Upper Saddle River, NJ: Prentice-Hall.

Turgeman-Goldschmidt, O. (2008). Meanings that hackers assign to their being a hacker. *International Journal of Cyber Criminology*, *2*(2), 382–396.

Turkiye Bankalar Birligi. (2016). Retrieved from https://www.tbb.org.tr/tr

UK Payments Administration. (2008). *Fact sheet for people who still write cheques backed by a guarantee card.* London, UK: UK Payments Administration.

United States Government Accountability Office USGA. (2015). *Bank and Other Depository Regulators Need Better Data Analytics and Depository Institutions Want More Usable Threat Information.* Report to Congressional Requesters. Retrieved from http://www.gao.gov/assets/680/671105.pdf

Usta, R. (2005). Tüketicilerin İnternet Bankacılığını Kullanmama Nedenleri Üzerine Bir Araştırma. *Doğuş Üniversitesi Dergisi*, *6*(2), 279–290.

Ustasüleyman, T., & Eyüboğlu, K. (2010). Bireylerin İnternet Bankacılığını Benimsemesini Etkileyen Faktörlerin Yapısal Eşitlik Modeli ile Belirlenmesi. *BDDK Bankacılık ve Finansal Piyasalar*, *2*(4), 11–38.

Van Iwaarden, J., van der Wiele, T., Ball, L., & Millen, R. (2003). Applying SERVQUAL to Web sites: An exploratory study. *International Journal of Quality & Reliability Management*, *20*(8), 919–935. doi:10.1108/02656710310493634

Venkatesh, V., Morris, M. G., Davis, G. B., & Davis, F. D. (2003). User acceptance of information technology: Toward a unified view. *Management Information Systems Quarterly*, *27*(3), 425–478.

Vines, J., Dunphy, P., Blythe, M., Lindsay, S., Monk, A., & Olivier, P. (2012). The Joy of Cheques: Trust, Paper and Eighty Somethings.*Proceedings of the ACM 2012 conference on Computer Supported Cooperative Work*, Seattle, Washington, USA (pp. 147-156). doi:10.1145/2145204.2145229

Vrechopoulous, A., & Atherinos, E. (2009). Web Banking Layout Effects on Consumer Behavioural Intentions. *International Journal of Bank Marketing*, *27*(7), 524–546. doi:10.1108/02652320911002340

W3C. (1998). SDML-Signed Document Markup Language, Version 2.0. Retrieved from http://www.w3.org/TR/NOTE-SDML/

Walker, P. (2012). UBS rogue trader Kweku Adoboli jailed over 'UK's biggest fraud'. *The Guardian.* Retrieved from http://www.theguardian.com/uk/2012/nov/20/ubs-trader-kweku-adoboli-jailed-fraud

Wall, D. S. (2015). The Internet as a conduit for criminal activity. In A. Pattavina (Ed.), Information Technology and the Criminal Justice System (pp. 77-98). London: Sage Publications.

Wang, W., Li, Z., Owens, R., & Bhargava, B. (2009). Secure and efficient access to outsourced data. Proceedings of the ACM Workshop on Cloud Computing Security (CCSW '09) (pp. 55-66). doi:10.1145/1655008.1655016

Wang, J., Gupta, M., & Raghav, H. (2015). Insider Threat in a Financial Institution: Analysis of Attack-Proneness of Information Systems Applications. *Journal of MIS Quarterly*, *39*(1), 91–112.

Wang, Y., Wang, Y., Lin, H., & Tang, T. (2003). Determinants of user acceptance of internet banking: An empirical study. *International Journal of Service Industry Management, 14*(5), 205–219. doi:10.1108/09564230310500192

webDEViL. (2008, October 20). Report on Internet Banking Flaws in India Banking.

Williamson, D. G. (2006). Enhanced authentication in online banking. *Journal of Economic Crime Management, 4*, 1–42.

Worring, M., Engl, A., & Smeria, C. (2012, October). A multimedia analytics framework for browsing image collections in digital forensics.*Proceedings of the 20th ACM international conference on Multimedia* (pp. 289-298). ACM. doi:10.1145/2393347.2393392

Worthen, B. (2009). Inside the head of Obama's CIO. *The Wall Street Journal Digits.*

Wu, J., Shen, W., Lin, L., Greenes, R., & Bates, D. (2008). Testing the technology acceptance model for evaluating healthcare professionals' intention to use an adverse event reporting system. *International Journal for Quality in Health Care, 20*(2), 123–129. doi:10.1093/intqhc/mzm074 PMID:18222963

Wyke, J., & Ajjan, A. (2015). The Current State of Ransomware. Sophos. Retrieved from https://www.sophos.com/en-us/medialibrary/PDFs/technical%20papers/sophos-current-state-of-ransomware.pdf

Xu, H., & Gupta, S. (2009). The effects of privacy concerns and personal innovativeness on potential and experienced customers' adoption of location-based services. *Electronic Markets, 19*(2), 137–149. doi:10.1007/s12525-009-0012-4

Xu, M. X., Wikes, S., & Shah, M. H. (2006). *E-Banking application and issues in Abbey National PLC. E-Technologies. Encyclopedia of E-Commerce, E-Government, and Mobile Commerce.* Hershey, PA, USA: IGI Global.

Yang, J. T., Huang, J. L., Wang, F. J., & Chu, W. C. (2002). Constructing an object-oriented architecture for Web application testing. *Journal of Information Science and Engineering, 18*(1), 59–84.

Yaseen, Q., & Panda, B. (2009). Knowledge Acquisition and Insider Threat Prediction in Relational Database Systems.*Proceedings of the 2009 International Conference on Computational Science and Engineering*, Vancouver, Canada. doi:10.1109/CSE.2009.159

Yaseen, Q., & Panda, B. (2012). Insider Threat Mitigation: Preventing Unauthorized Knowledge Acquisition. *International Journal of Information Security, 11*(4), 269–280. doi:10.1007/s10207-012-0165-6

Yee-Loong Chong, A., Ooi, K. B., Lin, B., & Tan, B. I. (2010). Online banking adoption: An empirical analysis. *International Journal of Bank Marketing, 28*(4), 267–287. doi:10.1108/02652321011054963

Yee, R. W. Y., Yeung, A. C. L., & Cheng, T. C. E. (2010). An empirical study of employee loyalty, service quality and firm performance in the service industry. *International Journal of Production Economics*, *124*(1), 109–120. doi:10.1016/j.ijpe.2009.10.015

Yıldırım, İ. (2015). Factors Affecting the Way Financial Consumers in Turkey Regard Internet Banking. *Journal of Business Research Turk*, *7*(3), 21–35. doi:10.20491/isader.2015315711

Yiu, C. S., Grant, K., & Edgar, D. (2007). Factors affecting the adoption of Internet banking in Hong Kong – Implications for the banking sector. *International Journal of Information Management*, *27*(5), 336–351. doi:10.1016/j.ijinfomgt.2007.03.002

Yoon, H. S., & Steege, L. M. B. (2013). Development of a quantitative model of the impact of customers' personality and perceptions on Internet banking use. *Computers in Human Behavior*, *29*(3), 1133–1141. doi:10.1016/j.chb.2012.10.005

Zaim, H., Bayyurt, N., & Zaim, S. (2010). Service quality and determinants of customer satisfaction in hospitals: Turkish experience. *The International Business & Economics Research Journal*, *9*(5), 51–58.

Zakaria, K., Karim, M. R., & Aliar, H. (2009). Towards Secure Information Systems in Online Banking. *Proceedings of the 2nd International Conference on Internet Technology and Secured Transactions*.

ZDNet. (2005). Security worries holding back online banking. Retrieved from http://news.zdnet.co.uk/Internet/security/0,39020375,39216740,00.htm

Zhou, T. (2012). Examining location based services usage from the perspectives of unified theory of acceptance and use of technology and privacy risk. *Journal of Electronic Commerce Research*, *13*(2), 135–144.

Zhu, D., Premkumar, G. X., Zhang, X., & Chu, C.-H. (2001). Data Mining for Network Intrusion Detection, A Comparison of Alternative Methods. Decision Sciences Journal, 32(4), 635–660. doi:10.1111/j.1540-5915.2001.tb00975.x

Zhu, F. (2009). Smart Card Based Solutions for Secure Internet Banking with a primitive reader or mobile phone, Retrieved from http://www.cs.ru.nl/bachelorscripties/2009/Feng_Zhu

Zhu, D. (2002). Security Control in Inter-Bank Fund Transfer. *Journal of Electronic Commerce Research*, *3*(1), 15–22.

About the Contributors

Shadi Aljawarneh is a ACM Senior member and an associate professor in Software Engineering, at Jordan University of Science and Technology. He holds a BSc degree in Computer Science from Jordan Yarmouk University, a MSc degree in Information Technology from Western Sydney University and a PhD in Software Engineering from Northumbria University-England. Aljawarneh has presented at and been on the organizing committees for a number of international conferences and is a board member of the International Community for ACM, Jordan ACM Chapter, ACS, and others. A number of his papers have been selected as "Best Papers" at conferences and journals.

* * *

Ahmad Alaiad is an assistant professor in computer information systems department at the Jordan University of Science and Technology, Jordan. His research focuses on information systems health informatics. He has various publications in reputed journals and conferences.

Khalid Alkhatib is an assistant professor in accounting and finance in the department of Computer Information Systems, Jordan University of Science and Technology. He obtained his PhD degree in accounting and finance and postgraduate diploma in social science research methods from Cardiff University in the United Kingdom. His master and bachelor degrees in management are also from the United Kingdom. He gained his financial experience from the banking industry in the UK where he worked. His teaching commitments are accounting, business planning and control, and accounting information systems. His research interests are financial reporting, information disclosure, and international accounting.

Akashdeep Bhardwaj, PhD research scholar from UPES, PGDM, B.E (Computer Science), is an Enterprise Risk and Resilience Technology professional working on Information Security and Infrastructure Operations domain having worked for various US based MNCs and trained and certified in Internal Information Security, Ethical Hacking, Microsoft, Cisco and VMware technologies.

Balamurugan Balusamy had completed his B.E. (computer science) from Bharathidasan University and M.E. (computer Science) from Anna University. He completed his Ph.D. in cloud security domain specifically on access control techniques. He has published papers and chapters in several renowned journals and conferences.

Ranjit Biswas has guided thirteen Ph.D.'s (degrees conferred) and published more than 120 research papers all being in foreign journals of international repute of USA, German, France, UK, Bulgaria, Italy in the field of Computer Science. He is having about 34 years of teaching experience in India and abroad at renowned universities viz. Calcutta University, IIT Kharagpur, Philadelphia University, IGNOU, NIT, etc. He is a Member in Editorial Board of 14 journals of high esteem international repute published from USA, German, France, UK, Bulgaria, Italy and Asian countries. Presently, he is Professor & Head of the Department of Computer Science & Engineering in Jamia Hamdard University, New Delhi, India.

Ernesto Damiani is a full professor at the Università degli Studi di Milano and Director of the Khalifa University Information Security Centre in Abu Dhabi, UAE. He has held visiting positions at a number of international institutions, including George Mason University in Virginia, LaTrobe University in Melbourne, Australia, and the University of Technology in Sydney, Australia. He has also done extensive research on advanced network infrastructure and protocols, taking part in the design and deployment of secure high performance networking environments, both as chief scientist and in management positions. His areas of interest include Web services security, processing of semi and unstructured information (e.g., XML), and semantics aware content engineering for multimedia. Also, he is interested in models and platforms supporting open source development. He has served and is serving in all capacities on many congress, conference, and workshop committees. He is a senior member of the IEEE and ACM distinguished scientist.

Dan DeFilippi was a black hat hacker in his teens and early twenties. In college he sold fake IDs, and later committed various scams, including phishing, credit card fraud, and identity theft. He was caught in December 2004. In order to avoid a significant jail sentence, DeFilippi decided to become an informant and work for the secret service for two years, providing training and consulting and helping them understand how hackers and fraudsters think. Today, DeFilippi is a successful director of engineering at a private organization. He continues to give his time toward raising awareness of cybercrime, particularly credit card fraud, presenting talks at international symposia, global media interviews, and guest lecturers at universities.

Fulvio Frati holds an administrative position at the Dipartimento di Informatica, Università degli Studi di Milano. He is the author of many international scientific publications in the field of Open Source, Service Oriented Architecture, Collaboration Environment, and Software Development Process Monitoring and Modeling. He has served as a PC member and publication chair of many International conferences and workshops.

Hayrünisa Gürel works in Marmara University Vocational School of Social Sciences, in Department of Foreign Trade in İstanbul, Turkey. She teaches courses on economics, insurance in foreign trade, banking law, communication. Her academic studies are on insurance and banking. She has been working as a lecturer in Marmara Unversity, the Vocational School of Social Sciences since 2010.

Shirley Jothi Mano majored in Computer Science and currently pursuing masters in Information Technology at VIT university Vellore. Her areas of interest are in networks and image processing.

Katina Michael is a professor in the School of Computing and Information Technology at the University of Wollongong. She is the IEEE Technology and Society Magazine editor-in-chief and also the senior editor of IEEE Consumer Electronics Magazine. Since 2008, Michael has been a board member of the Australian Privacy Foundation. Michael researches on the socio-ethical implications of emerging technologies and has cross-disciplinary qualifications in IT and Law. Michael is responsible for the creation of the human factors series of workshops hosted annually since 2006 on the "Social Implications of National Security". The workshops and proceedings were funded by the ARC's Research Network for a Secure Australia (RNSA) which embraced multidisciplinary collaboration.

Nitin Nagar has received a Master Degree in Computer Applications from Devi Ahilya University, Indore and perusing PhD Degree from Devi Ahilya University Indore, India. Presently he is the Assistant Professor at International Institute of Professional Studies, Devi Ahilya University Indore, India. He is having more than 7 years of teaching and 6 years of research experience. His areas of research are Cloud Computing, Advanced Database Management System, and Distributed Computing.

Saranya Nandagopal is currently pursuing her M.Tech at Vellore Institute of Technology, India.

Ahu Coşkun Özer has received her PhD degree from Istanbul University in Turkey. She has master degree on Theory of Economics. She has bachelor's degree from Marmara University. She is now Assistant Professor in Marmara University, Vocational School of Social Sciences. Economic policy, international economics, entrepreneurship are special interests of her.

Nilanjan Ray is from Kolkata, India. He has obtained his M.Com (Mktg), MBA (Mktg), STC FMRM (IIT-Kgp), PhD (Management) from The University of Burdwan Department of Business Administration). He has 8 years teaching experience in BBA, MBA, BCom and 6 years Research experience and guided around 56 Post Graduate students' project. Dr. Ray has contributed over 30 research papers in reputed National and International Referred, Peer Reviewed Journals and Proceedings. He has contributed 10 book Chapters and also Chief Editor of 4 Edited Book Volumes of IGI Global USA. He has also associated himself as a reviewer of Journal of Business and Economics, Research Journal of Business and Management Accounting and Journal of Service Marketing Emerald Group Publishing Limited, Research Journal of Business and Management Accounting, and as an Editorial Board Member of several referred Journals. He has also chaired in a technical session at IJAS Conference 2012, at Harvard University, Boston, USA. Dr. Ray is a life-member of the International Business Studies Academia.

Claudio Santacesaria is an experienced R&D manager with a focus on innovation. He has managed the R&D of big and small companies in various fields from Telecommunications to Banking applications.

Ugrasen Suman has received a Master Degree in Computer Applications from Rani Durgawati University Jabalpur and PhD Degree in Computer Science from Devi Ahilya University Indore, India. Presently, he is a Professor at School of Computer Science & Information Technology, Devi Ahilya University, Indore, India. He has more than 14 years of teaching and research experience. His areas of research are Software Engineering, Knowledge Management & Mining, Software Reuse, Software maintenance & reengineering and Service Oriented Computing. He has guided four PhD Scholars, four PG research scholars and 37 M.Tech thesis. Currently, he is guiding eight PhD Scholars. He has published more than 70 research papers in national & international journals/conferences. He is also working as Dy. Coordinator on a UGC-SAP research project on Distributed systems. He is a member of IEEE, IEEE-CS, Senior Member of IACSIT, Life Member of CSI and IAENG.

Malathi Velu completed her B.E. (Computer Science) from Panimalar Institute of Technology and is pursuing her M.Tech (IT-Networking) at Vellore Institute of Technology. She has published a conference paper in ACM Publication and a book in Lambert Publication.

Marta Vidal, BSc and MBA from ESADE Business School, PhD student in Management at Complutense University, Assistant Professor of Management at European University of Madrid.

Javier Vidal-García, Assistant Professor of Finance, University of Valladolid, has a BSc in Management from Queen´s University Belfast, MSc in Finance from Aston Business School, MA in Economics from Autonomous University of Madrid, Ph.D. in Financial Economics from Complutense University of Madrid and has been a postdoctoral fellow at the Harvard Business School.

Qussai Yaseen received his PhD in Computer Science from the University of Arkansas at Fayetteville, AR, USA in 2012, where he developed new approaches for mitigating insider threat in relational databases. At the U of A, he worked as a research assistant for Professor Brajendra Panda on a project funded by US AFOSR to tackle insider threat in relational database systems. Dr. Yaseen has published several papers in refereed journals and conferences. Prior to receiving his Ph.D., Dr. Yaseen worked at Al-Balqaa University, Jordan as an instructor, and at Irbid Private University as a lab administrator. Dr. Yaseen recieved his Bsc. and Msc. in Computer Science from Yarmouk Univeristy and Jordan University of Science and Technology in 2002 and 2006 respectively. After getting his Ph.D degree in 2012, Dr. Yaseen worked at Yarmouk University for two years. In 2014, Dr. Yaseen joined Jordan University of Science and Technology. Currently, he is working on Cloud Security and trying to develop new approaches that protect information stored in the Cloud, especially in Cloud Relational Databases.

İsmail Yıldırım is an assistant professor of finance at Hitit University, Department of Finance, Banking and Insurance, Corum, Turkey. He received PhD in Finance with his thesis entitled as *Stress Testing in the Risk Measurement of Insurance Companies: An Implementation in Turkish Insurance Sector*.

Index

www.ingramcontent.com/pod-product-compliance
Ingram Content Group UK Ltd.
Pitfield, Milton Keynes, MK11 3LW, UK
UKHW051028041026
15470UKWH00015B/1686

9 781522 508649